Curing
the
Incurable

Curing the Incurable

Vitamin C, Infectious Diseases, and Toxins

by Thomas E. Levy, MD, JD

*In memory of Frederick R. Klenner, M.D.,
a man of great vision and the truest of medical pioneers*

Acknowledgements

Frederick R. Klenner, M.D., to whom this book is dedicated, deserves the greatest credit for its writing. Without his keen insights and willingness to look beyond the limits of traditional medical teachings, the ability of vitamin C to cure some "incurable" infections and poisonings would remain completely unknown today. The primary purpose of this book is to clearly lay out the large body of scientific documentation showing that Dr. Klenner's principles of vitamin C therapy were completely right and need to be properly applied across the world.

Linus Pauling, Ph.D. also deserves an enormous amount of credit for helping to educate the world on the many benefits of vitamin C. Dr. Pauling won the Nobel Prize in Chemistry in 1954 and the Nobel Prize in Peace in 1962. Although his place in history was already assured, Dr. Pauling did not hesitate to put his credibility on the line in promoting vitamin C to the world and a medical profession that did not want to be advised by a non-physician. Maintaining complete personal and scientific integrity was of paramount importance to Dr. Pauling. Even though vitamin C is still greatly underutilized today, Dr. Pauling managed to get more people to take a good daily dose of vitamin C than any other individual in history. Although he was not a medical doctor, Dr. Pauling probably had a far greater positive effect on world health than he did in his chosen field of chemistry.

Albert Szent-Gyorgyi, M.D., Ph.D. won the Nobel Prize in Physiology or Medicine in 1937 for the discovery of vitamin C. His work

7

in defining the chemical structure of vitamin C, along with isolating and purifying it, allowed many subsequent researchers to study the continuing and expanding role of vitamin C in medicine and science.

Hal A. Huggins, D.D.S., M.S., a good friend, colleague, and co-author of my first book, *Uninformed Consent*, first introduced me to the amazing abilities of vitamin C in treating infections and neutralizing toxins in 1993. My life and my medical perspectives have never been the same.

Robert Kulacz, D.D.S., a good friend, excellent researcher, and co-author of my third book, *The Roots of Disease*, has contributed as much insight to me in medical matters as any of my medical colleagues. He has been invaluable to me as a sounding board for my many theories, thoughts, questions, and ideas.

My brother, John, read and thoroughly edited this book for me. Although he does not have a formal medical background, I adopted many of the insightful suggestions he made in order to better deliver the messages of this book.

My beautiful mother, Catherine, remains one of the greatest positive forces in my career. Her love and support have continued to motivate me throughout my entire life. My sister, Cathy, has always been supportive as well.

Many thanks to Char Longwell, Chris Prudhomme, and Bob Culp at the medical library of Memorial Hospital in Colorado Springs, CO. Their help to me in completing the necessary research for this book has been absolutely invaluable.

Preface

*In science the credit goes to the man who
convinces the world, not to the man to
whom the idea comes first.*

SIR WILLIAM OSLER

To paraphrase Sir William Osler, discovery without dissemination and assimilation is meaningless. If the greatest discovery touches only very few minds, or if it touches many minds but is never truly comprehended, it is of no real consequence. As the reader proceeds through this book, it will rapidly become apparent that much of the original research reported was first conducted 50 or more years ago. Many different researchers and authors have been involved in writing about vitamin C, or the "anti-scurvy" factor, for well over a century now. Vitamin C has been proven to be such a fascinating substance that a large amount of research on its effects even preceded its precise chemical isolation. The benefits of fresh fruits and vegetables on the health of both man and laboratory animals did not require a precise knowledge of what it was in such food that so greatly improved general health.

This book aims to do far more than just assemble much of the vast research on vitamin C, infectious diseases, and toxins in one volume. The overall presentation of the information on vitamin C in this book is felt to be fairly unique. Many of the concepts and much of the information presented on the following pages have resulted from my continuing goal to better understand the numerous and undeniable clinical results that I have witnessed resulting from the proper use of vitamin C. The book also cites many more remarkable clinical results that I have not directly witnessed but have discovered in the mountains of published research on vitamin C or have had reported to me by some of my colleagues. Such results continue to be either unknown to, or ignored by, most conventional medical practitioners. The literature is virtually overflowing with irrefutable evidence that vitamin C is the single most essential nutrient for achieving and maintaining optimal health and also the premier agent for curing or effectively treating a large number of the most common infectious diseases. Vitamin C is very arguably the *most* important therapy that *most* infected patients should receive, regardless of the diagnosis and whether other therapies and medications have already been started.

Many clinicians and researchers demand a precise explanation for every result that they observe from a treatment or research protocol. Such total comprehension is a very desirable goal, but a lack of complete understanding should never stand in the way of using a therapy that results in the achievement of consistent and reproducible positive clinical results. Results are results, and knowing why a result occurs is generally only a luxury for the clinician, and not a necessity for the patient's recovery. A lack of understanding can never negate a positive clinical result. Only the most intellectually insecure of clinicians would withhold a treatment that clearly works, especially when the treatment clearly and demonstrably is virtually harmless, as established by extensive administration worldwide for over 60 years.

While many other "vitamin C authors" have preceded me, the new millenium marks a period of time when more information is now available to researchers and clinicians than ever before existed in history. The Internet and the World Wide Web have provided an unprecedented availability of information on every conceivable topic. This veritable avalanche of information has resulted in every profession becoming much more liable for complete thoroughness and total integrity in the execution of its responsibilities to the public.

Many medical authors appear to be wary of ever using the term "cure." While this caution in an attempt not to misuse an important term is praiseworthy, it is completely appropriate to use the term "cure" when, in fact, the evidence demonstrates that a given medical condition has clearly and repeatedly been cured by a specific therapy. The format of Chapter 2, the primary chapter addressing vitamin C therapy and specific infectious diseases, is designed to make it readily apparent when an infectious disease is curable, reversible, or preventable by the proper dosing of vitamin C, as reflected in the world medical literature over the last century. An infectious disease will be considered reversible, as opposed to curable, when the optimal dosing of vitamin C clearly reverses some or all of the associated signs, symptoms, and abnormal chemistry tests. When such a reversal is complete and permanent, the medical condition will be considered curable. Such a system will allow the reader who is primarily concerned with a specific infectious disease to go directly to that section and see the effect that vitamin C has been documented to have on that disease. Avoiding the use of a term such as "cure" when it is absolutely appropriate does as much harm as using it inappropriately. Not realizing the incredible ability of vitamin C to cure a given infectious disease just perpetuates the usage of so many other needlessly applied toxic drugs and debilitating clinical protocols. If the shoe fits, wear it, and if the treatment works, proclaim it.

Where appropriate, the potential but unreported effects of properly dosed vitamin C on an infectious disease will also be proposed for the reader's consideration. Certainly, a reasonable inference can often be made on the clinical response of a given infectious disease to a more effective dosing (usually intravenous) and a more generous dosing of vitamin C. This clinical judgment is based on a more positive response of a similar infectious disease to that more optimal vitamin C dosing regimen. Although not having the same value as a controlled clinical research study, a competent clinician certainly should have the option to try a dosing regimen of vitamin C previously proven to be safe on another infectious disease that has not yet had that dosing regimen reported in the literature. In fact, a clinician is often expected to try a treatment regimen known generally to be very safe in one disease on a related disease that is largely unresponsive to other measures. This is the case even when clear evidence in the literature is insufficient to reach an unequivocal conclusion. Even though many clinicians might prefer the safe harbor of using only established therapies, the cautious use of therapies generally regarded as being safe for other diseases should be encouraged. This is especially true when the established therapies are arguably ineffective, and sometimes even harmful.

This book has been written with precisely the above points foremost in mind. When a hypothesis based on limited clinical and research information is being proposed, this will pointed out. However, when the totality of the evidence clearly indicates that vitamin C has cured a condition, this will also be asserted. The reader is always welcome and encouraged to check any of the many references cited in this book that support the assertions being made. Feedback from any reader is also welcome, especially when it represents an honest attempt to reconcile any of the incredible data cited that support the enormous role that vitamin C should be playing in the life and health of every human being. Challenging me about something, and supporting that statement with honest scientific data, never hurts my feelings. Such feedback will only make me a better physician, and it will improve the quality of my future medical treatments and medical writings. Conversely, it is my most ardent hope that all other doctors who encounter this book can assume the same open position. Let the results alone speak for or against vitamin C.

Obviously, propaganda and intellectual arrogance have no place in the esteemed practice of medicine. Researchers who are willing to speak against established medical concepts should be praised and encouraged by their peers, not isolated and ridiculed by them. If their new, radical medical theories prove to be wrong, then those results will speak for themselves. Medicine and science in general have rarely been significantly advanced by propositions offered by the majority versus the few. Only the truly independent minds, like Galileo, Tesla, Newton, and Pauling, have offered mankind opportunities to leap forward and not merely crawl along, or even slip backwards.

As Sir William Osler noted at the start of this preface, it is, unfortunately, far more important to convince the world that something is real rather than just to discover it and let the evidence speak for itself. Hopefully, this book will play a significant role in the "discovery" that vitamin C is an incredibly significant factor in maintaining and restoring the health of human beings. This book is also dedicated to the many still unrecognized vitamin C researchers who have contributed a few deft strokes of the paintbrush but have never had the opportunity to view the completed masterpiece, or perhaps, to even know the larger picture exists.

Table of Contents

Acknowledgements 7

Preface 9

Introduction 19

   References 32

Chapter One
Some Basic Concepts and Historical Perspectives

   A Theory of Life 33

   Entrenched Misconceptions 34

   Genetically Lacking 38

   Historical Background 45

   Summary 47

   References 48

Chapter Two
Curing, Reversing, and Preventing Infectious Diseases

   Paving the Way: Frederick R. Klenner, M.D. 51

   Polio (Curable and Preventable) 52

   Vitamin C and Polio: Supportive Research 59

   Additional Viral Diseases and Vitamin C 61

   Viral Hepatitis (Curable and Preventable) 61

   Measles (Curable and Preventable) 68

   Mumps (Curable and Preventable) 72

   Viral Encephalitis (Curable and Preventable) 74

   Chickenpox and Herpes Infections
      (Curable and Preventable) 82

   Viral Pneumonia (Curable and Preventable) 87

   Influenza (Curable and Preventable) 89

Rabies (Preventable; Curable-?, Reversible-?) 92

AIDS (Reversible and Preventable; Curable-?) 94

The Common Cold
  (Reversible and Preventable; Curable-?) 105

Ebola Virus (Curable-?, Reversible-?, Preventable?) 109

Non-Viral Infectious Diseases and Vitamin C 113

Diphtheria (Curable and Preventable) 113

Pertussis (Reversible and Preventable; Curable-?) 118

Tetanus (Curable and Preventable) 122

Tuberculosis (Reversible and Preventable; Curable-?) 127

Streptococcal Infections (Curable and Preventable) 143

Leprosy (Reversible and Preventable; Curable-?) 156

Typhoid Fever (Reversible and Preventable; Curable-?) 159

Malaria (Reversible; Curable-?, Preventable-?) 161

Brucellosis (Reversible: Curable-?, Preventable-?) 165

Trichinosis (Reversible; Curable-?, Preventable-?) 167

Other Infectious Diseases or
  Pathogenic Microorganisms and Vitamin C 169

Amebic Dysentery (Reversible and Preventable; Curable-?) 169

Bacillary Dysentery (Curable and Preventable) 172

Pseudomonas Infections (Curable and Preventable) 174

Rocky Mountain Spotted Fever (RMSF)
  (Curable; Preventable-?) 175

Staphylococcal Infections (Curable and Preventable) 177

Trypanosomal Infections
  (Reversible and Preventable; Curable-?) 179

Some Mechanisms of the Antimicrobial
  Effects of Vitamin C 180

Summary 184

References 185

Chapter Three
The Ultimate Antidote

Overview 217

Specific Toxins and Vitamin C 221

Alcohol (Ethanol)... 221

Barbiturates.. 227

Carbon Monoxide 228

Endotoxin 229

Methemoglobinemia 231

Fifty-One Miscellaneous Toxins 234

Mushroom Poisoning 266

Six Types of Pesticides 267

Radiation 271

Strychnine and Tetanus Toxin 279

Nine Toxic Elements 280

Venoms 312

Summary 317

References 319

Chapter Four
The Safety of High Doses of Vitamin C

Overview 371

Long-Term and High-Dose Supplementation 371

Does Vitamin C Cause Kidney Stones?.................... 375

A Typical Research Report Relating Vitamin C and
    Kidney Stone Formation.................................. 385

Vitamin C: Antioxidant and Prooxidant 389

Vitamin C and G6PD Deficiency 397

Vitamin C and Cancer.. 400

Vitamin C and Intentional Immune System Suppression 403

Vitamin C and the Rebound Effect 405

Summary 406

References 408

Chapter Five
Liposome Technology and

Intracellular Bioavailability... 435

Overview 435

The Liposome... 436

Liposome Characteristics (Conventional) 437

A Unique Marriage: Liposomes and Antioxidants............ 439

Intravenous Impact with Oral Administration................ 440

Summary 442

References 443

Chapter Six

Practical Suggestions 451

Balancing Antioxidant Supplementation 451

Vitamin C Optidosing 452

Treating Infections and Toxin Exposures 454

Patients with Kidney Disease 455

Summary 457

References 458

Resources

Suggested Readings 459

For Further Education and Assistance 461

About the Author.. 463

Introduction

*... it takes much more than logic and clear-cut
demonstrations to overcome the inertia
and dogma of established thought.*

IRWIN STONE

Amazingly, the medical literature already documents that vitamin C has readily and consistently cured both acute polio and acute hepatitis. Modern medicine still considers these two viral diseases to be incurable, regardless of the treatment used. It should be understood that both polio and hepatitis may sometimes spontaneously resolve, either relatively quickly or over a more prolonged period of time. However, modern medicine does not seem to be aware that properly dosed vitamin C will reliably and quickly cure nearly all cases of acute polio and acute hepatitis. Polio babies are completely well in less than a week, and hepatitis patients are sick for only a few days, not several months. Furthermore, chronic hepatitis does not develop in acute hepatitis patients treated with sufficient vitamin C.

properly dosed vitamin C will reliably and quickly cure nearly all cases of acute polio and acute hepatitis

Vitamin C has also reversed and often cured many of the other common viral and bacterial diseases that continue to plague both children and adults. While a great deal of evidence exists to further demonstrate that properly dosed vitamin C can reverse and almost always prevent other significant medical conditions such as cancer and heart disease, the best documented and most compelling evidence involves the cure of multiple infectious diseases that cause great suffering and often kill or incapacitate. As the reader witnesses a sampling of the enormous quantity of hard scientific evidence that has been virtually ignored on the effective treatment of infectious diseases with vitamin C, it will be much easier to comprehend that many more, although less well-documented, applications of vitamin C remain equally unappreciated.

Presently, modern medicine offers only a wide variety of vaccinations in the hope of affording protection against many of the infectious diseases. Little significant progress has been made in the actual treatment of nearly all the viral infectious diseases once they have been contracted.

Antibiotics have made a big difference in the treatment of different non-viral infectious diseases, but the hallmark treatment for most viral infections remains supportive, directed at treating symptoms only while hoping that the immune system can rally its forces. Either the body or the virus eventually wins, and the treating physician must wait along with the patient for the eventual result.

With vitamin C, however, such a scenario does not have to be continually repeated. For example, the scientific evidence presented in this book will conclusively show that the viral infection known as polio can be and has been completely *cured* by the proper administration of very high doses of vitamin C. The scientific evidence in this book will also conclusively show that vitamin C does much, much more than merely cure polio. Even though polio is largely an unknown disease to the younger generation and has become a forgotten disease to the older generation, any doctor, old or young, will tell you that polio was, and remains, a disease for which there is no effective treatment and definitely no cure.

It is in the light of these amazing clinical results that the past, present, and future credibility of the mainstream, traditional medical establishment must be evaluated. Most doctors probably have the best of intentions, but they must nevertheless be held totally liable for their collective and persistent ignoring of the inescapable conclusions on the enormous clinical benefit of properly dosed vitamin C. At the height of the polio epidemic in 1949, when all young parents lived in the fear that their babies and young children would be the next victims, Frederick R. Klenner, M.D., published that he had successfully cured 60 out of 60 polio patients who had presented to his office or to the emergency room! Furthermore, he reported that *none* of the 60 patients treated had any residual damage from the polio virus that often left its survivors crippled for life. This evidence was subsequently presented by Klenner in 1949 to an annual session of the American Medical Association that dealt with the treatment of polio patients.

Frederick R. Klenner, M.D. published that he had successfully cured 60 out of 60 polio patients

You will see that Klenner's research and data are clear-cut and straightforward, and it will then be completely left up to the reader to determine how such information was ignored in the past and remains ignored today. Landwehr (1991) addressed in some detail Klenner's attempt to inform the American Medical Association about the incredible response of polio to properly dosed vitamin C.

Klenner was also able to demonstrate repeatedly that vitamin C appears to be the ideal agent for killing any infecting virus. He repeatedly demonstrated that vitamin C is clearly the optimal choice to neutralize and often help eliminate nearly any toxic chemical or substance capable of poisoning the body, including the toxins associated with several of the infectious diseases. Additionally, you will see how Klenner and many other clinicians and researchers have conclusively shown that vitamin C appears to be the ideal agent for helping in the destruction of most bacteria, fungi, and other microbial agents that continue to afflict mankind.

In addition to the utility of vitamin C as a single agent, you will see that the effectiveness of many traditional therapies for most infectious diseases is tremendously improved with the proper addition of vitamin C therapy. Although vitamin C is an incredibly effective single therapy for many infectious diseases, there are virtually no medical treatments for any infectious disease that are not substantially improved by the addition of vitamin C.

The only absolute requirements are that vitamin C be given

1. in the right form,

2. with the proper technique,

3. in frequent enough doses,

4. in high enough doses,

5. along with certain additional agents, and

6. for a long enough period of time.

Anyone who has read the above information must surely be wondering how such a dramatic cure and treatment for polio, hepatitis, and other infectious diseases could possibly have been overlooked by so many caring, intelligent physicians and researchers. There is no simple explanation for such a situation.

Most people, especially highly schooled ones such as physicians, doggedly persist in thinking as a group rather than as individuals contributing to a collective fund of knowledge. Once something gets etched into the pages of the medical textbook, and medical school professors throughout the country teach it to medical students and doctors in post-graduate training, any contradictions to this orthodox body of knowledge get summarily ignored once these impressionable trainees become practicing physicians. This unquestioning faith in the "established" medical knowledge is so deeply engrained that many doctors simply will not even consider reading something that comes from sources that they do not consider worthy of producing new medical concepts. And if they do accidentally encounter and read such information, they quickly dismiss it as just being ridiculous if it conflicts with too many of the concepts that most of their colleagues and textbooks embrace.

As a practicing physician for more than 25 years, I can assure the reader that virtually all doctors fear being ridiculed by their colleagues more than anything else. This fear, more than any other factor that I can identify, appears to almost completely stifle independent medical thought. As Goethe once said: "We would rather admit our moral errors, mistakes and crimes than our scientific errors." Certainly, a small handful of dishonorable physicians may realize that some unwelcome but legitimate medical breakthroughs could reduce their income, and they may oppose those breakthroughs for that reason. However, most physicians really care about and want to help their patients. The problem that remains is how to get physicians and the complete medical truth together. Forman (1981) analyzed this resistance to innovation by some scientists, especially those who are physicians and clinicians.

> **doctors fear being ridiculed by their colleagues more than anything else...this fear appears to almost completely stifle independent medical thought**

Although this book will address the incredible ability of vitamin C to effectively treat and cure many different viral diseases and effectively treat a wide array of other infectious diseases, the following true story about another long-standing effective therapy will probably best illustrate why additional attempts to get the truth out about vitamin C must be made.

On Sunday, July 2, 2000, a made-for-TV movie aired during the primetime evening hours. Entitled *...First Do No Harm*, it starred Meryl Streep, one of the most acclaimed actresses of our day. It was a fictionalized story based on real events in the life of a mother (Streep) and her young child. The child developed epileptic seizures that proved to be progressively unresponsive to all of the prescription medicines that were used. Additionally, the child developed multiple side effects to the medications, with at least one being life-threatening. The child was finally offered brain surgery as a last resort, although not an option with much hope of long-term success.

The child's mother, not one to just accept fate but determined to mold it herself, threw herself into research at the medical library. She

"discovered" a treatment called the "ketogenic diet," which the literature said completely eliminated seizures in a significant percentage of
patients unsuccessfully treated with multiple seizure drugs. Her neurologist had not even mentioned diet as a possible therapy, even though
this treatment had been in the medical literature for about 75 years!

When the mother mentioned trying the diet, the neurologist only
ridiculed her, labeled the reports of success with the diet as "anecdotal,"
and even threatened to use legal action to keep her from transferring
her child to Johns Hopkins in Baltimore to try the diet and avoid surgery. As might now be expected, the diet worked dramatically, and the
child rapidly became seizure-free and remained off of all medications.

The next day in the doctor's lounge at one of the local hospitals in
Colorado Springs, it was very apparent that the doctors as a group were
indignant that their authority had been questioned by the movie, ...
First Do No Harm. When one of the younger doctors did assert that he
should "look into" this ketogenic diet, the remainder of them rapidly
built up a strong "group negativity" that welcomed only further negative comments about this treatment modality. Some of these real doctors' comments actually closely paralleled the negative comments of the
TV movie neurologist.

The doctors also assaulted the reports of positive responses to the
ketogenic diet as anecdotal, even though it was very obvious that most,
if not all, of them had never even heard of the ketogenic diet before seeing or hearing of the movie. This was in spite of the fact that many of
these positive responses to the diet had actually been published. One
doctor even referred to the Internet as just another "National Enquirer,"
implying that lay people are too hopelessly ignorant to ever discover
vital information on their own, and that they are easily deluded by
anything they might read.

Another older physician asserted that he would need a "full bibliography" of medical references before he would even give the ketogenic diet passing consideration. As a group, it was generally expressed
and accepted that it was impossible that any significant therapy for unresponsive seizure disorders could possibly have eluded them in the

course of their medical training. Rather than join in the conversation, I just listened, and then I left without commenting.

After I got home, it took all of about three minutes to get my computer online, access MEDLINE, and find 180 medical journal references on the "ketogenic diet." MEDLINE is the database of the National Library of Medicine, containing over 11 million citations and author abstracts from more than 4,000 biomedical journals throughout the world, dating from 1966 to the present. (See the references cited at the end of this introduction for a small sampling of these ketogenic diet references.)

In one of the more recent references in the April, 2000 issue of *Pediatrics* eleven studies on the ketogenic diet were reviewed. The authors concluded that the ketogenic diet *completely* stopped medically unresponsive seizures in a significant percentage of children. The diet also reduced seizure frequency by over 90% in an even greater percentage of children! Similar articles were found in the various neurology and epilepsy journals.

Sadly, it would seem that many pediatricians and pediatric neurologists do not know what is in the most current issues of their primary and specialty journals. At the very least, it appears that what is read is rarely independently evaluated and weighed in the mind of the doctor reader. Invariably, new and "radical" information simply must already be accepted by the majority of a doctor's medical peers to have any real chance of being utilized in patient care. Older, more "radical" information, ironically, seems to have even less chance of objective evaluation and practical application.

It is of further significance to note that there has always been a consistent push to use prescription drugs whenever possible for just about any medical condition. Modern epileptic drugs were not available when the ketogenic diet was first discovered. However, the proper application of the diet is demanding and requires much more of an investment in time and effort than needs to be taken in the writing of a prescription.

When the anti-seizure drugs first came along a few years later, the ketogenic diet quickly fell into disfavor. This is especially unfortunate since epileptic drugs frequently have severe side effects compared to many other prescription drugs. Suffice it to say, however, that the ordinary physician rarely strays from what is contained in the primary textbooks, even if the current journals with which the physician should be familiar assert otherwise.

A word about one of the most common physician criticisms of a concept that does not mesh with traditional medical information needs to be mentioned here. When something is labeled as an "anecdote," the person reporting the information is usually being told that he or she is incapable of accurately reporting the response of a patient to a treatment. In reality, the dictionary defines an anecdote as being a short narrative that is unpublished. The most esteemed journals of our day often contain what are called "case reports," which are nothing more than brief summarizations of the response(s) of one or a handful of patients to a certain treatment. A case report is absolutely nothing more than an anecdotal report that managed to get published. However, the published case report is typically written by a health care professional, and the information is often given the validity of a much more "scientifically" prepared study or article.

In the final analysis, however, a case report is an anecdote, and an anecdote is a case report. The only differences are the reporter and the reporter's ability to be published. The lay person reporter or the non-mainstream medical doctor reporter will only endure ridicule and struggle to get published, while the mainstream doctor reporter will often get published and be awarded greater respect from the medical community for making a significant observation of a noteworthy clinical event. New, cutting-edge medical concepts from "non-sanctioned sources" frequently struggle just to see the light of day.

The "power of the textbook" also plays a significant role in the perpetuation of one treatment and the continuing opposition toward another. Even though the current medical literature clearly identifies diet as a very viable treatment for epilepsy, as mentioned above, most doctors do not use treatments that are not yet in the textbooks, unless most of their peers are already doing so.

In the 21st edition of the *Cecil Textbook of Medicine,* copyright 2000, there is not even one mention of the ketogenic diet in the treatment of epilepsy. This medicine textbook has long been the "gold standard" for medical students and resident physicians nationwide. So how can it be that a legitimate epilepsy therapy of 75 years standing is not even *mentioned* anywhere on its pages, even when esteemed academic medical institutions such as Johns Hopkins and Stanford have championed the therapy and re-ported consistently positive re-sults? A good question, indeed.

most doctors do not use treatments that are not yet in the texbooks unless most of their peers are already doing so

It doesn't even seem to be of concern to the average physician that the typical chapter in the medicine textbook is written by usually one and rarely two or more authors. This means that usually only one or two people are being relied upon to condense all the relevant information on a certain subject into the most pertinent and useful information. Furthermore, those authors are being trusted as having reviewed all of the important articles in the medical literature on a given subject.

This book will readily demonstrate that a great deal of relevant information on the enormous value of vitamin C in the medical literature remains unacknowledged, or perhaps just ignored. Most reviews of vitamin C in the current medical literature mention or cite very little of the original research done on vitamin C. Sadly, this is a direct indicator that many other very relevant "old" concepts or other important pieces of information on any given medical topic never find their places in the pages of medical textbooks.

Also, whenever a new edition of a medical textbook is published, you can rest assured that the treatment of a given topic will only vary in the slightest from the previous edition. Typically, the differences will be contained in the literature of only the last few years. In other words, if an important concept in the older medical literature doesn't make it *immediately* into the first edition of the textbook of its own "time," it stands little chance of ever being properly appreciated, regardless of how important it may be.

Truth be known, many physicians have outright disdain for any medical literature that is more than a few years old. It almost seems that even the best of scientific data is considered to have a "shelf life," and if it is not immediately incorporated into a textbook it will never be appreciated unless a "modern" researcher decides to repeat the study and "rediscover" the information.

Under the entry "ascorbic acid," the medical term for vitamin C, a MEDLINE search promptly revealed a list of nearly 24,000 articles in its files (search made in 2002). Furthermore, about one new article a day involving ascorbic acid continues to be published. Vitamin C has been and continues to be one the most researched substances in the history of medical research. One indication of this popularity of vitamin C as a research focus came from King (1936), who wrote an extensive review on vitamin C. At that time, he noted that his review was "confined almost entirely to research papers which have appeared during the last four years." Nevertheless, he cited 169 papers.

Ironically, vitamin C remains one of the most ignored substances in terms of practical application, in spite of the massive amount of research that has been done, and continues to be done. The authors of many vitamin C research articles often end their discussions by encouraging "further research" and asserting that their articles are "preliminary" in nature only. This is in spite of the fact that tremendous positive responses to vitamin C for given clinical conditions may have been observed in the studies. An especially amazing example of this phenomenon is found in the study of Massell et al. (1950), which examined the clinical responses of seven patients with rheumatic fever to vitamin C.

ironically, vitamin C remains one of the most ignored substances in terms of practical application, in spite of the massive amount of research that has been done

All seven patients had dramatic responses to vitamin C. Case One's arthritis was gone within 24 hours of receiving vitamin C. Case Three had been ill for six weeks, and by day two of vitamin C treatment his temperature was normal, and his arthritis was also completely resolved. Case Seven, in the authors' own words, was "greatly improved" after vitamin C therapy was started. Case Five was noted to be "obviously much improved." The other three cases had similar positive responses. Yet at the end of this article the authors note that "no final assessments can yet be made regarding the possible therapeutic value" of vitamin C in the treatment of rheumatic fever. And although the authors acknowledge that vitamin C is "generally considered innocuous," they add that "there is obviously a need for careful toxicity studies." It seems as though there could have been no clinical response dramatic enough and devoid enough of side effects that would have allowed these authors to dare suggest the routine use of vitamin C in the treatment of rheumatic fever. It would appear, for some reason, that the water is always a little too cold for swimming. In general, nobody dares to recommend a regular high dosing of vitamin C, even though a logical examination of most vitamin C research would suggest precisely that.

There are very few human diseases or medical conditions that are not improved to at least some degree by the regular dosing of optimal amounts of vitamin C. There is only rarely a good reason for not immediately giving any patient large doses of vitamin C and then proceeding with the medical evaluation. In fact, Klenner reported that he would routinely treat with vitamin C first, and then proceed with his patient evaluation. Furthermore, Klenner reported always having good results with this clinical approach.

Basic research is certainly essential to achieve continued progress in medicine, but the landmark vitamin C studies that beg to be performed now should involve the use of only the highest of doses. Although Klenner achieved many amazing results with his vitamin C treatments, I could find no mainstream medical researcher who has performed *any* clinical studies on *any* infectious disease with vitamin C doses that even approached those used by Klenner.

Using a small enough dose of any therapeutic agent will demonstrate little or no effect on an infection or disease process. However, this information *cannot* be used in concluding what the effects of much larger doses of that agent would be. Klenner would often use daily doses of vitamin C on a patient that would be as much as 10,000 times more than the daily doses used in some of the many clinical studies in the literature! And even though such tiny doses of vitamin C would often still show some incredible clinical or laboratory effects, a lack of response was frequently reported as well. A scientifically valid comparison between the effects of such vastly different doses simply cannot be made fairly.

Klenner would often use daily doses of vitamin C on a patient... as much as 10,000 times more than the daily doses used in many clinical studies in the literature

The medical literature, as revealed on MEDLINE and in the literature that preceded the appearance of MEDLINE, reveals many long-lost, ignored, or otherwise neglected scientific facts and assorted pieces of information. The above examples of the ketogenic diet in the medical literature indexed on MEDLINE appear to have remained unknown or unappreciated to actively practicing pediatricians, internists, neurologists, and neurological surgeons.

It should come as no surprise, then, that numerous and dramatic pieces of medical and clinical information in vitamin C research can be found in 1990, as well as 1960, 1940, and even earlier. It should be easy to appreciate that when current research published in 1999 or 2000 is unknown to many physicians, even when it appears in their selected subspecialty journals, research data published in 1940 that never made it into the medical textbooks has no realistic chance of recognition by the vast majority of today's practicing doctors.

Vitamin C research is also somewhat unique in that a very large amount of research was accumulated on it before it was ever chemically identified. Prior to this identification, it was just known as the "anti-scurvy" factor present in many fruits, vegetables, and other plants. Scurvy is the uniformly fatal disease that appears after the passage of enough months without any ingested vitamin C. Much of this older and less well-defined research still produced some amazing information, as will be shown.

Every attempt will be made in this book to reference the old and new medical literature as much as possible. A motivated reader can check out a great deal of the information offered. In general, it will be clear when I am offering my own explanations on the actions and effects of vitamin C and when something is being directly cited from the medical literature. Often, a certain question is not clearly addressed in the literature, and I will attempt to use the existing information to reach a logical conclusion.

This book is intended to challenge you, upset you, and hopefully even motivate you to action. This intention applies to both the lay reader as well as to any health care practitioner reader.

Yes, vitamin C has been shown to cure, reverse and/or prevent many infectious diseases considered to be incurable and largely untreatable, except for some relief of associated symptoms. Yes, many viral infectious diseases have been cured and can continue to be cured by the proper administration of vitamin C.

Yes, the vaccinations for these treatable infectious diseases are completely unnecessary when one has the access to proper treatment with vitamin C.

And, yes, all of the side effects of vaccinations, whether you consider them to be many or few, are also completely unnecessary since the vaccinations do not have to be given in the first place with the availability of properly dosed vitamin C.

It is long, long overdue that vitamin C is given its proper recognition and utilization in mainstream medicine. Furthermore, vitamin C needs to be recognized not in the microdoses that have been typically researched for some 65 years, but in the much larger, optimal doses used by Frederick R. Klenner, M.D. and a few other noteworthy clinicians and researchers. Optimal vitamin C dosing should drastically reduce the use of many antibiotics and other medicines.

After you read this book, see if you don't agree that properly dosed vitamin C would prevent a large amount of needless disease and suffering.

References

Casey, J., J. McGrogan, D. Pillas, P. Pyzik, J. Freeman, and E. Vining. (1999) The implementation and maintenance of the Ketogenic Diet in children. *Journal of Neuroscience Nursing* 31(5):294-302.

Cecil Textbook of Medicine. (2000) 21st edition. Edited by Goldman, L. and J. Bennett. Philadelphia, PA: W. B. Saunders Company.

Forman, R. (1981) Medical resistance to innovation. *Medical Hypotheses* 7(8):1009-1017.

Freeman, J. and E. Vining. (1999) Seizures decrease rapidly after fasting: preliminary studies of the ketogenic diet. *Archives of Pediatrics & Adolescent Medicine* 153(9):946-949.

King, C. (1936) Vitamin C, ascorbic acid. *Physiological Reviews* 16: 238-262.

Klenner, F. (July 1949) The treatment of poliomyelitis and other virus diseases with vitamin C. *Southern Medicine & Surgery* 111(7): 209-214.

Landwehr, R. (1991) The origin of the 42-year stonewall of vitamin C. *Journal of Orthomolecular Medicine* 6(2):99-103.

Lefevre, F. and N. Aronson. (2000) Ketogenic diet for the treatment of refractory epilepsy in children: a systematic review of efficacy. *Pediatrics* 105(4):E46.

Massell, B., J. Warren, P. Patterson, and H. Lehmus. (1950) Antirheumatic activity of ascorbic acid in large doses. Preliminary observations on seven patients with rheumatic fever. *The New England Journal of Medicine* 242(16):614-615.

Sirven, J., B. Whedon, D. Caplan, J. Liporace, D. Glosser, J. O'Dwyer, and M. Sperling. (1999) The ketogenic diet for intractable epilepsy in adults: preliminary results. *Epilepsia* 40(12):1721-1726.

Stafstrom, C. and S. Spencer. (2000) The ketogenic diet: a therapy in search of an explanation. *Neurology* 54(2):282-283.

Chapter One

Some Basic Concepts and Historical Perspectives

Discovery consists in seeing what everybody else has seen and thinking what nobody has thought.

ALBERT SZENT-GYORGYI, M.D., PH.D.
AWARDED THE 1937 NOBEL PRIZE IN PHYSIOLOGY
OR MEDICINE FOR THE DISCOVERY OF VITAMIN C,
IN CONNECTION WITH BIOLOGICAL COMBUSTION

A Theory of Life

Szent-Gyorgyi (1978, 1980) proposed that the essence of the living state is that organic molecules such as the proteins in the tissues of the body must be maintained in a state of electron desaturation. All matter has varying proportions of electrons, protons, and neutrons, but Szent-Gyorgyi held that dead tissue had a full complement of electrons, while live tissue maintained a deficit of electrons. Vitamin C, known chemically as ascorbic acid, interacts with a wide variety of basic chemical substances in the body. Vitamin C literally appears to be one of the primary substances assuring that a vigorous, continuing electron exchange takes place among the body's tissues and molecules.

Szent-Gyorgyi asserted that energy exchange, arguably life's most important form of cellular communication, can only occur when there

33

is an imbalance of electrons between and among molecules. This imbalance of electrons causes the natural flow of electrons, a biological form of electricity, throughout the body. All of the body's functions are directed, controlled, and regulated by this physiological flow of electricity. Furthermore, this flow of electricity through the body also establishes and maintains the subtle magnetic fields in the body that appear to be involved with good health.

Vitamin C, although possessing other important qualities, appears to be a most important stimulus to this flow of electricity. A greater amount of vitamin C in the body enhances the flow of electricity in the body, thereby optimizing the ability of the cells in the body to maintain their health-sustaining communications. One definition of life, then, is that it is a state in which an optimal degree of electron interchange among cells can take place. Health exists when electrons flow fully and freely, illness exists when this flow is significantly impaired, and death occurs when this flow stops. Furthermore, when this electron flow is impaired, there is a need for more vitamin C to help remedy this impairment.

Since poor electron flow throughout the body's tissues appears to cause or be associated with disease, this also means that there is typically a vitamin C deficiency whenever the body is diseased. Because of this interrelationship vitamin C should always be a part of the treatment of virtually any disease state. Just as dehydration requires water, poor electron flow—a primary characteristic of the diseased state—requires vitamin C. This will virtually always apply, even when a deficiency of vitamin C was not necessarily involved in the development of a certain diseased state.

There are only a very few situations in which some restraint should be exerted in the administration of vitamin C, and these will be discussed in Chapter 4.

Entrenched Misconceptions

The enormous clinical usefulness of vitamin C remains little appreciated. This lack of appreciation is partially due to its classification as a vitamin, which is a very limiting definition. In the 28th edition of *Dorland's Illustrated Medical Dictionary* a vitamin is defined as

> a general term for a number of unrelated organic sub-
> stances that occur in many foods in small amounts and
> that are necessary in trace amounts for the normal meta-
> bolic functioning of the body.

While vitamin C is certainly necessary in at least trace amounts for the body to survive and to avoid the deficiency disease known as scurvy, much larger amounts are necessary for the body to achieve and maintain optimal health. The above definition pertains much more to other identified vitamins rather than vitamin C, and only trace amounts of vitamin C will *not* support the "normal metabolic functioning" of the body mentioned in the definition above. Rather, the chronic underdosing of vitamin C from minimal or no supplementation and from eating depleted food will facilitate the development of nearly all the chronic degenerative diseases that affect man.

chronic underdosing of vitamin C will facilitate the development of nearly all the chronic degenerative diseases that affect man

Furthermore, evidence that will be presented throughout this book will clearly and repeatedly demonstrate that chronic vitamin C depletion is often one of the primary reasons that many common infectious diseases are contracted in the first place. It will become apparent that many people throughout the world, including many in the seemingly well-fed United States, are suffering from the effects of a chronically deficient intake of vitamin C.

It is very possible that much of the success claimed by mainstream medicine in both improving lifespan and decreasing the incidence of infectious diseases has come from the addition of small amounts of vitamin C, along with other antioxidant nutrients, to many of our oth-erwise depleted packaged foods. The degree of this "success" should improve further as time goes by, as it is becoming increasingly accepted to supplement a greater variety of foods with even larger amounts of vitamin C.

As addressed in some length in the introduction, an established scientific concept, however wrong, is very difficult to correct once accepted and given the credibility of publication in medical textbooks. The information in this book will repeatedly demonstrate that a vitamin-like function is only one of multiple significant properties of vitamin C.

Arguably, since it will be shown that much larger than "trace amounts" of vitamin C are needed to be taken on a regular basis to maintain optimal health and "normal metabolic functioning," a strict interpretation of the definition of vitamin C can even support the argument that vitamin C is not a vitamin at all. Ultimately, it should become apparent to the reader that vitamin C is the single most important nutrient substance for the body, regardless of whether it is viewed as a vitamin. However, for purposes of discussing the massive amounts of literature that have been generated on this fascinating substance, I will continue to refer to it as vitamin C throughout this book. The scientific and medical literature contains a few other names for vitamin C based on the nature of its chemical composition, but they will not generally be used to avoid any possible confusion or appearance of inconsistency to the reader.

Another critical misconception regarding vitamin C involves how much of it should be used to achieve the intended therapeutic effect. Real estate agents frequently say that the three most important attributes of a home are "location, location, and location." Similarly, the three most important considerations in effective vitamin C therapy are "dose, dose, and dose."

the three most important considerations in effective vitamin C therapy are "dose, dose, and dose"

If you don't take enough, you won't get the desired effects. Period! On the other hand, you will rarely ever fail to observe a dramatic response to a wide variety of medical conditions if you take a large enough dose for a long enough time.

On the other hand, even the use of relatively tiny doses of vitamin C will frequently result in some clearly definable benefit in many infectious diseases. Nearly all of the past and present papers in the literature that declare the ineffectiveness of vitamin C for given conditions use incredibly small doses of vitamin C in their experiments and trials, while looking for dramatic and clear-cut benefits. The Recommended Dietary Allowance (RDA) of vitamin C ranges between 30 and 95 mg (milligrams) daily, with 60 mg being recommended for adult men and women. Often, the proper dose of vitamin C in the treatment of an infectious disease may be anywhere from several hundred-fold to several *thousand*-fold times the amount in this miniscule RDA dose! The RDA serves to prevent only the development of the full-blown clinical picture of scurvy in otherwise clinically healthy people, or to restore vitamin C blood levels in otherwise normal people to the levels deemed to be normal or acceptable.

nearly all the papers in the literature that declare the ineffectiveness of vitamin C use incredibly small doses in their experiments and trials

Indeed, in many people who have infectious diseases that metabolize unusually large amounts of vitamin C, keeping body stores of vitamin C depleted, the RDA for vitamin C will not even prevent many of the symptoms of scurvy from developing or restore the blood levels of vitamin C to the normal range.

Evidence contained in this book will actually demonstrate that many people with such vitamin C-depleting infectious diseases actually die from complications completely consistent with the symptoms of acute scurvy. For example, many people who eventually die from an infectious disease actually die from a bleeding complication. An acute and severe vitamin C deficiency is often the immediate underlying reason for either subtle bleeding or massive hemorrhage.

Many of the numerous vitamin C research papers are also especially misleading in their conclusions since they persist in labeling the small amounts of vitamin C used in their studies as "megadose." Even the amounts of vitamin C that are termed "megadose" in the literature often need to be increased a thousand-fold or more to reach the necessary dosage actually needed to achieve the desired therapeutic effect. Because of this continued mislabeling in the literature, I will refer to the amounts of vitamin C that really should be used as "optidoses" (optimal doses).

Although many of the optidoses recommended in this book will be substantially larger than most of the "megadoses" mentioned in the literature, use of the term optidose may gradually allow doctors and patients alike to realize that the recommended dose is really the *optimal* dose that the body needs at that time. It is also important to realize that the optidose of vitamin C, even for a single patient, can vary widely depending upon how sick the patient already is when therapy is initiated.

Furthermore, one optidose is not necessarily appropriate for two patients with seemingly similar clinical situations, since one patient may have underlying factors consuming vitamin C much more rapidly than the other patient. On the other hand, a megadose only implies that the treating physician feels that a large dose is being recommended, and the dose given may still not necessarily be the physiologically appropriate dose that will support or restore optimal health.

Taking regular optidoses of vitamin C tends to make the patient much more aware of the subtleties of good health. When something occurs that will compromise that good health, such as a new toxic or infectious challenge, it is not uncommon for the experienced vitamin C taker to almost reflexly increase the daily vitamin C optidose to the needed amount. The "chronically healthy" person almost always knows when even small reversals in good health are taking place, and taking enough additional vitamin C at such a time will almost always promptly restore good health, as well as make the contraction of any infectious disease extremely unlikely.

Genetically Lacking

Vitamin C must be directly ingested, usually in the form of supplementation as well as in the diet, to maintain adequate levels inside the cells in the tissues (versus the more commonly measured levels in the blood) throughout the body. Tissue cells contain greater concentrations of vitamin C than are found in the blood (Meiklejohn, 1953). As a result, ingesting only enough vitamin C to maintain a given blood level is no guarantee that many of the vitamin C-rich tissue cells will have enough vitamin C available to them from the blood to reach and maintain their proper concentrations.

It should also be realized that the human body does not have the ability to synthesize *any* vitamin C whatsoever. However, this is not the case with most other animals. Generally, nearly all mammals, reptiles, and amphibians have the ability to synthesize at least some of their daily requirement for vitamin C. Most mammals synthesize vitamin C in their livers, first measured experimentally by Grollman and Lehninger (1957), and other animals, primarily reptiles and amphibians, can achieve this synthesis in their kidneys (Chatterjee et al., 1975). This ability is felt to be completely lacking in humans, as well as in primates, fruit bats, and guinea pigs.

nearly all mammals, reptiles and amphibians have the ability to synthesize vitamin C ...this ability is felt to be completely lacking in humans

Interestingly, the very fact that the guinea pig cannot make any vitamin C for itself is one of the primary reasons that it has served scientific researchers so well. The guinea pig can be made ill or toxic much more easily than a vitamin C-producing research animal, and there is less variability in the guinea pig's response to a given stress compared to other animals that can respond with internally-produced vitamin C. Researchers quickly realized that guinea pigs and primates (including man) seemed uniquely susceptible to a wide variety of clinical syndromes, including life-threatening shock and infectious diseases such as tuberculosis, diphtheria, and polio. Of course, it eventually became apparent that experimentally-induced scurvy required an animal such as the guinea pig that could not produce its own vitamin C, or another animal that could produce only small amounts.

Chatterjee et al. (1975) examined the abilities of different species of animals to produce their own vitamin C. Among the mammals tested, they found that goats were especially capable of producing significant amounts of vitamin C. In fact, goats had a rate of production of vitamin C that was roughly 13 times greater than that of cats or dogs. All wild animals tested had at least a 4-fold greater rate of vitamin C production compared to cats or dogs. This is likely one of the primary reasons that these two most common domestic pets will keep the veterinarian busy with so many of the same diseases that afflict their human owners. Although they do produce some vitamin C,

goats are believed to produce as much as 100,000 mg of vitamin C daily when faced with life-threatening infectious or toxic stress

dogs and cats produce it less readily than many other animals, and compared with wild animals, they are much more easily stressed into a state of vitamin C deficiency. For example, the efficient vitamin C-producing adult goat can internally manufacture more than 13,000 mg of vitamin C daily to maintain its optimal health when it is not facing any significant challenges to its health (Stone, 1979). Even more amazingly, goats are also believed by some to produce as much as 100,000 mg of vitamin C daily when faced with life-threatening degrees of infectious or toxic stress! Researchers such as Levine (1986) have argued that it is quite difficult to recommend an optimal daily dose of vitamin C for the human being. However, few investigators familiar with the bulk of research on vitamin C would maintain that the human RDA dosage is nearly enough to meet all of the body's needs.

unlike many humans who spend much of their lives fighting a chronic disease, most wild animals synthesize enough vitamin C to exhibit good health throughout their life spans

Conney et al. (1961) demonstrated that animals having the ability to synthesize their own vitamin C could produce about 10 times more than their baseline levels when subjected to enough biochemical stress, such as from drugs. This automatic ability to adequately step up vitamin C production in the face of stress explains why so many wild animals tend to live healthy for their entire life spans until it is time to die. Conversely, generally vitamin C-depleted human beings will typically spend at least half of their lifetimes coping with one or more chronic diseases. Dogs and cats are generally somewhat healthier than people, but their limited vitamin C-synthesizing ability is eventually overwhelmed as they grow older and face greater cumulative toxic stresses, resulting in more disease than seen in wild animals.

Even the rabbit, which can produce roughly five times as much vitamin C internally as the dog or cat, can be malnourished to the point of eventually dying from what appears to be a metabolic condition closely akin to scurvy (Findlay, 1921). It should not be hard to understand, then, that an added vitamin C-utilizing condition, such as a significant infection, can push even vitamin C-producing animals to the point of clinical scurvy.

The specific genetic defect that prevents humans from internally synthesizing vitamin C is the lack of a liver enzyme known as L-gulonolactone oxidase (GLO). GLO is the last of a sequence of liver enzymes that ultimately transforms glucose (blood sugar) into vitamin C. Interestingly, the actual GLO genome, or sequence of coding DNA, has been identified to be present in humans (Nishikimi et al., 1988). For unclear reasons, this segment of human DNA remains "untranslated," meaning the recipe for GLO is present in the human but remains unprepared. This raises the possibility of potentially exciting new avenues of research for today's genetic researchers. If a way can eventually be found to get the already present genetic code for GLO to "turn on" and continually produce GLO, the health of the human population will leapfrog to levels that may seem literally unbelievable today. Human beings would then be able to continually synthesize vitamin C from glucose, and there would be far fewer toxic or infectious challenges that could cause illness. As is already seen with the many vitamin C-producing wild animals, such a human could then be expected to remain much healthier until the expected life span had run its course.

A thorough examination of the literature reveals another potentially exciting way to address the human being's inability to synthesize vitamin C that does not appear to have been seriously addressed. While not always practical or clinically effective, genetically-based enzyme defects can sometimes be addressed by the direct administration of the missing enzyme. Sato et al. (1986) administered GLO harvested from either chickens or rats to guinea pigs. Giving this enzyme to guinea pigs enabled them to survive vitamin C-deficient diets. At the very least, this should stimulate further research into the feasibility of giving such direct enzyme replacement therapy to humans. Hadley and Sato (1988) established a protocol involving long-term GLO administration to guinea pigs that was successful in maintaining a high proportion of those animals.

the recipe for synthesizing vitamin C is present in the human but remains unprepared

These results would certainly seem to warrant further serious research on similar treatment programs for humans. Assisting the liver in performing what should be a natural function is a very desirable clinical goal. Perhaps regular therapy with GLO enzyme replacement, supported by more vitamin C when toxic and other environmental stresses present themselves, might be a very good health-supporting regimen. Certainly, stimulating the liver to release vitamin C directly into the bloodstream would undoubtedly help support the oral and other non-intravenous forms of supplemental vitamin C. The scientific literature specifically addressed in Chapter 2 clearly shows the vast clinical superiority of intravenous vitamin C over any other form of vitamin C administration. Often a significantly smaller dose of intravenous vitamin C, compared to an oral administration, will promptly result in the clinical resolution of an infectious disease.

A human's inability to produce GLO must be considered something of an inborn error of metabolism. This metabolic error was also induced in the vitamin C-producing rat by Mizushima et al. (1984). They were able to establish a mutant rat colony that produced no GLO, the same defect "normally" found in guinea pigs and humans. As with other such inborn errors of metabolism, every attempt should routinely be made by a treating physician to consider this lack of enzyme activity in every medical condition. This translates into a very simple approach: always give vitamin C on a daily basis, and always give enough.

To date, there are NO infectious diseases that have ever been found in which vitamin C administration can be considered dangerous or inappropriate. This is the case even though there has already been roughly a century of research on vitamin C, involving the publishing of some 50,000 to 100,000 scientific articles. A handful of case reports, which will be addressed in more detail in Chapter 4, gives

to date, NO infectious diseases have been found in which vitamin C administration is dangerous or inappropriate

good reason to exert a minimal amount of caution when administering vitamin C under a very limited number of clinical circumstances.

However, no evidence has ever been produced to demonstrate that a regular optidose of vitamin C should be avoided by anybody. Everybody requires an optidosing of vitamin C on a daily basis to reach and maintain optimal health. No human body can operate effectively and stay healthy without such an optidose. The only real question that remains is what one's individual daily optidose should be. This, too, will be addressed later in more detail.

It is an incredibly rare situation for an inborn error of metabolism like the one resulting in GLO deficiency to be shared by all humans. There are many other inborn errors of metabolism, but these affect only certain unfortunate individuals. However, there appears to be a primary assumption in the medical community that a 100% GLO deficiency is a genetic trait shared by all human beings.

From my review of the scientific literature, however, it does not appear that a serious study was ever undertaken to see if all humans were equally lacking in this critical liver enzyme. Consider the anecdotal reports that one occasionally hears about a certain individual living to 100, while smoking and drinking every day of his adult life. Although one can be blessed with a much better immune system than others, the ability to synthesize GLO, at least to a limited degree, could also be the reason for an otherwise incredibly long and healthy life.

Any inborn error of metabolism is also not "completely expressed" all of the time. Certain enzyme levels may be depressed by 10%, 50%, or 90%, but not necessarily 100%. This must also be considered a possibility for the levels of GLO in different people possessed of great longevity, at least until careful studies can determine otherwise. Cummings (1981) pointed out that some individuals enrolled in vitamin C depletion studies were discontinued from those studies when no symptoms of scurvy developed or when vitamin C levels did not drop significantly over an extended period of time (Kline and Eheart, 1944; Pijoan and Lozner, 1944).

It seems that there was never any serious curiosity over whether these individuals could continue to have vitamin C in their bodies over even longer periods of time. If any individuals could be identified with even partial GLO production and internal vitamin C production during periods when dietary vitamin C restriction resulted in scurvy for the remainder of the individuals studied, even more exciting avenues of research could be pursued. It is always easier to research a condition that is not possessed by all.

Further support for the concept that all human beings might not be completely lacking in GLO and the internal production of vitamin C comes from studies with guinea pigs. Williams and Deason (1967) reported that one guinea pig continued to survive after eight weeks on a vitamin C-free diet, which should have produced scurvy. Before long, several other investigators concluded that some guinea pigs could synthesize vitamin C, thereby accounting for the occasional wide variability in the laboratory requirements needed to induce scurvy in these animals (Odumosu and Wilson, 1967; Ginter, 1976).

In spite of this research, there still does not appear to be any enthusiasm or significant interest in looking systematically for those occasional humans who can also synthesize some vitamin C.

Cummings (1981) further points out that if the lack of GLO in humans comes from the same recessive genetic trait as is found in other genetic enzyme deficiency states, then occasional mutations should be expected to occur that would again allow GLO to be expressed and vitamin C to be synthesized. However, if any of the above is true, a deliberate search should be made to find such vitamin C-synthesizing individuals. Some findings may fall into a researcher's lap, but many must be specifically sought out or they will not be found.

Historical Background

In its classical and full-blown form, scurvy is a painful, unrelenting, and uniformly fatal disease. Few physicians today ever get the opportunity to even see a case of classical scurvy of the kind that decimated navies, armies, and explorers of centuries ago. In *A Treatise on the Scurvy,* the classic work first published in 1753, James Lind, M.D. described the first symptoms he observed that heralded the appearance of scurvy:

> The first indication of the approach of this disease, is generally a change of colour in the face, from the natural and usual look, to a pale and bloated complexion; with a listlessness to action, or an aversion to any sort of exercise. When we examine narrowly the lips, or the corners of the eye, where the blood-vessels lie most exposed, they appear of a greenish tinge. Mean while, the person eats and drinks heartily, and seems in perfect health; except that his countenance and lazy inactive disposition may portend an approaching scurvy.

Classical scurvy in humans can only occur when vitamin C levels in the plasma, the fluid part of the blood free of cells, approach zero and remain so for a number of months.

Lund and Crandon (1941) and Crandon et al. (1940) reported on the deliberate induction of scurvy with a vitamin C-deficient diet. Crandon was able to eventually demonstrate in himself a complete absence of circulating plasma vitamin C. He developed small skin hemorrhages after about five months and demonstrated poor wound healing after six months. Other investigators (Baker et al., 1971) were able to induce the signs and symptoms of scurvy in a group of five prison volunteers before plasma vitamin C levels completely reached zero.

The ability of any given individual to develop scurvy will depend upon how absolutely the diet is deficient in vitamin C and how healthy and well-fed that individual was before the vitamin C intake was stopped. The body stores of vitamin C vary significantly, and the presence of underlying diseases and chronic toxin exposures will also substantially increase the rate of utilization of whatever vitamin C stores are present. As vitamin C levels in the plasma approach zero, the levels of vitamin C eventually become severely depleted throughout the tissues of the body.

When the depletion of vitamin C is severe enough, the scorbutic (scurvy-stricken) individual is incredibly weak and prone to very easy bleeding. Virtually all motion produces excruciating pain, and the gums are typically infected. Teeth are no longer soundly anchored in the gums, and the breath develops a putrid smell from the infection. The skin is mottled with spots, many of which relate to bleeding within the skin. The legs and knees also tend to be swollen in the late stages. The immune system is always severely compromised, and a secondary infectious disease, such as tuberculosis or pneumonia, will often take hold and end up being the immediate cause of death. Interestingly, many scurvy victims did not appear wasted and malnourished. Rather, full-blown scurvy would also occur in individuals who were overweight and considered well-fed in terms of the food amount eaten. This observation serves to underscore the important concept that a good quality and proper variety of foods are vastly more important for overall nutrition than the amount of food eaten.

Lind, who came to be known in Great Britain as "the father of nautical medicine," conducted what many consider to be one of the first experimental clinical trials that utilized a truly scientific methodology. While on board ship, he selected 12 sailors who already had scurvy and then formulated six different regimens of dietary supplementation to be given to six groups of two. All of the sailors were given the same basic diet throughout the day. Two sailors also received two oranges and one lemon daily for six days, while the remaining 10 men received other dietary supplementation that did not contain any significant amounts of vitamin C. Lind's other supplementations were termed "elixir vitriol," vinegar, sea water, "cyder," and a concoction containing nutmeg, garlic, mustard-seed, horseradish, barley, myrrh, and cream of tartar.

At the time, all of these concoctions were considered as candidates for having some anti-scurvy effects. After only six days the two fortunate recipients of the citrus fruits had already recovered to the extent that they could resume their normal on board duties. The trial could not continue any longer because Lind only had enough oranges and lemons to last six days. None of the other men showed any significant improvement, although the two men given what was only termed "cyder" along with the regular diet did show some lessening of their weakness.

Lind's trial also served to dramatically demonstrate that very little vitamin C given for a very short period of time can still be very effective in acutely relieving the symptoms of clinically full-blown scurvy. Because a vitamin is generally considered to be needed in only very small amounts to prevent a known deficiency disease, this dramatic clinical response of scurvy to very minimal vitamin C dosing is the primary reason that vitamin C first came to be considered a vitamin. As mentioned earlier in this chapter, however, such minimal doses of vitamin C are only enough to prevent the advanced symptoms and fatal complications of scurvy. Such small doses will not prevent the development and perpetuation of the many diseases associated with chronic vitamin C deficiency.

Summary

Vitamin C has long been mislabeled as a vitamin, at least in the strictest sense of the definition. This mislabeling has been one of the primary reasons that the proper dosing ("optidosing") of vitamin C remains largely unappreciated. Improper dosing of vitamin C continues to be the main reason for any scientific paper to claim that vitamin C was without effect in treating a given infectious disease or medical condition.

Genetically speaking, human beings and a few other animals cannot translate the DNA code for the vital enzyme, L-gulonolactone oxidase, which is needed to convert glucose into vitamin C internally. This genetic defect is the main reason why humans are so much more prone to infections and diseases than many wild animals. Humans are totally dependent on ingested sources of vitamin C. Repairing this genetic defect, or compensating for it, could improve the health of humans to an almost unimaginable degree.

Scurvy, a uniformly fatal disease when left untreated, results when a human has been completely deprived of vitamin C long enough to demonstrate little or no plasma vitamin C for several months. Relatively small amounts of vitamin C can save a scurvy victim from death, but much larger amounts are needed to optimize health.

References

Baker, E., R. Hodges, J. Hood, H. Sauberlich, S. March, and J. Canham. (1971) Metabolism of 14-C and 3-H-labeled L-ascorbic acid in human scurvy. *The American Journal of Clinical Nutrition* 24(4):444-454.

Chatterjee, I., A. Majumder, B. Nandi, and N. Subramanian. (1975) Synthesis and some major functions of vitamin C in animals. *Annals of the New York Academy of Sciences* 258:24-47.

Conney, A., G. Bray, C. Evans, and J. Burns. (1961) Metabolic interactions between L-ascorbic acid and drugs. *Annals of the New York Academy of Sciences* 92:115-127.

Crandon, J., C. Lund, and D. Dill. (1940) Experimental human scurvy. *The New England Journal of Medicine* 223:353-369.

Cummings, M. (1981) Can some people synthesize ascorbic acid? *The American Journal of Clinical Nutrition* 34(2):297-298.

Cuppage, F. (1994) *James Cook and the Conquest of Scurvy.* Westport, CT: Greenwood Press.

Davies, M., J. Austin, and D. Partridge. (1991) *Vitamin C: Its Chemistry and Biochemistry.* Cambridge: The Royal Society of Chemistry, Thomas Graham House.

Findlay, G. (1921) A note on experimental scurvy in the rabbit, and on the effects of antenatal nutrition. *The Journal of Pathology and Bacteriology* 24:454-455.

Ginter, E. (1976) Ascorbic acid synthesis in certain guinea pigs. *International Journal for Vitamin and Nutrition Research* 46(2): 173-179.

Grollman, A. and A. Lehninger. (1957) Enzymic synthesis of L-ascorbic acid in different animal species. *Archives of Biochemistry and Biophysics* 69:458-467.

Hadley, K. and P. Sato (1988) A protocol for the successful long-term enzyme replacement therapy of scurvy in guinea pigs. *Journal of Inherited Metabolic Disease* 11(4):387-396.

Kline, A. and M. Eheart. (1944) Variation in the ascorbic acid requirements for saturation of nine normal young women. *Journal of Nutrition* 28:413-419.

Levine, M. (1986) New concepts in the biology and biochemistry of ascorbic acid. *The New England Journal of Medicine* 314(14):892-902.

Lind, J. (1753) *A Treatise on the Scurvy.* [Special Edition for the Classics of Medicine Library] Birmingham, AL: Leslie B. Adams, Jr., Publisher, 1980.

Lund, C. and J. Crandon. (1941) Human experimental scurvy and the relation of vitamin C deficiency to postoperative pneumonia and wound healing. The *Journal of the American Medical Association* 116(8):663-668.

Meiklejohn, A. (1953) The physiology and biochemistry of ascorbic acid. *Vitamins and Hormones* 11:61-96.

Mizushima, Y., T. Harauchi, T. Yoshizaki, and S. Makino. (1984) A rat mutant unable to synthesize vitamin C. *Experientia* 40(4):359-361.

Nishikimi, M., T. Koshizaka, T. Ozawa, and K. Yagi. (1988) Occurrence in humans and guinea pigs of the gene related to their missing enzyme L-gulonolactone oxidase. *Archives of Biochemistry and Biophysics* 267(2):842-846.

Odumosu, A. and C. Wilson. (1973) Metabolic availability of vitamin C in the guinea-pig. *Nature* 242(5399):519-521.

Pijoan, M. and E. Lozner. (1944) Vitamin C economy in the human subject. *Bulletin of the Johns Hopkins Hospital* 75:303-314.

Sato, P., A. Roth, and D. Walton. (1986) Treatment of a metabolic disease, scurvy, by administration of the missing enzyme. *Biochemical Medicine and Metabolic Biology* 35(1):59-64.

Stone, I. (1979) Homo sapiens ascorbicus, a biochemically corrected robust human mutant. *Medical Hypotheses* 5(6):711-721.

Szent-Gyorgyi, A. (1978) How new understandings about the biological function of ascorbic acid may profoundly affect our lives.
Executive Health 14(8):1-4.

Szent-Gyorgyi, A. (1980) The living state and cancer. *Physiological
Chemistry and Physics* 12(2):99-110.

Williams, R. and G. Deason. (1967) Individuality in vitamin C needs.
*Proceedings of the National Academy of Sciences of the United
States of America* 57(6):1638-1641.

Chapter Two

Curing, Reversing, and Preventing Infectious Diseases

Everything that is written in books is worth much less than the experience of one physician who reflects and reasons.

RBAZES (850-923 A.D.)

Paving the Way: Frederick R. Klenner, M.D.

Even today only a very small number of medical researchers and clinicians completely appreciate the enormous benefit that can be obtained for a wide variety of infections and diseases by the proper use of what is considered very large doses of vitamin C. Frederick R. Klenner, M.D. led the way in both advocating and using the routine administration of these high doses of vitamin C for a wide variety of diseases, many of them infectious. Although primarily a clinical doctor rather than an institution-based researcher, Klenner also managed to publish at least 20 significant papers that documented the successful outcomes that he repeatedly achieved with many patients in Reidsville, North Carolina (see references at the end of this chapter).

After obtaining bachelor's and master's degrees in biology, Klenner went on to earn his medical degree from Duke University in 1936. He spent three more years in postgraduate training before deciding to go into the general practice of medicine. It was only in the late 1930s and early 1940s that vitamin C became readily available and economically affordable as a pharmaceutical. In his early medical practice Klenner subjected only himself to the initial large doses that he would later use on his patients. He then proceeded to use similarly large doses on his patients, and the results were absolutely unprecedented.

Polio (Curable and Preventable)

Although the viral syndrome known as polio is seen only very infrequently in the United States anymore, it still takes a substantial toll in some of the poorer countries around the world. However, even though the terror that polio inflicted on so many babies and children was at its peak about 50 years ago, many individuals in the younger generation who did not see its effects firsthand still appreciate that it was (and is) considered an incurable disease. In fact, the 21st edition (copyright 2000) of the *Cecil Textbook of Medicine* clearly asserts that "no specific treatment is available" for polio, adding that "supportive care" is essential for dealing with pain and increasing the chances of survival.

the 2000 edition of the Cecil Textbook of Medicine clearly asserts that "no specific treatment is available" for polio

Both the general public and the medical specialists share the view that polio has to "run its course" if it cannot be prevented by vaccination or otherwise avoided. It is also generally appreciated that many of the polio victims fortunate enough to survive the acute infection have to subsequently endure a lifetime of being crippled to a lesser or greater degree. A great deal of the public awareness of this disease also stems from the vivid images of our polio-stricken former president, Franklin D. Roosevelt, who struggled greatly to be seen in his wheelchair as little as possible in public. President Roosevelt's condition also made it clear to the public that polio and its crippling side effects were not limited to only babies and small children, but included unfortunate adults as well.

The data demonstrating the ability of vitamin C to cure polio is of worldwide concern, since polio outbreaks still occur. From August 16 to October 17, 2000, 33 cases of "acute flaccid paralysis" considered to be secondary to polio were reported in Cape Verde (MMWR, 2000). From July 12, 2000 to February 8, 2001, 12 "laboratory-confirmed poliomyelitis cases" were reported in the Dominican Republic (MMWR, 2001). These latter cases were attributed to "vaccine-derived poliovirus type 1." Regardless of the cause, however, polio continues to infect babies and children, and doctors must be prepared to treat these patients with the best therapy available.

When I first came across Klenner's work on polio patients, I was absolutely amazed and even a bit overwhelmed at what I read. I had already worked on a number of different medical conditions with large intravenous doses of vitamin C, so I was not completely surprised by the fact that the poliovirus could be easily eradicated by vitamin C. However, I was not prepared to easily deal with the spectrum of emotions that would grip me. To know that polio had been easily cured and so many babies, children, and some adults still continued to die or survive to be permanently crippled by this virus was extremely difficult to accept. As a child, I swallowed the little sugar cube polio vaccination along with all of my elementary school buddies, and we all prayed the same prayer, hoping against hope that the virus bogeyman wouldn't attack us as we slept.

Even more incredibly, Klenner briefly presented a summarization of his work on polio at the Annual Session of the American Medical Association on June 10, 1949 in Atlantic City, New Jersey. Galloway and Seifert (1949) reported on Klenner and the other presenters in their article in *The Journal of the American Medical Association*. Landwehr (1991) discussed this occasion and commented on its possible significance. Klenner's comments followed an extensive presentation on the best-known ways to support the ability of advanced polio patients to continue breathing. Klenner made the following remarks:

It might be interesting to learn how poliomyelitis was treated in Reidsville, N.C., during the 1948 epidemic. In the past seven years, virus infections have been treated and cured in a period of seventy-two hours by the employment of massive frequent injections of ascorbic acid, or vitamin C. I believe that if vitamin C in these massive doses—6,000 to 20,000 mg in a twenty-four hour period—is given to these patients with poliomyelitis none will be paralyzed and there will be no further maiming or epidemics of poliomyelitis.

One doctor made comments before Klenner, and four doctors made comments following him. The four doctors who commented after Klenner did not have anything to say about his assertions. They were only concerned with making their own observations about how a polio patient who had difficulty breathing could best be assisted and given a better chance to survive.

Although Klenner managed to publish his landmark article only a month later, which documented his cure of 60 out of 60 cases of polio during the 1948 polio epidemic, his comments at the Annual Session apparently were little heeded and quickly forgotten. Perhaps his results were just too fantastic to be believed.

Klenner published his landmark article one month after his presentation of his results to the AMA in June of 1949 which documented his cure of 60 out of 60 cases of polio

In the journal *Southern Medicine & Surgery* Klenner (July 1949) gave an in-depth accounting of his impressive treatment and results on polio patients. He noted that all 60 of his patients presented with all or almost all of the same signs and symptoms during the epidemic: fever of 101°F to 104.6°F, headache and pain behind the eyes, bloodshot eyes, reddened throat, nausea, vomiting, constipation, and pain between the shoulder blades, in the back of the neck, in the lower back, and in one or more limbs. Fifteen cases had confirmatory spinal taps, and eight had been in contact with another proven case of polio, helping to confirm the clinical diagnoses.

Spinal taps were generally avoided since they were felt to promote the access of the blood-borne virus into the nervous system through the puncture site. Also, with the sameness of symptoms occurring during an acknowledged epidemic of polio, spinal taps were not justifiable for diagnosis. Even if a skeptical reader does not think that all 60 of the patients had polio, there is no question that the vast majority of them did indeed have the disease.

After diagnosis, Klenner promptly initiated the massive vitamin C therapy. He even noted that the administration of the vitamin was much like that of an ordinary antibiotic. For children and babies under the age of four, the vitamin C was given as an intramuscular injection. The initial dose varied between 1,000 and 2,000 mg (one or two grams). Body temperature was utilized as a practical guide to continuing treatment, and the same dose was repeated in two hours if no drop in fever had been observed. If the temperature did show a clear drop, the next dose was held back for another two hours. This dosing schedule was followed strictly for the first 24 hours. Klenner noted that the presenting fevers were consistently down after the first 24 hours, and vitamin C was then given at the same dose but only every six hours. This dosing schedule was continued for 48 more hours. Klenner noted that *all* of the patients were clinically well after this 72-hour period of treatment.

However, when three patients had a subsequent clinical relapse of symptoms, Klenner decided it was best to continue the vitamin C administration for all of the patients under treatment at the same dosage for an additional 48 hours. During this final 48-hour period, vitamin C was dosed at either eight-hour or 12-hour intervals, and a complete and permanent resolution of the symptoms resulted. It is also very significant to note that *none* of the 60 patients treated by Klenner had any of the residual deformities so characteristic of many polio survivors. It would appear that the cure of all 60 polio patients was complete and absolute.

Klenner even noted that two of the patients already had advanced disease to the point where fluids were coming back through the nose. This was a symptom that typically heralded the progression of the disease to the point that breathing support would be required, and the chance of deformity and even death would be significantly increased. However, the recoveries of these two patients were also complete.

Klenner (September 1956) also published some of his clinical observations on the use of vitamin C to treat polio in two older patients. One 21-year-old woman presented with deep eye pain, leg pain in the hamstring area, pain in the neck and lower back, and a general desire to keep her entire body in a fixed position to avoid painful movements. She had a fever that reached 104.6°F, along with a sore throat that had relapsed after an initial treatment with antibiotics, aspirin, and fruit juice two weeks earlier. It is interesting to note that the small amounts of vitamin C in the fruit juice may very well have kept the symptoms from evolving more quickly and definitively.

In any event, Klenner felt the clinical diagnosis of polio was straightforward, and this 118-pound patient was immediately given 22,000 mg of vitamin C by slow intravenous injection with a 100 cc syringe. She then took 1,500 mg of vitamin C with juice every two hours at home. Twelve hours later she was free of her headache and had a fever of only 101.4°F. Klenner then gave her another 22,000 mg injection of vitamin C. There was some nausea and vomiting for the next 30 minutes, but after 24 hours she had a temperature of 100.8°F, with definite clinical improvement noted. Seven 18,000 mg injections of vitamin C were then given every 12 hours. Then five 10,000 mg injections were given every other day. Oral vitamin C was continued for an additional week at 1,500 mg every three to four hours. Klenner noted that the patient had an almost complete elimination of pain, except at the knees, after the first 48 hours. Temperature had normalized after 84 hours. Other than some thiamine (vitamin B_1) injections to help nervous tissue recovery, vitamin C was the only medication given to achieve a prompt and complete recovery.

Another patient, a 28-year-old female, presented with a very comparable clinical picture. She also demonstrated the same type of response after 96 hours of similarly dosed intravenous and oral vitamin C therapy. Even if one were to argue that both of these patients had a severe form of influenza rather than polio, the clinical responses they demonstrated to these large doses of vitamin C are nonetheless very dramatic. Getting over the flu in only three to four days would still be a modern medical miracle, regardless of the treatment used.

In another case reported by Klenner (1953), an eight-year-old boy presented to Klenner's office with a history of flu-like symptoms during the prior week. The child was continuing to be bothered by nausea and vomiting, sore throat, and a deep-seated headache at the back of his eyes that had even failed to respond to adult-sized doses of aspirin from his mother. Klenner took note of this clinical picture along with a few other classical symptoms, and he had little doubt the boy was having difficulty recovering from the poliovirus.

By any standards the boy's recovery was remarkable even if the syndrome had been due to another virus. He had a fever of 104°F and continued to cradle his head in his own hands in an attempt to find relief. He was also beginning to have some localizing symptoms characteristic of polio in his lumbar area (lower back) and left hamstring. Klenner gave 2,000 mg of vitamin C intravenously immediately in the office. The boy was then sent to the hospital where he promptly received another 2,000 mg of vitamin C intravenously. Repeated injections were then given every four hours. Only six hours later, with no other pain medication, the severe headache was completely relieved. The nausea and vomiting had resolved as well. Klenner commented that this previously miserable child was actually now in a "jovial" mood. The boy was discharged after a hospital stay of 48 hours during which he had received a total of 26,000 mg of vitamin C. A lesser oral regimen was continued to prevent a relapse that Klenner realized could occur whenever vitamin C therapy was severely tapered or discontinued too soon. Whether it was flu or polio, the response was prompt, and the cure was complete. Even today, modern medicine does not have a single effective and non-toxic virus-killing drug.

In an especially incredible case, Klenner (1951) described a five-year-old girl stricken with polio. This child had already been *paralyzed* in both her lower legs for over four days! The right leg was completely flaccid (limp), and the left leg was determined to be 85% flaccid. Pain was noticed especially in the knee and lumbar areas. Four consulting physicians confirmed the diagnosis of polio. Other than massage, vitamin C was the only therapy initiated. After four days of vitamin C injections the child was again moving both legs, but with only very slow and deliberate movement. Klenner also noted that there was a "definite response" after only the first injection of vitamin C. The child was discharged from the hospital after four days, and 1,000 mg of oral vitamin C was continued every two hours with fruit juice for seven days. The child was walking about, although slowly, on the 11th day of treatment. By the 19th day of treatment there was a "complete return of sensory and motor function," and no long-term impairment ever resulted. Vitamin C not only completely cured this case of polio, it completely reversed what would undoubtedly have been a devastating, crippling result for the remainder of this girl's life.

vitamin C not only completely cured this case of polio, it completely reversed what would undoubtedly have been a devastating, crippling result for the remainder of this girl's life

As one reviews the work of Klenner, it can readily be seen that he did not stick to hard and fast formulas on how much vitamin C to give to a certain patient. He always based subsequent dosing on the degree of general clinical response and the extent to which a elevated temperature had been lowered from the previous vitamin C dose. Although this is completely appropriate, it may make some potentially adventurous physician readers a bit reluctant to try using large doses of vitamin C on different viral syndromes without a fixed schedule of dosing based on diagnosis and body size. As will be shown later in this book, this fear is completely groundless due to the lack of toxicity of vitamin C at even the highest doses.

The greatest practical concern of high-dose vitamin C therapy is not an overdose of vitamin C, but an underdose. Typically, the acutely ill patient will not get a high enough dose of vitamin C for a long enough period of time, and the treating physician will then think that the less aggressive vitamin C dosing represents all that can be done with this agent. Some viral diseases, to be discussed later, can metabolize as much as 300,000 to 400,000 mg of vitamin C daily. In these cases the only way to assure a complete recovery, or even survival, is to maintain such an elevated dose until the virus has been completely destroyed. There are some viral syndromes that may even require still larger amounts of vitamin C. The rule of thumb in vitamin C treatment of viral diseases is to continue increasing the dose as long as the clinical response is inadequate or unsatisfactory, and to continue the treatment period until all clinical symptoms have disappeared.

Vitamin C and Polio: Supportive Research

Although the clinical cures that Klenner achieved with the vitamin C treatment of polio stand completely on their own merits, it should be of interest to note that earlier basic research had already suggested that vitamin C was a very effective killer of the poliovirus. Jungeblut (1935) demonstrated that vitamin C could completely inactivate the poliovirus outside of the body ("in vitro"), rendering it non-infectious even when injected directly into the brains of monkeys.

Salo and Cliver (1978) demonstrated this in vitro inactivation of the poliovirus by vitamin C more recently. Peloux et al. (1962) also showed that vitamin C, along with hydrogen peroxide, inactivated the poliovirus. Jungeblut (1937) later induced experimental polio in monkeys by this same direct injection technique into the brain. He found that about 30% of the 62 infected monkeys, which had also received injections of vitamin C, escaped developing paralysis. In the control group only about 5% of the survivors escaped paralysis. This demonstrated that vitamin C could kill the poliovirus in an infected animal ("in vivo") as well as in a test tube ("in vitro").

Although Jungeblut's use of lower doses of vitamin C, relative to Klenner's dose levels, did not demonstrate the level of clinical efficacy achieved by Klenner, Jungeblut's results clearly showed that vitamin C was an agent capable of killing the poliovirus in research animals and preventing subsequent neurological damage. This virus-killing effect alone deserved significant recognition since vitamin C was such a non-toxic therapy. Furthermore, Jungeblut's much smaller doses of vitamin C were given by a different route of administration than used by Klenner. Also, the virus had already been injected directly into the brain before the vitamin C treatment began, thereby giving the virus the ability to quickly progress to an advanced state of infection. Jungeblut (1937a), desiring to make sure that the data in his work was statistically significant, repeated his efforts with another 181 monkeys and again found that approximately 30% of them survived their infections without paralysis. Jungeblut (1939) later demonstrated a comparable virus-killing ability of vitamin C in monkeys when a different infecting strain of the poliovirus was used. These studies allowed Jungeblut to clearly confirm that vitamin C by itself could kill the poliovirus in infected monkeys. It remained only for doctors such as Klenner to discover the most effective protocols for the administration of vitamin C in humans for diseases such as polio.

Greer (1955) also reported excellent clinical results in his treatment of five polio victims with only oral vitamin C, given 10,000 mg at a time. This vitamin C dose was given as often as every three hours for up to 10 days. The total daily oral dose of vitamin C would range from 50,000 to 80,000 mg. His patients ranged in age from five to 43 years of age, and two of the patients did have slight residual weakness in a leg after treatment was complete. Baur (1952) also reported positive effects using only 10,000 to 20,000 mg of vitamin C daily, shortening both the total time of illness and the time it took to normalize the elevated body temperatures. However, in light of Klenner's success at seeing no residual damage in 60 out of 60 patients, it would appear that intramuscular and intravenous administrations of vitamin C get tissue levels of vitamin C to an optimal range more effectively than only oral administrations.

Using oral vitamin C appears to best serve as an adjunct to the other forms of vitamin C administration, and oral vitamin C is obviously the form of choice for long-term daily usage to stay healthy and prevent disease.

Additional Viral Diseases and Vitamin C

Viral Hepatitis (Curable and Preventable)

Acute viral hepatitis, a serious infection of the liver, afflicts between 0.5 and 1.0% of the United States population annually. Conservatively, this incidence of hepatitis translates to at least one million new cases every year. The current medical textbooks still maintain that there are no specific curative therapies for this disease, and provide only nonspecific recommendations aiming to treat symptoms while avoiding whatever might aggravate the underlying process. When the acute syndrome has not completely resolved or subsided on its own after a six-month period, the patient is generally considered by definition to have chronic hepatitis. Roughly 2% of the United States population is felt to have chronic hepatitis. Chronic hepatitis results in upwards of 10,000 deaths annually in the United States, and roughly another 1,500 patients with this disease survive to receive liver transplantation.

Acute viral hepatitis, which keeps many people sick for extended periods of time even if it does not result in chronic hepatitis, is easily and readily completely *curable* if treated promptly with adequate doses of vitamin C. The effects of vitamin C on hepatitis patients who have already proceeded to the chronic stage is less well-defined, although some evidence indicates that a high enough dose of vitamin C for a long enough period of time would probably resolve this disease as well in many of the cases.

Klenner (1974) considered vitamin C the drug of choice for viral hepatitis. His general recommended dosing of vitamin C for hepatitis was 500 to 700 mg per kilogram of body weight, given every eight to 12 hours by vein. He would also give at least another 10,000 mg daily by mouth in divided doses. Routinely, a complete resolution of the hepatitis could be expected in two to four days. On occasion, Klenner would achieve a cure of viral hepatitis with only oral vitamin C (as sodium ascorbate). Presumably, such patients were less ill or more reluctant about being stuck with needles. One case reported by Klenner was given only 5,000 mg of vitamin C in water or juice every four hours. All signs and symptoms of the hepatitis were gone by 96 hours. This involved a total of 120,000 mg of vitamin C by mouth over the four-day period.

Smith (1988) reported on further dramatic successes that Klenner had with viral hepatitis. One 27-year-old male who was acutely ill with jaundice (yellowed eyes and skin), nausea, and 103°F temperature received a total of 270,000 mg of vitamin C intravenously and 45,000 mg of vitamin C orally over the next 30 hours. After this relatively brief period of time, the patient stopped spilling bile in his urine, his temperature was no longer elevated, and he returned to work. Another Klenner hepatitis patient, a 22-year-old male acutely ill with chills and fever, was treated over a six-day period. He received a total of 135,000 mg of vitamin C intravenously and 180,000 mg of vitamin C orally. He, too, had resolution of his symptoms and went back to work. Of particular interest was that this man's roommate also contracted hepatitis, but he had to remain in the hospital for 26 days with only bed rest as treatment. Klenner treated another male hepatitis patient over a six-day period with a total of 170,000 mg of vitamin C intravenously and 90,000 mg orally. During this six-day period, the patient's SGOT (a liver function test abnormal in acute hepatitis) had gone from 450 to 45 (very high to near-normal).

Smith also reported on a case of chronic hepatitis that Klenner treated successfully. This 42-year-old male had already been treated unsuccessfully with steroids over a seven-month period. Although Klenner wanted to treat this patient much more aggressively, he was wary that some of the other doctors on the hospital staff would eventually deny the patient any vitamin C therapy if too large a dosing regimen of vitamin C was ordered. Nevertheless, he still managed to administer 45,000 mg of vitamin C intravenously three times a week and 30,000 mg of vitamin C orally daily for about five months, finally achieving resolution of the disease. Chronic hepatitis will generally prove more difficult to completely eradicate than acute hepatitis with vitamin C therapy, even though the acute viral form of this disease is virtually always a completely curable disease if treated promptly and vigorously with vitamin C. As you may surmise from the above information, Klenner would always use his clinical expertise in determining how vigorously to treat his patients with vitamin C. He prescribed vitamin C by general guidelines according to clinical and temperature responses. Part of the reason for this clinical approach pertains to how deficient the patient was in vitamin C body stores before the disease ever took hold. Any given patient can require far more vitamin C than a seemingly comparable patient if the body stores of the two patients were not comparable in amount prior to the onset of the infection. However, patients with chronic active hepatitis have decreased blood vitamin C levels and laboratory indicators of increased oxidative stress (Yamamoto et al., 1998), and this indicates that some vitamin C supplementation is always appropriate in such patients.

Other clinicians have achieved clinical successes similar to those of Klenner in the vitamin C treatment of acute viral hepatitis, and often much less total vitamin C was administered. Dalton (1962) reports on a 20-year-old female presenting with the typical clinical picture of acute hepatitis. For the first three days of her illness, while she received only complete bed rest as her primary treatment, little clinical improvement was seen. However, she was then started on a series of vitamin C injections, and over the remaining six days of her hospitalization received a total of six 2,000 mg vitamin C injections. After only the second injection, she remarked that she no longer had the feeling of "being sick." Although she remained hospitalized for several more days, she wanted to go home the next day. Dalton, a medical doctor, commented that this case was the most dramatic recovery from hepatitis that he had ever observed. Even though the patient appeared to be completely cured of hepatitis, she did require a longer period of treatment with vitamin C than Klenner typically needed with his higher dosing regimen.

A dentist, Orens (1983), reported on his personal experience with hepatitis B. By taking a combination of 25,000 mg of vitamin C intravenously and 20,000 mg orally Orens had a near-normalization of extremely elevated liver enzymes (SGOT, SGPT, and LDH) over only a five-day treatment period. Orens also indicated that he only took vitamin C for a period of 10 days. Although Orens was originally advised by his physician that he might be out of the dental office for a period of six to 12 weeks, he was back to working full-time by the end of his 10-day course of vitamin C. By the time two additional months had passed there was a total normalization of his liver function tests. Bauer and Staub (1954) also reported

Baetgen reported excellent clinical responses in 245 children with acute hepatitis using only 10,000 mg of vitamin C per day

that acute viral hepatitis responded positively to 10,000 mg of vitamin C a day, accelerating the resolution of symptoms and shortening the overall duration of the illness. Kirchmair (1957, 1957a, 1957b) similarly reported that 10,000 mg of vitamin C daily for only five days markedly improved the clinical status of 63 children with acute hepatitis. The vitamin C was administered either intravenously, by rectal infusion, or both. The jaundice was noted to clear more rapidly, and hospitalization times were cut roughly in half. Swollen livers were noted to subside much more quickly as well. Baetgen (1961), again using 10,000 mg of vitamin C a day, reported similar excellent clinical responses in 245 children with acute hepatitis.

Calleja and Brooks (1960) reported on a case of acute hepatitis treated with intravenous vitamin C. A liver biopsy on this patient revealed that he already had cirrhosis (chronic scarring) of the liver with superimposed acute hepatitis. The cirrhosis was attributed to long-term heavy alcohol intake. A 5,000 mg dose of vitamin C was given intravenously daily for 24 days. On this regimen the patient had a dramatic clinical response. His anemia (low blood count) resolved, and his white blood cell count and analysis returned to normal. He gained weight, recovered his appetite, and lost all of the abdominal fluid that he had been accumulating due to the progressive failure of his liver. His only liver function test that did not normalize with the treatment was the one that reflected the irreversible cirrhosis part of this liver disease. Perhaps most significant was the complete resolution of the inflammatory changes on a repeat liver biopsy. Such changes classically accompany acute hepatitis and end up persisting to some degree whenever chronic hepatitis subsequently develops. Of further interest is that this study utilized much smaller doses of vitamin C compared to those used by Klenner. Nevertheless, a complete clinical success was eventually achieved.

Cathcart (1981) is another physician who has repeatedly witnessed the ability of vitamin C to easily eradicate the infecting virus in acute viral hepatitis and achieve a complete clinical cure. He reported that he never had a single case of acute viral hepatitis fail to respond to properly dosed intravenous vitamin C. Cathcart also noted that he has never observed any of his vitamin C-treated acute hepatitis patients subsequently develop chronic hepatitis. He noted that the acutely elevated liver enzyme levels (SGOT and SGPT) typically started dropping dramatically after only the first intravenous administration of vitamin C. He also noted that the yellowing effect of the associated jaundice would take four to five days to clear, well after the patient feels better. He attributed this to an actual staining of the skin by the excessive amounts of bilirubin that circulate in the blood during acute hepatitis. Cathcart lamented in his writings that he was simply confounded by the fact that such an inexpensive, simple, non-toxic, and extraordinarily effective therapy was not routinely used for a disease that disables and/or kills so many people worldwide.

Cathcart reported that he never had a single case of acute viral hepatitis fail to respond to properly dosed intravenous vitamin C

Further evidence for the ability of vitamin C to destroy hepatitis-causing viruses can be found in the work of Morishige and Murata (1978). From 1967 to 1973 hospitalized patients who received whole blood transfusions also received anywhere from 2,000 to 6,000 mg of vitamin C daily after the transfusions were given. Twelve cases of hepatitis were seen in a group of 170 patients who received little or no vitamin C after their transfusions (incidence 7%), and only three cases of hepatitis were seen in a group of 1,367 patients who received 2,000 mg or more of vitamin C daily after their transfusions (incidence 0.2%)! With even higher doses of vitamin C, especially if given intravenously, this incidence of post-transfusion hepatitis should be virtually zero. Knodell et al. (1981) published data claiming to refute the positive data outlined above. However, the vitamin C dosing administered by these investigators continued only 16 days after the transfusions as contrasted to almost six months by Morishige and Murata.

Also, Morishige and Murata gave their patients substantially larger daily doses of vitamin C for this longer period of time. Unfortunately, the scientific literature on vitamin C, both past and present, continues to attempt to debunk the many incredible clinical effects of vitamin C on various conditions by conducting studies that use much smaller doses for much shorter periods of time. Furthermore, few debunking studies ever use the highly effective intravenous administration of vitamin C, at any dose.

few debunking studies ever use the highly effective intravenous administration of vitamin C at any dose

Russian investigators, using much smaller doses of vitamin C in their viral hepatitis patients than the curative doses noted earlier, nevertheless documented significant improvements in laboratory test results. Komar and Vasil'ev (1992) administered only 300 or 400 mg of vitamin C daily along with several other vitamins (B3, B6, and B12). They noted significant improvements in levels of immune proteins in the blood as well as in the function of immune cells. Vasil'ev et al. (1989) had earlier made the same finding using only 300 mg of vitamin C daily for two to three weeks. Vasil'ev and Komar (1988) also determined that this same dose of vitamin C clearly resulted in a more rapid recovery of the depressed T-lymphocyte levels seen in acute viral hepatitis.

a reason for vigorous vitamin C therapy is the disease process itself rapidly utilizes the stores and blood levels of vitamin C present prior to the disease

Part of the reason for vigorous vitamin C therapy in acute hepatitis is that the disease process itself rapidly utilizes the existing body tissue stores and blood levels of vitamin C present prior to the disease. This increased rate of vitamin C utilization is actually seen in all infectious diseases and virtually all non-infectious medical diseases. Dubey et al. (1987) looked at the plasma levels of vitamin C in patients with viral hepatitis and found those levels to also be significantly decreased.

The scientific evidence has clearly established that acute viral hepatitis can be easily cured when enough vitamin C is administered in the early stages of the disease. This early treatment also provides strong assurance that the acute hepatitis will not just appear to spontaneously resolve while actually evolving into the long-term infection of chronic hepatitis, which can sometimes occur in acute hepatitis untreated by vitamin C and given only supportive care. The symptoms of chronic hepatitis nearly always respond well to vitamin C therapy, and some cases of chronic hepatitis may actually be curable if enough vitamin C is given for a long enough period of time. However, clearly supporting data for the cure of chronic hepatitis by vitamin C could not be found and probably has yet to be definitively gathered.

the scientific evidence has clearly established that acute viral hepatitis can be easily cured when enough vitamin C is administered in the early stages of the disease

The data on the decreased incidence of post-transfusion hepatitis in patients taking enough daily vitamin C is also compelling evidence that a high enough daily dose of vitamin C should ensure that acute viral hepatitis is a completely preventable and curable disease. Although less readily apparent, a very significant benefit of properly dosed vitamin C would be the elimination of any need or reason to vaccinate people against hepatitis. This would further protect the population from any of the negative consequences that are sometimes seen with such vaccinations.

Klenner also had striking success in the effective symptomatic treatment and eventual cure of virtually all viral diseases that he treated with vitamin C. More viral diseases, only some of which Klenner had the opportunity to treat with vitamin C, will now be addressed and discussed separately.

Measles (Curable and Preventable)

The 21st edition of the *Cecil Textbook of Medicine* characterizes measles as an acute and highly contagious disease accompanied by fever, cough, runny nose, inflamed eyes, and a rash. Although significant complications are relatively rare, measles can sometimes be fatal when the disease proceeds to a viral pneumonia or to a viral brain infection. The *Cecil Textbook of Medicine* states that there is "no specific antiviral therapy" for measles, and bed rest remains the recommended treatment in the absence of complications. Attempted prevention of measles by the use of the measles, mumps, and rubella (MMR) vaccine is the primary intervention offered by modern medicine for this disease.

Klenner (1953) dealt with the treatment of measles in the care of his own young daughters. They contracted the disease during an epidemic in North Carolina during the spring of 1948. Vitamin C therapy was started as soon as the diagnosis of measles was clinically certain. Klenner was very confident that high doses of vitamin C would destroy the virus at any point, and he proceeded to see what smaller doses of vitamin C would do to the development of the disease. Doses of 1,000 mg by mouth every four hours clearly improved the symptoms, although smaller doses were noted to allow the disease to progress.

this single clinical experiment probably best exemplifies that vitamin C simply must be given in high enough doses for a long enough period of time to effectively kill an invading virus

When Klenner proceeded to administer 1,000 mg by mouth every two hours, all evidence of the infection was cleared within 48 hours. However, discontinuation of the vitamin C at this point allowed a return of the disease. Klenner was able to demonstrate that the measles could be symptomatically controlled but not eradicated by this pattern of vitamin C dosing for a period of 30 days. At this point he again gave 1,000 mg every two hours around the clock for four days, and the infections were permanently eradicated. Klenner noted that for "the first time a virus infection could be handled as if it were a dog on a leash." This single clinical experiment conducted by Klenner probably best exemplifies that vitamin C simply must be given in high enough doses for a long enough period of time to effectively kill an invading virus.

Following the successful treatment of measles in his daughters, Klenner proceeded to treat new cases of measles with intravenous or intramuscular vitamin C. He noted that he could achieve complete control of the disease within 24 to 36 hours after starting the treatment, with the response differing only because of variable doses and frequencies of administration. Klenner also noted that his patients were able to develop complete immunity to recontracting measles even when he had intervened early and cured the disease before the rash was ever allowed to develop.

Klenner (1951, 1953) reported the case of a 10-month-old infant with reddened eyes and throat, high fever (105°F), cough, runny nose, and Koplik's spots. Koplik's spots are essentially the typical rash spots seen in measles that appear on the mucous membranes inside the mouth prior to skin eruptions. A 1,000 mg dose of vitamin C was given intramuscularly every four hours. After only 12 hours the cough had subsided, the red eyes and throat had cleared, and the temperature had normalized. However, Klenner wanted to see whether the fever was just fluctuating or actually responding to the vitamin C like an antibiotic. No vitamin C was given over the next eight hours, and the fever went back to 103.4°F. After vitamin C therapy was restarted, the fever promptly decreased, and the baby made a complete and rapid recovery. No measles rash ever developed on the skin, and Klenner noted that over the next four years the baby did not contract measles. This is consistent with an acquired immunity to the disease even though the disease never became completely expressed clinically.

Klenner also treated a 22-month-old baby with a similar clinical picture to the 10-month-old baby noted above. This baby responded rapidly in the same manner to vitamin C therapy, and the parents insisted on hospital discharge after only 36 hours. Apparently still infectious, the baby's brother and sister developed measles four days later, and the baby broke out with measles seven days later. This again rein-

forces the absolute need to use enough vitamin C for a long enough period of time. Paez de la Torre (1945) also reported good results treating
measles with vitamin C. Kalokerinos (1976) reported the responsiveness
of measles to vitamin C, and he added the importance of using the intravenous or intramuscular form of administration for optimal and re-
liable effect.

As mentioned earlier, measles can kill when it invades the brain
or the lungs. Klenner (1953) discussed the case of an eight-year-old boy
who presented with encephalitis, a viral infection and inflammation of
the brain, as a complication of measles and mumps. The boy was nota-
bly drowsy and listless, and his mother related that the child's increasing stupor, which was associated with headache, had developed over
the prior four or five days. Although a very active child, he went to bed
on his own with a temperature of 104°F.

Klenner immediately gave 2,000 mg of vitamin C intravenously,
and since no hospital beds were available, the child was then sent
home. After two hours, the child developed an appetite, began playing around the house, and for several hours looked as though he had
completely recovered. However, after six hours, his symptoms began to
return. About 18 hours after the initial vitamin C injection in the office,
Klenner gave another 2,000 mg dose of vitamin C intravenously and
added 1,000 mg to be given orally every two hours. Consequently, the
following day found the child free of fever and symptoms. Wary of a
relapse, however, Klenner gave yet another 2,000 mg of vitamin C by
vein and continued the oral regimen for another 48 hours.

The child made a complete recovery, and never demonstrated any
evidence of brain damage, even as long as five years later. Such damage is very common after surviving encephalitis. Klenner added that
"similar cases" to this boy had shown even more rapid and dramatic
responses when the vitamin C was given by injection every two to four
hours.

Klenner (July 1949) also published some observations on the ability of vitamin C to protect those at risk from contracting measles during an epidemic. Not unexpectedly, the primary consideration was
dose. Klenner found that 1,000 mg of vitamin C by injection every six

hours gave complete protection. However, as much as 1,000 mg given in fruit juice every two hours did *not* provide complete protection. This is further dramatic evidence that many of the so-called "megadoses" of vitamin C that are researched and published are very insufficient in the face of an enormous viral exposure.

many of the so-called "megadoses" of vitamin C that are researched and published are insufficient in the face of an enormous viral exposure

Anything in gram (versus milligram) doses is considered megadose in much of the literature, even if it is only one or two grams (1,000 to 2,000 mg). However, acute diseases, especially infectious ones, metabolize and utilize vitamin C at a seemingly astronomical rate. Measles is an infectious disease especially notorious for causing nosebleeds. Bleeding caused by the fragility of tiny blood vessels (capillaries) is also one of the characteristic findings in scurvy. This bleeding tendency resolves very reliably and promptly after the first or second injection of vitamin C. The overwhelming virus load seen in an acute case of measles may well often induce an acute case of scurvy, at least with regard to a greater likelihood of bleeding.

Whenever a "maintenance" dose of several thousand milligrams of vitamin C still allows some infectious disease such as measles to take hold, vastly higher doses of vitamin C must still be immediately instituted to deal with the infection. The fact that the disease took hold while the individual was faithfully taking several thousand milligrams of vitamin C daily does not negate a much higher dosing of vitamin C as the treatment of choice.

The immune function in patients with measles was also demonstrated to be enhanced by the administration of vitamin C. Joffe et al. (1983) were able to demonstrate that vitamin C allowed for a more rapid recovery of certain lymphocyte subsets. This information alone might not seem to be very significant, but it makes a lot of sense in the context of the clinical responses that Klenner reported.

Like polio and hepatitis, measles is one more disease that is completely curable by properly dosed vitamin C given by the proper route. Also, when adequate doses are ingested regularly, measles can also be prevented. Other vitamin supplementation is also a good idea. Goskowitz and Eichenfield (1993) noted that an acute vitamin A deficiency can be seen in children with measles, usually associated with more severe disease. However, because vitamin C can promptly cure a fully developed case of measles, the ability to prevent the infection is not nearly so important. In fact, a valid argument can be made that contracting the disease, curing it with vitamin C, and then attaining the resultant long-term immunity to the disease might be the most desirable way to proceed. This is especially true since adequate vitamin C may not always be readily available and/or there may not be a doctor willing to dose it properly when the disease strikes.

Mumps (Curable and Preventable)

Mumps is another common viral disease that most commonly afflicts children. The disease is usually self-limited, and it is characterized by the swelling of the parotid glands, giving a "chipmunk-like" appearance to the face. In the susceptible child, mumps can also end up involving the brain. Glands other than the parotids, including the pancreas and the thyroid, can sometimes become inflamed. In some boys, and often in men, the virus can affect one or both testicles. According to the *Cecil Textbook of Medicine*, mumps is another viral disease for which there is "currently no established role for antiviral drugs, corticosteroids, or passive immunotherapy." Immunization remains the primary intervention offered by modern medicine to deal with this disease. In patients who have already contracted mumps, supportive measures are the main therapeutic interventions.

Klenner noted that 33 out of 33 cases of mumps responded promptly

Klenner (July 1949) reported tremendous success with the vitamin C treatment of mumps. Using a vitamin C treatment protocol comparable to that used with the other viral diseases already mentioned, Klenner noted that 33 out of 33 cases of mumps responded promptly. The general profile of clinical response was remarkably similar in these patients. Fever was gone after 24 hours, pain was gone after 36 hours, and the parotid swelling was resolved after 48 to 72 hours. Klenner also noted that two of these rapidly responding 33 cases were already complicated by orchitis, or testicular inflammation. One of these cases was a 23-year-old man who developed severe swelling ("the size of tennis balls") and pain in both testicles. This patient also had a fever of 105°F. Klenner gave him 1,000 mg of vitamin C by vein every two hours. The severe testicular pain began to subside after the first injection and was completely gone within 12 hours. The high fever was resolved after 36 hours, and the patient was out of bed feeling "his old self" by 60 hours. A total of 25,000 mg of vitamin C was given to this man during this 60-hour period.

Klenner (July 1949) reported on the differing clinical courses he observed in three cousins with mumps and receiving different therapeutic regimens. A seven-year-old boy was given the "old routine of bed rest, aspirin, and warm camphor oil applications," and was noted to have a "rough time" for a week. An 11-year-old boy was allowed to develop his mumps without any therapy to the "point of maximum swelling." At this point he was given 1,000 mg of vitamin C intramuscularly every two to four hours. Klenner found the boy to be entirely well in only 48 hours. The third cousin, a nine-year-old girl, had vitamin C started when the parotid gland swelling was felt to be still increasing, having reached only about 60% of its anticipated enlargement. This patient was given 1,000 mg of vitamin C intravenously every four hours and was considered to be completely well in 72 hours.

Klenner (July 1949) observed that some children would present to him with what he termed a "mixed-virus picture." For example, he characterized one such clinical presentation as one

any given viral load requires its own amount of vitamin C to be killed and/or neutralized — if double the viral load is present, then double the dose of vitamin C will be needed

of "receding mumps and developing measles." Whenever he encountered such a mixed picture, he found that he generally needed to use approximately double the dose of vitamin C that he would use for either disease singly. Klenner's clinical observation meshes well with the concept that any given viral load requires its own amount of vitamin C to be killed and/or neutralized. If double the viral load is present, then double the dose of vitamin C will be needed; otherwise, the likelihood of a therapeutic "failure" of the vitamin C will increase.

Mumps appears to be yet another viral disease that can routinely be cured by the proper administration of vitamin C. Although no specific studies can be cited, it seems very logical to conclude that if vitamin C can so readily cure mumps and its worst complications, then preventing mumps with vitamin C should be easy to accomplish. A mere exposure to the mumps virus will always involve an exposure to a lower total viral count than that encountered after the disease has already taken hold and massive viral multiplication has taken place. If vitamin C can kill huge challenges of mumps virus, then substantially smaller challenges should also easily be met. Even the complicated cases of mumps, such as those with orchitis, appear to respond extremely well.

The next disease to be examined, viral encephalitis, also responds very dramatically to vitamin C. Many such cases of encephalitis are never completely diagnosed as to the identity of the infecting virus. These cases represent not only complicated cases of mumps, but also of measles and other childhood viral diseases that encounter individuals with depleted vitamin C stores or otherwise sickly immune systems. Whenever a given therapy can readily cure the significant complications of an infectious disease, curing the routine presentation of that disease presents no obstacle.

Viral Encephalitis (Curable and Preventable)

Viral encephalitis refers to a viral infection and inflammation of the brain. Depending upon how far the infection has progressed, the patient may be confused, lethargic, or even comatose. Fever and headache are almost always present, and the remainder of the symptoms will depend largely upon which virus is responsible for the infection. Virtually any virus has the capability of infecting the brain if there exists enough compromise of the patient's immune system. The *Cecil Textbook of Medicine* lists over 40 different viruses that can infect the central nervous system, adding that more than 50 viruses have been found to be associated with such infections.

The central nervous system refers to the brain and all of its directly related nervous tissues. Except for the viral encephalitis that can be associated with a herpes infection, the recommended treatment from the medicine textbooks for viral encephalitis in general is once again supportive and aimed at relief of symptoms only. Although most cases of encephalitis are not fatal statistically, the encephalitis associated with AIDS or rabies is almost always uniformly fatal. Furthermore, encephalitis associated with certain other viruses has anywhere from a 10% to a 50% rate of fatality. For this reason, encephalitis is never a condition for which one can assume a favorable outcome. The offending virus in many cases of encephalitis goes undiagnosed, and all cases should be treated as vigorously as possible.

Klenner (July 1949, 1951, 1953, June 1957, 1958, 1960, 1971) reported a great deal of success in treating viral encephalitis with vitamin C. Once again, high enough doses of vitamin C given over an adequate period of time will routinely cure this disease. Klenner termed the response that he repeatedly witnessed when treating viral encephalitis with vitamin C as "dramatic." Even though it may seem that some given patients should already have progressed too far to

Klenner repeatedly used vitamin C to cure patients who were already comatose with viral encephalitis

be brought back with vitamin C therapy, Klenner never reported this happening, and many of his patients had very advanced infections. Indeed, Klenner repeatedly cured patients who were already comatose with encephalitis.

The dramatic response of viral encephalitis to vitamin C is especially impressive when one considers how many medicines cannot penetrate into the nervous system either partially or totally. This blockade to certain substances and medicines is called the blood-brain barrier, and many molecules are incapable of gaining access to the brain and nervous tissues to any significant degree because of this barrier.

However, ready access to the nervous tissues by vitamin C represents one more reason why it is such an ideal therapeutic agent.

Klenner reported on the complete cure of six cases of viral encephalitis. Two were associated with viral pneumonia, while one followed measles, one followed mumps, one followed chickenpox, and one followed a combined presentation of measles and mumps. The encephalitis patient following the mumps was a 12-year-old boy who developed a headache one week after his mumps had seemed to resolve. Within 12 hours of developing the headache, the boy had become lethargic and had a fever of 105°F. Upon being admitted to the hospital he was given an injection of 2,000 mg of vitamin C. Repeat injections of 1,000 mg of vitamin C were then given every two hours. Following the third vitamin C injection, the boy was, in Klenner's words, "sitting up in bed, laughing, talking, begging for food and completely without pain." The boy was discharged 24 hours later, continuing on a maintenance regimen of vitamin C for 48 hours to guard against any possible relapse.

Klenner also described the dramatic responses of two patients who developed encephalitis as a complication of viral pneumonia. A 28-year-old woman first had fever, chills, and a head and chest cold for 14 days. She then developed a severe headache for the last three days of this illness. Klenner commented that she was in a "stupor" when first seen and had a "white foam" in her mouth. Temperature measured in her armpit was 106.8°F, even though she had already been through extensive courses of penicillin, streptomycin, and sulfa drug antibiotics. Since she was also very dehydrated, she was given her first 4,000 mg dose of vitamin C in 1,000 cc of intravenous fluids. Eleven hours later her temperature was down to 100°F, and 15 hours after the first dose of vitamin C further doses of 2,000 to 4,000 mg were given every two to three hours "depending upon the response."

The patient had clinically recovered after only 72 hours, although maintenance vitamin C was given for two more weeks. Her abnormal chest X-ray took another three months to completely normalize. Klenner commented that in five other cases with viral lung involvement the resolution of the chest X-ray could be expected to lag behind the normalization of the clinical symptoms, depending upon how abnormal the chest X-ray had become.

Another dramatic case of viral encephalitis treated by Klenner involved a 19-month-old baby. This baby had been sick with a "little cold" for about two weeks when a fever began over the prior 24 hours. Twelve hours before admission the baby had some focal seizures involving the right arm and leg. Klenner described the baby as an "undernourished infant, lying rigid in its mother's arms, skin cold to touch, color cadaver-like, eyes closed, grade-2 mucopurulent nasal discharge, throat red." The temperature was 103.8°F, and Klenner further commented that some areas of skin over the infant's back resembled "rigor mortis."

A 1,000 mg dose of vitamin C was given intramuscularly and repeated every four to six hours. Klenner noted that with the first vitamin C injection the baby "did not move and the sensation was like that of sticking an orange." Two hours after this first injection the baby took 240 cc of orange juice, its first nourishment in 24 hours. Total paralysis of the right arm and right leg was noted at this time, but this lost function was subsequently regained within about 12 hours of admission. The rest of the recovery was uneventful.

Klenner (1960) compiled one study that dealt solely with viral encephalitis as a complication of pneumonia. One patient, a 58-year-old female, had suffered with a head and chest cold for 10 days. She was hospitalized after having a "convulsive seizure," and was given 24,000 mg of vitamin C in an intravenous infusion for a total of three doses at eight-hour intervals. A 4,000 mg oral dose of vitamin C was given every four hours, and 24 hours after admission the patient had developed a complete paralysis of her right arm and right leg. Fortunately, this completely resolved after 48 more hours. Although the patient had associated cardiac problems, her viral infection nevertheless completely resolved.

Klenner described another dramatic case. A 23-year-old male was brought to the emergency room in a "semi-coma." His friends had found him unconscious in a telephone booth. It was later determined that the man had been bothered with a cold for two weeks and a severe headache for the past five days for which he had consulted another physician earlier on the same day. Upon admission 30,000 mg of vitamin C was given in an infusion of 350 cc of glucose and water. Five more doses were repeated at eight-hour intervals. He was also given 4,000 to 6,000 mg orally every four to six hours. After six days of hospitalization his parents had him transferred to a teaching hospital, which verified the diagnosis of viral encephalitis. He received no further treatment there and was discharged to home.

Klenner treated another patient, a 22-year-old male, initially described as being unconscious at another emergency room. When Klenner saw him, however, he was wildly delirious, thrashing about and needing to be subdued. History later revealed that the man had endured a dull to severe headache for several days. He later collapsed, and the ambulance driver actually thought the man was dead, but still needed to be pronounced dead by a doctor. A 100,000 mg dose of vitamin C was given by vein over the first 24 hours. A 4,000 mg oral dose every four to six hours followed this and led to the patient's recovery.

Ironically, even Klenner didn't always use enough vitamin C. His own seven-year-old son developed lethargy and fever after about six weeks of flu-like symptoms. The child had received only "moderate" doses of vitamin C for those weeks along with sulfa drugs, which had some minimal effectiveness until the traditional breakthrough symptoms of encephalitis appeared. Klenner then gave 6,000 mg dose of vitamin C intravenously every six hours. A 10,000 mg dose of vitamin C was also given by mouth, and recovery was noted to be complete by 24 hours.

Klenner also described an especially deadly syndrome of viral encephalitis that he attributed to an "insidious" virus. As mentioned previously, few cases of viral encephalitis get specifically diagnosed with regard to the precise identity of the infecting virus. Klenner frequently saw viral encephalitis that started with either the "flu" for two to four days prior, or with a mild cold that lingered for several weeks prior to presentation. Klenner further noted that the onset of the encephalitis was typically heralded by any of a number of symptoms, including seizures, extreme excitability and agitation, severe chills, strangling while trying to eat or drink, collapse, and/or stupor. He repeatedly observed that viral encephalitis presenting in such a manner was especially capable of killing the patient in very short order. Klenner felt the syndrome was similar if not identical to the syndrome of acute hemorrhagic encephalitis.

Any time hemorrhage complicates any disease process, it is a very strong indication that the body stores of vitamin C have been especially

any time hemorrhage complicates any disease process, it is a very strong indication that the body stores of vitamin C have been severely depleted

severely depleted, and because death can be rapid, the initial and subsequent vitamin C dosing must be even more aggressive than usual. Klenner was particularly sensitized in this regard, as he reported that he had seen children die "within 30 minutes to two hours" after being admitted to the hospital for encephalitis without receiving vitamin C. In his paper of October, 1958 dealing with viral encephalitis Klenner asserted that, in spite of the very real possibility of sudden death, he had never yet failed to see full recovery from encephalitis with the use of very large doses of vitamin C.

Klenner also treated a 16-month-old infant who suddenly collapsed and was unconscious after having had a mild cold for two weeks prior to presentation. The baby received 2,000 mg of vitamin C intramuscularly and regained consciousness in ten minutes. An additional 2,000 mg was injected after the baby was moved to the hospital room. These injections were continued every two hours for five doses, and then extended to every four hours for 12 more doses. The fever noted on admission had normalized within 60 hours, and discharge was on the seventh day. Klenner also often used antibiotics along with vitamin C if he had any suspicion at all that any superimposed bacterial infection was playing a role in the illness.

One especially interesting case treated by Klenner was a 73-year-old male who ended up being hospitalized three times in a 24-day period. The patient was first brought in by ambulance unconscious after having a cold for 10 days, followed over the next few hours by a severe headache, a chill, and then sudden unconsciousness. Fever, rapid heart rate, and rapid breathing rate were all noted on admission. An initial dose of 20,000 mg of vitamin C was slowly infused. This was repeated eight hours later. The patient regained consciousness about 18 hours after admission, and he was discharged on the third hospital day. Two weeks later, the patient presented in a similar fashion, was treated the same way, and then went home on the fourth hospital day. Once again the patient was readmitted a week later in a similar state, except that he was conscious. On this third visit he received virtually the same treatment except that the 20,000 mg dose of vitamin C was increased to 24,000 mg. He was discharged on the third hospital day, with a 10,000 mg daily dosage of vitamin C being prescribed. The patient remained well, and had no further relapses. Once again, this case report from Klenner demonstrates unequivocally that enough vitamin C must be used for a long enough period of time, or the viral disease will not be eradicated and can be expected to recur.

Klenner is particularly emphatic about the treatment of viral encephalitis when he asserts that it must be treated "heroically." In contrast to other less grave diseases, Klenner is absolutely clear that the initial doses of vitamin C must be given by needle (intravenous or intramuscular), and the subsequent initial dosing must be maintained around the clock on an uninterrupted schedule.

Destro and Sharma (1977) reported on their experience in treating bacterial and "viral" meningitis with vitamin C. As diseases go, meningitis is closely akin to encephalitis, since both infections involve the central nervous system. The doses of vitamin C necessary to properly treat a case of meningitis are comparable to those needed for a case of encephalitis. These researchers found "no appreciable ameliorating effect" of the vitamin C that they administered compared to placebo. However, none of Klenner's work was cited in their bibliography, which was readily apparent from the vitamin C doses they used. They never exceeded an initial intravenous dose of 100 mg/kg (Klenner would go as high as 700 mg/kg), and their subsequent doses were only 50 mg/kg. Also, the frequency of dosing was less often than that of Klenner, who continued to dose vigorously until the patient clearly improved and the fever came down. Only then did Klenner start spacing out his doses as infrequently as Destro and Sharma. Given these comparisons with

Klenner's dosage levels, the lack of effect that these researchers found was exactly what would be expected. Klenner and many other clinicians repeatedly emphasized that if you don't use enough vitamin C, especially in life-threatening infectious diseases, you will see little or *no* beneficial effect. It is truly a shame that these researchers were not aware of Klenner's work, as a replication of Klenner's protocols would have been invaluable in educating the medical world on what properly dosed vitamin C could achieve.

if you don't use enough vitamin C, especially in life-threatening infectious diseases, you will see little or no beneficial effect

As a specialist in both cardiology and internal medicine, I have had the opportunity to witness at least two cases of aggressive encephalitis, presumably viral in origin. One case was a friend of the family with a history of headaches over a short period of time before he went to his doctor and ended up in the hospital. When I visited him, he was already intermittently slipping into unconsciousness. He was in a complete coma by the next day, and died about a week later. In the second case I was the treating physician. A middle-aged man was noted to be "not right" by his wife. He seemed perfectly normal to me, but I did a spinal tap since the wife was so concerned. A few cells were seen in the spinal fluid, which represented only the most minimal of abnormalities. Nevertheless, I trusted the wife's intuition and admitted her husband to the hospital. Within 24 hours, he was dead. I stayed up all night helplessly witnessing his rapid deterioration. Even today, it amazes me that a virus can take someone's life so quickly. Viral encephalitis is a very dangerous disease, capable of progressing to death very quickly. Klenner's observations on this disease are especially impressive to me, and I only wish I had known then what I know now.

Viral encephalitis, which can be rapidly fatal or often leave its victim with a variable degree of brain and neurological damage, is another disease that is completely curable by the aggressive dosing of vitamin C. Also, using the same reasoning that was utilized on the previously discussed viral diseases, viral encephalitis is a completely preventable disease when adequate doses of vitamin C are taken on a regular basis.

Chickenpox and Herpes Infections
(Curable and Preventable)

These diseases are being addressed together since the infecting viruses are closely related to one another. Chickenpox, also known as varicella, is a common viral childhood disease typically identified by its characteristic rash. Depending upon the immune status of the patient, the disease can range from being almost inconsequential to causing death. Herpes zoster (shingles) results from a reactivation of the varicella-zoster virus already lying dormant in the body. It also has a characteristic rash that overlies the distribution of an affected nerve. Typically, herpes zoster is an exceptionally painful condition. As with the other viral infections, treatment is generally only supportive.

Another type of herpesvirus, herpes simplex (fever blisters, genital herpes), is felt to be responsive to the antiviral drugs vidarabine and acyclovir. However, these agents cannot be relied upon to actually cure the viral infection. Infectious mononucleosis will also be addressed here, as this disease is also typically caused by a herpes virus. Mononucleosis is characterized by fatigue, headache, fever, sore throat, generalized swelling of the lymph nodes, and mild hepatitis. The symptoms of mononucleosis will often persist for months, and the *Cecil Textbook of Medicine* asserts that almost all "normal" people will completely recover from this disease within three to four months.

Klenner (July 1949, 1953, 1974) reported having excellent results in the vitamin C treatment of chickenpox, shingles, and herpes simplex.

seven of eight shingles patients experienced total pain relief within two hours of the first vitamin C injection

Klenner treated a series of eight adults who had shingles. A 2,000 to 3,000 mg dose of vitamin C was given by injection every 12 hours, and 1,000 mg was given orally every two hours. The severe pain associated with the skin lesions, which can often persist for weeks before completely resolving, was completely gone in seven of eight patients within two hours of the first vitamin C injection. Although no pain-killing medications were administered, the pain relief was permanent. The skin lesions, which can persist for weeks, had completely resolved in seven out of eight patients within 72 hours. Each patient received from five to seven total injections of vitamin C. One of the patients had the skin lesions of shingles over his abdomen. For 36 hours he had been taking opiate pain medications without any significant relief. Within four hours of the initial 3,000 mg intravenous injection of vitamin C he was pain-free. Dainow (1943) reported success in the treatment of 14 cases of shingles with vitamin C injections. Zureick (1950), noting a clinical response like that of Klenner, published the results of 327 shingle cases treated with vitamin C. Complete resolution of the disease in all of these patients was seen within 72 hours after administering vitamin C injections.

published results show complete resolution of 327 of 327 shingle cases within 72 hours after administering vitamin C injections

Klenner emphasized the importance of continuing the vitamin C treatment for herpes infections for a sufficient period of time. With fever blisters, healing would appear complete after two vitamin C injections, but recurrence was noted when the vitamin C was discontinued after only 24 hours.

Chickenpox showed a similar response as that of shingles to Klenner's vitamin C therapy. The itching wet rash would show some drying in the first 24 hours, and clinical wellness was restored by the third or fourth day. Smith (1988) described Klenner's experience in treating his own daughter for chickenpox. Although the child was given 24,000 mg of vitamin C orally each day, the rash appeared to worsen, and the itch increased. After only 1,000 mg was administered intravenously, the itch stopped, and the child was able to sleep well for eight hours. Another intravenous dose was then given, and there was no further progression of the rash. Perhaps by wanting to avoid sticking his own daughter with a needle Klenner was able to provide one more especially striking example of the superiority of injected vitamin C over oral vitamin C, especially when prompt control over infection is needed.

Klenner also pointed out that viral encephalitis, which can occur following a wide variety of viral infections, is an especially severe disease when the infecting virus is herpes simplex. Lerner et al. (1972) published estimates that one third of such cases of encephalitis result in death, and approximately eight of nine survivors have some residual brain damage. The current *Cecil Textbook of Medicine* asserts that only 15% of herpes simplex encephalitis patients die. Perhaps the recently introduced antiviral drugs have helped reduce this number. However, Klenner reported no failures in the treatment of encephalitis, regardless of the offending virus. The recoveries of the vitamin C-treated encephalitis victims were complete, and Klenner observed no long-term brain or neurological damage.

Cathcart (1981) also reported success with the treatment of acute herpes infections using oral vitamin C. Cathcart often used large oral doses of vitamin C in the treatment of other infections as well. Specific cases were not outlined, and Cathcart noted that recurrent disease was especially common if the disease had already entered a chronic phase. He suggested that intravenous vitamin C might be of benefit for chronic herpes infections. This appears to be yet another example of the need to initially attack any significant viral infection with intravenous vitamin C in order to obtain an optimal clinical response.

Klenner (1971) did not address mononucleosis with the same detail that he provided for many of the other viral diseases. He did, however, assert that "large" doses of vitamin C given intravenously had a "striking" influence on the typically prolonged course of this disease. He briefly described one interesting case in which a hospitalized patient was in a bad enough condition that she had already been given the last rites of her church. She was not Klenner's patient, however, and the attending physician refused the mother's request to give vitamin C. However, since the patient's mother was a nurse and an ardent advocate of the benefits of vitamin C, she decided for herself to add 20,000 to 30,000 mg of vitamin C to every bottle of intravenous fluids administered to her daughter. Klenner noted that the girl went on to make an "uneventful recovery."

Dalton (1962) reported the case of a 36-year-old woman who contracted mononucleosis. The symptoms were pronounced, and her diagnosis was verified by blood testing. Only three daily 2,000 mg injections of vitamin C were given, and her symptoms were resolved within one week.

Cathcart (1981) reported good results with the administration of large oral doses of vitamin C for mononucleosis. However, significant maintenance oral vitamin C (20,000 to 30,000 mg daily) was necessary for about two months to complete the treatment in one specific patient he described. Cathcart noted that many other cases did not require significant maintenance therapy for more than two to three weeks in order to assure no recurrence or relapse occurred. Cathcart's experience, especially when compared to the result that Dalton achieved with small intravenous doses of vitamin C, would appear to be another good example of the importance of administering at least the initial doses intravenously when treating mononucleosis or any other acute and severe viral infection.

Further experimental evidence supports the ability of vitamin C to inactivate herpesviruses. Sagripanti et al. (1997) found that vitamin C in association with cupric (copper) ions would kill at least one form of herpesvirus, herpes simplex. Furthermore, the authors suggested that the concentrations of vitamin C and copper needed to kill this herpesvirus indicated that preparations for human ingestion could be administered with only a minimal risk of any toxicity. Such suggestions indicate a lack of awareness of vitamin C 's already well-established nontoxic profile. However, it is good to see that current basic researchers are reaching a conclusion that agrees with the absence of side effects already noted in many earlier clinical applications.

White et al. (1986) were also able to demonstrate that vitamin C, with the assistance of ionic copper, was able to inactivate all of the viruses tested. In addition to the inactivation of herpes simplex virus types 1 and 2, vitamin C also completely terminated the infectivity of cytomegalovirus, parainfluenzavirus type 2, and respiratory syncytial virus.

Still further evidence of the ability of vitamin C to effectively treat herpesvirus infections comes from studies performed on different applications of vitamin C directly on herpetic lesions. Hamuy and Berman (1998) reported that the treatment of herpes simplex virus infections with topical vitamin C "shows promising effects." Hovi et al. (1995) did a double-blind, placebo-controlled clinical trial that applied a vitamin C-containing solution against herpes lesions that erupt on mucous membranes, such as in the mouth. Based on symptom control, length of scab formation, and viral cultures, it was determined that this preparation resulted in statistically significant clinical and antiviral effects. Terezhalmy et al. (1978) demonstrated a positive effect of oral vitamin C on recurrent herpes labialis (cold sores). This study showed a clear remission in the related symptoms from the administration of only 600 mg of vitamin C (along with bioflavonoids) three times daily.

Some of the important initial groundwork establishing the likelihood that herpesviruses were killed (inactivated) by vitamin C in the body came from the work of Holden and Resnick (1936). Their research clearly demonstrated that vitamin C in the test tube inactivated the strain of herpesvirus tested. This conclusion was again tested and published a year later (Holden and Molloy, 1937). In the 1937 paper, an attempt was also made to determine if the test tube neutralization of the herpesvirus was a valid indicator that vitamin C could also cure rabbits directly infected with this virus. Unfortunately, after an injection of the virus into the rabbits, only a very tiny dose (5 mg) of vitamin C was given subcutaneous daily for six days, and no demonstrable effect of this minimal vitamin C dosing on the disease development could be detected. Nevertheless, the test tube aspect of the research of Holden and Molloy was quite significant.

Like other viruses discussed in this chapter, herpes and closely related viruses are extremely susceptible to the administration of vitamin C. Klenner and other researchers have reported curing such diseases with vitamin C injections. Presumably, enough daily vitamin C would also prevent such diseases from taking hold. If at all possible, it would seem prudent to always initially attack viruses of this family with intravenous or intramuscular vitamin C to achieve complete virus eradication and avoid the emergence of chronic disease due to incomplete treatment. The data for treating chronic herpetic disease, such as recurrent fever blisters or genital herpes, with high-dose intravenous vitamin C was not found. However, there is no reason to believe that this virus cannot be completely eliminated from the body if enough intravenous vitamin C is given for a long enough period of time.

Viral Pneumonia (Curable and Preventable)

Viral pneumonia is a viral infection of the lungs. The diagnosis is often one of exclusion, concluding that a virus is the infecting agent after other common infecting agents such as bacteria have been ruled out. Viral pneumonia is often the result of a cold or upper respiratory tract infection that eventually extends into the lungs.

Klenner (1948) reported on 42 cases of viral pneumonia treated with vitamin C over a five-year period. As with the other viral infections already examined, Klenner had excellent results. Once the diagnosis was entertained, Klenner started with 1,000 mg of vitamin C intravenously and repeated this dosage every six to twelve hours. For infants and smaller children, he would give 500 mg of vitamin C intramuscularly every six to twelve hours. In all of his cases, Klenner had "complete clinical and x-ray response" after only three to seven vitamin C injections. Interestingly, he gave additional oral vitamin C in about a third of the patients, but observed no definite additional benefit. Nearly all of the patients reported feeling better within an hour of the first injection.

It was for a case of viral pneumonia that Klenner (1953) first used vitamin C as an antiviral therapy in the early 1940s. A patient being treated at home with the usual supportive measures suddenly became cyanotic (turning bluish due to low oxygen). The patient refused Klenner's offer of hospitalization for oxygen therapy. Klenner, theorizing that vitamin C would somehow help improve the delivery of oxygen to the cells of the body, gave 2,000 mg of vitamin C intramuscularly. Within 30 minutes the breathing had improved, and the cyanosis had cleared. When Klenner saw the patient again six hours later, the patient was eating and looking so much better that he gave another 1,000 mg of vitamin C intramuscularly. Over the next three days, this 1,000 mg injection was repeated every six hours. Klenner wrote that the patient appeared well after only 36 hours. Klenner only happened to have vitamin C in his black bag because he had been using it to help treat diarrhea in children. Regardless, through Klenner's inventiveness a therapy of unequaled importance was born.

Dalton (1962) reported excellent results using vitamin C on three cases of viral pneumonia and one case he termed a "general viremia." His dosing of vitamin C was less than that of Klenner, but his patients resolved their illnesses much more quickly than would have been otherwise anticipated. One of the cases, a 60-year-old physician, had fever, cough, generalized aching, and an X-ray confirming viral lung involvement. His clinical picture actually appeared to be very much an influenza that had become complicated by viral pneumonia. In addition to bed rest and aspirin, the patient received only 2,000 mg of vitamin C intravenously daily for three days. Dalton termed the response "excellent," noting the return of strength on the fourth day and the patient's return to work on the fifth day.

Another of Dalton's cases, a 47-year-old woman, also had severe symptomatic disease, with exhaustion limiting her to bed, loss of appetite, and generalized chest pain. Dalton termed her "completely debilitated." Over the next 15 days she received a total of six 2,000 mg injections of vitamin C. No other medications were given. After only the second injection she was feeling better, and she was insistent on receiving additional injections. Of particular interest in this case was that this patient had a history of recurrent bouts of pneumonia, although in this instance her condition improved much more rapidly than it ever had before.

Dalton described a 41-year-old man who had headache, generalized muscular aching, and exhaustion. Clinically, he was felt to have acute viral pneumonia, and the clinical description again suggested a diagnosis of influenza complicated by pneumonia. The patient was given a 2,000 mg injection of vitamin C for three consecutive days. Seen in follow-up a week later, he was found to be symptom-free, and he had already returned to work a couple of days earlier. Dalton also treated a 72-year-old man for what he termed a general viremia. Three 2,000 mg vitamin C injections were given over an 11-day period, and a "marked improvement" in the presenting symptoms was noted.

While the descriptions of Dalton's cases are not as impressive as those of Klenner, significant responses were still obtained with a much less aggressive dosing of vitamin C. It also reinforces the importance of having as much of the vitamin C given by needle as possible. It is very doubtful Dalton would have seen equivalent patient responses with the same number of 2,000 mg vitamin C doses given orally.

Viral pneumonia is another infection readily curable by vitamin C. Adequate daily doses of vitamin C should also prove effective in preventing it from being contracted in the first place.

Influenza (Curable and Preventable)

Influenza ("flu") is a very common viral infection that is often associated with, or evolves from, a head cold. Even though influenza can sometimes also affect the lungs and resemble viral pneumonia, it should be noted that viral pneumonia primarily affects the lungs while influenza seems to affect more of the body in general. Diffuse muscular pain is especially characteristic of influenza, accompanying the less specific symptoms of headache, weakness, fever, and chills. While no traditional treatments are known to cure influenza, rimantadine and amantadine are antiviral drugs that are felt to lessen symptoms and speed recovery in uncomplicated cases.

Klenner (July 1949) did not specifically detail his vitamin C treatment of influenza. Probably one reason for this was because he had reported such profound successes with so many other advanced and life-threatening viral diseases. Certainly, curing a comatose patient with encephalitis or eliminating the paralysis of a polio patient must have had precedence over Klenner's

Klenner implied complete success with influenza commenting that the "size of the dose" and "number of injections" of vitamin C needed were directly related to the fever response to therapy

vitamin C experience with the flu. Klenner did say, however, that he treated many cases of influenza with vitamin C. He also implied complete success with this disease as well, commenting only that the "size of the dose" and the "number of injections" of vitamin C needed were directly related to the fever response to therapy and to the duration of the disease.

Magne (1963) reported on the vitamin C treatment of 130 cases of influenza. Males and females, ranging in age from 10 to 40 years, were treated. Treatment was given for one to three days with doses of vitamin C up to 45,000 mg. In spite of this variable approach, Magne reported good success, with 114 recovering and only 16 not significantly responding. As has already been seen repeatedly in Klenner's work, failing to provide an adequate dose of vitamin C can be expected to show little or no clinical effect.

Another virus somewhat akin to the influenza virus is the one that causes the dog and cat distemper complex. Distemper is an infectious disease of the respiratory tract and sometimes the gastrointestinal tract, with associated fever, dullness, loss of appetite, and discharge from the eyes and nose. When dogs and cats get sick enough with distemper and do not recover spontaneously, they are often put to sleep. As with so many human viral infections, this animal viral disease is readily and easily curable with adequate doses of vitamin C.

Belfield (1967) reported excellent results in the treatment of 12 dogs and cats. He generally gave dogs 2,000 mg of intravenous vitamin C each day for three days. For cats and small dogs he gave 1,000 mg of vitamin C intravenously per day for three days. All 12 animals recovered completely, even though two of them had been given no hope of recovery by other veterinarians. Amazingly, the editor made some explanatory comments at the start of Belfield's article to justify its publication, stating that veterinarians were "still plagued by the age-old problem of what to do with the dog that is already sick with distemper." It was also noted that editors were especially "inclined to view this subject as a hot potato and to apply themselves to less controversial matters."

Obviously anticipating negative feedback from Belfield's article, the editor added that "the chuckles of our friends in research as they read these words" could almost be heard. In a defensive posture, the editor challenged readers not to brand the journal editors as "cracked" or the reporting clinicians as "quacks," but to keep their minds open. The editor asserted that the "fate of the unattended distemper-sick dog is well known, and euthanasia just doesn't carry the professional dignity it did 25 years ago." This editor realized that readers of the journal did not have the most open of minds, but that the information still had to be published. If science is not open-minded, it has no dignity and little validity.

Motivated by the clinical successes reported by Belfield in 1967, Leveque (1969) decided to start treating his dogs suffering from distemper with vitamin C. Leveque treated a total of 67 cases of canine distemper complex, and he also reported very good results. He commented that recovery from this disease "can be markedly improved" by including vitamin C in the treatment regimen.

Klenner (1974) was able to later corroborate Belfield's work. Klenner noted that he had "cured many dogs suffering with distemper" by giving injections of several grams of vitamin C every two hours. Klenner also noted that vitamin C had been discounted as being of little or no value against distemper since dogs are animals that can make their own vitamin C. However, dogs (and cats) cannot produce the massive amounts of vitamin C that some wild animals can make, and Klenner demonstrated repeatedly in his work that many viral infections will not show a positive response until a certain threshold of vitamin C administration is reached. This means that dogs and cats can only be expected to protect themselves from mild viral and infectious challenges. Large challenges, however, can rapidly and irreversibly sicken them if additional amounts of vitamin C are not forthcoming.

The ability of vitamin C to effectively treat the influenza virus is consistent with the fact that significant influenza infections are associated with a great deal of oxidative stress, a condition ideally suited for the potent antioxidant properties of vitamin C. Buffinton et al. (1992) showed that an influenza virus infection in mice was associated with increased oxidative stress in the lungs. In a similar experimental model, Hennet et al. (1992) also showed that influenza-infected mice had lowered levels of vitamin C and an overall lowered antioxidant status. This is especially significant since mice readily synthesize substantial amounts of their own vitamin C. It would appear that a virus such as the influenza virus can rapidly overwhelm the resistance of even a vitamin C-synthesizing animal like the mouse. This further underscores the need to supplement vitamin C promptly and in very high doses to effectively combat influenza and other viral diseases.

Although reported in less detail than some of the other viral diseases, it nevertheless appears that influenza responds rapidly to optimal vitamin C dosing. Some of the viral diseases cured by Klenner and others were most likely mixed viral combinations that included influenza. As was noted earlier, mixed viral syndromes generally have a greater viral load and require more intensive vitamin C therapy. Therefore, any time that Klenner cured a mixed viral syndrome that included influenza viruses, it is probably reasonable to conclude that the influenza virus alone could have been eradicated with less aggressive vitamin C dosing. Influenza is yet another viral disease that is curable, and adequate maintenance vitamin C should easily prevent it from ever being contracted in the first place.

Rabies (Preventable; Curable-?, Reversible-?)

Rabies is an especially feared viral disease that results in a relentless and almost invariably fatal encephalitis. The incubation period preceding development of initial symptoms is unusually long, averaging from one to two months. Traditional therapy is directed at attempting to prevent the viral penetration of the nervous system after initial exposure to the virus, using vaccines and other forms of immunotherapy. The *Cecil Textbook of Medicine* asserts that rabies cannot be cured once the disease has already invaded the nervous system.

the only "failures" Klenner ever had were overcome by giving more vitamin C, often by the intravenous route

Klenner did not report on the treatment of any rabies patients in his publications. As might be expected considering the successes he had with so many other viral diseases, Klenner was very adamant that the administration of the proper amounts of vitamin C would destroy all viruses encountered. The only "failures" that Klenner ever had were overcome by giving more vitamin C, often by the intravenous route.

Amato (1937) demonstrated that the rabies virus could be inactivated (killed) by vitamin C. Much later, Banic (1975) studied the effects of vitamin C on the rabies virus with guinea pigs. With 48 animals in the test group (using vitamin C) and 50 animals as a control group (without vitamin C), Banic found a statistically significant greater survival rate among the vitamin C-treated animals versus those who received no vitamin C. He concluded that vitamin C was effective in the prevention of rabies. Banic also noted that no therapeutic effect for "continued" vitamin C usage was achieved in animals that had already developed paralysis.

However, Banic used only 100 mg of vitamin C per kilogram animal body weight administered intramuscularly twice daily for seven days. Recall that Klenner would use as much as 700 mg of intravenous vitamin C per kilogram body weight in some of his patients. Also, Klenner's dosing would be repeated as often as every two hours until a favorable clinical response appeared. Furthermore, Klenner would often add significant amounts of oral vitamin C to go along with the intravenous doses. Had Banic used a more aggressive dosing of vitamin C, his results could certainly have been even more dramatic. When one considers that variable degrees of paralysis associated with other viral diseases were also completely reversed by Klenner-sized doses of vitamin C, higher dosing by Banic could likely have salvaged some of the animals even after the paralysis had developed.

even if the medical practitioner wants to use an extended rabies vaccine therapy, which is highly toxic in itself, the co-administration of vitamin C should be mandatory

In any event, there is absolutely no justification for not treating all rabies victims with high doses of intravenous vitamin C. Even if the medical practitioner still wants to heed the present recommendations of using an extended vaccine therapy that is highly toxic in itself, the co-administration of vitamin C should be mandatory.

Even though rabies certainly appears to be a preventable disease, the studies simply have not been conducted that would justify calling rabies either a reversible or a curable disease with the administration of vitamin C. However, this would appear to be due only to the lack of documented attempts to treat rabies with large doses of intravenous vitamin C. There is no reason to suspect that rabies would not respond in as equally dramatic a fashion as the other life-threatening viral diseases already discussed.

AIDS (Reversible and Preventable; Curable-?)

In the approximately two decades of its known existence, the acquired immunodeficiency syndrome (AIDS) has arguably become the most widely recognized disease syndrome in the history of the planet. AIDS is the disease that commonly eventually develops in those who become infected with the human immunodeficiency virus (HIV). The worldwide epidemic of HIV-infected individuals has shown no signs of significant slowing, except in areas where a large percentage of the population has already become infected.

Consider the following figures from the World Health Organization (WHO). In 1991 the WHO estimated that there were eight to 10 million HIV-infected persons in the world. The WHO increased this estimate to 12 to 14 million HIV infections in 1993. The WHO estimated the number of cases would be up to 36 million by the end of the year 2000. The WHO also estimated that three million people would die in 2000, as 2.6 million had already died in 1999.

the amount of vitamin C taken daily and subsequently stored in the body will be a primary determinate as to whether HIV or any other virus takes hold inside the body

Although the majority of deaths from earlier infections and new infections continues to occur in Africa, the rest of the world should not feel safe from this virus. Like any other virus, HIV attacks and infects those with the weakest immune systems. Poor nutrition and poor general health are always precursors to any viral infection. Furthermore, the amount of vitamin C taken daily and subsequently stored in the body will also be a primary determinant as to whether HIV or any other virus takes hold inside the body. Therefore, even though viruses like HIV (and Ebola, for another example) can be pandemic in many of the starving, weakened African nations, they will also attack nutritionally and immunologically deficient people anywhere else in the world.

Cathcart (1984) reported on his experience in treating AIDS patients with vitamin C. His results clearly indicate that AIDS and HIV infection are *preventable* and *reversible* conditions, and he postulates that the cure of AIDS might be possible if aggressive vitamin C therapy is continued for a long enough period of time. The reversibility of AIDS with vitamin C can vary from minimal symptom alleviation and reversal to a complete suppression of AIDS-associated symptoms. This complete suppression is distinguished from a cure, however, as the AIDS syndrome will typically reappear when Cathcart's suggested high-dose maintenance regimen of vitamin C is either discontinued or significantly cut back.

Although Cathcart did occasionally use intravenous vitamin C in treating AIDS, his most consistent administration of vitamin C was by mouth. He found that roughly 50,000 to 200,000 mg of vitamin C (as ascorbic acid powder) daily could suppress the symptoms of many AIDS patients. Not surprisingly, he

Cathcart found that roughly 50,000 to 200,000 mg of vitamin C daily could suppress the symptoms of many AIDS patients

also found that this dosage level of vitamin C markedly reduced the incidence of secondary infections in the AIDS patients. Such infections are often the immediate causes of death in AIDS, and they also are responsible for much of the suffering associated with the disease. Also, even though these patients were sustaining good symptom relief, the helper T-cell (an important immune cell) count would still show evidence of being suppressed even when the high-dose vitamin C protocol had resolved the clinical symptoms. This indicated an ongoing control of the disease process but not a cure.

Cathcart (1981) first described the method of adjusting vitamin C dosage according to bowel tolerance. Oral vitamin C, whether as ascorbic acid or as an ascorbate salt like sodium ascorbate, will reliably cause a watery diarrhea when a large enough dose is given. This occurs when a high concentration of unabsorbed vitamin C manages to reach the lower bowel and rectum. The high concentration of vitamin C naturally draws fluid into it from the surrounding tissues, resulting in a large volume of fluid in the rectum, which generally requires urgent evacuation. This process is also one of the reasons that large amounts of purified water must be faithfully ingested during this process. Significant fluid loss can occur in short order, and vitamin C exerts its own mild diuretic (urine production-stimulating) action as well. Only rarely will vitamin C ever manifest negative side effects, but when it does (see Chapter 4), it is often because a patient who is dehydrated simply will not ingest enough water and fluids.

Cathcart also found that stressful conditions of any kind, but especially viral infections, would greatly increase the utilization rate of vitamin C in the body. Such stressful conditions would allow a patient to take vastly more vitamin C orally than would normally trigger the diarrhea response. The vitamin C-depleted individual absorbs enough of the vitamin C in the early segments of the gut so that a high enough concentration to cause the diarrhea never reaches the lower gut. As a general rule, the sicker or more stressed the patient, the more vitamin C will be absorbed and utilized before enough of it reaches the lower gut, or colon, and stimulates the diarrhea reaction. Cathcart reported that over a 10-year period he had treated more than 9,000 patients with vitamin C doses using this concept of bowel tolerance. AIDS was one of the diseases treated by Cathcart with vitamin C that consistently showed the highest bowel tolerances. In other words, AIDS showed an ability to utilize and metabolize vitamin C more rapidly than most other diseases, infectious or otherwise. Probably only an acute and massive viral infection such as Ebola would consistently require more.

not surprisingly, Cathcart noted that clinical improvement in HIV patients seemed proportional to the amount of vitamin C given and how clinically ill the patient was at the beginning of treatment

From his experience in the vitamin C treatment of over 250 HIV-positive patients, including ones with full-blown AIDS, Cathcart (1990) was able to outline some fairly well-defined patterns of response. Not surprisingly, he noted that clinical improvement seemed proportional to the amount of vitamin C given and relative to how clinically ill the patient was at the beginning of treatment. Cathcart asserted that any AIDS patient could be put into remission if enough vitamin C is taken to neutralize the toxicity of the disease process, and any secondary infections are adequately treated. Furthermore, Cathcart noted that the CD4 cell count, an important immune cell that is depleted in HIV-infected patients, often responds posi-

declining CD4 cell count in HIV-infected patients... can be slowed, stopped, or even reversed for several years when vitamin C is dosed optimally

tively to the vitamin C therapy. The depletion of the CD4 count can be slowed, stopped, or even reversed for several years when vitamin C is dosed optimally. This is especially significant since the CD4 count is an important indicator of immediate prognosis. When it drops below a certain level and it does not rebound, any of several life-threatening infections can be contracted at any time.

When AIDS patients presented to Cathcart in a critically ill fashion (for example, with *Pneumocystis carinii* pneumonia or with a widely disseminated additional viral infection such as herpes or cytomegalovirus) he would give as much as 180,000 mg of vitamin C intravenously per day until there was enough clinical stability to switch to oral maintenance vitamin C therapy. Like Klenner, the oral vitamin C would typically be initiated at the outset along with the intravenous therapy. Cathcart would also start with the intravenous administration if the patient had a stomach condition that would not allow significant amounts of vitamin C (as ascorbic acid) to be given orally. As the overall condition of the patient improved, the oral dosing would usually become better tolerated. To prevent relapses, Cathcart emphasized the importance of educating the patient as to the lifelong need for high-dose oral vitamin C as determined by bowel tolerance.

Cathcart also noted that AIDS could be a syndrome in which eliminating the virus completely might not necessarily eliminate the disease. Just as juvenile-onset diabetes is felt to be possibly due to virus-facilitated damage to the insulin-secreting cells of the pancreas, AIDS may represent a form of incurable damage to the immune system. But even if this is the case, there is probably still good reason to believe that all cases of AIDS might not have sustained the same levels of permanent damage to the immune system. Therefore, completely eliminating the offending virus might still result in cures for some patients.

Cathcart suggests that giving a minimum of 180,000 mg of vitamin C intravenously daily for at least two weeks while simultaneously taking bowel tolerance doses of vitamin C orally may very well completely eliminate HIV and even lead to a clinical cure of AIDS. He does add, however, that this regimen was not successful in curing at least one AIDS patient on whom it was tried.

In general, all acute viral syndromes can probably be cured with prompt and vigorous vitamin C therapy. However, when some viral infections are not immediately and definitively addressed and become chronic, the disease processes are no longer pathologically the same as when they were acute. Consequences such as secondary damage to tissues and the provocation of autoimmune reactions not seen with acute infections can change the basic disease process. This, in turn, can change the response to vitamin C and any other medication or treatment. However, if the opportunity exists, any AIDS patients would be best served by going on a prolonged daily regimen of high-dose intravenous vitamin C, perhaps for a month or more, before transferring to daily maintenance on oral vitamin C at bowel tolerance levels for life.

One possible reason that AIDS is so much more difficult to completely eradicate than other viral infections is because of harboring of the virus in the CD4 lymphocytes mentioned earlier. The *Cecil Textbook of Medicine* notes that approximately one million lymphocytes having the CD4 antigen in any given infected person contain "stably integrated provirus" in a latent state. Provirus is the nucleic acid (DNA or RNA) of the infecting virus that has actually been integrated into the chromosome of the patient's host cells. This allows it to be reproduced indefinitely along with the rest of the cell's DNA every time cell replication takes place. However, until the CD4 cell is activated by any of several stimuli, the viral nucleic acid will not again be activated to produce a complete virus. As a result, this reservoir of inactive virus will remain much less accessible to any therapy, including vitamin C. Logic dictates that the intravenous administration of vitamin C would be required to extend beyond the lifetimes of the CD4 cell and any other cells of the body in which the virus might have become incorporated. The administration of vitamin C by vein would be expected to neutralize any viral DNA or RNA released by the dying cells; otherwise, it would be expected to neutralize any viral particles that are re-formed upon the release of the DNA or RNA.

This same reasoning may apply to some of the cancers that are known to be associated with viral infections. The intravenous application of vitamin C may have to be continued for one or more months on a daily basis to result in the cure of some cancers. Less aggressive dosing may result in the improvement of clinical symptoms only or in the achievement of a remission that could later relapse.

As AIDS is a syndrome characterized by immune compromise, the potential for curing a case of AIDS with vitamin C would be optimized if identifiable sources of significant daily immune-suppressing toxins are also eliminated. Huggins and Levy (1999), as well as other investigators, have long observed the enormous negative health impact of a daily exposure to potent dental toxins. Not only do such toxins directly utilize and metabolize a large amount of vitamin C that could otherwise be directed to the support of general health, but these toxins further exert their own unrelenting negative effect on the immune system and the body in general. Such dental toxins include mercury in amalgam fillings and the toxins of anaerobic bacterial metabolism found in root canal treated teeth, cavitations, and gum (periodontal) disease (Kulacz and Levy, 2002). In addition, the toxicity of other biologically incompatible and toxic dental materials, such as the nickel in many crowns and braces, remain in the mouth for many years. If an AIDS patient can be relieved of this enormous daily toxic stress before undergoing the intensive course of vitamin C therapy outlined above, dramatic reversals and even clinical cures might become commonplace.

A sizable amount of research has been performed that supports the benefits of vitamin C in HIV-infected patients. With regard to

HIV-infected men, Tang et al. (1993) reported "that high intakes of several nutrients (niacin, vitamin C, and vitamin B1) were associated with slower progression to AIDS, after adjustment for confounding variables." Allard et al. (1998) were able to demonstrate that fairly small doses of oral vitamin C (relative to the bowel tolerance doses used by Cathcart, see above), along with vitamin E, showed positive effects.

The administration of merely 1,000 mg of vitamin C and 800 IU of vitamin E daily for three months to HIV-infected patients resulted in a lessened evidence of oxidative stress and a trend toward a reduction in the actual viral load. The authors, along with Kotler (1998), suggest considering the routine use of antioxidants such as vitamin C and vitamin E in HIV-infected individuals, since only about 10% of those infected individuals can currently afford to buy the existing prescription AIDS drugs. Semba et al. (1993) also reported that a deficiency of vitamin A "seems to be an important risk factor for disease progression during HIV-1 infection." Certainly, it would seem wise to take reasonable daily doses of all the other antioxidant vitamins to help vitamin C's support of the immune system.

Although Cathcart's extensive experience with very large doses of vitamin C in AIDS conclusively demonstrates that prolonged administration benefits the patients, including even raising the CD4 T-lymphocyte cell count, research continues that attempts to discredit the benefits of vitamin C and discourage its use.

Eylar et al. (1996), looking at purified human T cells in culture, found that incubating these cells with vitamin C in the test tube at variable concentrations damaged the cells in an irreversible fashion after an exposure of at least 18 hours. On this basis alone, these authors cautioned against the use of large doses of vitamin C in the treatment of patients with AIDS and cancer. Furthermore, the title of their article, which is all that many readers and reviewers often read, simply states that vitamin C is toxic and immunosuppressive to human T cells. The researchers never even mention that this effect was observed only in the test tube and not the body. A treatment period of only 18 hours is inconsequential, and any familiarity at all with the vitamin C ingestion of Cathcart's HIV-infected patients for years permits a total dismissal of the extremely over-extrapolated conclusion reached by these research-ers. Test tube research can be very valuable, but it cannot always be di-rectly correlated and applied to what happens inside the body. These researchers have an obligation to be aware of the volumes of positive clinical data already amassed before warning AIDS and cancer patients against the use of large doses of vitamin C, which is quite possibly the best therapeutic option available to them.

Vitamin C has been demonstrated to kill HIV directly in both whole blood and in a culture medium. Rawal et al. (1995) conclud-ed that concentrations of vitamin C that completely in-activated HIV did not demon-strate any definable harmful effects. Furthermore, there was no negative effect seen on the platelets in the vitamin C-medi-ated HIV inactivation in the blood. Platelets are sticky elements in the blood that help to initiate blood clotting. The possibility exists that a routine addition of vitamin C to blood products to be transfused would not only disinfect them, but would also improve the nutrient benefit to the patient. Having a way to routinely eliminate HIV from blood and blood product transfusions would also effectively eliminate the occa-sional transfusion of HIV-tainted blood from a donor who had not yet developed HIV antibodies, which would allow the tainted blood to es-cape detection by routine testing. Such effective treatment of blood to be transfused could possibly complete eliminate the need for routinely checking such blood for infective agents.

vitamin C has been demonstrated to kill HIV directly in whole blood and in a culture medium... there was no negative effect seen on the platelets in the vitamin C-mediated HIV inactivation

Cumming et al. (1989) noted that the risk of such an unwelcome transfusion appears to be decreasing over time. However, such transfu-sions still occur, even though there is no satisfactory reason for not pre-treating the blood with vitamin C and significantly dosing the patient to be transfused with vitamin C before and after transfusion for added protection against any transmitted infection.

In addition to its ability to kill HIV directly as noted above, vita-min C has demonstrated the ability to be toxic to cells already infected with HIV. Rivas et al. (1997) showed that exposure to pharmacological concentrations of vitamin C *preferentially* lessened the ability of HIV-infected cells to reproduce or survive. This effect resulted further in decreased viral production. Earlier, Harakeh et al. (1990) indicated that concentrations of vitamin C not directly toxic to the infected cells still resulted in a significant inhibition of virus reproduction inside the cells. Furthermore, vitamin C has been shown to suppress the viral enzyme (reverse transcriptase) that allows viral DNA to reproduce itself.

While these experimental studies do not provide clear guidelines for treating HIV-infected patients with vitamin C, they still indicate that achieving optimal concentrations of vitamin C in the body can inhibit HIV viral activity inside infected cells and preferentially kill or retard the proliferation of infected cells.

Harakeh and Jariwalla (1991) looked at the effects of vitamin C on the ability of HIV to replicate in chronically infected T-lymphocytes. Their results further supported "the potent antiviral activity" of vitamin C. The authors also suggested that vitamin C had "therapeutic value in controlling HIV infection." Harakeh and Jariwalla (1997) later further investigated the ability of vitamin C to inhibit HIV activity in infected T-lymphocyte cells. They reported that vitamin C appeared to facilitate this effect by a mechanism not shared with other antioxidants, which further supports the concept that vitamin C offers more benefit than just a potent antioxidant activity.

Vitamin C has also been shown to help the clinical status of an HIV-infected patient by helping to repair damage that occurs as a side effect of drug therapy traditionally given to such patients. A frequent side effect of zidovudine (AZT), which is often used in the treatment of HIV-positive patients, is myopathy that is typically manifested as muscle

"supranutritional" dosing of vitamin C and vitamin E protected against AZT-mediated oxidative muscle damage in both AIDS patients and in mice treated with AZT

weakness. De la Asuncion et al. (1998) speculate that this myopathy is due largely to oxidative damage to the DNA found in the mitochondria in the muscle tissue. Mitochondria are the principal sites of cellular energy generation, accounting for muscular weakness perceived by a patient when their function is impaired. These researchers concluded that "supranutritional" dosing of vitamin C and vitamin E protected against AZT-mediated oxidative muscle damage in both AIDS patients and in mice treated with AZT. Gogu et al. (1989) had earlier published that vitamin E alone also increased the therapeutic efficacy of AZT. Both vitamin C and vitamin E are antioxidants, which is probably why both lessen the toxicity of AZT.

A myelopathy, or pathology of the spinal cord, syndrome is associated with human T-lymphotropic virus, type 1 (HTLV-1). HTLV is often associated with HIV, existing as a coinfection. In fact, HTLV-III was an early designation for HIV. Kataoka et al. (1993, 1993a) reported that seven of seven patients with myelopathy "responded well" to vitamin C therapy.

Although it has already been stated that any form of stress, especially infective stress, will utilize and metabolize vitamin C at a greater rate, it is useful to note that this has been studied specifically in HIV infection. Treitinger et al. (2000) found that HIV-infected patients had lower plasma concentrations of vitamin C than found in controls. Their results suggested that abnormalities of antioxidant defense were directly related to the progression of HIV infection. In similar fashion, Muller et al. (2000) found that antioxidant supplementation with vitamin C and N-acetyl cysteine for only six days in eight HIV-infected patients had striking effects on certain immune functions and virus activity indicators. Specifically, in five patients who had the most advanced disease, the CD4 T-lymphocyte count rose significantly, and the glutathione (another significant antioxidant) content of those CD4 cells also increased. Conversely, the plasma content of virus-related RNA declined.

Everall et al. (1997) found that AIDS patients who died of nervous system toxicity had significantly reduced levels of vitamin C in the most affected areas of the brain. As with other infective diseases, sufficient doses of vitamin C must be taken to deal with preexisting depletions as well as to deal with the infection itself. Skurnick et al. (1996) reported that in a survey of HIV-positive patients and controls, almost a third of the HIV-positive patients had subnormal levels of one or more antioxidants even though supplemental vitamins were being taken. Bogden et al. (1990) also reported that 27% of HIV-positive patients they studied had below normal plasma concentrations of vitamin C. Looking more generally at overall antioxidant levels, McLemore et al. (1998) found that HIV-positive subjects had significantly lower levels than control subjects. Bagchi et al. (2000) noted that AIDS is only one of many diseases with high levels of free radicals and oxidative stress causing at least part of the clinical symptoms.

The issue of supplementation is an especially important consideration when doing any kind of study on AIDS or other diseases. Vitamin C is very commonly taken currently as a supplement by millions of people, and many studies that look at the effects of different drugs on certain conditions never consider how diligently the patients are already self-medicating with vitamin C and other nutrients. Also, such patients often begin this vigorous supplementation immediately after they are first diagnosed, and this further obscures a determination of the singular effectiveness of any simultaneously prescribed medication. Modern medicine makes many claims as to the causes of improved clinical responses seen with many diseases today. It may well be that much of this improvement is due to increased self-dosing of vitamin C and other vital nutrients, as well as to the increased amounts of antioxidants and other nutrients being put into packaged foods.

A reasonable conclusion would be that HIV infection and even full-blown AIDS are diseases that can be controlled quite effectively if a high enough chronic dosing of vitamin C is maintained. Indeed, with enough vitamin C, the evidence indicates that much of the disease pathology and many of the laboratory abnormalities can be reversed significantly or even normalized. Just as with all other viruses, there is also no reason not to believe that a high enough daily dose of vitamin C would prevent most HIV infections from ever even starting.

Curing AIDS and HIV infection with vitamin C, however, remains yet to be clearly demonstrated. The unique nature of the HIV infection, with its dormancy in the CD4 positive lymphocytes (and very likely in other immune cells and tissues), makes the complete eradication of the infecting virus more difficult. Dental and other toxins that keep the immune system suppressed must first be properly removed. Once all readily removable toxicity is absent from the body, a prolonged series of high dose intravenous injections of vitamin C along with oral doses that approach bowel tolerance may actually cure the HIV-infected patient.

The Common Cold
(Reversible and Preventable; Curable-?)

The common cold is an acute viral disease typically characterized by cough, sore throat, and nasal symptoms (runny, difficult air passage). This disease is also known as acute coryza, or upper respiratory tract infection. Multiple viruses are capable of producing the common cold, and some of them do not produce an immunity, which subjects an individual to possible repeated infections with the same virus. As with most other viral infections, the medical textbook asserts that no antiviral agents are available for treating colds.

The common cold is usually self-limited, with the most prominent symptoms characteristically persisting for about a week. Not uncommonly, however, significant colds can seriously depress the immune system, and substantially deplete vitamin C stores in the body. Colds can lead to other superimposed infections or progress to additional organ involvement in the body as is seen in some cases of viral pneumonia, encephalitis, or meningitis.

Linus Pauling (1970), the only individual to ever win two unshared Nobel Prizes, probably generated more attention in advocating high doses of vitamin C for the common cold than for anything else he did. It certainly brought him an enormous amount of criticism from members of the medical establishment.

The book that Pauling wrote regarding vitamin C's beneficial effects on the common cold stimulated numerous subsequent publications on the subject. Unfortunately, Pauling's publication and many others did not look at dosing the common cold with the amounts of vitamin C that Klenner effectively used on so many different viruses. As already noted in this chapter, many of the viral diseases cured by Klenner with vitamin C were far more serious and had much greater viral loads spread throughout the body than seen with the common cold. However, a severe cold probably has a comparable viral load to an uncomplicated case of the flu, and Klenner demonstrated that curing the flu required substantially more vitamin C than recommended by Pauling for the common cold, and at least some of the vitamin C had to be injected rather than just taken orally. Nevertheless, Pauling was able to show a positive effect of vitamin C on the common cold with doses far lower than those utilized by Klenner.

Cathcart (1981), in describing his bowel tolerance method of determining the best doses of vitamin C for a given condition (discussed above in his treatment of AIDS), found that colds seemed to require much more vitamin C than was suggested in any published study before or since this observation. Specifically, Cathcart described a "mild cold" as typically requiring 30,000 to 60,000 mg of vitamin C to reach bowel tolerance. He also noted that a "severe cold" could require from 60,000 to more than 100,000 mg of vitamin C to reach bowel tolerance. Depending upon the amount required for bowel tolerance, Cathcart recommended administering the vitamin in six to 15 divided doses daily to maintain optimal blood and body tissue levels. It should also be noted that Cathcart found that most normal adults without apparent infection or disease would tolerate from 4,000 to 15,000 mg of vitamin C before reaching bowel tolerance.

In a review article Hemila and Douglas (1999) noted that more than 60 studies on the effects of vitamin C on the common cold had been published as of the time of their writing. Douglas et al. (2000) reviewed 30 studies looking at the effects of oral vitamin C in treating the common cold. They concluded that although colds were not prevented by the doses of vitamin C given, a modest benefit of reduced symptom duration was seen, and some of the evidence indicated that larger doses resulted in even greater benefits.

Hemila (1994) earlier reviewed 21 placebo-controlled studies examining the effects of vitamin C on the common cold performed since 1971. He concluded that vitamin C consistently lessened cold symptoms but did not reduce the incidence of the common cold. The daily doses in these studies were either equal to or somewhat in excess of 1,000 mg of vitamin C. In terms of disease duration and severity of symptoms, an average of 23% reduction was observed.

Gorton and Jarvis (1999) designed a prospective, controlled study to look at how effective vitamin C would be in both preventing and relieving symptoms of already contracted colds and flu. A test group was compared with a control group. The test group regularly received 1,000 mg of vitamin C three times a day. If cold or flu symptoms developed in the test group, 1,000 mg of vitamin C was immediately given hourly for the first six hours, and the maintenance schedule was resumed. Relative to the control group, the cold and flu symptoms in the vitamin C-receiving test group were decreased by 85%. This study is also significant in that the importance of a "loading dose" of vitamin C above and beyond a maintenance dose was recognized. Although the dose sizes were still well below those routinely used by Klenner and were given orally rather than intravenously, this study, when compared to most of the earlier vitamin C-cold studies, helps to independently establish the importance of acutely giving a larger dose of vitamin C. After the loading dose has been administered, one may proceed to a maintenance dose in order to achieve clinical benefit.

Karlowski et al. (1975) published a study from the National Institutes of Health that has long served to supposedly "debunk" the idea that vitamin C is of definite use in treating the common cold. Hemila (1996), in analyzing the oft-cited results of Karlowski et al., found that the study actually showed a 17% decrease in the duration of colds in those patients given an additional 3,000 mg of vitamin C daily to a existing maintenance dose of 3,000 mg daily. Karlowski and his coworkers had dismissed this as being secondary to the placebo effect. They concluded this because the placebo had a different taste from the vitamin C. Hemila points out that this placebo explanation is not likely valid since the decrease in symptoms very closely paralleled the decreases seen in other studies with non-detectable placebos. Also, the 17% improvement is very close to the average 23% improvement seen in the series of 21 placebo-controlled studies referred to by Hemila (1994).

Carr et al. (1981) also generated data consistent with the finding noted above. They looked at the effects of vitamin C on the com-

mon cold, using identical twins as controls. It was concluded that the
vitamin C was effective in "shortening the average duration of cold episodes by 19%."

Murphy et al. (1974) looked at the effects of vitamin C in alleviat-
ing the symptoms of a virus that could cause cold-like symptoms in the
marmoset, a primate susceptible to cold viruses of human origin. The
mean body weight of the animals was 400 grams, and the vitamin C-
supplemented animals received 100 mg of vitamin C twice a day
orally, which would equate to approximately 35,000 mg daily for a 70-
kilogram man. The authors concluded that while the vitamin C did not
prevent virus infection, it did delay the onset of disease, reduce clinical
symptoms, and decrease the chances of death from the infection.

Edwards (1968) treated cats with feline rhinotracheitis, a type of
viral cold, with vitamin C. A 1,000 mg daily dose of vitamin C was
given intravenously until clinical recovery, and then 250 mg daily oral
doses were continued for a few days after recovery. The average recovery time for the treated cats was 4.9 days compared to 13 days for the
untreated controls. Povey (1969) also reported on the treatment of feline
viral rhinotracheitis with vitamin C. Although Povey used much smaller daily doses of vitamin C (100 mg) than Edwards, Povey was still able
to assert that there was "some evidence" that these "high levels" of vitamin C were shortening recovery times.

Belfield and Stone (1975) reported on the vitamin C treatment of
a Siamese cat that was very ill with rhinotracheitis. The initial dose of
vitamin C was 8,000 mg intravenously (1,000 mg per pound of body
weight) in two divided doses. Two more 4,000 mg injections were given
after the first day, and 2,000 to 4,000 mg were also given orally daily in
the cat's food. The cat recovered quickly, and the authors asserted that
they had "similarly successfully treated about 100 cases" like this one.

There is certainly no reason to believe that the viruses responsible
for the common cold would respond any less positively to the large
doses of vitamin C used by Klenner for the other viral diseases that he
successfully treated. If one wanted to recover from a cold in 72 hours
or less, significant doses of intravenous vitamin C would typically
have to be part of the protocol. A very light cold treated very promptly

with bowel tolerance doses of vitamin C would also likely be cured in 72 hours or less. However, once the viral load has been allowed to become substantially large, initial dosing should be intravenous in order to quickly get "ahead" of the virus. While the literature does not directly assure that the common cold is curable with vitamin C, the indirect evidence would indicate that this is the case. The symptoms definitely show reversibility with adequate doses of vitamin C, and taking daily bowel tolerance doses of vitamin C should suffice in preventing most colds from ever being contracted. A recently developed form of oral vitamin C encapsulated in liposomes is now demonstrating superior bioavailability and clinical response relative to intravenous vitamin C (see Chapter 5).

Ebola Virus
(Curable-?, Reversible-?, Preventable-?)

Due to news coverage in recent years that seems designed to induce fear that a new, uncontrollable killer virus has suddenly appeared, Ebola virus is now generally well-known throughout the world. Ebola is probably the best known of a class of viruses known as hemorrhagic fever viruses. In fact, Ebola virus was initially recognized in 1976. Other less known but related viral syndromes include yellow fever, dengue hemorrhagic fever, Rift Valley fever, Crimean-Congo hemorrhagic fever, Kyasanur Forest disease, Omsk hemorrhagic fever, hemorrhagic fever with renal syndrome, Hantavirus pulmonary syndrome, Venezuelan hemorrhagic fever, Brazilian hemorrhagic fever, Argentine hemorrhagic fever, Bolivian hemorrhagic fever, and Lassa fever. The Ebola virus infection, also known as African hemorrhagic fever, has the distinction of having the highest case-fatality rate of the viral infections noted above, ranging from 53% to 88%.

the clinical presentation of these viral hemorrhagic fever diseases is similar to scurvy, which is also characterized by capillary fragility and a tendency to bleed easily

These viral hemorrhagic fever syndromes share certain clinical features. The *Cecil Textbook of Medicine* notes that these diseases are characterized by capillary fragility, which translates to easy bleeding, that can frequently lead to severe shock and death. These diseases also tend to consume and/or destroy the platelets, which play an integral role in blood clotting. The clinical presentation of these viral diseases is similar to scurvy, which is also characterized by capillary fragility and a tendency to bleed easily. Characteristic skin lesions develop, which are actually multiple tiny areas of bleeding into the skin that surround the hair follicles. Some cases even include bleeding into already healed scars.

In the classic form of scurvy that evolves very slowly from the gradual depletion of vitamin C body stores, the immune system will be sufficiently compromised for infection to claim the patient's life before the extensive hemorrhage that occurs after all vitamin C stores have been completely exhausted. Ebola virus and the other viral hemorrhagic fevers are much more likely to cause hemorrhaging before any other fatal infection has a chance to become established. This is because the virus so rapidly and totally metabolizes and consumes all available vitamin C in the bodies of the victims that an advanced stage of scurvy is literally produced after only a few days of the disease.

the virus so rapidly and totally metabolizes and consumes all available vitamin C in the bodies of the victims that an advanced stage of scurvy is produced after only a few days

The scurvy is so complete that the blood vessels generally cannot keep from hemorrhaging long enough to allow an infective complication to develop. Also, the viral hemorrhagic fevers typically only take hold and reach epidemic proportions in those populations that would already be expected to have low body stores of vitamin C, such as is found in many of the severely malnourished Africans. In such individuals, an infecting hemorrhagic virus will often wipe out any remaining vitamin C stores before the immune systems can get the upper hand and initiate recovery. When the vitamin C stores are rapidly depleted by large infecting doses of an aggressive virus, the immune system gets similarly depleted and compromised. However, this point is largely academic after hemorrhaging throughout the body has begun.

To date, *no* viral infection has been demonstrated to be resistant to the proper dosing of vitamin C as classically demonstrated by Klenner. However, not all viruses have been treated with Klenner-sized vitamin C doses, or at least the results have not been published. Ebola viral infection and the other acute viral hemorrhagic fevers appear to be diseases that fall into this category. Because of the seemingly exceptional ability of these viruses to rapidly deplete vitamin C stores, even larger doses of vitamin C would likely be required in order to effectively reverse and eventually cure infections caused by these viruses. Cathcart (1981), who introduced the concept of bowel tolerance to vitamin C discussed earlier, hypothesized that Ebola and the other acute viral hemorrhagic fevers may well require 500,000 mg of vitamin C daily to reach bowel tolerance! It would be very interesting to examine the effects of oral liposome encapsulated vitamin C on these rapidly progressing viral syndromes.

Whether this estimate is accurate, it seems clear as evidenced by the scurvy-like clinical manifestations of these infections that vitamin C dosing must be vigorous and given in extremely high doses. If the disease seems to be winning, then even more vitamin C should be given until symptoms begin to lessen. Obviously, these are viral diseases that would absolutely require high doses of vitamin C intravenously as the initial therapy. The oral administration should begin simultaneously, but the intravenous route should not be abandoned until the clinical response is complete. Death occurs too quickly with the hemorrhagic fevers to be conservative when dosing the vitamin C.

Belfield and Stone (1975) reported enormous success in the treatment of a variety of viral infections in animals, emphasizing that they had found no virus to be unresponsive to intravenous vitamin C. Specifically, with regard to viral diseases, they asserted:

> The intravenous use of ascorbate [vitamin C] is especially valuable in the therapy of the viral diseases as it appears to be an effective, non-specific, non-toxic virucidal

> agent. We have not seen any viral disease that did not
> respond to this treatment. Successful therapy appears to
> depend on using it in sufficiently large doses.

The experience of Belfield and Stone with vitamin C and viral infections in animals certainly seems to agree with the phenomenal success that Klenner reported in his treatment of viral infections with vitamin C in humans. It also implies that Ebola viral infection and the other acute viral hemorrhagic fevers should respond to large enough doses of intravenous vitamin C.

Another viral disease that has the capability of producing Ebola-like hemorrhagic complications is smallpox. Akin to chickenpox but much more deadly, smallpox has probably killed approximately 100 million people throughout history. Not surprisingly, smallpox has historically been the most deadly in those populations of people who have the poorest nutritional status and, logically, the lowest body reservoirs of vitamin C.

Although no direct evidence of the effects of vitamin C on the smallpox virus could be found in the literature, the virus in the smallpox vaccine is readily killed by vitamin C. This virus, known as the vaccinia virus, is related closely enough to the smallpox virus that inoculation with it will typically produce an immunity to smallpox. However, this fortunate similarity between vaccinia and smallpox virus prevents the need for direct inoculation with some weakened or attenuated form of smallpox virus, eliminating the chance of an accidental smallpox infection.

Kligler and Bernkopf (1937) and Turner (1964) found that this related vaccinia virus was easily killed by relatively small amounts of vitamin C. They noted that the degree of viral inactivation depended on the vitamin C concentration and time period it was in contact with the virus. These studies were done shortly after Jungeblut (1935) had demonstrated that vitamin C could similarly inactivate the poliovirus. All of this research represented initial efforts to show the wide-ranging ability of vitamin C to neutralize and/or kill different microbes. Although the vaccinia virus is not the smallpox virus, all of the evidence presented so far would argue strongly that enough vitamin C properly administered should control and cure smallpox as readily as any other of the deadly viral syndromes.

For those who still fear that the Ebola virus is the untreatable disease just waiting to strike down their perfect health, consider the recently published evidence that indicates a symptom-free Ebola infection can and does occur in human beings. Leroy et al. (2000) looked at a number of individuals who were in direct contact with patients sick with Ebola but who had never developed symptoms. Evidence in the blood testing of these patients revealed that a strong inflammatory response early in the course of the infectious process had taken place, and that roughly half of the symptom-free group also developed Ebola virus-specific antibodies. All of this evidence lends further support to the notion that encountering the Ebola virus does not mean instant death. It is also highly unlikely that Ebola virus could successfully sicken an individual with a good general nutritional status, and who is taking a daily bowel tolerance dosage of vitamin C, or a reasonable daily dose of liposome encapsulated vitamin C.

Non-Viral Infectious Diseases and Vitamin C

Diphtheria (Curable and Preventable)

Diphtheria is an acute bacterial infectious disease that is most commonly found in infants and children. Diphtheria usually affects primarily the upper respiratory tract, where a tough membrane will typically cover the most affected tissues. In fact, the word diphtheria literally means "leather hide," referring to how notoriously tough this characteristic membrane is. The infecting organism, a gram-positive bacillus, also produces a potentially lethal toxin that can spread rapidly to the heart, the nerves, and/or the kidneys. Diphtheria is one of several infectious diseases that produces illness both from the primary infection and from the production of a disease-specific toxin. Vitamin C is especially appropriate for the treatment of a disease like diphtheria, since it is uniquely capable of both eradicating the infection and neutralizing the associated toxin without any significant toxicity of its own.

vitamin C is especially appropriate for the treatment of a disease like diphtheria since it is uniquely capable of both eradicating the infection and neutralizing the associated toxin without toxicity of its own

Over the past few decades, diphtheria has continued to have a case-fatality rate that runs between 5% and 10%. The primary traditional treatment for this infection is a horse serum-derived antitoxin along with antibiotics such as penicillin, erythromycin, or clindamycin. Immediate allergic reactions to the antitoxin have an overall incidence of 15%. In older children, a syndrome called serum sickness can follow the use of the antitoxin in 20% to 30% of the cases. This will typically last an additional one to two weeks, featuring joint inflammation and further fever. Furthermore, there can also be a significant adverse reaction or side effect from any of the antibiotics given.

Klenner (July 1949) also had a great deal of success in treating diphtheria with vitamin C. He was quite emphatic, however, that "massive frequent doses" of vitamin C needed to be given intravenously or intramuscularly. Generally, when the patient was four years of age or older, Klenner would opt for an intravenous administration if at all possible. This intravenous route was used whenever the child seemed ill enough, regardless of the diagnosis.

In treating diphtheria Klenner specifically noted that giving only 1,000 to 2,000 mg of vitamin C orally every two hours typically produced little response. However, he asserted that curing diphtheria was routine if enough vitamin C was given by vein or in the muscle. Klenner (1974) later declared that he had witnessed the clearing of diphtheria, hemolytic streptococcus, and staphylococcus infections within hours when a vitamin C dose range of 500 to 700 mg/kg body weight was given intravenously and allowed to run through a 20 gauge needle "as fast as the patient's cardiovascular system would allow." Antitoxin was not needed, since vitamin C, as will be discussed at length in Chapter 3, is also the ultimate toxin neutralizer or inactivator. Vitamin C negates the effects of a wider variety of toxic poisonings than any other known agent, by far. This is another reason why vitamin C is exceptionally well suited to treat diphtheria as well as other infectious diseases that produce not only specific toxins, but also less well-identified toxic by-products that result from both the metabolism of the microbe and its interactions with the host. Multiple German investigators (Bamberger and Wendt, 1935; Bamberger and Zell, 1936; Dieckhoff and Schuler, 1938; Szirmai, 1940) all documented beneficial results from the treatment of diphtheria with vitamin C.

the clearing of diphtheria, hemolytic streptococcus, and staphylococcus infections was witnessed within hours when 500 to 700 mg/kg body weight of vitamin C was given intravenously

Klenner (July 1949) also noted that the tough membrane that adhered to the most affected tissues in the throat tended to gradually decompose as the disease responded to the vitamin C rather than break off more suddenly (slough) when the antitoxin was used. He also commented that diphtheria could be cured in about half the time normally needed to remove the membrane with the antitoxin treatment.

McCormick (1951) commented on the bleeding tendencies seen in diphtheria, and he also noted the association between scurvy and a proneness to hemorrhage. Any infectious disease that also produces a potent toxin can be expected to even more rapidly and completely deplete vitamin C stores, and bleeding from different sites can be expected from this acutely induced state of scurvy if vitamin C is not quickly and generously administered. Diphtheria patients are prone to easy nosebleeds, and when the membrane is removed it is not uncommon to see profuse bleeding. McCormick also noted that diphtheria in 18th century central and northern Europe was an especially dreaded disease with about an 80% case-fatality rate. He attributed this to the prevalence of widespread vitamin C depletion from the lack of fresh fruits available at that time.

Klenner (1971) also reported on three children living in the same neighborhood with nasal diphtheria, which specifically affects the nasal lining and produces a characteristic bloody discharge from the nose. In nasal diphtheria the membrane will develop in this area rather than in the throat. All three children had different doctors. The little girl under Klenner's care was given 10,000 mg of vitamin C as a slow intravenous "push" with a 50 cc syringe every eight hours for the first 24 hours and then every 12 hours for two more doses. Following this she was given 1,000 mg of vitamin C every two hours by mouth. Klenner also notes that a 40,000-unit dose of antitoxin was injected into the little girl's abdomen. The other two children received the antitoxin as well, but they did not receive any vitamin C. They both died but Klenner's patient survived, later becoming a nurse.

The outstanding clinical success of Klenner in treating diphtheria with vitamin C was supported by some impressive basic research reported in the 1930s. Harde and Philippe (1934) demonstrated that lethal doses of diphtheria toxin premixed with vitamin C were no longer lethal in the guinea pigs they injected. The toxin doses without the vitamin C killed the guinea pigs in four to eight days. Jungeblut and Zwemer (1935) found that vitamin C inactivated diphtheria toxin in the test tube, and also helped to protect many of the guinea pigs against the fatal outcome of being injected with diphtheria toxin. The authors concluded that vitamin C played an important role in the mechanism of natural resistance to diphtheria toxin. Greenwald and Harde (1935) were also able to demonstrate that vitamin C could increase the resistance of guinea pigs to injections of standardized diphtheria toxin. Furthermore, they demonstrated that mixtures of toxin and vitamin C had less toxicity than pure toxin upon injection. Hanzlik and Terada (1936), stimulated to further investigate the work of the two research groups just cited, found that about 50% of pigeons injected with fatal doses of diphtheria toxin survived when given a single 100 mg intramuscular injection of vitamin C. They also found that pigeons injected with toxin premixed with vitamin C all survived. They concluded that vitamin C was a legitimate inactivator of diphtheria toxin.

Sigal and King (1937) looked at the effect that vitamin C has in lessening the negative impact of diphtheria toxin on glucose (sugar) metabolism in guinea pigs. Compared to animals receiving larger doses, these researchers were able to demonstrate that sublethal injections of toxin did cause greater metabolic disturbances in animals receiving only enough vitamin C to prevent scurvy. This conclusion was especially significant since it demonstrated that the healthiest dose of vitamin C was clearly in excess of the tiny amount capable only of preventing scurvy. Similarly, King and Menten (1935) were able to demonstrate that actual survival times for scurvy-stricken guinea pigs infected with diphtheria were only half that of normal, control animals. This finding was consistent with the fact that the guinea pig cannot manufacture any vitamin C for itself. On the other hand, the mouse is a vitamin C-synthesizing research animal that has a natural resistance to diphtheria.

Kligler et al. (1937) looked at the effects of vitamin C on growing cultures of diphtheria bacteria as opposed to purified diphtheria toxin. They found that a given amount of vitamin C has a specific effect in reducing the toxicity of diphtheria cultures. However, they could not clearly determine the mechanism utilized by vitamin C in reducing the toxicity of the cultures. They suggested that vitamin C could be either affecting the metabolism of the bacteria to stop producing toxin, or that vitamin C could be modifying or destroying the toxin as rapidly as it was formed. Another researcher, von Gagyi (1936), found that enough vitamin C added to cultures of diphtheria bacteria in an acidic medium could kill the bacteria within six hours of exposure. Pakter and Schick (1938) put together a good review of much of this early information concerning the effects of vitamin C on diphtheria and its associated toxin.

The incredible clinical success that Klenner had in treating diphtheria with vitamin C, along with early laboratory evidence looking at the interactions of vitamin C and diphtheria, clearly shows that diphtheria is a disease that can be readily cured with properly dosed and administered vitamin C. Because diphtheria is both an infectious disease and a producer of a severe toxin, vitamin C should be given initially by vein or in the muscle prior to settling on any oral dosage regimen.

Also, as with any other infectious disease curable by vitamin C, maintenance dosing up to bowel tolerance should be highly effective in preventing diphtheria from ever being contracted. A much smaller daily dose of liposome encapsulated vitamin C should also prove to be a highly effective preventive therapy.

Pertussis (Reversible and Preventable; Curable-?)

Pertussis, commonly known as whooping cough, is a bacterial respiratory illness that occurs most commonly and most severely in infants and young children. The common name derives from the sound of the prolonged, distressed efforts to take a breath that follows repeated coughing. Even today, pertussis is estimated to cause 500,000 deaths yearly, primarily in infants. Antibiotic treatment of this disease is primarily directed at rendering the patient non-infectious to others. Even when the microbes are eliminated by antibiotics in an infected infant, the remaining course of the illness is typically unaltered. Pertussis is somewhat prolonged, with an incubation stage of one to two weeks characterized by fever, runny nose, and cough.

The severe phase of the illness, with the frightening episodes of coughing and whooping, lasts another three to four weeks. The convalescent stage, marked by a slow recovery with a gradually lessened frequency of whooping episodes, can last another four to 12 weeks. Following this final stage, for many more months, even a mild, unrelated respiratory infection can induce a return of the characteristic pertussis cough and whoop. Pertussis is also another disease with an associated toxin even though no traditional antitoxin treatments have been developed for it. However, the pertussis toxin is not considered to have the severe, bodywide effect of the diphtheria toxin.

Unfortunately, no evidence could be found indicating that Klenner had the opportunity to treat pertussis. Other investigators and clinicians have had some success in treating pertussis with vitamin C, but it has been qualified by the use of significantly smaller doses than would have been used by Klenner. However, as should be apparent from the evidence already reviewed, there is no good reason to believe that Klenner-sized doses of vitamin C would not be as effective in the treatment of pertussis as in the treatment of so many other infectious diseases.

Otani (1936) found that pertussis bacteria seemed to be especially susceptible to the effects of vitamin C in the test tube, with a high enough dose having a killing, bactericidal effect. It was also demonstrated that a culture of pertussis bacteria in which vitamin C had been added possessed a "strongly reduced" infectivity in test animals. Furthermore, when the vitamin C-treated bacteria were injected by vein into test animals, a lessened white blood cell response resulted. Most likely, this was an indication that the treated bacteria were less infectious and toxic than the untreated bacteria. Because of these results, Otani proceeded to use vitamin C in the treatment of children with pertussis. Otani's treatment ranged from 50 to 200 mg of vitamin C once or twice daily, and total injections ranged from five to 12. Otani reported that in 81 patients treated in this fashion, 34 showed a clear improvement of symptoms or "perfect healing," 32 showed a lesser symptom improvement, and 15 showed an "indeterminate" response. It appears that Otani got fairly dramatic responses in many pertussis patients with vitamin C doses well below what Klenner would have routinely used. It would also seem that the neutralizing effect that vitamin C has on pertussis toxin is an additional reason why symptoms responded so well to its administration, since eliminating the bacteria with antibiotics has long been noted *not* to effect the duration or severity of the clinical illness.

One hypothesis, advanced by Brown (1936), is that the symptoms of pertussis are prolonged because the pertussis toxin becomes bound to the nervous tissue that involves the mucous membranes of the respiratory tract, thereby maintaining a prolonged irritability. Otani (1939) later reported on the treatment of 109 pertussis cases. He found "some efficiency" to "remarkable efficiency" in over 80% of the patients treated. Some of the less responsive patients had had additional infections or other medical complications that would be expected to require increased amounts of vitamin C in order to show a good clinical response.

Ormerod and Unkauf (1937) also reported on the treatment of pertussis with vitamin C. They found that vitamin C "definitely shortens" the severest symptoms of pertussis, particularly if relatively "large" doses are used shortly after the first symptoms of the disease appear. Nine children and one adult were treated. The oral dosing was somewhat minimal, ranging from 150 to 500 mg of vitamin C daily over an eight-day to 15-day period.

Woringer and Sala (1928) had earlier reported that in a number of infants seen for pertussis in their clinic, four of them developed scurvy as a result of their infections. This is further evidence that the combination of infection and toxicity is an especially effective way to rapidly and completely deplete the body's limited stores of vitamin C. It is also an important additional reason to add vitamin C therapy to the treatment of any infectious disease, regardless of cause. A recurring theme throughout this book is that infection and stress of any sort will significantly increase the rate at which vitamin C is metabolized and utilized. As a result, unrecognized acute scurvy is a relatively common complication of many fatal diseases, infectious or otherwise.

Ormerod et al. (1937), in following up the earlier work just mentioned, presented their results on the treatment of 17 more cases of pertussis with oral doses of vitamin C. Although they acknowledged the likely superiority of giving vitamin C by vein, they especially wanted to evaluate the oral route since it would provide a less expensive treatment with wider applicability. The oral schedule was a prolonged, tapered regimen. A 350 mg dose of vitamin C was given on the first day, and on subsequent days 250, 250, 200, 200, 150, 150, 125, 125, and finally 100 mg were given. A 100 mg daily dose was then maintained until there was a "complete remission of symptoms for two days." The average total dose ended up being about 2,700 mg. This vitamin C treatment protocol was found to "markedly" decrease the intensity, frequency, and length of the characteristic pertussis symptoms.

Vermillion and Stafford (1938) reported on the vitamin C treatment of 26 infants and small children with pertussis. They appeared to be particularly interested in trying to duplicate the earlier work of Otani, Ormerod, Unkauf, and White, already cited. The first 16 patients were treated with 150 mg of oral vitamin C daily for the first three days. Then 120 mg daily was given for the next three days, and finally 90 mg daily was given until symptoms entirely subsided. The remaining patients were given comparable but variable oral doses of vitamin C. The researchers concluded that vitamin C appeared to be "strikingly effective" in the relief of symptoms in all but two patients. They further concluded that vitamin C should be given in all cases of pertussis regardless of patient age or the length of time elapsed since the onset of symptoms.

Two other researchers who utilized injectable vitamin C in treating infants with pertussis also reported success in controlling the disease symptoms. Sessa (1940) reported that injecting 100 to 500 mg of vitamin C daily appeared to reduce the convulsive coughing and accelerate the overall rate of recovery. Meier (1945), using both injectable and oral doses of vitamin C, found that coughing was reduced with a quicker restoration of appetite and disappearance of vomiting. The benefit appeared to be especially pronounced in infected infants.

The evidence clearly supports a beneficial role for vitamin C in the treatment of pertussis. Doses probably adequate to achieve a complete and rapid cure, as used routinely by Klenner in other infectious diseases, were not found in the literature for the treatment of pertussis. However, much smaller doses consistently had positive effects in lessening both the intensity and duration of symptoms, and often the duration of the illness was also clearly shortened. The bacteria causing pertussis can be killed in culture by vitamin C, and the effects of the pertussis toxin also appear to be lessened by vitamin C. Furthermore, scurvy has been shown to be precipitated by pertussis infection. Vitamin C needs to be administered in pertussis and all infectious diseases, and adequate regular dosing of vitamin C should prevent pertussis from ever being contracted. It remains to be seen what Klenner-sized doses of vitamin C would do for the acutely infected pertussis patient.

Tetanus (Curable and Preventable)

Tetanus is an acute bacterial infectious disease that results in an often fatal neurological syndrome. The primary clinical manifestations of tetanus are caused by the extremely potent neurotoxin that is produced by the germinating spores of the bacteria causing the infection, known as *Clostridium tetani*. The neurotoxin, known as tetanospasmin, is among the most potent toxins known to man, including botulism toxin. One mg of tetanospasmin is capable of killing 50 to 70 million mice!

one mg of tetanospasmin, the neurotoxin produced by the tetanus bacteria — among the most potent toxins known to man — is capable of killing 50 to 70 million mice

Symptoms of this toxin come from the progressive muscular spasms that can eventually evolve to seizures, respiratory difficulty, and paralysis. Tetanus is traditionally treated with a combination of antibiotics, tetanus antitoxin, and tetanus toxoid immunization. The tetanus toxoid is given to induce antibodies that neutralize newly produced toxin not yet bound to target tissues. As tetanus typically comes from deep physical wounds that allow the oxygen-deprived bacteria to germinate and multiply, local wound cleaning and care is also important in the proper treatment of this infection.

Klenner (July 1954) felt the need to dispel the general belief that tetanus was a difficult disease to cure. He was also convinced that tetanus antitoxin had "no curative value" and was actually harmful, especially when given frequently by vein. Klenner described the case of a six-year-old boy who was already demonstrating toxin-related symptoms and muscle spasms when he first saw the child. The child could not open his mouth more than 30% due to jaw spasm, and a sudden, involuntary clamping of the jaws shut ("lockjaw") would follow any attempt to open his mouth. Vital signs revealed a low-grade temperature, rapid and shallow breathing, and a rapid pulse, ranging from 120 to 130 per minute. In addition to vitamin C, Klenner also used a skeletal muscle relaxant known as Tolserol to prevent convulsive seizures and help relieve the muscle spasms. Klenner also noted that the antitoxin therapy administered to this child was the result of "outside pressure" and not his decision.

All vitamin C was given intravenously to this patient. During the first 24 hours a total of 22,000 mg of vitamin C was given in multiple doses ranging from three to five hours apart. A total of 24,000 mg of vitamin C was given over the next 24 hours. Throughout these first two days, the child was taking progressively more nutrition and was bothered with only mild abdominal cramps. Over the next two days comparable amounts of vitamin C were given, but five separate doses of tetanus antitoxin were also given intravenously. After each dose of antitoxin the child deteriorated clinically with severe abdominal pain and initially a reactivation of fever. Intermittent doses of penicillin and calcium gluconate were also given. Much of the child's discomfort was alleviated by the Tolserol. Ultimately the child was discharged on the 18th hospital day, although Klenner felt the child could have been safely discharged 10 days earlier. Klenner was very convinced that the antitoxin actually continued to compromise health rather than improve it.

While no other cases of tetanus treated by Klenner could be found in the literature, he did comment on the tetanus case of an adult white female who died from the inability to breathe less than one hour after receiving a single intravenous dose of tetanus antitoxin. Undoubtedly, this also affected Klenner's attitude toward antitoxin. He did feel that a single intramuscular (rather than intravenous) dose of antitoxin above a wound suspected to be the site of the infecting tetanus bacteria was reasonable for the purpose of dealing more effectively at the presumed site where new toxin was being formed.

When considering the response of Klenner's tetanus-infected child described above, it should be kept in mind that the overall mortality for generalized tetanus is 20% to 25% with even the best modern medical care. Furthermore, those who do survive will generally require from three to six weeks for complete recovery.

Jahan et al. (1984) conducted a simple study on the effects of vitamin C in the treatment of tetanus. In 31 tetanus patients aged from one to 12 years, a daily intravenous vitamin C administration of 1,000 mg was given in addition to antitoxin. Although none of the vitamin C-treated patients died, almost 75% of those who did not receive the vitamin C did. In older patients, aged from 13 to 30 years, 68% of those not receiving vitamin C died, while only 37% of those who received the vitamin C expired. Undoubtedly, larger doses of vitamin C would have completely protected the older group as well. The need for vitamin C is directly proportional to the size of one's body. A 1,000 mg dose of intravenous vitamin C goes a lot further in an infant or small child than in a much larger teenager or adult.

none of the vitamin C-treated [tetanus] patients died, while almost 75% of those not treated with vitamin C did

One very impressive animal study on tetanus toxicity strongly supports Klenner's conviction that antitoxin treatment is, at best, unnecessary, and that vitamin C alone should remedy the condition without any resulting toxicity. Dey (1966) studied the effects of vitamin C on the toxicity of twice the minimal lethal dose of tetanus toxin injected into rats. There were five groups of rats. Group 1 was given only the tetanus toxin. Group 2 received toxin and intraabdominal vitamin C simultaneously, *followed* by more vitamin C for three more days. Group 3 received vitamin C *first* for three days, then was dosed with the toxin, and vitamin C was continued for three more days. Group 4 was given the toxin and the symptoms of local tetanus were allowed to develop over the next 16 to 26 hours. Vitamin C was then initiated and continued for three days. Group 5 was given the toxin, and the symptoms of generalized, severe tetanus were allowed to develop over the next 40 to 47 hours. Intravenous vitamin C, rather than intraabdominal, was then given.

Except for group 1 animals, which received toxin and no vitamin C, all animals survived. Group 1 animals died from 47 to 65 hours after the toxin administration. In the group 2 survivors some very mild local tetanus symptoms were seen in the affected legs. In group 3 survivors, which also received vitamin C before the toxin was given, there were no symptoms of toxicity. The group 4 survivors had no further spread of the initial symptoms. No symptom description was given for the group 5 survivors.

What does this experiment mean? One reasonable conclusion is that totally non-toxic vitamin C dosages can completely neutralize fatal amounts of tetanus toxin in an animal model. There was no need for the administration of any antitoxin to help in reaching this outcome. Dey (1967) had earlier demonstrated that vitamin C was most effective as a prophylactic and a therapeutic agent in negating the lethal and convulsive properties of strychnine, an agent that produces a clinical syndrome very similar to that produced by tetanus toxin. Furthermore, adequate doses of vitamin C given prior to tetanus toxin administration proved to be completely protective in preventing any manifestation of toxin effect. Also, considering the rat is an animal that can produce its own vitamin C, this experiment gives even greater support for the vigorous treatment of suspected tetanus infection with vitamin C. Animals producing vitamin C can still get sick from tetanus or any other infectious disease if enough of a microbe challenge and/or microbe-associated toxicity confronts them. Humans, with no inherent vitamin C-producing abilities, need the prompt high dosing of vitamin C in the face of such challenges to survive the infection and minimize the toxic effects.

Some earlier research suggested the likelihood that the positive clinical effects noted above would occur in the treatment of tetanus-stricken patients. Jungeblut (1937b) demonstrated that vitamin C could inactivate tetanus toxin in the test tube. Prior to the isolation and commercial availability of vitamin C, Imamura (1929) demonstrated that ovarian follicular fluid could inactivate tetanus toxin as well. It is now known that such fluid contains a high concentration of vitamin C.

Kligler et al. (1938) found that vitamin C added to growing cultures of tetanus bacteria reduced the toxicity of those cultures in proportion to the amount of vitamin C added. The authors also found that the vitamin C added to purified tetanus toxin neutralized the toxin, with the degree of neutralization depending upon temperature, vitamin C concentration, and time of vitamin C exposure. More recently, Eller et al. (1968) looked at the abilities of vitamin C to kill the spores of a number of different bacteria in the genus *Clostridium,* including the spores of the bacteria responsible for botulism and its enormous toxicity. The botulism bacteria are in the same genus as those of tetanus bacteria. Not only did the researchers demonstrate that vitamin C would kill the bacterial spores in a dose-dependent fashion, they also noted that vitamin C did not appear to provoke the toxin-releasing state of spore germination, which a large number of diverse compounds will induce (Wynne, 1957; Ward and Carroll, 1966).

The totality of the evidence would indicate that vitamin C is an ideal agent for the treatment of patients infected with the tetanus microbe. The tetanus toxin appears to be neutralized by vitamin C in the body, in laboratory animals, and in the test tube. A significant amount of the sickness related to a tetanus infection can come from antitoxin, one of its standard treatments. Undoubtedly, fatal reactions to this antitoxin still occur, and some of these deaths end up being blamed on the tetanus toxin itself and not its antitoxin treatment. Fortunately, vitamin C does not share this toxicity. While the volume of evidence documenting a vitamin C cure for tetanus is limited, it would certainly appear that tetanus is another infectious/toxic disease that vitamin C can cure, reverse, and prevent.

It should also be noted that the last three diseases addressed— diphtheria, pertussis, and tetanus—are the same three diseases targeted by the DPT (diphtheria-pertussis-tetanus) vaccinations routinely administered to infants in the United States and across the world. Many individual reports of adverse reactions to this vaccine have been reported, including encephalopathy with permanent brain damage and sometimes autism. Vaccinations also generally present some degree of toxin insult to the body.

Kalokerinos (1981) observed that vitamin C-deficient Aboriginal infants were often pushed into an acute state of scurvy because of the additional vitamin C demands placed on their bodies by the vaccination injections, resulting in sudden death. Kalokerinos was also able to determine that regular administrations of vitamin C would prevent sudden death and eliminate many of the toxic effects associated with vaccination.

The work of Kalokerinos argues strongly that sudden infant death syndrome (SIDS) is often a complication of too many vaccinations given over too short a time and injected into bodies that are just too small to cope with the cumulative toxic insult. However, regardless of the actual frequency of such vaccination complications, it is important to keep in mind that the proper use of vitamin C would probably completely prevent any need (perceived or otherwise) to vaccinate against these diseases at all.

if you must receive a vaccination, the toxicity is greatly lessened and the desired immune response enhanced with generous doses of vitamin C before and after

It is doubtful that there are any diseases for which vaccinations are presently administered that will not be easily prevented and/or cured by the optimal dosing of vitamin C. No negative outcomes following a vaccination will ever occur if no vaccination is ever given. However, if you must receive a vaccination, the toxicity is greatly lessened and the desired immune response definitely enhanced by giving generous doses of vitamin C before and after the vaccination.

Tuberculosis
(Reversible and Preventable; Curable-?)

Tuberculosis is an infectious disease caused by a type of bacteria called *Mycobacterium tuberculosis*. Tuberculosis bacteria, known as mycobacteria, are characterized by a slower rate of growth than is seen with many other types of bacteria. Accordingly, tuberculosis is a chronic disease, developing slowly and responding slowly to treatment when compared with the acute and rapidly developing syndromes seen with many of the other infectious diseases. Although tuberculosis can involve many different organs and tissues in the body, the classic form predominantly features the infectious involvement of the lungs.

Worldwide, tuberculosis is the leading infectious cause of both illness and death. The World Health Organization (WHO) estimates that about 33% of the world's population is latently infected with tuberculosis, and from this reservoir approximately 8 to 10 million new and active cases of tuberculosis develop each year. Of these cases, about half are the more readily communicable pulmonary (lung) forms of tuberculosis.

The symptoms of pulmonary tuberculosis include a cough that progresses to cough-produced secretions streaked with blood. Often bright red blood alone is coughed up, and night sweats with variable amounts of fever can also be seen. Standard medical therapy usually involves two or more drugs to which a patient's infecting strain of tuberculosis bacteria proves to be sensitive. Drug-resistant strains of tuberculosis have become relatively common.

No reports could be found of Klenner or any other researchers treating tuberculosis with Klenner's uniquely high amounts of vitamin C. However, without further qualification, Klenner (1974) did assert that "massive daily doses" of vitamin C "will also cure tuberculosis by removal of the organisms' polysaccharide coat." This was the same assertion made by Klenner when vitamin C was used to cure a pneumococcal infection. While a fairly large amount of research has been done on the effects of vitamin C in both human and animal tuberculosis, the doses of vitamin C used never resulted in what could be considered a cure for well-established cases of pulmonary tuberculosis. However, a significant amount of early research showed that vitamin C was capable of effectively controlling both the clinical aspects of tuberculous infections as well as the actual growth of the tuberculosis bacteria. At the very least, it would seem that adequate doses of vitamin C can be expected to put most active cases of tuberculosis into a contained, latent phase. Such contained cases of tuberculosis can be expected to have little adverse effect on long-term health as long as daily vitamin C dosing remains adequate.

mammals lacking the ability to synthesize vitamin C are the same mammals most susceptible to bovine and human tuberculosis bacteria infections

Osborn and Gear (1940) made the simple observation that mammals lacking the ability to synthesize vitamin C were the same mammals most susceptible to bovine and human tuberculosis bacteria infections. These mammals were identified as man, monkey, and guinea pig. This simple fact also explains why so much of the tuberculosis research has utilized human and guinea pig subjects.

A number of early researchers looked at the effects of vitamin C on tuberculosis patients. Even though the doses were generally very small, positive benefits were still often seen. Petter (1937) treated both tuberculous adults and children with an oral dose of only 150 mg vitamin C daily. Even this small dosage was noted to definitely improve 30 of the 49 adults treated (61%). Of the 24 children treated, 21 (88%) were felt to have improved on the same dosage. The better improvement among the children can be explained by the fixed dosage of vitamin C having a greater effect in a smaller body. Petter also noted improvement in the weight and general condition of the responding children.

Another investigator, Albrecht (1938), gave only 100 mg of vitamin C, although by injection, to his patients and noted positive responses in temperature, weight, general well-being, appetite, and some blood tests. Bakhsh and Rabbani (1939) also had good results giving tuberculous patients from 150 to 200 mg of oral vitamin C daily for six weeks. They also gave an additional 500 mg of vitamin C intramuscularly each day for the first four days of treatment. The researchers concluded that vitamin C was a valuable added treatment when there was low vitamin C excretion in the urine. They also noted that patients with preexisting anemia generally responded with an increase in the blood count. The sedimentation rate, a test than can indicate the level of inflammation activity associated with infection, was lowered in more than half of the vitamin C-treated patients. Heise et al. (1937) found that the intravenous administration of vitamin C often reduced an elevated sedimentation rate.

Hasselbach (1935) reported seeing some positive effects from the administration of 100 mg of vitamin C daily. Hasselbach (1936) also advocated vitamin C as a "tonic" in tuberculosis patients, noting favorable results in certain forms of pulmonary hemorrhage. Radford et al. (1937) studied 111 tuberculosis patients described as having far-advanced disease. In addition to having vitamin C-untreated control patients, they administered either orange juice or 250 mg of vitamin C in an orange-flavored drink. Generally, both the orange juice group and the vitamin C-supplemented orange drink group showed a more favorable response clinically, as judged by red blood cell count, hemoglobin level, and several other blood tests. Hurford (1938), in studying 66 cases of tuberculosis, found 64% of them to be suffering from vitamin C deficiency, as determined by urinary vitamin C excretion. Of 42 patients treated with vitamin C, seven who suffered from anemia were felt to show a significant improvement.

Babbar (1948) looked at 74 patients with tuberculosis and found that the vitamin C-treated patients showed a "marked increase" in hemoglobin content and red blood cell counts. Dosage levels were only 200 mg orally in four divided doses daily for a period of 10 weeks. Rudra and Roy (1946) looked at the effects of giving 250 mg of oral vitamin C daily over a 10-week period to patients with pulmonary tuberculosis. After reviewing before and after blood tests on the white and red blood cell counts, they concluded that the additional vitamin C appeared to have improved the overall "blood picture" of the treated patients. Based on this improvement, they also suggested that a "large intake" of vitamin C by patients with pulmonary tuberculosis would be likely to increase resistance to infection.

Some insight as to the effects of much larger doses of vitamin C on tuberculosis was submitted by Charpy (1948). Although the dosing was not nearly the equivalent of Klenner-sized dosing, Charpy did give 15,000 mg of vitamin C daily to six very advanced tuberculosis patients. As the selected patients were already considered terminal, one patient died before the test was even significantly underway. However, the other five patients were still alive a half year later, gaining anywhere from 20 to 70 pounds in the process. They were no longer bedridden, and they were generally considered to have undergone an enormous degree of improvement in their general condition. Although Charpy noted that the tuberculous lesions had not

total vitamin C dosing was roughly 3,000,000 mg per patient and there was no evidence of any toxicity or side effect

resolved during the treatment period, he commented that the patients seemed to be "unaware of the enormous tuberculous lesions they harbored." He also commented that the total vitamin C dosing was roughly 3,000,000 mg per patient, and there was no evidence of any toxicity or side effect.

As mentioned earlier in this section, it would appear that the administration of enough vitamin C can certainly be expected to enable a tuberculosis patient to coexist with the chronic infection in an overall healthy manner. It should also be noted that tuberculous lesions in the lung of an advanced patient destroy a significant amount of lung tissue, resulting in a scarred appearance on the chest X-ray. Since scarring would remain even if every tubercular organism was eradicated in a long-infected patient, a normal chest X-ray examination would never result.

McCormick (1951) described one case of active tuberculosis treated with vitamin C. A dose of 1,000 mg was given intravenously, either daily or every other day, for a period of three weeks. This intravenous regimen was combined with 500 mg of oral vitamin C, along with a large amount of citrus juices. McCormick noted that the temperature was reduced and maintained at a normal level from the outset of treatment. Furthermore, the patient completely stopped having the characteristic tuberculosis cough, and the associated coughing up of the accumulated products of the tuberculosis infection in the lungs. In addition, the patient gained about ten pounds over the treatment period.

It should also be noted that traditional antituberculosis drugs are given for years. No traditional form of tuberculosis treatment is ever prescribed for only a few weeks or even months. Like any other antituberculosis drug, vitamin C needs to be given to the tuberculosis patient for life, with the extra-high dosing extending for a year or more. It must be kept in mind that the tubercular organisms grow very slowly, and any form of therapy will not show dramatic changes over a short period of treatment. This is in direct contrast to the vitamin C or antibiotic treatment of many of the other more acute infectious diseases.

As was noted earlier, pulmonary tuberculosis is typically characterized by the coughing up of bright red blood or blood-streaked sputum. Whenever bright red blood appears in any context, there is a general assumption that some degree of acute hemorrhage, however localized, has occurred. Borsalino (1937), in working with 140 tuberculous patients, found that injections of 100 mg of vitamin C were able to rapidly control the coughing up of blood, presumably by strengthening the capillaries in the lungs. Furthermore, this symptom regularly reappeared once the vitamin C treatment was discontinued.

One interpretation of this response is that pulmonary tuberculosis induces a state of focal scurvy in the capillaries of affected areas of the lungs. This focal scurvy directly facilitates the rupture of capillaries as they lose their structural integrity, resulting in the coughing up of blood. Also, just as with generalized scurvy, administering vitamin C produces a very rapid and positive clinical response in the stopping of this focal bleeding.

The effects of vitamin C on some of the non-pulmonary forms of tuberculosis have also been studied. Vitorero and Doyle (1938) reported positive benefits in the vitamin C treatment of intestinal tuberculosis. Their initial regimen was the injection of 500 to 600 mg of vitamin C daily, with gradual reductions to 400 mg daily and finally 200 mg daily as improvement was demonstrated. Bogen et al. (1941) looked at the response of tuberculosis lesions to vitamin C therapy in different mucous membranes. They found that only 150 mg of vitamin C supplemented daily with whatever was already present in the diet appeared to have a beneficial effect on tuberculous lesions that could be visualized in the respiratory passages, intestines, and rectum. This was in spite of the fact that the general condition of the lung involvement from the tuberculosis showed little difference.

tuberculosis patients with the most clinically active disease had the lowest vitamin C levels in the urine

As with many other diseases, researchers have also determined that tuberculosis patients generally have lower levels of vitamin C. This is an additional argument that all tuberculosis patients should be supplemented regularly with vitamin C, with only the amount remaining in question. Plit et al. (1998) found that tuberculosis patients had persistent evidence of ongoing oxidative stress, which consumes vitamin C at greater than normal rates, even after six months of "apparently successful" antimicrobial therapy.

Faulkner and Taylor (1937), looking at two patients with active tuberculosis, found that roughly three times more vitamin C than normal was required to maintain normal plasma levels and urinary excretion levels of vitamin C. Furthermore, they found the same increased vitamin C needs applied to two other patients, one with rheumatic fever, and one with lung abscess, indicating the increased utilization of vitamin C in other infections as well. Abbasy et al. (1937) and Chang and Lan (1940) not only noted lowered urinary excretion of vitamin C in their tuberculosis patients, but they also saw that the patients with the most clinically active disease had the lowest vitamin C levels in the urine. Banerjee et al. (1940) also noted much lower urinary vitamin C excretion in acute tuberculosis patients.

In a study on Navajo Indians with tuberculosis, Pijoan and Sedlacek (1943) concluded that a minimum of twice as much vitamin C was needed on a daily basis by the tuberculosis patients to maintain the same plasma levels as normal subjects. Jetter and Bumbalo (1938), in examining the excretion of vitamin C in the urine, found that 37 out of 37 children with "active tuberculosis" were suffering from vitamin C deficiency. They logically concluded that vitamin C supplementation in such patients "would seem advisable." In another publication, Bumbalo and Jetter (1938) noted that vitamin C supplementation raised the urinary excretion of vitamin C in children with tuberculosis a small amount, but not nearly to the levels of their normal control children. Stopping the supplementation promptly dropped the urinary excretion to pretreatment levels. They concluded that "hypovitaminosis C" was a part of active tuberculosis, and increased vitamin C intake was an indicated therapeutic measure. Bumbalo (1938) also concluded that there is probably "some vitamin C deficiency in all forms of tuberculosis in children."

37 out of 37 children with "active tuberculosis" were suffering from vitamin C deficiency

Babbar (1948), in treating 74 tuberculosis patients, also found that the vast majority of patients treated had low plasma concentrations of vitamin C. Furthermore, plasma levels were highest after a full ten weeks of oral supplementation, giving further support to the need for prolonged (lifelong) supplementation in such a chronic infection as tuberculosis. Getz and Koerner (1941, 1943) also noted lower blood vitamin C levels in their tuberculosis patients.

In patients with tuberculous involvement of the intestines, Dubey et al. (1985) found that both plasma and white blood cell levels of vitamin C were significantly lowered, and the urinary excretion of vitamin C was also "markedly decreased," presumably representing an attempt to conserve the depleted vitamin C stores remaining in the body. In tubercular meningitis patients, Bhaduri and Banerjee (1960) documented low blood levels of vitamin C.

Abbasy et al. (1936) also showed that the vitamin C status in tuberculosis appeared to directly correlate with the activity level of the disease. Looking at urinary excretion levels of vitamin C, they found that 23 cases of active tuberculosis had low levels of excretion, 46 cases of clinically inactive tuberculosis had normal excretion levels, and 19 cases deemed to be "half-active" clinically had intermediate readings. These observations also can be interpreted to indicate that vitamin C status in the body is actually what determines whether active tuberculosis ever evolves to the inactive, or latent state.

Heise and Martin (1936) were able to correlate the daily urinary excretion of vitamin C with the activity level of the tuberculous infection. By looking at patient X-rays, they found that the lowest levels of urinary vitamin C (indicating low body levels) were associated with the greatest disease activity. Awotedu et al. (1984) demonstrated that patients with pulmonary tuberculosis have "significantly lower" plasma vitamin C levels than the normal population. Furthermore, they were able to find a correlation between the low plasma vitamin C levels and extensiveness of the lung disease on X-ray.

The ability of vitamin C to decrease the likelihood of contracting tuberculosis has also been examined. Downes (1950) found that a daily supplementation of vitamins and minerals that included vitamin C resulted in an "appreciably lower" incidence of new cases of tuberculosis in a treated group of people when compared to a control group not receiving the supplementation. Nevertheless, Downes was not convinced the study had statistical significance.

Getz et al. (1951) provided good statistical evidence that one's vitamin C level is a very significant indicator of the susceptibility to new tuberculous infection. They looked at a group of 1,100 men who were free of pulmonary tuberculosis when first examined. Over the next seven years 28 of these men developed X-ray evidence of pulmonary tuberculosis. By looking at previously gathered data, all 28 cases of tuberculosis had demonstrated low plasma levels of vitamin C. Furthermore, the cases of "clearly active" tuberculosis had "markedly substandard" levels of both vitamin C and vitamin A. Hemila et al. (1999) found that individuals who had a dietary vitamin C intake greater than merely 90 mg daily and who consumed "more than the average" amount of fruits, vegetables, and berries had a significantly lower risk of contracting tuberculosis.

a daily vitamin C intake greater than 90 mg and eating "more than the average" amount of fruits, vegetables, and berries lowers risk of contracting tuberculosis

In animal studies the evidence for vitamin C 's ability to prevent tuberculosis infections is compelling as well. In both susceptible people and animals, the swallowing of sputum with tuberculous bacteria coming from an already existing pulmonary infection can lead to tuberculous infection in the intestines. McConkey and Smith (1933) conducted an experiment that can be interpreted as indicating that it is the vitamin C level in the body that determines the likelihood of contracting intestinal tuberculosis. They fed guinea pigs tuberculous sputum for periods ranging from six weeks to four months. Of the 37 animals maintained on a diet partially deficient in vitamin C, 36 developed ulcerative intestinal tuberculosis. Furthermore, in the 35 animals supplemented with an "adequate" amount of vitamin C, only two animals developed this intestinal infection.

Birkhaug (1938, 1939) published a series of studies looking at the role vitamin C plays in the tuberculous disease process in guinea pigs. He was able to demonstrate a "significant and progressive" deficiency of vitamin C in guinea pigs infected with tuberculosis. He also found that a significant vitamin C deficit developed in the adrenal glands of infected animals. The adrenal glands are tissues that especially concentrate vitamin C in the normal animal. Birkhaug also noted some blood changes in vitamin C-treated tuberculous guinea pigs that approximated the changes seen in similarly treated humans with tuberculosis. Over a period of seven weeks of treatment the red blood cell counts and hemoglobin levels in treated guinea pigs increased slightly, and white blood cell counts became more normal in the same group. The overall effect of vitamin C administration on the clinical course of tuberculosis in the guinea pigs was evaluated as well. Birkhaug determined that 10 mg of vitamin C daily caused a significant weight gain, accompanied by a reduction in the development of a more generalized tubercular infection, which indicates a reduction in the clinical invasiveness of tuberculous lesions.

Since tuberculosis was once known as "consumption" because it involves a gradual wasting away of the body in its advanced stages, and weight gain is always a very positive response to a tuberculosis treatment. As early as 1689, Richard Morton made the observation in his work *Phthisiologia* that "scurvy is wont to occasion a consumption of the lungs," indicating that scurvy predisposes the patient to contracting tuberculosis. Birkhaug was also able to demonstrate under the microscope that his treated guinea pigs had fewer lesions, more collagen (connective tissue requiring vitamin C for synthesis) encapsulating and walling-off the lesions, and less tuberculous bacteria throughout the tissue. In other words, this dose of vitamin C, while not curing the guinea pigs of their tuberculous infection, did show clear evidence that the infection had been made much more dormant and clinically less consequential without any evidence of active or aggressive infection. In effect, the infection had been quarantined within the bodies of the infected animals themselves.

Grant (1930) also reported that increased amounts of vitamin C seemed to decrease the severity and extent of tuberculous lesions in the lungs of guinea pigs. This was likely due to a more effective encapsulation of the tuberculous lesions. Leichtentritt (1924) fed tuberculous guinea pigs large amounts of orange juice. Although this study preceded the discovery of vitamin C, orange juice was known to contain an unidentified "anti-scurvy" substance in it. The guinea pigs with this orange juice supplemented in their normal diet survived twice as long as animals fed only the normal diet. Also, the orange juice group was found to have encapsulated their infections, with a walling-off of the tuberculous lesions in the fashion noted above. Those animals deprived of orange juice had a very unchecked, widespread tuberculous infection ("miliary tuberculosis").

Miliary tuberculosis is a very aggressive form of tuberculosis that can quickly result in the death of the infected person or animal if not promptly brought under control. Hojer (1924) noticed an interesting microscopic appearance of the infected tissues in tuberculous guinea pigs also afflicted with scurvy. The sites of tuberculous infection in muscular, lymph glandular, or splenic tissue were neither surrounded nor penetrated by any connective tissue. Literally, the sites of infected and dead tissue made a direct transition into normal, non-infected tissue without any evidence of borders or demarcation. It would appear that vitamin C plays an integral role in the natural walling-off and isolation of tuberculous lesions, perhaps largely due to its essential role in the formation of collagen, which is the body's primary connective tissue. Vitamin C has similarly been implicated in the walling-off of focal sites of cancer as well. It is likely that vitamin C is the primary force in isolating and lessening the impact of any foreign or unwelcome presence perceived by the body.

Even if large enough doses of vitamin C do not prove to cure tuberculosis, optimal vitamin C dosing would appear to be essential in allowing the coexistence of relative good health and a chronic tuberculous infection. Certainly, the aggressive and rapidly fatal miliary tubercular infections show little or no evidence of walling-off any tuberculous lesions. This strongly implies that a severe vitamin C deficiency is an essential precondition for the development of this unrelenting form of tuberculosis. The present availability of oral liposome encapsulated vitamin C could prove to have an enormous impact in controlling and possibly even curing tuberculosis.

Not surprisingly, Mouriquand et al. (1925) were able to show that scurvy-stricken guinea pigs given oral doses of tuberculosis bacteria had a more rapid progression of the disease than in guinea pigs fed normal diets. Greene et al. (1936) were also able to demonstrate that a chronic vitamin C deficiency in the face of active tuberculosis resulted in a significant loss of body weight and shortened survival in guinea pigs.

Heise and Martin (1936a) showed that even though the tuberculosis infection was not eliminated, a 20 mg daily injection of vitamin C into the abdomens of infected guinea pigs controlled the clinical course of the disease very well. The treated animals given a subcutaneous injection of tubercular organisms grew at a "normal rate" and "behaved in every way just as the controls" over a five-month period, even though the autopsy studies documented the presence of tubercular infection in various tissues.

Even more basic research has been conducted that has examined the effect that vitamin C has on the growth of tuberculosis bacteria. Boissevain and Spillane (1937) were able to demonstrate that an artificial growth medium that otherwise readily supported the growth of tuberculosis bacteria showed no growth at a fairly low concentration of added vitamin C (0.001%). Myrvik et al. (1954) also found that vitamin C added to a tuberculosis bacteria culture medium was able to inhibit growth. They further determined that it was a breakdown product of vitamin C exerting the antibacterial effect in this system. Their research was stimulated by the earlier observations of Bjornesjo (1951, 1952), who reported that the majority of urine specimens tested had the ability to kill tuberculosis bacteria. The conclusion was that vitamin C and vitamin C metabolites in the urine were the bacteria-killing elements.

Tuberculosis is another infectious disease that has a toxic component as well, although it is not as pronounced and well-defined as other classically toxic diseases such as diphtheria or tetanus. Tuberculin, a sterile solution containing the growth products of tuberculosis bacteria, is presently used in skin testing to help determine whether an individual is at high risk of developing active tuberculosis. A positive skin reaction to tuberculin generally means that the individual has already had a significant exposure to tuberculosis and is capable of demonstrating an immune response to the now-familiar products of tubercular infection. Typically, about 10% of such positive reactors will eventually develop active tuberculosis. This same tuberculin solution has also been demonstrated in early studies to have a directly toxic effect on laboratory animals, an effect that can be negated by vitamin C.

Steinbach and Klein (1936) looked at the effect of vitamin C on the ability of guinea pigs to tolerate tuberculin, which in sufficient doses is fatal to these animals. Capillary hemorrhaging, a classical finding in acute scurvy, was found in all tissues examined in tuberculous animals after toxic doses of tuberculin were administered. Interestingly, they found that their regimen of vitamin C did not neutralize the toxicity of tuberculin when mixed directly with it prior to injection into the animals. However, they were able to show that 5 mg daily injections of vitamin C were adequate to protect tuberculous guinea pigs against otherwise lethal doses of tuberculin that would have readily killed the unsupplemented control animals. Steinbach and Klein (1941) later demonstrated a similar result, with 13 of 16 (81%) control tuberculous guinea pigs dying from tuberculin shock after a regimen of repeated doses. However, only three of 17 (18%) infected animals succumbed to the tuberculin doses when also treated with vitamin C.

Birkhaug (1939) found that skin reaction to subcutaneous injections of tuberculin was also significantly inhibited by the daily oral dosing of vitamin C in tuberculous guinea pigs. This skin testing is comparable to the skin testing used in humans to determine past tuberculosis exposure. Apparently enough vitamin C effectively neutralizes the toxicity of the bacterial products in the tuberculin solution once it is in the animal. This effectively negates the need or the stimulus for the immune system to cause the typical inflammatory reaction in the skin (termed a "positive tuberculin skin test" in humans).

Boyden and Andersen (1956) hypothesized that vitamin C reduced the metabolic injury to cells in the tuberculous host that is caused by the antigen-antibody complexes formed by the immune system's reaction to the release of bacterial by-products. These by-products are essentially what is in the purified tuberculin solution. This conforms with Birkhaug's observation that vitamin C lessens the reaction to tuberculin in sensitive animals and man. It also helps to explain why generalized, miliary tuberculosis is so unrelenting. Severe vitamin C deficiency allows it to develop to begin with, and then there is a resultant release of massive amounts of bacterial by-products as the infection goes unchecked. The final result is advanced tuberculin toxicity and shock that require even more vitamin C to counteract.

Birkhaug also noted that the degree of inhibition of the inflammatory skin reaction to tuberculin was definitely correlated with the content of vitamin C in the urine and adrenal glands, which are two measurements used to effectively assess the animal's vitamin C stores. Bieling (1925) had earlier noted a similar protective effect against the toxicity of tuberculin by merely placing tuberculous guinea pigs on a normal diet known to prevent scurvy.

Some additional evidence on a toxic component of the tuberculous infection was published by Kato (1967). Kato was able to demonstrate that both live tuberculosis bacteria as well as the "toxic constituents" of tuberculosis bacteria could impair oxidative phosphorylation. This is a chemical process that is essential for the production of ATP, one the most important molecules in the body involving the production of energy.

A number of other early investigators did not have the same success in the treatment of tuberculosis with small doses of vitamin C as detailed earlier. Martin and Heise (1937) did not report achieving a beneficial effect using only 200 mg of vitamin C daily, according to their evaluation of patient X-rays, sputum examinations, sedimentation rates, and tuberculin skin tests. They also did not feel that the coughing up of blood by the treated patients was favorably affected. Josewich (1939) reported little success when treating tuberculous patients with vitamin C doses ranging from 100 to 200 mg daily. Sweany et al. (1941) also reported little success when treating tuberculosis patients with vitamin C doses ranging from 100 to 200 mg daily. Erwin et al. (1940) also concluded that a 100 to 200 mg daily dose of vitamin C was not useful in the treatment of tuberculosis, although they excluded improved appetite and lessened cough as symptoms of improvement. Kaplan and Zonnis (1940), administering 200 mg of vitamin C daily for a six-month period, somehow concluded that "no significant favorable effects" could be ascribed to this therapy. This conclusion was made even though the investigators acknowledged that "subjectively" and by X-ray, "the experimental group seems to have done considerably better." Even the conclusions of some researchers need to be examined in more detail before being taken at face value.

It is likely that the lack of success in most of the negative tuberculosis-vitamin C studies relates primarily to the small doses of vitamin C used. However, whether the route of administration is oral or injected is another important factor. Duration of therapy is also important, as tuberculosis bacteria grow slowly, and the clinical responses to any therapy cannot be expected to be as immediate or pronounced as in a more acute disease. Tuberculosis requires years of traditional antituberculosis drug therapy for optimal effects. Expecting vitamin C to accomplish in a few weeks or even months what no other drug can achieve in the same time frame is not a fair evaluation of the utility of vitamin C in the treatment of tuberculosis. Also, the stage of the disease will also play a role. Advanced tuberculous lung changes, with increasing cavitational disease and breakdown of lung tissue, will also help determine whether a small dose of vitamin C can possibly make a difference.

Such advanced, active disease will generally require larger doses of vitamin C to show a definitive, positive response. Finally, the increased destruction of vitamin C by the tubercular infection pushes the necessary daily antiscurvy dose of vitamin C into the range of 100 to 200 mg daily. When the patients in a given study are less well nourished, this small daily dosing of vitamin C will likely just prevent only the overt manifestations of scurvy rather than make an obvious difference in the clinical course of the disease. However, the terminal symptoms of tuberculosis and other potentially fatal infectious diseases are often the symptoms of scurvy. Therefore, only preventing the overt appearance of scurvy with very small doses of vitamin C is still of benefit in the management of tuberculosis. A little vitamin C is definitely much better than none at all.

the terminal symptoms of tuberculosis and other potentially fatal infectious diseases are often the symptoms of scurvy

Overall, tuberculosis has not proved to be an infectious disease that is clearly curable by vitamin C. However, any prolonged intravenous administrations of Klenner-sized doses of vitamin C could not be found in the literature. Even though evidence of scarring at focal sites of tuberculous infection would not be eliminated by any regimen of vitamin C, the question of whether vitamin C could completely and reliably eradicate advanced tuberculous infections remains unanswered. Nevertheless, the vast majority of the research done on vitamin C and tuberculosis would certainly indicate that even moderate, suboptimal vitamin C dosing results in clear clinical benefits for the tuberculosis patient.

The most aggressive forms of tuberculosis seem to be directly associated with the lowest body levels of vitamin C. Regular vitamin C dosing appears to convert active tuberculosis into a more latent, manageable form, where one's overall life span and general health can be expected to be normal or near-normal. Finally, it also appears that tuberculosis, like many other infectious diseases, is an opportunistic disease that prefers a vitamin C-deficient body as a host. Malnutrition, especially in the absence of any supplementation, is the primary precursor for contracting tuberculosis. Malnutrition is defined here only as a poor choice of foods with suboptimal intake of vitamin C. Starvation would also be a predisposition for tuberculosis, but such severe caloric restriction is not necessary to contract the disease. Regular dosing of vitamin C at nearly one's bowel tolerance can be expected to prevent not only tuberculosis, but also virtually all other infectious diseases. Taking the oral liposome encapsulated form of vitamin C regularly may well eliminate tuberculosis as a prominant world-wide killer.

Streptococcal Infections
(Curable and Preventable)

Streptococci are bacteria that can produce a great deal of disease and pathology in humans. Interestingly, streptococci are frequently found colonizing the skin and mucous membranes of people who are clinically healthy. Kelly (1944) noted that a wide variety of microorganisms capable of causing severe disease in a susceptible host, including different types of streptococcal bacteria, was found on the tonsils of all her healthy research monkeys. It would appear that many clinically significant streptococcal and other infections are initiated when the host's natural resistance to infection becomes compromised, and the normally benign bacteria already present "take hold" and produce any of a number of different disease presentations.

Smith (1913) long ago noted that his guinea pigs were much more susceptible to streptococcal pneumonia when they were on poor diets. When "fresh green fodder" was added to the diet, the pneumonia incidence promptly lessened. McCullough (1938) wrote a review that noted the susceptibility of vitamin C-deprived guinea pigs to the streptococcus and a number of other infectious agents.

All of the different streptococcal infections will not be covered here. However, rheumatic fever, which results from an unchecked streptococcal infection, deserves special attention, as it still causes a significant amount of disease today. Also, understanding the mechanisms by which rheumatic fever causes illness and responds to vitamin C therapy will facilitate the understanding of the pathology and treatment of many other less known streptococcal infections.

Rheumatic fever occurs as a result of an infection with what are known as group A beta-hemolytic streptococci. As a delayed result of infection with these bacteria, multiple sites of inflammation characteristically appear in connective tissue structures, especially in the heart, joints, skin, and nervous system. Although rheumatic fever can be contracted as an adult, individuals in the age range of five to 15 years are most commonly stricken. Recurrent bouts of rheumatic fever are also commonly seen, and long-term heart valve damage can occur when these recurrent bouts of disease cannot be prevented.

A bout of rheumatic fever typically assumes a prolonged clinical course, averaging about three months. When the heart involvement is more pronounced, the duration of a bout of the illness can persist as long as six months. Penicillin is generally given to eradicate any streptococci that are still present, even though antibiotic treatment has not been shown to either modify the course of a rheumatic fever attack or lessen the likelihood of eventual heart involvement. However, penicillin does play a significant role in lessening the likelihood of a recurrent attack of rheumatic fever.

The streptococcal infections probably initiate their widespread inflammatory effects by multiple mechanisms. Many investigators feel that much of the damage associated with a rheumatic fever attack comes from the direct toxic effects of streptococcal bacterial products, particularly streptolysins S and O (Manders, 1998).

Rosenow (1912) long ago outlined a number of different toxic substances obtainable from pneumococci (a type of streptococcus) that could promptly put guinea pigs into life-threatening shock. Many researchers also feel that the streptococcal infection initiates immune system-mediated damage in which the immune system attacks some normal tissue as though it were a foreign invader. Another possible immune mechanism is one in which tissue inflammation is initiated and sustained by antigen-antibody complexes depositing in the affected tissues. As will be discussed further, some investigators make a very good case that much or most of the rheumatic fever pathology is caused by a severe deficiency of vitamin C in those individuals with a significant streptococcal infection. Furthermore, such a vitamin C deficiency would make the patient much more susceptible to any of the toxins produced by the infection.

Devasena et al. (2001) showed that children who had streptococcal infections affecting their kidneys had significantly low levels of vitamin C in the plasma and red blood cells and significant increases in tests indicating oxidative stress. As a general rule, the more oxidative stress present, the less vitamin C present, and vice versa. Oran et al.

(2001) also showed that acute rheumatic fever is associated with a great deal of increased oxidative stress and increased free radicals. Further back, Rinehart et al. (1936) had already observed the low vitamin C levels in the blood of patients with rheumatic fever. Also, Rinehart (1936) made a good case for the conclusion that both infection and vitamin C deficiency were necessary to cause the classic tissue damage seen in guinea pigs with rheumatic fever, which will be discussed below in more detail.

Although no report of Klenner specifically treating rheumatic fever could be found, he did report having excellent results in treating streptococcal infections with vitamin C. Klenner (1974) stated that he had cured "hemolytic streptococcus" infections by administering vitamin C intravenously in a dose range of 500 to 700 mg/kg body weight.

Cathcart (1981) reported success in the treatment of three cases of scarlet fever, another disease caused by the group A beta-hemolytic streptococcal bacteria. The typical rash associated with the disease is felt to be directly due to a toxin produced by the bacteria. Cathcart asserted that all three of his patients had a "typical sandpaper-like rash," along with peeling skin, and laboratory findings diagnostic for scarlet fever. His vitamin C administration result-

Cathcart's administration of vitamin C to three scarlet fever patients resulted in a rapid clinical response in only one hour

ed in a rapid clinical response in only one hour. He felt that this very prompt response was due to the neutralization of the associated toxin by the vitamin C. He added that he had not personally seen a case of rheumatic fever but would anticipate a rapid response of the disease to vitamin C. McCormick (1951) also reported success in treating several cases of scarlet fever. A 2,000 mg of vitamin C daily was administered both intravenously and orally. McCormick noted that in each case the fever dropped to normal within a few hours, and the patients became symptom-free in three to four days.

Massell et al. (1950) reported on seven patients with rheumatic fever treated with vitamin C. Only 1,000 mg of vitamin C was given four times daily for treatment periods that ranged from eight to 26 days. A 13-year-old boy treated with vitamin C had his joint pain completely relieved in 24 hours, along with a prompt lessening of fever. The fever was completely resolved after the second day of therapy. A 14-year-old boy who had already suffered for many months was also treated with vitamin C. There was a complete resolution of his fever within the first 48 hours of treatment. A 15-year-old boy already ill for six weeks with rheumatic fever showed a complete resolution of fever by the second day of therapy, and his other general symptoms promptly improved. Another 14-year-old boy with rheumatic fever and a painful, swollen knee became gradually free of symptoms and fever during the first four days of vitamin C therapy.

rheumatic fever, a disease that typically causes severe suffering for months, was symptomatically controlled with vitamin C in a few days in seven out of seven cases

His elevated sedimentation rate also showed a dramatic drop. An 11-year-old girl who was acutely ill with rheumatic fever responded quite dramatically to the vitamin C therapy. She had a temperature of 104°F rectally, an enlarged heart and liver, swollen and painful finger joints, swelling of her legs from heart failure, and a heart rate of 160 per minute. Over the next seven days, the vitamin C therapy gradually lessened the fever and joint symptoms until they were completely absent. The heart rate dropped to 120 per minute within 24 hours, and swelling in the legs completely resolved. An 18-year-old male showed complete resolution of fever and joint pain by the fourth day of vitamin C treatment.

Finally, a five-year-old boy with recurrent rheumatic fever had joint pain in his right knee and both ankles disappear promptly, while the fever steadily declined until it was absent by the eighth day of treatment. Individually, each of the above patients demonstrated a dramatic response to the administration of relatively small amounts of vitamin C. Collectively, the message is even more compelling. A disease that typically causes severe suffering for months was symptomatically controlled with vitamin C in a few days in seven out of seven cases! Even more incredible, however, was the way the authors downplayed the results, commenting that the observations only suggested the 4,000 mg daily dose of vitamin C had "antirheumatic activity," and that "no final assessments can yet be made regarding the possible therapeutic value" of vitamin C in rheumatic fever. They also emphasized a need for "careful toxicity studies" even though they acknowledged having no problems whatsoever in the treatment of their seven patients. If one were to read only the conclusions reached by the authors in this paper, there would be little reason to suspect that vitamin C actually produced such incredible clinical responses. Even though no such official recommendation exists, this paper alone should mandate that at least some minimal dosing of vitamin C be given regularly to rheumatic fever patients.

Glazebrook and Thomson (1942) looked at the effects of regular doses of vitamin C in a large group of students ranging in age from 15 to 20 years. Over a period of several months, a group of 335 youths received from 100 to 200 mg daily of supplemental vitamin C. A larger control group of 1,100 youths received only the standard diet at their educational institution without any vitamin C supplementation. The results were significant. None of the 335 supplemented youths developed rheumatic fever, while 16 cases occurred in the control group. Also, none of the supplemented youths developed pneumonia, while 17 of the students in the control group contracted the disease. Pneumonia in an institutional setting can often be secondary to a streptococcal organism. Tonsillitis, a streptococcal infection of the tonsils that often sets the stage for rheumatic fever, occurred in about 9% of both groups. However, the tonsillitis infections in the control group lasted longer than in the vitamin C-treated group. The authors also noted that the incidence of the common cold as well as its average duration was the same in both groups.

The interesting conclusion that can be drawn from this study is that even minimal doses of vitamin C are highly effective in keeping streptococcal bacteria from taking hold in the first place, such as is the case in the initial stages of rheumatic fever and pneumonia. Furthermore, it appears that small doses of vitamin C are also highly effective in keeping the predisposing streptococcal infection in tonsillitis from progressing to the more generalized streptococcal infection of rheumatic fever. Finally, the results are consistent with the fact that significant viral infections like the common cold require significantly more vitamin C than 100 to 200 mg daily to produce a clear-cut benefit. Also, streptococcal bacterial infections appear to be very susceptible to low-dose supplemental vitamin C.

Other investigators have also found that vitamin C can prevent pneumonia. Kimbarowski and Mokrow (1967) looked at military recruits who had contracted the flu (influenza A). Those recruits who received vitamin C had significantly fewer cases of pneumonia complicating their flu. Pitt and Costrini (1979) conducted a randomized double-blind placebo-controlled trial with 674 marine recruits in a training camp during an eight-week period. Although their primary aim was to see if vitamin C affected the incidence of the common cold, they were able to determine that 2,000 mg of vitamin C daily resulted in fewer cases of pneumonia. Eight recruits who received no additional vitamin C contracted pneumonia, and only one recruit who took the vitamin C supplementation developed the disease. In reviewing these two studies as well as the work of Glazebrook and Thomson noted above, Hemila (1997) found that each of these three trials revealed approximately an 80% lower incidence of pneumonia in the vitamin C groups. This degree of lessened incidence of pneumonia is highly unlikely to have occurred by chance. Sabin (1939), in placing rhesus monkeys on vitamin C-deficient diets, reported that five cases of pneumonia occurred in a group of 25 monkeys, while none of 21 monkeys with adequate vitamin C developed pneumonia. In another animal/pneumonia study, Hamdy et al. (1967) found that lambs given intramuscular injections of vitamin C had 83% less pneumonia than control lambs. Multiple early investigators publishing in German journals (Gander and Niederberger, 1936; Vogl, 1937; Bonnholtzer, 1937; Hochwald, 1937; Gunzel and Kroehnert, 1937; Sennewald, 1938; Szirmai, 1940) also found vitamin C to be of benefit in the treatment of pneumonia. It was also noted that vitamin C was especially effective in shortening the clinical course of the disease. Szirmai also demonstrated that evidence of tissue saturation was necessary to obtain maximal benefit in the vitamin C treatment of pneumonia although patients with typhoid fever and diphtheria were noted to improve on vitamin C doses that did not produce tissue saturation.

Esposito (1986) looked at the effects of vitamin C on experimental pneumococcal pneumonia in mice. He found that a vitamin C dosage of 200 mg/kg body weight/day allowed the supplemented animals to significantly enhance their ability to clear bacteria from their lungs within 24 hours after the infective challenge.

Although pneumonia can be caused by non-bacterial microorganisms, bacterial pneumonia, often involving more than one infecting microorganism, continues to be a fairly common potentially fatal disease in older and more immunocompromised patients. Several studies looked at the effects of vitamin C on pneumonia without identifying the infecting microorganisms.

Slotkin and Fletcher (1944) reported on the effects of vitamin C on pulmonary (lung) complications after urological surgery in elderly patients. One 73-year-old patient, who already had experienced life-threatening bouts of pneumonia following two previous hernia surgeries, underwent an extensive prostate surgery procedure. He again rapidly developed lung symptoms after the surgery along with fever and rapid heart rate. He was given only 100 mg of vitamin C daily in divided doses, with "spectacular results" noted within 40 hours. Two other patients had similar postoperative symptoms, and both of them responded similarly.

In a randomized double-blind trial looking at the effect of vitamin C on the clinical course of elderly patients hospitalized with acute respiratory infections (bronchitis and pneumonia), Hunt et al. (1994) found vitamin C to be of benefit. Using a fairly small amount of vitamin C supplementation (100 mg twice daily), the authors found that the patients supplemented with vitamin C "fared significantly better" than those who received placebo. All 57 patients in the study received their normal medication as well.

Otitis media, a middle ear infection commonly afflicting children, is commonly secondary to *Streptococcus pneumoniae*. Ruskin (1938) reported on his striking success in treating such middle ear infections with vitamin C. Although the infecting microorganisms were not reported, his clinical success was consistent. In reporting on ten cases, Ruskin noted that the ten patients he treated over a one-year period "all showed signs of improvement within 12 hours and had resolved within four to five days." He added that "the results were too striking" to even question "the therapeutic effect of the parenteral administration" of vitamin C. All ten patients received intramuscular injections of vitamin C.

Rheumatic fever, as with other infectious diseases, has been found to be associated with low urinary excretion of vitamin C, which is an indication of overall low body stores of the vitamin. Abbasy et al. (1936) looked at 107 patients with active rheumatic fever and another 86 patients in the recovery and convalescent phase of rheumatic fever. In both groups there was a significant deficit of urinary vitamin C relative to an uninfected control group of 64 individuals. Most likely, it is the continued deficiency of vitamin C in the convalescing cases of rheumatic fever that makes them so liable to have active recurrences of the disease. The authors pose the question of whether vitamin C deficiency is a cause or effect of the infective process. The most accurate answer is that it is probably both a cause and an effect of the infective process. The infective process will always consume more vitamin C, and, at least in the case of rheumatic fever, it appears that vitamin C deficiency directly predisposes to catching both primary rheumatic fever and recurrent rheumatic fever, and to sustaining the specific types of internal damage caused by rheumatic fever.

Streptococcal tonsillitis and streptococcal pharyngitis (throat infection) are conditions that can precede the development of rheumatic fever. Coulehan et al. (1976) performed a double-blind, placebo-controlled trial of vitamin C administration in a group of 868 children. The authors found that fewer children receiving the vitamin C had positive throat cultures for beta-hemolytic streptococci than did the children receiving placebo. The vitamin C administration was also noted to result in higher plasma vitamin C levels in the supplemented children compared to the placebo group.

Kaiser and Slavin (1938) found an overall higher incidence of streptococci in the tonsils of children who had lower blood levels of vitamin C. Furthermore, the children with higher blood levels of vitamin C were found to have streptococcal bacteria that were less virulent (capable of producing clinical infection and disease) on their tonsils. Specifically, 40% of the streptococci found in the children with the lowest vitamin C levels were virulent, as determined by injection into mice. In the children with average vitamin C levels 30% were virulent, and only 10% were virulent in those children with above average levels of vitamin C. The authors also looked at vitamin C levels in tonsils that were surgically removed. Not surprisingly, the tonsils with the highest levels of vitamin C showed the lowest incidence of hemolytic streptococci presence. The authors concluded that the decreased incidence of streptococcal bacteria in the tonsils of children with the higher levels of vitamin C in the tonsil tissue suggested that vitamin C had an inhibitory relationship on the proliferation of those bacteria in the body.

In the same paper, the authors also looked at the inhibitory effect of various dilutions of vitamin C on the growth of virulent hemolytic streptococci. They found that the streptococci were completely inhibited in 21 consecutive experiments while in all instances the control bacteria grew freely. Similar results were obtained with pneumococci bacteria, a pneumonia-causing strain of streptococcal bacteria. Gnarpe et al. (1968) looked at the growth of different types of bacteria in urine. They found that vitamin C had a killing effect ("bactericidal") on the one type of streptococcus tested (*Streptococcus faecalis*).

As with a number of other experimentally-produced diseases, the guinea pig, with its inability to produce vitamin C, has been especially useful in evaluating the treatment of streptococcal infections with vitamin C. Streptococcal infections are often very virulent in guinea pigs. Witt et al. (1988) reported that vitamin C-deficient guinea pigs were significantly more likely to contract severe streptococcal infections that often resulted in death.

Much earlier, Findlay (1923) had noticed a similar result with his guinea pigs. He found that scurvy-stricken (scorbutic) guinea pigs appeared to cope as well as normal guinea pigs with small injections of pneumococci (a streptococcal bacteria). However, when the numbers of injected microbes were slightly increased, the resistance of the scorbutic guinea pigs broke down more rapidly than that of the control group. The control animals lived longer and had a more localized infection. Findlay repeated this experiment with hemolytic streptococci and was able to find a dose of bacteria that killed the scorbutic animals while allowing the controls to survive, demonstrating a probable protective effect of vitamin C against the toxicity and lethality of streptococcal infection.

In rabbits, Locke et al. (1937) were able to demonstrate very elegantly that an intravenous injection of vitamin C about 10 minutes before an intravenous injection of pneumococcal bacteria was followed by a "substantial" increase in the ability of the animal to remove the bacteria from the blood. In seven of 11 rabbits treated in this fashion, blood cultures showed no bacterial growth 30 minutes later, while nine out of 12 control animals not treated with vitamin C did demonstrate bacterial growth. This is a clear demonstration that vitamin C has a strong antibiotic-like effect on pneumococcal bacteria in the blood stream.

In guinea pig studies, Rinehart and Mettier (1934) looked at the abilities of scurvy alone, scurvy combined with beta streptococcal infection, and the streptococcal infection alone to produce the types of heart valve and muscle lesions seen in human rheumatic fever. They found that the streptococcal infection alone in animals on an adequate diet usually produced "no significant lesions" in the heart valves. In scurvy alone, without the introduction of any infection, "definite atrophic and degenerative changes" were found in the connective tissue (collagen-containing) matrix forming the foundation for the heart valves. In the animals with both scurvy and streptococcal infection, "striking lesions" of a "combined degenerative and proliferative" nature developed in the heart valves with "considerable frequency." This terminology is especially significant, since the lesions of rheumatic fever seen in the heart and elsewhere throughout the body of the rheumatic fever patient have been described as initial areas of degeneration, sometimes involving tissue death (necrosis), followed by an inflammatory, "proliferative" phase.

Presumably one reason for the proliferative phase is to have multiplying cells help strengthen the supporting tissue matrix that has been depleted of collagen, which is the vital connective tissue that normally gives significant mechanical strength to the tissues containing it. Recall that collagen is absolutely dependent on vitamin C for its synthesis. As Rinehart and Mettier (1934) pointed out, it would appear that there is a primary degenerative pathological lesion seen in both human rheumatic fever and in scurvy combined with streptococcal infection in guinea pigs. Furthermore, several guinea pigs developed similar lesions with just the scurvy and *no* added streptococcal infection. Probably one reason why the severity of disease can seem to vary so widely from one host to another is that similar test conditions can produce different levels of pathological response to specific stresses depending on the initial vitamin C body stores, which also vary widely.

Rinehart and Mettier (1934) also looked at the effects of another organism, "*B. aertrycke*," injected into two guinea pigs with scurvy. Once again, some degree of the above mentioned degenerative/proliferative changes were seen in the mitral valves of both animals. When the same organism was injected into guinea pigs with adequate vitamin C supplementation, the heart valves remained normal. The authors suggested that infections other than streptococcus had the potential to be especially damaging when combined with a severe enough deficiency of vitamin C.

Rinehart et al. (1934) also pointed out that scurvy alone would produce a functional impairment in the joints of guinea pigs. They found that the addition of streptococcal infection accentuated these joint changes, and joint lesions were also noted to be of a type consistent with rheumatic fever. Furthermore, the authors noted that joint lesions were not caused by infection alone when adequate vitamin C was present in the diet. Rinehart and Mettier (1933) and McBroom et al. (1937)

also determined that acute scurvy alone, without superimposed infection, would produce rheumatic-like degenerative changes in the heart valves and heart tissue of guinea pigs. Rinehart et al. (1938), however, noted that infection alone, "in the presence of an adequate diet, does not produce rheumatic-like lesions." Stimson et al. (1934) were able to show that some guinea pigs kept vitamin C-deficient would show rheumatic heart lesions while being given only the toxin harvested from a streptococcal infection.

Rinehart et al. (1934) also pointed out that epidemiological data on rheumatic fever in humans gave strong support for the conclusions they reached on the experimental interactions between infection and varying degrees of vitamin C deficiency. Campbell and Warner (1930) pointed that the malnourished, or "debilitated" child is the one most likely to develop rheumatic fever. Certainly, such a child is more likely to be vitamin C-deficient. They also noted that rheumatic fever has been a disease that predominantly affects the poor, another factor likely to be associated with poor nutrition and vitamin C deficiency. Dalldorf (1933), using capillary resistance determinations, estimated a 35% to 66% incidence of "subclinical scurvy" among children from poor homes in New York.

Rinehart et al. also pointed out that the age incidence of rheumatic fever probably parallels the preexisting body stores of vitamin C in the patients. The *Cecil Textbook of Medicine* asserts that acute rheumatic fever most commonly strikes between five and 15 years of age. Falk et al. (1932) pointed out that children between the ages of five and 14 years of age require approximately two times more vitamin C per kilogram of body weight than adults to prevent "latent scurvy." This is probably due to the surge of active growth seen during these years. The greater the requirement of vitamin C, the easier it is to fall short and induce a subclinical state of scurvy that increases susceptibility to rheumatic fever.

Further evidence that vitamin C deficiency is a primary risk factor for developing rheumatic fever comes from the seasonal incidence of the disease. Rheumatic fever occurs commonly in late winter and early spring. These are the same times of the year when vitamin C-rich fresh fruits and vegetables are least available, especially for the poor.

Geographic distributions of rheumatic fever incidence also support the idea that vitamin C helps to prevent the contraction of rheumatic fever. Clarke (1930) asserted that in the "true tropics" rheumatic fever is not seen. In such areas, even the poor and the otherwise malnourished still get most of their calories from fresh fruits and vegetables, and vitamin C deficiency is not a problem. In thousands of patients, Clarke could not find one case of rheumatic fever in the tropics over a 30-year period. Clarke further cites Rogers (1927), who was able to find evidence of only one case of rheumatic heart involvement in the 4,800 autopsies conducted over a period of 37 years in Calcutta, India. In India, cabbage and a number of other green leafy vegetables are consumed frequently, and they are usually subjected to only minimal amounts of cooking that would lessen the content of vitamin C.

Rinehart et al. (1934) further pointed out that the symptoms of "latent scurvy" and the "prerheumatic or early rheumatic state" are very similar and have much in common. They asserted that children with either condition are often found to have "general undernutrition, fatigue, loss of appetite, loss of weight, myopathy, nervousness, and anemia." It may be that the two conditions are essentially the same, awaiting only a sufficient exposure to virulent streptococci bacteria in order to develop rheumatic fever.

Finally, Rinehart et al. (1934) asserted that preexisting infection plays an important role in the development of rheumatic fever. Although the streptococcal infections, manifesting as tonsillitis, sinusitis, and other upper respiratory tract infections, are most commonly associated with the development of rheumatic fever, other organisms have been found to be associated with the disease. Any state of infection further depletes the stores of vitamin C in the body. Rinehart and his co-authors suggested that both latent scurvy and infection are necessary for the development of rheumatic fever. Mild scurvy with a severe infection, or more advanced scurvy with a mild infection both seem to promote the development of rheumatic fever. The interaction of the two conditions assures an especially severe depletion of vitamin C.

Furthermore, the authors claim that the extent of each of the two conditions would help explain the known wide variability in clinical severity of any given case of rheumatic fever.

Streptococcal bacterial infections appear to be especially responsive to vitamin C therapy. High enough doses can be expected to cure most streptococcal infections, although rheumatic fever has not clearly been shown to be curable. However, the resolution of rheumatic fever is clearly accelerated by the administration of vitamin C, even at doses that are well below those utilized by Klenner in other infectious diseases. The evidence is also strong that streptococcal infections, including rheumatic fever, should be easy to prevent if enough vitamin C is taken on a daily basis. The associated toxins seen with different streptococcal infections also seem to be readily neutralized by vitamin C, making it the ideal agent for treating streptococcal infections. Antibiotic therapy can be utilized as well, but it is probably unnecessary in most cases.

Leprosy (Reversible and Preventable; Curable-?)

Leprosy is another infectious disease caused by very slow-growing bacteria in the same family as tuberculosis bacteria. It is a disease characterized by both low infectivity and great chronicity. In humans the infecting agent, *Mycobacterium leprae*, accumulates significantly in the skin and the peripheral nerves. This leads to a variety of skin lesions and loss of nerve conduction. The loss of nerve conduction can keep the patient from having any feeling in the areas most affected, and this can lead to further inadvertent damage to those areas, since the patient cannot feel the pain or discomfort that allows protection from trauma. Serious disfigurement and loss of digits can result, giving the dreaded physical appearances that have long been associated with this disease. However, the long-standing history of the total isolation of leprosy patients is probably not warranted, since disease transmission is not likely to occur in a hospital or ward setting, and years of exposure often seem to be necessary to develop the disease.

Only a limited amount of research on the effects of vitamin C on leprosy and its associated microorganism could be found. As with most diseases not reported to have been treated by Klenner, no studies using his range of vitamin C doses could be found. Indeed, the long-term effects of vitamin C on the clinical course of this disease would appear still to be largely unresearched.

Matsuo et al. (1975) and Skinsnes and Matsuo (1976) reported what they termed as only "suggestive findings" in the treatment of five leprosy patients with vitamin C. One received only 1,500 mg of vitamin C daily for 4.5 months, and the other four received this vitamin C regimen for up to 24 months along with dapsone, an antibacterial drug used to treat leprosy. All five patients had a comparable amount of lesion regression, with changes in bacterial appearance under the microscope felt to be consistent with lesion regression. When measured by these findings, it appears that vitamin C was able to regress the lesions as much by itself as when added to the more traditional dapsone treatment.

Hastings et al. (1976), who further investigated the findings of Matsuo et al., looked at the response of mice that had foot pads infected with leprosy bacteria to variable amounts of vitamin C. The researchers gave the mice doses of vitamin C that were equivalent to a 500 mg, a 1,500 mg, or a 4,500 mg dose of vitamin C in a human. They found that the vitamin C had a "statistically significant" effect in inhibiting the multiplication of leprosy bacteria when the foot pads were examined after six months. Furthermore, they asserted that the multiplication of the bacteria suggested a dose-response relationship, implying that still higher doses of vitamin C could have produced even more pronounced effects. It should also be noted that no bacteria were seen in those animals at six months treated with the established antileprosy drugs, dapsone, clofazimine, or rifampin. However, with the established safety profile of vitamin C there should be no hesitation to add it in sizeable doses to the traditional therapy for leprosy until more information on the effects of higher doses of vitamin C is obtained.

Other researchers have used relatively small doses of vitamin C in leprosy with clinical improvement generally observed. Bechelli (1939) reported positive results in over half of the 20 leprosy patients that he treated with intramuscular injections of 50 to 100 mg of vitamin C.

Gatti and Gaona (1939) also noted good results in two leprosy patients injected with 100 mg of vitamin C for several weeks. Undoubtedly, some of these responses represented general improvements in overall health from the addition of the vitamin C, since the slow growth of the leprosy bacteria would not be expected to directly respond in a very quick or clinically dramatic fashion. In fact, Sinha et al. (1984), in studying 70 leprosy patients, found significant reductions in their blood levels of vitamin C. Giving vitamin C to any vitamin C-depleted patient, with or without a backdrop of leprosy, should show improvements in general health.

Some other investigators also found vitamin C to be of benefit in the treatment of leprosy. Ferreira (1950), working with a group of leprosy patients in Brazil, found that daily injections of 500 mg of vitamin C were of clear clinical benefit. The patients had an improved sense of well-being, an improved appetite with weight gain, fewer nosebleeds, and an improved tolerance to their regular antileprosy medications. Floch and Sureau (1952) also reported good results using 500 mg injections of vitamin C over extended periods of time. They also tried using 1,000 mg of vitamin C daily and claimed to have still better results. They even suggested that the use of "two or even four grams daily" of vitamin C in this disease would be worth investigating.

Another benefit of vitamin C therapy in the treatment of leprosy was reported by Sahu and Das (1994). These researchers found that vitamin C was very effective in protecting against clofazimine-induced chromosomal damage in mice. Clofazimine remains one of the important drugs commonly used for very extended periods of time in the treatment of leprosy. Using vitamin C in all leprosy patients would not only address the commonly found disease-associated vitamin C deficiency, it would also protect against significant side effects of the standard leprosy drug therapy.

It would appear that high enough doses of vitamin C do retard the growth of leprosy bacteria, and patients clinically improve, at least indicating a stabilization of the disease process, along with some reversibility of symptomatology. Since the leprosy bacterium is in the same family as tuberculosis, and leprosy transmission is so difficult, logic would also dictate that a daily intake of adequate amounts of vitamin C should prove to be just as protective against the primary contraction of leprosy as tuberculosis.

Typhoid Fever
(Reversible and Preventable; Curable-?)

Typhoid fever is a bacterial disease caused by the bacteria *Salmonella typhi*. Also called enteric fever, typhoid fever is characterized by prolonged fever, diarrhea, and abdominal pain. Complications can include intestinal bleeding and perforation. Typhoid fever has been almost eliminated in developed countries due to modern sewage and water treatment facilities. However, it still remains a problem today in less developed countries. Also, typhoid fever has a case-fatality rate in underdeveloped countries of about 10%, while the developed countries, which have antibiotic therapy and better nutrition, have a case-fatality rate of less than 1%.

No reports of Klenner treating typhoid fever could be found. Farah (1938) treated 18 cases of typhoid with intravenous vitamin C and adrenal gland extract, reporting great success in reducing both the length of the illness as well as the chance of death. Farah noted that the effect of vitamin C and adrenal extract administration "is dramatic from the first injection." Szirmai (1940) administered 300 mg injections of vitamin C in clinically severe cases of typhoid fever, achieving a complete protection against the complication of intestinal hemorrhaging. Drummond (1943) reported success in the treatment of 106 cases of typhoid fever. The daily dose of vitamin C was 1,200 mg, with 400 mg given by injection and 800 mg given by mouth. Although when this paper was written the mortality rate for typhoid fever in South Africa was 15%, only two of the 106 patients died with the vitamin C treatment regimen. Furthermore, Drummond commented that the autopsy on these two patients revealed "complications to be present which in no way discredited the efficacy of the treatment." Drummond also noted that there was a "demonstrable lessening of toxicity" in all but two patients, who turned out to have hyperthyroidism. Not surpris-

ingly, Drummond was also able to determine that vitamin C could kill
the typhoid bacteria in the test tube, finding that 50 mg of vitamin C
added to 5 cc of a "virulent culture" would rapidly destroy all growth.
Also, no bacterial growth could
be initiated in the culture broth
when vitamin C had been added
to the inoculation ahead of time.
Drummond concluded that
vitamin C treatment of typhoid
fever allowed it to be considered
"a comparatively safe illness." These results certainly suggest there is
an excellent chance that even more dramatic responses could be obtained routinely with much higher doses of vitamin C, as achieved
with many infectious diseases by Klenner and others.

vitamin C killed the typhoid bacteria in the test tube... 50 mg of vitamin C added to 5 cc of a "virulent culture" rapidly destroyed all growth

As pointed out by Stone (1972) a number of different strains of
Salmonella bacteria produce significant toxins as well. These toxins characteristically affect the cells lining the intestines, further aggravating
the abdominal symptoms that accompany *Salmonella* infections. Stone
further points out that this added toxic component with such infections
would make vitamin C an especially good treatment agent, since it has
proved to be effective against so many other toxins, bacteria-produced
or otherwise. Furthermore, even though typhoid fever is responsive to
antibiotics, it would be desirable to avoid any unexpected side effects
from these drugs by not having to use them. Very likely this goal could
be achieved if high enough doses of vitamin C prove to be an adequate
single therapy, as seems likely.

Hill and Garren (1955) reported on the effects of high vitamin levels on the resistance of chicks to typhoid. They found that "high levels
of all the known required vitamins" increased this resistance. They
also noted that vitamin C can serve the function of "the required antioxidant."

Although it cannot be unequivocally stated that vitamin C can
cure typhoid fever, there is no doubt that vitamin C can quickly and effectively reverse symptomatology and lessen the likelihood and degree
of complications, including death. Klenner-sized doses would likely re-

sult in a prompt and complete eradication of this infection. This is especially important in light of the observations of Foster et al. (1974). They point out that chloramphenicol, one of the first-line antibiotics used in the treatment of typhoid fever, will often result in the development of anemia in the patient, thereby adding to the total illness burden. Using vitamin C as the sole therapy for typhoid fever would prevent this possible side effect. Furthermore, it would seem very unlikely that this infection would ever be contracted in the first place as long as adequate daily doses of vitamin C were taken.

Malaria (Reversible; Curable-?, Preventable-?)

Malaria is one of the world's most common infectious diseases, with 200 to 300 million cases every year that result in one to two million deaths annually. Malaria is caused by microorganisms known as protozoa, from the genus *Plasmodium*. These microbes typically cause a malarial syndrome when they are introduced into the body by the bites of infected mosquitoes, and are subsequently incorporated into the red blood cells. Protozoa are the simplest organisms of the animal kingdom. They are single-celled, and they range in size from visibility by the naked eye to invisibility under the light microscope. Typically, they are free-living, but some types can assume a parasitic existence. In malaria the protozoa parasitize the red blood cells of the infected human, essentially using these cells as a culture medium to propagate their own life cycles, which results in the eventual rupture and destruction of the host red blood cells. Repetitive infections with these malarial protozoa are also common since the primary infection does not produce a protective immune response. Recently, malaria has been showing a resurgence due to increasing resistance of the infecting microbe to the drug chloroquine and due to an increasing resistance of the infecting mosquito to some of the more economical insecticides.

Lotze (1938) treated malaria patients with injections of vitamin C. Following 300 mg intravenous doses, he found that healthy individuals excreted about 50% of it in 24 hours while patients with acute malarial infection excreted very little. Just as with the other infectious diseases, this finding demonstrated that the malarial patient uses greater quantities than normal of vitamin C. Lotze also gave 1,000 mg doses of vitamin C intravenously to his malaria patients. He found that this dose prevented the chills, lowered the elevated temperatures seen with the disease, and improved the overall sense of well-being. He also noted that hemoglobin levels and red blood cell counts were stable during treatment.

1,000 mg intravenous doses of vitamin C in malaria patients prevented chills, lowered elevated temperatures, and improved sense of well-being

A "hemolytic crisis," or massive destruction of the infected red blood cells, did not occur during the treatment, even though there has been some speculation that this reaction might occur in the vitamin C therapy of malaria. In fact, Lotze commented that vitamin C appeared to have an antihemolytic effect on the infected red blood cells.

Although hemoglobin levels and red blood cell counts were noted to decline after treatment, this probably represented a healing response more than a crisis response since the malarial infection can never be completely resolved until all infected red blood cells eventually die and are replaced by newly formed, uninfected ones. Abnormal serum protein tests were also seen to normalize on this vitamin C therapy.

Other authors also looked at the association between vitamin C levels and malarial infections. Millet (1940) observed that inadequate nutrition, along with poor vitamin C intake, lead to suboptimal adrenal function. This is probably due to the fact that the adrenal glands normally have very high concentrations of vitamin C, implying an important role of vitamin C in adrenal function. The author noted that a subsequent malarial infection could then lead to a syndrome characterized by the symptoms of adrenal insufficiency.

Millet suggested that a closer attention to an adequate diet should be given in the proper treatment of malaria. Krishnan (1938) also looked at vitamin C excretion and saturation in normal and malarial subjects in Bengal, India. It was noted that most of the healthy children had normal vitamin C saturation while most of the malarial patients had a marked deficiency of vitamin C. The author felt that in chronic malaria there is a subscurvy state that is further aggravated during the acute attacks of malarial fever. Njoku et al. (1995) also noted that the vitamin C levels in the blood of malarial patients were significantly decreased during and after infection.

Mohr (1941) also found that malarial patients demonstrated an increased consumption of vitamin C. He found that the administration of vitamin C (250 mg) along with iron supplementation accelerated the rate of normalization of anemia seen with malaria. Furthermore, he found that this regimen increased the reticulocyte count, which is an index of the rate of regeneration of new red blood cell formation. Mohr stressed that the addition of vitamin C therapy to the traditional antimalarial drug therapy is appropriate, and Levander and Ager (1993) made a similar suggestion.

Suggestions that vitamin C should be added to antimalarial therapy also comes from Das et al. (1993). These researchers showed that while vitamin C blood levels dropped in malaria patients, there was evidence of increasing oxidative stress. Regardless of which situation came first, vitamin C is always a logical addition to whatever other treatment is being given when increased oxidative stress and increased free radicals are shown to be present. This increase in oxidative stress in malaria has also been documented by other researchers (Sarin et al., 1993; Mishra et al., 1994). Winter et al. (1997) has demonstrated that vitamin C enhances the effect of exifone, an antimalarial drug used against multidrug-resistant strains of *Plasmodium falciparum*.

McKee and Geiman (1946) looked at the vitamin C status in monkeys infected with malarial parasites. They found that the average plasma vitamin C levels in infected animals were less than half the average seen in uninfected animals. Bourke et al. (1980) looked at the effect of vitamin C on the ability of mice to resist malarial infection. They gave infected mice daily intraabdominal injections of vitamin C in a dose of 500 mg/kg body weight, starting the injections five days before the infection was introduced. These mice exhibited a 38% depression in the parasite count in the blood, and they had a mean survival time that was 67% longer than that of the infected control group receiving no treatment.

They gave another group of mice vitamin C injections in a dose of 1,000 mg/kg, but starting on the same day that infection was introduced. The larger dose of vitamin C was slightly less effective in lowering the blood parasite count (23% versus 38%), but these animals survived substantially longer. Their mean survival time was increased by 133% over the control group. It would appear that the larger doses of vitamin C needed some time to "catch up" to the effects of the lower doses of vitamin C, which were started well before the infection was introduced. As revealed by the improved survival times, the clinical response was ultimately much better with the larger doses of vitamin C, even though they were started later.

Even more basic research has looked at the effects of vitamin C on the malaria parasite itself and malaria-infected red blood cells in a test tube setting. Marva et al. (1989) found that vitamin C in the presence of copper had a destructive effect on the parasitic growth of *Plasmodium falciparum*, a microorganism responsible for an especially aggressive form of human malaria. Marva et al. (1992) looked further at the effects that vitamin C has on red blood cells parasitized in malaria. They noted that parasitized red blood cells concentrated two and a half times more vitamin C than non-infected red blood cells. Furthermore, they found that vitamin C *selectively* has a prooxidant effect inside infected red blood cells, allowing for parasite destruction.

In non-infected red blood cells, however, vitamin C has its more typical antioxidant effects of promoting and protecting normal cellular function. It would appear that vitamin C becomes capable of a destructive, prooxidant role against the parasite in infected red blood cells because of the increasing amounts of iron released as the parasite proceeds with its multiplication. The right ratio of iron to vitamin C can promote prooxidant rather than antioxidant activity (Hershko, 1989). The iron can serve the same function as copper in promoting the destructive effect of vitamin C on the malarial parasite as demonstrated by Marva et al. (1989) and noted above.

Vitamin C can also be an important nutrient in the prevention and effective treatment of a certain malaria therapy complication. Naraqi et al. (1992) reported a case of acute blindness after intravenous quinine therapy. Use of vitamin C, vitamin B complex, and steroids ultimately resulted in a complete restoration of vision in this patient.

The literature on malaria and vitamin C appears to clearly indicate that vitamin C can help to reverse the clinical and laboratory indicators of a malarial infection. No evidence of either Klenner-sized doses of vitamin C or even of modestly high vitamin C doses was found in reviewing the literature. It cannot be asserted definitively that vitamin C can cure malaria, but the possibility also cannot be ruled out. As with many of the other infectious diseases already examined, the literature is strongly suggestive that a person with a better nutritional status and better body stores of vitamin C would be far less likely to contract malaria in the first place. However, the protective effect of vitamin C in this instance cannot be regarded as absolute at this time. If one or more infected mosquitoes can deliver a sufficient parasite load acutely, malaria will likely be contracted in spite of the individual's vitamin C status. Nevertheless, recovery should still proceed more quickly and efficiently if the victim is not vitamin C-depleted.

Brucellosis (Reversible; Curable-?, Preventable-?)

Brucellosis is an infectious disease caused by bacteria of the genus *Brucella*. Transmission of the disease to humans comes from infected animals. A common source of transmission is through contaminated dairy products, such as milk, cheese, and butter. Initially, brucellosis presents as a fever syndrome, usually without evidence of a specific focus of infection. Joint and muscle pains are often present. Brucellosis is difficult to diagnose unless there is a high index of suspicion, and the patient lives in an area of the world where such infections are common. The infection in its active phase can be located in any organ, preventing a completely typical presentation of this disease. Antibiotic treatment of this disease will shorten its duration and reduce the incidence of complications. However, relapses still occur in many cases even with antibiotic treatment. The common name for brucellosis, undulant fever, comes from the frequent relapses seen with this disease. Many individuals contract brucellosis as children and have episodic relapses for the rest of their lives. The endemic areas with the highest incidences of brucellosis are in the Mediterranean basin, the Arabic peninsula, India, and Latin America.

Mick (1955) reported on the treatment of 12 brucellosis patients with vitamin C. One 35-year-old woman had been plagued with extreme fatigue for about 15 years. She had regular headaches, as well as joint and abdominal pains. Every six to eight weeks, she would have a three-day to five-day bout of fever, ranging from 99°F to 102°F, during which her chronic symptoms became more intense. After a "definite diagnosis" of brucellosis was made, and more than ten years after the initial onset of the symptoms, a 3,000 mg daily dose of vitamin C was started. After about 15 months the patient finally reported that she had not had any fever since about four months after starting the vitamin C therapy. She claimed to feel better than at any time in the past 11 years, and except for occasional headaches, she reported that all of her earlier symptoms had disappeared.

Another 52-year-old man who had been sick for at least six years and unable to work for three years was also started on 3,000 mg of vitamin C daily with no other treatment. He eventually regained about 70 pounds, initially weighing only 129 pounds on a six foot, two inch frame. He became symptom-free, and was able to work full-time again. When Mick did not get a good response with oral vitamin C, he would add 1,000 mg of intravenous vitamin C two to three times a week. Only one of the 12 patients he reported on did not have dramatic responses to the vitamin C therapy, and this patient refused the intravenous injections. All 12 patients described by Mick were very ill, and they had been so for years or even decades. Mick concluded that the vitamin C treatment of brucellosis "has much to offer."

Boura et al. (1989) reported that the levels of vitamin C in both the blood and certain white blood cells (monocytes) of 14 chronic brucellosis patients "were significantly beneath normal." They also showed that only 15 days of vitamin C supplementation significantly restored some specific parameters of monocyte immune function helpful in combating brucellosis.

The doses of vitamin C that Mick used clearly demonstrated that the symptoms of brucellosis and the disease process itself could be reversed. However, it cannot be definitively stated that brucellosis is curable by vitamin C. The prevention of brucellosis by adequate doses of vitamin C seems to be a likely possibility since the disease symptoms can so readily be reversed on relatively low-dose vitamin C therapy. Unfortunately, no clear data to support this assertion could be found in the literature.

Trichinosis (Reversible; Curable-?, Preventable-?)

Trichinosis is a disease that results from eating raw or undercooked pork containing the cysts of *Trichinella spiralis,* one of the smallest parasitic roundworms. Once swallowed, the cysts dissolve, and the parasite matures. The larvae of the mature parasite then get deposited in the intestinal lining, and from here the lymphatic system delivers the parasites bodywide, where they can return to their cystic form. Clinically, the patient initially experiences diarrhea, nausea, abdominal pain, and fever. After the parasite progresses past the intestinal stage, symptoms may include pain and swelling of the muscles, sweating, insomnia, swelling of the eyelids, depressed appetite, cough, and profound weakness.

Klenner (April 1954) described the case of a 31-year-old male who presented with most of the classical signs and symptoms of trichinosis. Only after the patient recovered did he finally remember that he had eaten raw sausage. Without being specific as to dosage size, Klenner stated that "massive doses of vitamin C were given by needle" to this patient. At least five different antibiotics were given over a 10-day period during which the patient's condition was observed to worsen. After the patient slipped into a "state of semi-coma" para-aminobenzoic acid (PABA) was added to the treatment. He then started to respond well and subsequently recovered. It is unclear whether the PABA also required the administration of the vitamin C to bring about this patient's recovery. Certainly, the patient was sick enough to rapidly deplete vitamin C body stores, and vitamin C therapy on this basis alone would be justified to support the general immune status of the patient.

Daoud et al. (2000) looked at the effects of an antioxidant combination that included vitamin C on the course of *Trichinella spiralis* infection in albino rats. The combination included vitamins A, C, and E, along with selenium. The daily dose of vitamin C was fairly small, being equivalent to approximately 200 mg for a 70-kilogram person. Nevertheless, even at this low dose, several significant effects were observed. The authors found that the initial (intestinal) phase of the trichinosis infection was somewhat enhanced by the antioxidants, presumably because the natural oxidant attack against the parasites was lessened. However, they found that after the trichinosis parasites reached the muscles, the antioxidants in combination with an antiparasite drug (mebendazole) resulted in the number of larvae in the muscles being "highly decreased" relative to no treatment. The larvae were also significantly lessened relative to treatment with only the antiparasite drug.

the vitamin C-treated trichinosis-infected animals had about a 40% reduction in worm (larvae) count in the muscles after 30 days of treatment

Senutaite and Biziulevicius (1986) also looked at the effects of vitamin C on the resistance of rats to the trichinosis infection. They administered a daily dose of vitamin C (50 mg) to each rat, which equates to approximately a 35,000 mg dose in a 70-kilogram man or animal. Relative to infected animals that were not given vitamin C, a higher antibody titer was seen in the infected animals given vitamin C. Most significantly, the vitamin C-treated infected animals had about a 40% reduction in worm (larvae) count in the muscles after 30 days of treatment. This significant decrease took place with vitamin C treatment alone since no traditional antiparasite medications were given.

Once the initial challenge of parasites has been presented to the intestine and parasite assimilation has taken place, it would appear that vitamin C, as well as other antioxidants, can play a significant role in shortening the course of trichinosis and lessening the acute intensity of the infection. It would also appear that vitamin C would probably best serve as a significant addition to the traditional therapies already in use for this infection, rather than just being used as the sole treating agent. There was no evidence found in the literature to specifically support the assertion that vitamin C would prevent the contraction of a trichinosis infection. As with microbes, enough of an acute challenge to the intestinal tract with cysts of *Trichinella spiralis* would be expected to initiate an infection in spite of significant amounts of vitamin C being present.

Other Infectious Diseases or Pathogenic Microorganisms and Vitamin C

Amebic Dysentery
(Reversible and Preventable; Curable-?)

Amebic dysentery is a disease caused by a pathogenic strain of protozoa, *Entamoeba histolytica*. This parasite continues to infect approximately 1% of the world's population, with the highest incidence in poor and underdeveloped countries. Symptomatically, this infection can result in severe gastrointestinal symptoms, including inflammation of the intestines that can proceed to ulceration in the colon. Diarrhea containing blood and mucus is common along with associated abdominal pain. Some patients will go on to develop amebic liver abscesses.

Veselovskaia (1957), using only 150 mg of vitamin C daily, found a clear relationship between the severity of amebic disease and vitamin C levels in 106 patients. Bloody bowel movements were seen more often in the vitamin C-deficient patients. Sokolova (1958) treated ameba-infected patients with 500 mg of vitamin C daily. Combined with other routine treatments, the patients receiving vitamin C had shorter illness durations and a quicker elimination of the symptoms associated with severe dysentery. Ivanov et al. (1991), in looking at 287 patients with amebic intestinal infections, noted that the disease "assumed a fulminant course" in five patients with evidence of "vitamin C and B deficiency." A fulminant course is an extremely rapid, unchecked progression of disease.

As with a number of other infectious diseases already discussed, the acuteness and clinical activity level of amebic disease can vary widely. Just as tuberculosis can be either very active and clinically debilitating or latent and relatively inconsequential, amebic infections can also range between dormancy and a very active infection. Alexander and Meleney (1935) found equally high incidences of amebic infection in two rural Tennessee communities. However, one of the communities was noted to be especially lacking in dietary vitamin and caloric content, and the acute amebic infection with dysentery was found to be common. However, in the community with the higher quality diet, this acute presentation of amebic infection was found to be rare.

Elsdon-Dew (1949) observed Bantus, Indians, and Europeans living in the same community in South Africa, noting that amebic infections affected the three races in different ways. The Bantus, who consume large amounts of maize, most typically have acute fulminating dysentery as a result of amebic infection. The Indians, eating significant amounts of curry and rice, only rarely had acute dysentery but often ended up with liver abscesses. The Europeans, with a much more balanced and full diet, rarely had severe amebic infections. Elsdon-Dew (1950), in comparing Africans from two different areas of the country, also found strikingly lower rates of amebic dysentery among those with a multitude of vegetables in their diet. Fresh vegetables are a significant source of dietary vitamin C.

Faust et al. (1934) found that dogs fed only salmon would lose their resistance to being infected with ameba. Recall that dogs can make some vitamin C, but the amounts produced are relatively little compared to an animal such as a goat. Apparently, having a diet that is chronically deficient in vitamin C can make a dog more prone to amebic infection in spite of the dog's ability to internally synthesize limited amounts of vitamin C. A salmon-only diet will not supply very much vitamin C. When fed with raw liver and liver extract, the intestinal ulcers of dogs with amebiasis tended to heal (Faust and Kagy, 1934; Faust and Swartzwelder, 1936). Monkeys fed only raw milk showed either a reduction in intestinal ameba count, or, in some instances, a complete elimination of the infecting parasite (Kessel and K'e-Kang, 1925).

The above studies clearly demonstrate that adequate nutrition bears a direct relation to the severity of an amebic infection. Although the most important nutrients cannot be precisely determined from the above information, all of the diets mentioned above that were associated with the less severe infections would be expected to have the higher amounts of vitamin C. Sadun et al. (1950) found that guinea pigs fed a diet deficient in vitamin C were especially susceptible to ameba infection, even when the microbe count in the inoculating dose was decidedly small. Sadun et al. (1951) were able to demonstrate the relationship between vitamin C intake and the infectivity and virulence of amebic infection even more definitively.

In 43 guinea pigs fed a vitamin C-deficient diet and inoculated with a given dose of amebas, 87% developed intestinal lesions, and 100% died from the infection. However, in 48 guinea pigs fed the same diet plus a supplement of vitamin C, only 67% ended up with the infection, and only 27% eventually died from the infection. An "intermediate" effect was seen in 19 guinea pigs fed a "mildly scorbutogenic" diet. The authors concluded that vitamin C deficiency made the amebic infection much more severe. They also noted that the average time from inoculation to death among the vitamin C-supplemented animals was about 33% longer than in the vitamin C-deficient animals. Overall the vitamin C-deficient animals more easily contracted the amebic infections, had more severe clinical courses, and died sooner than those animals given vitamin C.

It would appear that amebic dysentery is very responsive to the administration of fairly small doses of vitamin C. Larger doses, up to Klenner-sized levels, should be expected to have even quicker and more dramatic clinical responses. The symptoms of amebic dysentery are definitely reversible by vitamin C administration, and a prompt curing of this disease is likely with high enough doses. Although hard evidence for a cure could not be found in the literature, the studies cited strongly imply that this is another infectious disease that should be preventable by large enough daily doses of vitamin C. This is suggested by the compelling relationship found between vitamin C deficiency and both the infectivity and severity of amebic dysentery.

Bacillary Dysentery (Curable and Preventable)

This is a syndrome of intestinal infection and inflammation caused by bacteria of the genus *Shigella*. Several strains of *Shigella* also produce bacterial toxins that further complicate the severity of the clinical pictures. The combined infectious/toxic nature of *Shigella* infections makes vitamin C an especially useful agent for treating this infection, whether alone or in combination with the more traditional antimicrobial drugs.

Klenner (July 1949) reported great success in the treatment of this type of dysentery with vitamin C. He repeatedly found that "vitamin C in 500 to 1000 mg doses" given by intramuscular injection would readily cure this infection. He also noted that children having "10 to 15 bloody stools per day" would clear up in 48 hours, and at the same time they would revert to normal feedings.

Honjo et al. (1969) gave 11 monkeys small doses of *Shigella*. Of the seven monkeys given no vitamin C for 20 weeks, three developed "pronounced clinical dysentery" in four to 12 days after the bacterial challenge. By contrast none of the four control monkeys exposed to the same bacterial challenges but who received vitamin C regularly developed any signs of clinical dysentery. Interestingly, two of the four monkeys challenged with the bacteria and deprived of vitamin C developed severe scurvy during the observation period, with one of them dying. Perhaps individual susceptibilities among the monkeys determined whether the infection became pronounced because of the vitamin C deficiency. Also, the vitamin C deficiency could have developed into full scurvy because of the added stress of the bacterial challenge. This would appear to be analogous to the interactions between degrees of infection and degrees of vitamin C deficiency discussed earlier in the clinical course of rheumatic fever.

Honjo and Imaizumi (1967) looked at monkeys that died from natural dysentery (not experimentally produced). They found that the average vitamin C content of the adrenal glands was about 60% lower than in healthy control animals. Similarly, in animals with experimentally-induced *Shigella* dysentery, adrenal gland content of vitamin C was decreased to about 55% of the normal control by the peak of the disease. Conversely, the average liver vitamin C levels of infected monkeys *markedly rose* relative to the healthy control animals. Perhaps the high concentrations of vitamin C normally found in the adrenal glands serves to some extent as a reservoir that acutely supplements other areas of the body in greater need of vitamin C. The liver is a primary site where toxins are neutralized, and vitamin C is a primary neutralizer of toxicity. Other investigators have documented that ACTH (an adrenal gland-stimulating hormone) can also increase liver vitamin C content (Forbes and Duncan, 1954; Kameta, 1959), as can exposure to a bacterial endotoxin (Jefferies, 1965). Perhaps many of the infectious diseases with a toxic component, such as some *Shigella* infections, will show this increase in liver vitamin C as long as adrenal stores of vitamin C are not already too depleted.

It would appear that vitamin C is clearly capable of lessening the symptoms associated with *Shigella* infections. Klenner's work indicates this disease can probably be readily cured with adequate vitamin C. The ability of the *Shigella* infection to deplete adrenal vitamin C stores and fortify liver vitamin C stores, however, appears to be more of a nonspecific reaction to an infectious disease, particularly one capable of producing a bacterial toxin as well. Certainly, the limited data found on the treatment of *Shigella* infections with vitamin C should at least warrant adding vitamin C to whatever other medications and supportive measures that are usually offered to such patients. Klenner's success also strongly suggests that regular optidoses of vitamin C should prevent *Shigella* from taking hold unless the degree of acute exposure is very great.

Pseudomonas Infections
(Curable and Preventable)

Klenner (1971) had some experience in the treatment of *Pseudomonas* infections. *Pseudomonas* is a type of bacteria that appears most commonly in debilitated and weakened patients, and it is generally a very difficult infection to control and eradicate. *Pseudomonas aeruginosa*, a fairly common strain, is also associated with the production of a variety of toxins.

Klenner saw *Pseudomonas* in association with severe burns. He asserted that either the toxin or the spread of the bacteria into the blood could result in the death of the patient. Klenner would spray a 3% vitamin C solution over the entire area of the burn every two to four hours for a period of roughly five days. He would also administer both oral and intravenous vitamin C. The intravenous vitamin C, in an amount of 500 mg/kg body weight, was diluted to at least 18 cc per 1,000 mg of vitamin C in an injectable solution. The first injection was given as rapidly as a 20-gauge needle would allow. Repeat injections were given every eight hours for the first few days, and then every 12 hours. The oral vitamin C was given to bowel tolerance in a fashion similar to that of Cathcart (1981) described earlier. Since large doses of vitamin C could lower calcium levels, one gram of calcium gluconate was also given daily. Klenner stated that under this regimen *Pseudomonas* infection was not a problem. He also added that even when the burn was seen late in its course, a *Pseudomonas* infection that was already present would be destroyed within a few days, "leaving a clean healthy surface" to the burned area and minimizing the chances of significant scarring.

Carlsson et al. (2001) found that vitamin C worked well with nitrite in markedly inhibiting the growth of *Pseudomonas aeruginosa* in human urine. The authors asserted that their results might help to explain the benefits of vitamin C in the treatment and prevention of urinary tract infection. Rawal et al. (1974) found that vitamin C could inhibit the growth of 16 different strains of *Pseudomonas aeruginosa* in the test tube. They also demonstrated that vitamin C worked well in enhancing the effects of a number of different antibiotics on the growth of *Pseudomonas aeruginosa* in culture. The authors demonstrated that vitamin C alone could cure mice infected with *Pseudomonas aeruginosa*, but less vitamin C was needed for a curative effect when erythromycin was added to the treatment. Finally, they were able to show that cystic fibrosis patients infected in their lungs with *Pseudomonas aeruginosa* were easily clinically controlled with a combination of vitamin C and antibiotic therapy. Four of the five test patients wanted to continue the combination therapy at the end of the clinical trial, which further indicated the effectiveness of the therapy.

Clinically, cystic fibrosis patients suffer a great deal with their lung infections. Rawal (1978) later showed that *Pseudomonas aeruginosa* cells became "increasingly susceptible" to the effects of five different antibiotics when exposed at the same time to vitamin C. Rawal and Charles (1972) showed that vitamin C worked well *in vitro* with the antibacterial agents sulfamethoxazole and trimethoprim in killing *Pseudomonas aeruginosa*.

Nakanishi (1992, 1993) found that the topical application of vitamin C along with antibiotics ensured the absence of *Pseudomonas aeruginosa* from a treated bedsore.

Vitamin C appears to be an excellent agent for the treatment of *Pseudomonas* infections since it appears to eradicate the infection and neutralize any associated toxins. Furthermore, as these bacteria tend to infect only when the patient's immune system is compromised, an adequate daily dosing of vitamin C should prevent most *Pseudomonas* infections from ever starting.

Rocky Mountain Spotted Fever (RMSF) (Curable; Preventable-?)

This is an acute infectious disease that is sometimes fatal, caused by the bacteria *Rickettsia rickettsii*. Also known as tick fever, RMSF is usually transmitted by the bites of infected ticks. Clinically, RMSF is characterized by sudden onset, with fever lasting two to three weeks. A rash generally appears in the first week of illness, initially involving the peripheral parts of the body and then gradually spreading inwards to the trunk of the body. Muscle soreness, severe headache, and extreme exhaustion are all associated symptoms.

Smith (1988) reported that Klenner was an authority on treating RMSF because his medical practice was in an area of the country where infected ticks were often found. Smith wrote that Klenner treated an advanced case of RMSF with a dramatic clinical response. This patient had 104.4°F temperature, a characteristic rash over the body, a positive blood test, and was in a coma when seen by Klenner.

a comatose RMSF patient was cons, conscious and rational within six hours of starting vitamin C/ PABA treatment... he was fully recovered on the sixth day

Klenner gave 30,000 mg of vitamin C intravenously every six hours. He also gave large oral doses of para-aminobenzoic acid (PABA). The PABA treatment schedule was 6,000 mg every two hours for three doses, then 4,000 mg every two hours for 12 doses, and finally 4,000 mg every four hours until the fever was gone for a full 24 hours. With this vitamin C /PABA treatment, this patient was conscious and rational within about six hours of starting treatment. The patient was sent home fully recovered on the sixth day.

Klenner treated a 12-year-old girl with RMSF. She had a characteristic rash and 105°F temperature. By the third day she was doing poorly in spite of PABA and chloramphenicol therapy. She was then given 30,000 mg of vitamin C intravenously, and in only two hours she was cheerful and responsive, seeming to be "almost well." She continued to receive 30,000 mg doses of vitamin C intravenously and was home and recovered within seven days.

Klenner also treated his son for RMSF. Even though his son was gravely ill, he eventually responded to vitamin C, vibramycin, and PABA, recovering by the fourth day. With RMSF, Klenner found that the disease could always be reversed when vitamin C was given around the clock at the 500-900 mg/kg body weight level. It would appear that RMSF is another infectious disease that is readily curable by vitamin C, even though traditional therapies do not even assure survival. Preventing the disease by taking vitamin C is less clear since a very large dose of the microbes can be delivered at the time of the tick bite.

Typhus *(not "typhoid fever")* is another infectious disease caused by rickettsia bacteria. Zinsser et al. (1931) noted that the "average guinea pig" seemed to possess some resistance against typhus infection that limited the spread of the organism and lead to "almost invariable recovery" of the animals. However, in animals fed on "vitamin-deficient diets," the response to typhus infection was typically dramatic. Illness was severe and widespread—usually without a temperature rise and sometimes with a temperature drop, and death sometimes occurring without any of the clinical characteristics of a typhus infection. The authors noted that there was a historical association of high typhus mortality with war and famine, both of which would be associated with vitamin C and other nutrient deprivation.

Staphylococcal Infections
(Curable and Preventable)

Klenner (1974) did not address staphylococcal infections in any detail. However, he did report the prompt resolution of "staphylococcus infections" following intravenous injections of vitamin C in a dose range between 500 to 700 mg/kg body weight, given through "a 20G needle as fast as the patient's cardiovascular system will allow."

Rebora et al. (1980) looked at two children with defective abilities of their white blood cells to kill bacteria. These two children were especially susceptible to repeated skin infections with *Staphylococcus*. These authors reported that vitamin C "was effective in delaying and eventually suppressing infectious episodes." Nakanishi (1992, 1993) reported that the application of vitamin C directly in a topical fashion to a bedsore was able to "remarkably" enhance the bacteria-killing effect of antibiotics. Nakanishi also noted that *Staphylococcus aureus*, which had been antibiotic-resistant prior to the addition of vitamin C, subsequently disappeared from the wound.

Ledermann (1962) reported on the case of an elderly woman with an ulcer on her left cheek. Multiple treatments were attempted to heal this lesion. Cultures detected the presence of *Staphylococcus aureus*. After the ulcer had been present for over three years, even becoming larger, vitamin C therapy was initiated and healing was complete in several weeks. Ledermann also noted that "no signs of scurvy were observed." This is strong support for the importance of vitamin C in healing, especially when a pathogenic organism must be treated at the same time.

Gupta and Guha (1941) were able to demonstrate an inhibition of the growth of *Staphylococcus aureus* at concentrations of vitamin C lower than that needed to inhibit certain diphtheria and streptococcal bacteria that result in clinical infections readily responsive to vitamin C therapy. Staphylococcal infections can also produce toxins that can magnify the severity of the clinical disease resulting from the infection. Kodama and Kojima (1939) were able to demonstrate the ability of vitamin C to render staphylococcus-related toxin harmless.

Andreasen and Frank (1999) looked at infection-fighting white blood cells in broiler chickens. They found that the treatment of these white blood cells in the test tube with vitamin C significantly increased the ability of these cells to kill *Staphylococcus aureus*. In guinea pigs Nelson et al. (1992) showed that a sufficient dose of vitamin C (375 mg/kg body weight/day) allowed burned animals to gain body weight and lower their metabolic rates in spite of being deliberately infected with *Staphylococcus aureus* at the time of the burn trauma.

It would appear that Klenner-sized doses of vitamin C should also be utilized in staphylococcal infections. As with a number of the other infectious diseases, vitamin C is especially valuable here since it can neutralize bacterial toxins while eradicating the organism. As with so many of the other infectious diseases, vitamin C can always be used to optimize the performance of traditional antibiotic therapy. However, antibiotics can have very undesirable side effects, and vitamin C as a single-agent therapy should be considered if the attending physician feels that the patient is not so critically ill as to be possibly harmed by an antibiotic-free treatment. Because of its ability to cure staphylococcal infections, maintenance doses of vitamin C should be very effective in preventing such infections from taking hold.

Trypanosomal Infections
(Reversible and Preventable; Curable-?)

Trypanosomal infections are due to a type of protozoa. Umar et al. (1999) reported that a fairly small dose of vitamin C (100 mg/kg body weight) prevented the elevation in liver enzymes that otherwise attended the infections of rabbits with *Trypanosoma brucei brucei*. The authors used this information to infer that the liver injury from this infection might be principally due to increased oxidative stress.

Chagas' disease is a trypanosomal disease that infects approximately 18 million people in Central and South America alone. Many of the cases are initially contracted because of contaminated blood transfusions. Ramirez et al. (1995) found that the addition of vitamin C to the gentian violet treatment of collected blood deliberately infected with *Trypanosoma cruzi* before transfusion allowed sterilization with less gentian violet than is typically needed to achieve sterilization. Although the authors noted that gentian violet is already regarded as being free of serious side effects, they concluded that using vitamin C with it could minimize or eliminate the possibility of a cancer-causing side effect seen in some animal studies. Docampo et al. (1988) previously concluded that vitamin C had a similar contribution to the sterilization of *Trypanosoma cruzi*-infected blood. Moraes-Souza and Bordin (1996) also reported that gentian violet, vitamin C, and light will "effectively inactivate" *Trypanosoma cruzi* present in donor blood.

In guinea pig studies, Perla (1937) found that a fairly small dose of vitamin C (approximately 20 mg/kg body weight) raised the natural resistance of this animal to *Trypanosoma brucei* infection. In the test tube, Strangeways (1937) found that vitamin C, along with glutathione, readily killed trypanosomes in culture.

The above data indicate that even low concentrations of vitamin C can be toxic for trypanosomal infections. It seems likely that higher doses of vitamin C would certainly have more pronounced positive effects. It remains to be clearly established whether it could cure such an infection. Based on the transfusion-sterilization studies, it also seems logical that such infections could be prevented if enough vitamin C were taken regularly.

Some Mechanisms of the Antimicrobial Effects of Vitamin C

In addition to the potent antioxidant, reducing ability of vitamin C, which accounts for a great deal of its positive antimicrobial clinical effects, vitamin C has been observed to have many other positive effects as well. Indeed, some of these positive effects on various infections may ultimately be due to the antioxidant properties of vitamin C, although this might not always be readily apparent. However, many other antioxidants simply cannot accomplish what vitamin C does in the intact biological system. To dismiss vitamin C as nothing more than an antioxidant greatly understates and misrepresents the range of vitamin C's positive effects on the body. Some of the mechanisms contributing to vitamin C's potent antimicrobial effects likely include the following (It should be noted that some of the research is on animals, which does not always allow a conclusive extrapolation to vitamin C function in humans.):

1. Enhancement of interferon production (Siegel, 1974; Siegel, 1975; Geber et al., 1975; Dahl and Degre, 1976; Stone, 1980; Karpinska et al., 1982). Interferons are naturally produced antiviral glycoproteins. Interferons are produced by cells that get infected with a virus, and they subsequently increase the resistance of nearby cells to virus attack.

2. Enhancement of phagocytic function (Nungester and Ames, 1948; Goetzl et al., 1974; Sandler et al., 1975; Boxer et al., 1976; Ganguly et al., 1976; Anderson and Dittrich, 1979; Anderson and Theron, 1979; Boxer et al., 1979; Anderson

et al., 1980; Anderson et al., 1980a; Dallegri et al., 1980; Corberand et al., 1982; Patrone et al., 1982; Cunningham-Rundles, 1982; Oberritter et al., 1986; Levy and Schlaeffer, 1993; Levy et al., 1996; Ciocoiu et al., 1998; De la Fuente et al., 1998). A phagocyte is the kind of white blood cell that ingests microorganisms and infection-related cellular debris.

3. Selective concentration of vitamin C in white blood cells (Glick and Hosoda, 1965; Thomas and Holt, 1978; Evans et al., 1982; Goldschmidt, 1991, Washko et al., 1993). Some of the primary cells in the immune system concentrate vitamin C as much as 80 times higher than the level in plasma. This assures extra delivery of vitamin C to the sites of infection by the migration of the vitamin C-rich white blood cells.

4. Enhancement of cell-mediated immune response (Siegel and Morton, 1979). Cell-mediated immune response refers to the T-lymphocytes and how active they are in attacking a given infectious agent.

5. Enhancement of cytokine production by white blood cells (Jeng et al., 1996). Cytokines are nonantibody proteins released by certain white blood cells that serve as intercellular mediators, or agents, in the generation of an immune response.

6. Inhibition of various forms of T-lymphocyte death (Campbell et al., 1999). T-lymphocytes are an integral part of the immune system; increasing their numbers and viability strongly supports the immune system.

7. Enhancement of nitric oxide production by phagocytes (Mizutani et al., 1998; Mizutani and Tsukagoshi, 1999). Nitric oxide is produced in large amounts in white blood cells, and it is one of the agents that will kill invading microorganisms.

8. Enhancement of T-lymphocyte proliferation (Fraser et al., 1980; Kennes et al., 1983; Wu et al., 2000).

9. Enhancement of B-lymphocyte proliferation (Schwager and Schulze, 1997).

10. Inhibition of neuraminidase (Rotman, 1978). Some pathogenic viruses and bacteria utilize the enzyme neuraminidase to keep from being trapped in mucus, one of the natural lines of defense. By inhibiting neuraminidase, vitamin C helps the host optimize this defensive mechanism.

11. Enhancement of antibody production and complement activity (Ecker and Pillemer, 1940; Bourne, 1949; Prinz et al., 1977; Vallance, 1977; Sakamoto et al., 1980; Feigen et al., 1982; Li and Lovell, 1985; Wahli et al., 1986; Johnston et al., 1987; Haskell and Johnston, 1991; Wu et al., 2000). Good antibody function is important to combat both infections and toxins. The complement system is a complex group of proteins that interact to kill targeted cells and mediate other functions of the immune system.

12. Enhancement of natural killer cell activity (Heuser and Vojdani, 1997). Natural killer cells are small lymphocytes that can directly attack cells, such as tumor cells, and kill them. This activity is not antibody-dependent.

13. Enhancement of prostaglandin formation (Horrobin et al., 1979; Scott, 1982; Siegel and Morton, 1984). Prostaglandins are potent mediators of a variety of physiologic processes, including the regulation of T-lymphocyte function.

14. Enhancement of cyclic GMP levels in lymphocytes (Atkinson et al., 1979; Panush et al., 1982). Cyclic GMP plays a central role in the regulation of different physiologic responses, including the modulation of immune responses. Cyclic GMP is important for normal cell proliferation and differentiation. Cyclic GMP also mediates the action of many hormones, and it appears to mediate the relaxation of smooth muscle.

15. Enhanced localized generation of and/or interaction with hydrogen peroxide, which can kill microorganisms (Strangeways, 1937; Miller, 1969; Tappel, 1973; Kraut et al.,

1980). Vitamin C and hydrogen peroxide can dissolve the protective capsules of some bacteria, such as pneumococci (Robertson et al., 1941).

16. Detoxification of histamine (Nandi et al., 1974; Johnston et al., 1992). This antihistamine effect of vitamin C is important in the support of local immune factors.

17. Neutralization of oxidative stress further enhancing the infective process (Kastenbauer et al., 2002). Infections can produce free radicals locally that further promote and entrench the infective process.

18. Nonspecific immunopotentiation and improvement of the vaccination effect (Versteeg, 1970; Banic, 1982; Wu et al., 2000). Vitamin C can improve the immune response achieved with vaccination.

19. Mucolytic effect of vitamin C (Ericsson, 1954). This property helps liquefy thick secretions, increasing immune access to infection.

20. Possible alteration of bacteria cell surface qualities (Rawal, 1978). It has been suggested that vitamin C can alter the bacteria cell surfaces to become more permeable to some antibiotics.

If you conduct your own literature search, you may find a few articles that are not supportive of the conclusions reached in the articles cited above. However, it must be stressed that the vast majority of such discrepancies are related to vitamin C dose. A sizeable amount of research has been performed that concludes vitamin C is not useful or important in various research models. Virtually all of this research has utilized vitamin C doses that are anywhere from slightly to vastly less than what would be required to achieve a given positive outcome or effect. Unfortunately, many of these researchers persist in making unqualified statements that vitamin C is of little or no value in a given research application when the only really valid conclusion is that a very small dose of vitamin C had little or no value in that given research application.

Summary

A very large amount of research has been conducted regarding the effects of vitamin C on a wide variety of microorganisms and the diseases they produce. Many of the infectious agents and their associated diseases can be completely prevented, readily reversed, and often cured by vitamin C alone. Frederick Klenner, M.D. pioneered the usage of doses of vitamin C beyond what most other investigators employed or even imagined. In doing so, Klenner often obtained singularly incredible results in his patients, while many other clinicians achieved positive, but less compelling, results with much smaller doses of vitamin C.

Vitamin C is undoubtedly the ideal agent for treating virtually any viral infection. There are many documented cases showing that the prompt administration of very large doses of vitamin C can bring back heavily infected individuals from even comatose states, ultimately resulting in complete cures. Regardless of whether other medication is given to the victim of an aggressive, relentless viral syndrome, vitamin C should be given in generous doses to all such patients. Furthermore, in a very acute case the intravenous administration of vitamin C simply must be employed since complete curative success can still often be obtained even after seeing oral vitamin C fail to improve the clinical situation.

Many infectious diseases also produce toxins that increase the degree of illness and chance of death. Vitamin C is an extremely potent antitoxin, which makes it an ideal agent to treat infectious diseases that also produce toxins. Unfortunately, antibiotic therapy has no such ability. The use of vitamin C as an antitoxic agent will be more fully discussed in the following chapter.

For the clinician or patient who simply cannot "defy" what modern textbooks and clinical manuals dictate, vitamin C becomes the perfect agent to add to whatever other recommended standard treatments are being administered. This certainly includes antibiotics, which Klenner often used in conjunction with his vitamin C administrations. As Klenner (1974) said: "Ascorbic acid [vitamin C] is the safest and the most valuable substance available to the physician. Many headaches and many heartaches will be avoided with its proper use."

References

Abbasy, M., L. Harris, and P. Ellman. (1937) Vitamin C and infection. Excretion of vitamin C in pulmonary tuberculosis and in rheumatoid arthritis. *The Lancet* 2:181-183.

Abbasy, M., N. Hill, M. Lond, and L. Harris. (1936) Vitamin C and juvenile rheumatism with some observations on the vitamin-C reserves in surgical tuberculosis. *The Lancet* 2:1413-1417.

Albrecht, E. (1938) Vitamin C as an adjuvant in the therapy of lung tuberculosis. *Medizinische Klinic* (Munchen) 34:972-973.

Alexander, F. and H. Meleney. (1935) A study of diets in two rural communities in Tennessee in which amebiasis was prevalent. *American Journal of Hygiene* 22:704-730.

Allard, J., E. Aghdassi, J. Chau, C. Tam, C. Kovacs, I. Salit, and S. Walmsley. (1998) Effects of vitamin E and C supplementation on oxidative stress and viral load in HIV infected subjects. *AIDS* 12(13):1653-1659.

Amato, G. (1937) Azione dell'acido ascorbico sul virus fisso della rabbia e sulla tossina tetanica. *Giornale di Batteriologia, Virologia et Immunologia* (Torino) 19:843-847.

Anderson, R. and O. Dittrich. (1979) Effects of ascorbate on leucocytes. Part IV. Increased neutrophil function and clinical improvement after oral ascorbate in 2 patients with chronic granulomatous disease. *South African Medical Journal* 56(12):476-480.

Anderson, R. and A. Theron. (1979) Effects of ascorbate on leucocytes. Part III. *In vitro* and *in vivo* stimulation of abnormal neutrophil motility by ascorbate. *South African Medical Journal* 56(11):429-433.

Anderson, R., R. Oosthuizen, R. Maritz, A. Theron, and A. Van Rensburg. (1980) The effects of increasing weekly doses of ascorbate on certain cellular and humoral immune functions in normal volunteers. *The American Journal of Clinical Nutrition* 33(1):71-76.

Anderson, R., I. Hay, H. van Wyk, R. Oosthuizen, and A. Theron. (1980a) The effect of ascorbate on cellular humoral immunity in asthmatic children. *South African Medical Journal* 58(24):974-977.

Andreasen, C. and D. Frank. (1999) The effects of ascorbic acid on in vitro heterophil function. *Avian Diseases* 43(4):656-663.

Atkinson, J., A. Weiss, M. Ito, J. Kelly, and C. Parker. (1979) Effects of ascorbic acid and sodium ascorbate on cyclic nucleotide metabolism in human lymphocytes. *Journal of Cyclic Nucleotide Research* 5(2):107-123.

Awotedu, A., E. Sofowora, and S. Ette. (1984) Ascorbic acid deficiency in pulmonary tuberculosis. *East African Medical Journal* 61(4): 283-287.

Babbar, I. (1948) Observations of ascorbic acid. Part XI. Therapeutic effect of ascorbic acid in tuberculosis. *The Indian Medical Gazette* 83:409-410.

Baetgen, D. (1961) [Results of the treatment of epidemic hepatitis in children with high doses of ascorbic acid in the years 1957-1958]. German. *Medizinische Monatschrift* 15:30-36.

Bagchi, D., M. Bagchi, S. Stohs, D. Das, S. Ray, C. Kuszynski, S. Joshi, and H. Pruess. (2000) Free radicals and grape seed proanthocyanidin extract: importance in human health and disease prevention. *Toxicology* 148(2-3):187-197.

Bakhsh, I. and M. Rabbani. (1939) Vitamin C in pulmonary tuberculosis. *The Indian Medical Gazette* 74:274-277.

Bamberger, P. and L. Wendt. (1935) *Klinische Wochenschrift* 14:846.

Bamberger, P. and W. Zell. (1936) *Zeitschrift Kinderheilk* 58:307.

Banerjee, S., P. Sen, and B. Guha. (1940) Urinary excretion of combined ascorbic acid in pulmonary tuberculosis. *Nature* 145(3679): 706-707.

Banic, S. (1975) Prevention of rabies by vitamin C. *Nature* 258(5531):153-154.

Banic, S. (1982) Immunostimulation by vitamin C. *International Journal for Vitamin and Nutrition Research*. Supplement 23:49-52.

Baur, H. (1952) [Poliomyelitis therapy with ascorbic acid]. German. *Helvetia Medica Acta* 19:470-474.

Baur, H. and H. Staub. (1954) [Therapy of hepatitis with ascorbic acid infusions]. Article in German. *Schweizerische Medizinische Wochenschrift* 84:595-597.

Bechelli, L. (1939) Vitamin C therapy of the lepra reaction. *Revista Brasileira de Leprologia* (Sao Paulo) 7:251-255.

Belfield, W. (1967) Vitamin C in treatment of canine and feline distemper complex. *Veterinary Medicine/Small Animal Clinician* 62(4):345-348.

Belfield, W. and I. Stone. (1975) Megascorbic prophylaxis and megascorbic therapy: a new orthomolecular modality in veterinary medicine. *Journal of the International Academy of Preventive Medicine* 2:10-26.

Bhaduri, J. and S. Banerjee. (1960) Ascorbic acid, dehydro-ascorbic acid and glutathione levels in blood of patients suffering from infectious diseases. *The Indian Journal of Medical Research* 48: 208-211.

Bieling, R. (1925) *Zeitschrift fur Hyg* 104:518.

Birkhaug, K. (1938) The role of vitamin C in the pathogenesis of tuberculosis in the guinea-pig. I. Daily excretion of vitamin C in urine of L-ascorbic acid treated and control tuberculous animals. II. Vitamin C content of suprarenals of L-ascorbic acid treated and control tuberculous animals. *Acta Tuberculosea Scandinavica* 12: 89-104.

(1938) III. Quantitative variations in the haemogram of L-ascorbic acid treated and control tuberculous animals. *Acta Tuberculosea Scandinavica* 12:359-372.

(1939) IV. Effect of L-ascorbic acid on the tuberculin reaction in tuberculous animals. *Acta Tuberculosea Scandinavica* 13:45-51.

(1939) V. Degree of tuberculosis in L-ascorbic acid treated and control tuberculosis animals. *Acta Tuberculosea Scandinavica* 13:52-66.

Bjornesjo, K. (1951) On the effect of human urine on tubercle bacilli. II. The tuberculostatic effect of various urine constituents. *Acta Tuberculosea Scandinavica* 25:447.

(1951) III. The solubility of the tuberculostatic factor in organic solvents, and its behavior in dialysis and electrodialysis. *Acta Tuberculosea Scandinavica* 25:457.

(1952) IV. Some attempts to concentrate and purify the tuberculostatic factor. *Acta Tuberculosea Scandinavica* 27:116.

(1952) V. Experiments with the tuberculostatic factor purified from urine. *Acta Tuberculosea Scandinavica* 27:123.

Bogden, J., H. Baker, O. Frank, G. Perez, F. Kemp, K. Bruening, and D. Louria. (1990) Micronutrient status and human immunodeficiency virus (HIV) infection. *Annals of the New York Academy of Science* 587:189-195.

Bogen, E., L. Hawkins, and E. Bennett. (1941) Vitamin C treatment of mucous membrane tuberculosis. *American Review of Tuberculosis* 44:596-603.

Bonnholtzer, E. (1937) *Deutsches Med Wochenschrift* 26:1001.

Borsalino, G. (1937) La fragilita capillare nella tubercolosi polmonare e le sue modificazioni per azione della vitamin C. *Giornale di Clinica Medica* (Bologna) 18:273-294.

Bossevain, C. and J. Spillane. (1937) A note on the effect of synthetic ascorbic acid (vitamin C) on the growth of the tubercle bacillus. *American Review of Tuberculosis* 35:661-662.

Boura, P., G. Tsapas, A. Papadopoulou, I. Magoula, and G. Kountouras. (1989) Monocyte locomotion in anergic chronic brucellosis patients: the *in vivo* effect of ascorbic acid. *Immunopharmacology and Immunotoxicology* 11(1):119-129.

Bourke, G., R. Coleman, and N. Rencricca. (1980) Effect of ascorbic acid on host resistance in virulent rodent malaria. *Clinical Research* 28(3):642A.

Bourne, G. (1949) Vitamin C and immunity. *The British Journal of Nutrition* 2:342.

Boxer, L., A. Watanabe, M. Rister, H. Besch, J. Allen, and R. Baehner. (1976) Correction of leukocyte function in Chediak-Higashi syndrome by ascorbate. *The New England Journal of Medicine* 295(19):1041-1045.

Boxer, L., B. Vanderbilt, S. Bonsib, R. Jersild, H. Yang, and R. Baehner. (1979) Enhancement of chemotactic response and microtubule assembly in human leukocytes by ascorbic acid. *Journal of Cellular Physiology* 100(1):119-126.

Boyden, S. and M. Andersen. (1956) Diet and experimental tuberculosis in the guinea pig. The importance of the source of ascorbic acid. *Acta Pathologica et Microbiologica Scandinavica* 39:107-116.

Brown, H. (1936) Whooping cough. *Clin J* 65:246.

Buffinton, G., S. Christen, E. Peterhans, and R. Stocker. (1992) Oxidative stress in lungs of mice infected with influenza A virus. *Free Radical Research Communications* 16(2):99-110.

Bumbalo, T. (1938) Urinary output of vitamin C of normal and of sick children. With a laboratory test for its estimation. *American Journal of Diseases of Children* 55:1212-1220.

Bumbalo, T. and W. Jetter. (1938) Vitamin C in tuberculosis. The effect of supplementary synthetic vitamin C on the urinary output of this vitamin by tuberculous children. *The Journal of Pediatrics* 13:334-340.

Calleja, H. and R. Brooks. (1960) Acute hepatitis treated with high doses of vitamin C. *The Ohio State Medical Journal* 56:821-823.

Campbell, J., M. Cole, B. Bunditrutavorn, and A. Vella. (1999) Ascorbic acid is a potent inhibitor of various forms of T cell apoptosis. *Cellular Immunology* 194(1):1-5.

Campbell, M. and E. Warner. (1930) *Lancet* 1:61.

Carlsson, S., N. Wiklund, L. Engstrand, E. Weitzberg, and J. Lundberg. (2001) Effects of pH, nitrite, and ascorbic acid on nonenzymatic nitric oxide generation and bacterial growth in urine. *Nitric Oxide: Biology and Chemistry* 5(6):580-586.

Carr, A., R. Einstein, L. Lai, N. Martin, and G. Starmer. (1981) Vitamin C and the common cold: using identical twins as controls. *The Medical Journal of Australia* 2(8):411-412.

Cathcart, R. (1981) Vitamin C, titrating to bowel tolerance, anascorbemia, and acute induced scurvy. *Medical Hypotheses* 7(11):1359-1376.

Cathcart, R. (1984) Vitamin C in the treatment of acquired immune deficiency syndrome (AIDS). *Medical Hypotheses* 14(4):423-433.

Cathcart, R. (1990) Letter to the Editor. *Lancet* 335:235.

Cecil Textbook of Medicine (2000) 21st ed. Edited by Goldman, L. and J. Bennett, Philadelphia, PA: W.B. Saunders Company.

Chang, C. and T. Lan. (1940) Vitamin C in tuberculosis. Ascorbic acid content of blood and urine of tuberculosis patients. *American Review of Tuberculosis* 41:494-506.

Charpy, J. (1948) Ascorbic acid in very large doses alone or with vitamin D2 in tuberculosis. *Bulletin de l'academie Nationale de Medecine* (Paris) 132:421-423.

Clarke, J. (1930) *Journal of Tropical Medicine and Hygiene* 33:249.

Ciocoiu, M., E. Lupusoru, V. Colev, M. Badescu, and I. Paduraru. (1998) [The involvement of vitamins C and E in changing the immune response]. Article in Romanian. *Revista Medico-Chirurgicala a Societatii de Medici si Naturalisti din Iasi* 102(1-2): 93-96.

Corberand, J., F. Nguyen, B. Fraysse, and L. Enjalbert. (1982) Malignant external otitis and polymorphonuclear leukocyte migration impairment. Improvement with ascorbic acid. *Archives of Otolaryngology* 108(2):122-124.

Coulehan, J., S. Eberhard, L. Kapner, F. Taylor, K. Rogers, and P. Garry. (1976) Vitamin C and acute illness in Navajo school children. *The New England Journal of Medicine* 295(18):973-977.

Cumming, P., E. Wallace, J. Schorr, and R. Dodd. (1989) Exposure of patients to human immunodeficiency virus through the transfusion of blood components that test antibody-negative. *The New England Journal of Medicine* 321(14):941-946.

Cunningham-Rundles, S. (1982) Effects of nutritional status on immunological function. *The American Journal of Clinical Nutrition* 35(5 Suppl):1202-1210.

Dahl, H. and M. Degre. (1976) The effect of ascorbic acid on production of human interferon and the antiviral activity in vitro. *Acta Pathologica et Microbiologica Scandinavica*. Section B, Microbiology 84(5):280-284.

Dainow, I. (1943) Treatment of herpes zoster with vitamin C. *Dermatologia* 68:197-201.

Dalldorf, G. (1933) *American Journal of Diseases of Children* 46:794.

Dallegri, F., G. Lanzi, and F. Patrone. (1980) Effects of ascorbic acid on neutrophil locomotion. *International Archives of Allergy and Applied Immunology* 61(1):40-45.

Dalton, W. (1962) Massive doses of vitamin C in the treatment of viral diseases. *Journal of the Indiana State Medical Association* August, pp. 1151-1154.

Daoud, A., A. Abdel-Ghaffar, F. Deyab, and T. Essa. (2000) The effect of antioxidant preparation (antox) on the course and efficacy of treatment of trichinosis. *Journal of the Egyptian Society of Parasitology* 30(1):305-314.

Das, B., J. Patnaik, S. Mohanty, S. Mishra, D. Mohanty, S. Satpathy, and T. Bose. (1993) Plasma antioxidants and lipid peroxidation products in falciparum malaria. *The American Journal of Tropical Medicine and Hygiene* 49(6):720-725.

De la Asuncion, J., M. del Olmo, J. Sastre, A. Millan, A. Pellin, F. Pallardo, and J. Vina. (1998) AZT treatment induces molecular and ultrastructural oxidative damage to muscle mitochondria. Prevention by antioxidant vitamins. *The Journal of Clinical Investigation* 102(1):4-9.

De la Fuente, M., M. Ferrandez, M. Burgos, A. Soler, A. Prieto, and J. Miquel. (1998) Immune function in aged women is improved by ingestion of vitamins C and E. *Canadian Journal of Physiology and Pharmacology* 76(4):373-380.

Destro, R. and V. Sharma. (1977) An appraisal of vitamin C in adjunct therapy of bacterial and "viral" meningitis. *Clinical Pediatrics* 16(10):936-939.

Devasena, T., S. Lalitha, and K. Padma. (2001) Lipid peroxidation, osmotic fragility and antioxidant status in children with acute post-streptococcal glomerulonephritis. *Clinica Chimica Acta* 308(1-2):155-161.

Dey, P. (1966) Efficacy of vitamin C in counteracting tetanus toxicity. *Die Naturwissenschaften* 53(12):310.

Dey, P. (1967) Protective action of ascorbic acid & its precursors on the convulsive & lethal actions of strychnine. *Indian Journal of Experimental Biology* 5(2):110-112.

Dieckhoff, J. and K. Schuler. (1938) *Klinische Wochenschrift* 17:936.

Docampo, R., S. Moreno, and F. Cruz. (1988) Enhancement of the cytotoxicity of crystal violet against *Trypanosoma cruzi* in the blood by ascorbate. *Molecular and Biochemical Parasitology* 27(2-3):241-247.

Douglas, R., E. Chalker, and B. Treacy. (2000) Vitamin C for preventing and treating the common cold. *Cochrane Database of Systematic Reviews* (2):CD000980.

Downes, J. (1950) An experiment in the control of tuberculosis among Negroes. *The Milbank Memorial Fund Quarterly* 28:127-159.

Drummond, J. (1943) Recent advances in the treatment of enteric fever. *Clinical Proceedings* (South Africa) 2:65-93.

Dubey, S., K. Sinha, and J. Gupta. (1985) Vitamin C status, glutathione and histamine in gastric carcinoma, tuberculous enteritis and non-specific ulcerative colitis. *Indian Journal of Physiology and Pharmacology* 29(2):111-114.

Dubey, S., G. Palodhi, and A. Jain. (1987) Ascorbic acid, dehydroascorbic acid and glutathione in liver disease. *Indian Journal of Physiology and Pharmacology* 31(4):279-283.

Ecker, E. and L. Pillemer. (1940) Vitamin C requirement of the guinea pig. *Proceedings of the Society for Experimental Biology and Medicine* 44:262.

Edwards, W. (1968) Ascorbic acid for treatment of feline rhinotracheitis. *Veterinary Medicine/Small Animal Clinician* 63:696-698.

Eller, C., F. Edwards, and E. Wynne. (1968) Sporicidal action of autooxidized ascorbic acid for *Clostridium*. *Applied Microbiology* 16(2): 349-354.

Elsdon-Dew, R. (1949) Endemic fulminating amebic dysentery. *American Journal of Tropical Medicine* 29:337-340.

Elsdon-Dew, R. (1950) Amoebiasis in Natal. *South African Medical Journal* 24:160.

Ericsson, Y. (1954) The effect of ascorbic acid oxidation on mucoids and bacteria in body secretions. *Acta Pathologica et Microbiologica Scandinavica* 35:573-583.

Erwin, G., R. Wright, and C. Doherty. (1940) Hypovitaminosis C and pulmonary tuberculosis. *British Medical Journal* 1:688-689.

Esposito, A. (1986) Ascorbate modulates antibacterial mechanisms in experimental pneumococcal pneumonia. *The American Review of Respiratory Disease* 133(4):643-647.

Evans, R., L. Currie, and A. Campbell. (1982) The distribution of ascorbic acid between various cellular components of blood, in normal individuals, and its relation to the plasma concentration. *The British Journal of Nutrition* 47(3):473-482.

Everall, I., L. Hudson, and R. Kerwin. (1997) Decreased absolute levels of ascorbic acid and unaltered vasoactive intestinal polypeptide receptor binding in the frontal cortex in acquired immunodeficiency syndrome. *Neuroscience Letters* 224(2):119-122.

Eylar, E., I. Baez, J. Navas, and C. Mercado. (1996) Sustained levels of ascorbic acid are toxic and immunosuppressive for human T cells. *Puerto Rico Health Sciences Journal* 15(1):21-26.

Falk, G., K. Gedda, and G. Gothlin. (1932) *Upsala Lakaref Forh* 38:1.

Farah, N. (1938) Enteric fever treated with suprarenal cortex extract and vitamin C intravenously. *Lancet* 1:777-779.

Faulkner, J. and F. Taylor. (1937) Vitamin C and infection. *Annals of Internal Medicine* 10:1867-1873.

Faust, E. and E. Kagy. (1934) Studies on the pathology of amebic enteritis in dogs. *American Journal of Tropical Medicine* 14:221-233.

Faust, E., L. Scott, and J. Swartzwelder. (1934) Influence of certain foodstuffs on lesions of *Entamoeba histolytica* infection. *Proceedings of the Society for Experimental Biology and Medicine* 32:540-542.

Faust, E. and J. Swartzwelder. (1936) Use of liver extract intramuscularly in the course of acute amebiasis in dogs. *Proceedings of the Society for Experimental Biology and Medicine* 33:514-518.

Feigen, G., B. Smith, C. Dix, C. Flynn, N. Peterson, L. Rosenberg, S. Pavlovic, and B. Leibovitz. (1982) Enhancement of antibody production and protection against systemic anaphylaxis by large doses of vitamin C. *Research Communications in Chemical Pathology and Pharmacology* 38(2):313-333.

Ferreira, D. (1950) Vitamin C in leprosy. *Publicacoes Medicas* 20:25-28.

Findlay, G. (1923) The relation of vitamin C to bacterial infection. *Journal of Pathology and Bacteriology* 26(1):1-19.

Floch, H. and P. Sureau. (1952) Vitamin C therapy in leprosy. *Bulletin de la Societe de Pathologie Exotique et de Ses Filiales* (Paris) 45:443-446.

Forbes, J. and G. Duncan. (1954) Effect of alcohol intoxication and ACTH on liver ascorbic acid in the guinea pig. *Endocrinology* 55:822-827.

Foster, D., E. Obineche, and N. Traub. (1974) The effect of pyridoxine, folic acid and ascorbic acid therapy on the incidence of sideroblastic anaemia in Zambians with chloramphenicol treated typhoid. A preliminary report. *East African Medical Journal* 51(1):20-25.

Fraser, R., S. Pavlovic, C. Kurahara, A. Murata, N. Peterson, K. Taylor, and G. Feigen. (1980) The effect of variations in vitamin C intake on the cellular immune response of guinea pigs. *The American Journal of Clinical Nutrition* 33(4):839-847.

Galloway, T. and M. Seifert. (1949) Bulbar poliomyelitis: favorable results in its treatment as a problem in respiratory obstruction. *Journal of the American Medical Association* 141(1):1-8.

Gander, J. and W. Niederberger. (1936) *Munchener Medizinische Wochenschrift* 83:1386.

Ganguly, R., M. Durieux, and R. Waldman. (1976) Macrophage function in vitamin C -deficient guinea pigs. *The American Journal of Clinical Nutrition* 29(7):762-765.

Gatti, C. and R. Gaona. (1939) Ascorbic acid in the treatment of leprosy. *Archiv Schiffe-und Tropenhygiene* 43:32-33.

Geber, W., S. Lefkowitz, and C. Hung. (1975) Effect of ascorbic acid, sodium salicylate, and caffeine on the serum interferon level in response to viral infection. *Pharmacology* 13(3):228-233.

Getz, H. and T. Koerner. (1941) Vitamin A and ascorbic acid in pulmonary tuberculosis. Determination in plasma by the photoelectric colorimeter. *The American Journal of the Medical Sciences* 202:831-847.

Getz, H. and T. Koerner. (1943) Vitamin nutrition in tuberculosis. *American Review of Tuberculosis* 47:274-283.

Getz, H., E. Long, and H. Henderson. (1951) A study of the relation of nutrition to the development of tuberculosis. Influence of ascorbic acid and vitamin A. *American Review of Tuberculosis* 64:381-393.

Glazebrook, A. and S. Thomson. (1942) The administration of vitamin C in a large institution and its effect on general health and resistance to infection. *Journal of Hygiene* 42(1):1-19.

Glick, D. and S. Hosoda. (1965) Histochemistry. LXXViii. Ascorbic acid in normal mast cells and macrophages and neoplastic mast cells. *Proceedings of the Society for Experimental Biology and Medicine* 119:52-56.

Gnarpe, H., M. Michaelsson, and S. Dreborg. (1968) The *in vitro* effect of ascorbic acid on the bacterial growth in urine. *Acta Pathologica et Microbiologica Scandinavica* 74(1):41-50.

Goetzl, E., S. Wasserman, I. Gigli, and K. Austen. (1974) Enhancement of random migration and chemotactic response of human leukocytes by ascorbic acid. *The Journal of Clinical Investigation* 53(3):813-818.

Gogu, S., B. Beckman, S. Rangan, and K. Agrawal. (1989) Increased therapeutic efficacy of zidovudine in combination with vitamin E. *Biochemical and Biophysical Research Communications* 165(1): 401-407.

Goldschmidt, M. (1991) Reduced bactericidal activity in neutrophils from scorbutic animals and the effect of ascorbic acid on these target bacteria *in vivo* and *in vitro*. *The American Journal of Clinical Nutrition* 54(6 Suppl):1214S-1220S.

Gorton, H. and K. Jarvis. (1999) The effectiveness of vitamin C in preventing and relieving the symptoms of virus-induced respiratory infections. *Journal of Manipulative and Physiological Therapeutics* 22(8):530-533.

Goskowicz, M. and L. Eichenfield. (1993) Cutaneous findings of nutritional deficiencies in children. *Current Opinion in Pediatrics* 5(4): 441-445.

Grant, A. (1930) *American Review of Tuberculosis* 21:115.

Greene, M., M. Steiner, and B. Kramer. (1936) The role of chronic vitamin-C deficiency in the pathogenesis of tuberculosis in the guinea pig. *American Review of Tuberculosis* 33:585-624.

Greenwald, C. and E. Harde. (1935) Vitamin C and diphtheria toxin. *Proceedings of the Society for Experimental Biology and Medicine* 32:1157-1160.

Greer, E. (1955) Vitamin C in acute poliomyelitis. *Medical Times* 83(11):1160-1161.

Gunzel, W. and G. Kroehnert. (1937) Experiences in the treatment of pneumonia with vitamin C. *Fortschrifte der Therapie* 13:460-463.

Gupta, G. and B. Guha. (1941) The effect of vitamin C and certain other substances on the growth of microorganisms. *Annals of Biochemistry and Experimental Medicine* 1(1):14-26.

Hamdy, A., W. Pounden, A. Trapp, D. Redman, and D. Bell. (1967) Effect of vitamin C on lamb pneumonia and mortality. *The Cornell Veterinarian* 57(1):12-20.

Hamuy, R. and B. Berman. (1998) Treatment of Herpes simplex virus infections with topical antiviral agents. *European Journal of Dermatology* 8(5):310-319.

Hanzlik, P. and B. Terada. (1936) Protective measures in diphtheria intoxication. *Journal of Pharmacology and Experimental Therapeutics* 56:269-277.

Harakeh, S., R. Jariwalla, and L. Pauling. (1990) Suppression of human immunodeficiency virus replication by ascorbate in chronically and acutely infected cells. *Proceedings of the National Academy of Sciences of the United States of America* 87(18): 7245-7249.

Harakeh, S. and R. Jariwalla. (1991) Comparative study of the anti-HIV activities of ascorbate and thiol-containing reducing agents in chronically HIV-infected cells. *The American Journal of Clinical Nutrition* 54(6 Suppl):1231S-1235S.

Harakeh, S. and R. Jariwalla. (1997) NF-kappa B-independent suppression of HIV expression by ascorbic acid. *AIDS Research and Human Retroviruses* 13(3):235-239.

Harde, E. and M. Philippe. (1934) Observations sur le pouvoir antigene du melange toxine diphtherique et vitamin C. *Compt rend Acad d sc* 199:738-739.

Haskell, B. and C. Johnston. (1991) Complement component C1q activity and ascorbic acid nutriture in guinea pigs. *The American Journal of Clinical Nutrition* 54(6 Suppl):1228S-1230S.

Hasselbach, F. (1935) Therapy of tuberculosis pulmonary hemorrhages with vitamin C. *Fortschrift der Therapie* 7:407-411.

Hasselbach, F. (1936) *Zeitschrift Tuberkulose* 75:336.

Hastings, R., V. Richard, Jr., S. Christy, and M. Morales. (1976) Activity of ascorbic acid in inhibiting the multiplication of *M. leprae* in the mouse foot pad. *International Journal of Leprosy and Other Mycobacterial Diseases* 44(4):427-430.

Heise, F. and G. Martin. (1936) Ascorbic acid metabolism in tuberculosis. *Proceedings of the Society for Experimental Biology and Medicine* 34:642-644.

Heise, F. and G. Martin. (1936a) Supervitaminosis C in tuberculosis. *Proceedings of the Society for Experimental Biology and Medicine* 35:337-338.

Heise, F., G. Martin, and S. Schwartz. (1937) The influence of the administration of vitamin C on blood sedimentation and sensitivity to tuberculin. *British Journal of Tuberculosis* 31:23-31.

Hemila, H. (1994) Does vitamin C alleviate the symptoms of the common cold?—a review of current evidence. *Scandinavian Journal of Infectious Disease* 26(1):1-6.

Hemila, H. (1996) Vitamin C, the placebo effect, and the common cold: a case study of how preconceptions influence the analysis of results. *Journal of Clinical Epidemiology* 49(10):1079-1084.

Hemila, H. (1997) Vitamin C intake and susceptibility to pneumonia. *The Pediatric Infectious Disease Journal* 16(9):836-837.

Hemila, H. and R. Douglas. (1999) Vitamin C and acute respiratory infections. *The International Journal of Tuberculosis and Lung Disease* 3(9):756-761.

Hemila, H., J. Kaprio, P. Pietinen, D. Albanes, and O. Heinonen. (1999) Vitamin C and other compounds in vitamin C rich food in relation to risk of tuberculosis in male smokers. *American Journal of Epidemiology* 150(6):632-641.

Hennet, T., E. Peterhans, and R. Stocker. (1992) Alterations in antioxidant defences in lung and liver of mice infected with influenza A virus. *The Journal of General Virology* 73(Pt 1):39-46.

Hershko, C. (1989) Mechanism of iron toxicity and its possible role in red cell membrane damage. *Seminars in Hematology* 26(4): 277-285.

Heuser, G. and A. Vojdani. (1997) Enhancement of natural killer cell activity and T and B cell function by buffered vitamin C in patients exposed to toxic chemicals: the role of protein kinase-C. *Immunopharmacology and Immunotoxicology* 19(3):291-312.

Hill, C. and H. Garren. (1955) The effect of high levels of vitamins on the resistance of chicks to fowl typhoid. *Annals of the New York Academy of Sciences* 63:186-194.

Hochwald, A. (1937) *Deutsches Med Wochenschrift* 63:182.

Hojer, J. (1924) Studies in scurvy. Part IV. Scurvy and tuberculosis. *Acta Paediatr* 3(suppl):140-171.

Holden, M. and R. Resnick. (1936) The *in vitro* action of synthetic crystalline vitamin C (ascorbic acid) on herpes virus. *Journal of Immunology* 31:455-462.

Holden, M. and E. Molloy. (1937) Further experiments on the inactivation of herpes virus by vitamin C (L-ascorbic acid). *Journal of Immunology* 33:251-257.

Honjo, S. and K. Imaizumi. (1967) Ascorbic acid content of adrenal and liver in cynomolgus monkeys suffering from bacillary dysentery. *Japanese Journal of Medical Science & Biology* 20(1):97-102.

Honjo, S., M. Takasaka, T. Fujiwara, K. Imaizumi, and H. Ogawa. (1969) Shigellosis in cynomolgus monkeys (Macaca irus) VII. Experimental production of dysentery with a relatively small dose of Shigella flexneri 2a in ascorbic acid deficient monkeys. Japanese Journal of Medical Science & Biology 22(3):149-162.

Horrobin, D., M. Manku, M. Oka, R. Morgan, S. Cunnane, A. Ally, T. Ghayur, M. Schweitzer, and R. Karmali. (1979) The nutritional regulation of T lymphocyte function. Medical Hypotheses 5(9): 969-985.

Hovi, T., A. Hirvimies, M. Stenvik, E. Vuola, and R. Pippuri. (1995) Topical treatment of recurrent mucocutaneous herpes with ascorbic acid-containing solution. Antiviral Research 27(3):263-270.

Huggins, H. and T. Levy. (1999) Uninformed Consent: The Hidden Dangers in Dental Care. Charlottesville, VA: Hampton Roads Publishing Company, Inc.

Hunt, C., N. Chakravorty, G. Annan, N. Habibzadeh, and C. Schorah. (1994) The clinical effects of vitamin C supplementation in elderly hospitalized patients with acute respiratory infections. International Journal for Vitamin and Nutrition Research 64(3): 212-219.

Hurford, J. (1938) Lancet I:498.

Imamura, T. (1929) Acta Medicin Keijo 12:249.

Ivanov, K., S. Ponomarev, A. Gorelov, I. Volchek, S. Basos, V. Volzhanin, and E. Samgina. (1991) [The clinical picture of the initial period of intestinal amebiasis]. Article in Russian. Meditsinskaia Parazitologiia i Parazitarnye Bolezni 2:38-40.

Jahan, K., K. Ahmad, and M. Ali. (1984) Effect of ascorbic acid in the treatment of tetanus. Bangladesh Medical Research Council Bulletin 10(1):24-28.

Jefferies, C. (1965) Effect of endotoxin on liver ascorbic acid of mice. Journal of Bacteriology 89: 922-923.

Jeng, K., C. Yang, W. Siu, Y. Tsai, W. Liao, and J. Kuo. (1996) Supplementation with vitamins C and E enhances cytokine production by peripheral blood mononuclear cells in healthy adults. The American Journal of Clinical Nutrition 64(6):960-965.

Jetter, T. and T. Bumbalo. (1938) The urinary output of vitamin C in active tuberculosis in children. American Journal of Medical Science 195:362-366.

Joffe, M., N. Sukha, and A. Rabson. (1983) Lymphocyte subsets in measles. Depressed helper/inducer subpopulation reversed by in vitro treatment with levamisole and ascorbic acid. *The Journal of Clinical Investigation* 72(3):971-980.

Johnston, C., W. Kolb, and B. Haskell. (1987) The effect of vitamin C nutriture on complement component C1q concentrations in guinea pig plasma. *The Journal of Nutrition* 117(4):764-768.

Johnston, C., L. Martin, and X. Cai. (1992) Antihistamine effect of supplemental ascorbic acid and neutrophil chemotaxis. *Journal of the American College of Nutrition* 11(2):172-176.

Josewich, A. (1939) Value of vitamin C therapy in lung tuberculosis. *Medical Bulletin of the Veterans Administration* 16:8-11.

Jungeblut, C. (1935) Inactivation of poliomyelitis virus *in vitro* by crystalline vitamin C (ascorbic acid). *Journal of Experimental Medicine* 62:517-521.

Jungeblut, C. (1937) Vitamin C therapy and prophylaxis in experimental poliomyelitis. *Journal of Experimental Medicine* 65:127-146.

Jungeblut, C. (1937a) Further observations on vitamin C therapy in experimental poliomyelitis. *Journal of Experimental Medicine* 66: 459-477.

Jungeblut, C. (1937b) Inactivation of tetanus toxin by crystalline vitamin C (L-ascorbic acid). *Journal of Immunology* 33:203-214.

Jungeblut, C. (1939) A further contribution to vitamin C therapy in experimental poliomyelitis. *Journal of Experimental Medicine* 70: 315-332.

Jungeblut, C. and R. Zwemer. (1935) Inactivation of diphtheria toxin *in vivo* and *in vitro* by crystalline vitamin C (ascorbic acid). *Proceedings of the Society for Experimental Biology and Medicine* 32:1229-1234.

Kaiser, A. and B. Slavin. (1938) The incidence of hemolytic streptococci in the tonsils of children as related to the vitamin C content of tonsils and blood. *Journal of Pediatrics* 13:322-333.

Kalokerinos, A. (1976) Letter: Severe measles in Vietnam. *The Medical Journal of Australia* 1(16):593-594.

Kalokerinos, A. (1981) *Every Second Child.* New Canaan, CT: Keats Publishing, Inc.

Kameta, T. (1959) Studies on the effects of ACTH, cortisone and adrenaline on ascorbic acid in rabbits' organs. [Japanese] *Japanese Journal of Urology* 50:1214-1224.

Kaplan, A. and M. Zonnis. (1940) Vitamin C in pulmonary tuberculosis. *American Review of Tuberculosis* 42:667-673.

Karlowski, T., T. Chalmers, L. Frenkel, A. Kapakian, T. Lewis, and J. Lynch. (1975) Ascorbic acid for the common cold. A prophylactic and therapeutic trial. *The Journal of the American Medical Association* 231(10):1038-1042.

Karpinska, T., Z. Kawecki, and M. Kandefer-Szerszen. (1982) The influence of ultraviolet irradiation, L-ascorbic acid and calcium chloride on the induction of interferon in human embryo fibroblasts. *Archivum Immunologiae et Therapiae Experimentalis* 30(1-2)33-37.

Kastenbauer, S., U. Koedel, B. Becker, and H. Pfister. (2002) Oxidative stress in bacterial meningitis in humans. *Neurology* 58(2):186-191.

Kataoka, A., H. Imai, S. Inayoshi, and T. Tsuda. (1993) Intermittent high-dose vitamin C therapy in patients with HTLV-1 associated myelopathy. *Journal of Neurology, Neurosurgery, and Psychiatry* 56(11):1213-1216.

Kataoka, A., H. Imai, S. Inayoshi, and T. Tsuda. (1993a) [Intermittent high-dose vitamin C therapy in patients with HTLV-1-associated myelopathy]. Article in Japanese. *Rinsho Shinkeigaku. Clinical Neurology* 33(3):282-288.

Kato, M. (1967) Studies of a biochemical lesion in experimental tuberculosis in mice. VI. Effect of toxic bacterial constituents of tubercle bacilli on oxidative phosphorylation in host cell. *American Review of Respiratory Disease* 96(5):998-1008.

Kelly, F. (1944) Bacteriology of artificially produced necrotic lesions in the oropharynx of the monkey. *Journal of Infectious Diseases* 74: 93-108.

Kennes, B., I. Dumont, D. Brohee, C. Hubert, and P. Neve. (1983) Effect of vitamin C supplements on cell-mediated immunity in old people. *Gerontology* 29(5):305-310.

Kessel, J. and H. K'e-Kang. (1925) The effect of an exclusive milk diet on intestinal amoebae. *Proceedings of the Society for Experimental Biology and Medicine* 23:388-391.

Kimbarowski, J. and N. Mokrow. (1967) [Colored precipitation reaction of the urine according to Kimbarowski (FARK) as an index of the effect of ascorbic acid during treatment of viral influenza]. Article in German. *Das Deutsche Gesundheitswesen* 22(51):2413-2418.

King, C. and M. Menten. (1935) Influence of vitamin level on resistance to diphtheria toxin. *Journal of Nutrition* 10:129-155.

Kirchmair, H. (1957) [Treatment of epidemic hepatitis in children with high doses of ascorbic acid]. Article in German. *Medizinische Monatschrift* 11:353-357.

Kirchmair, H. (1957a) [Ascorbic acid treatment of epidemic hepatitis in children]. Article in German. *Das Deutsche Gesundheitswesen* 12:773-774.

Kirchmair, H. (1957b) [Epidemic hepatitis in children and its treatment with high doses of ascorbic acid]. Article in German. *Das Deutsche Gesundheitswesen* 12:1525-1536.

Klenner, F. (February 1948) Virus pneumonia and its treatment with vitamin C. *Southern Medicine & Surgery* 110(2):36-38,46.

Klenner, F. (July 1949) The treatment of poliomyelitis and other virus diseases with vitamin C. *Southern Medicine & Surgery* 111(7):209-214.

Klenner, F. (September 1949) Fatigue-normal and pathological with special consideration of myasthenia gravis and multiple sclerosis. *Southern Medicine & Surgery* 111(9):273-277.

Klenner, F. (April 1951) Massive doses of vitamin C and the virus diseases. *Southern Medicine & Surgery* 103(4):101-107.

Klenner, F. (August 1952) The vitamin and massage treatment for acute poliomyelitis. *Southern Medicine & Surgery* 114:194-197.

Klenner, F. (1953) The use of vitamin C as an antibiotic. *Journal of Applied Nutrition* 6:274-278.

Klenner, F. (April 1954) The treatment of trichinosis with massive doses of vitamin C and para-aminobenzoic acid. *Tri-State Medical Journal* pp. 25-30.

Klenner, F. (July 1954) Case history: cure of a 4-year-old child bitten by a mature highland moccasin with vitamin C. *Tri-State Medical Journal*

Klenner, F. (July 1954) Recent discoveries in the treatment of lockjaw with vitamin C and Tolserol. *Tri-State Medical Journal* pp. 7-11.

Klenner, F. (November 1955) The role of ascorbic acid in therapeutics. (Letter to the Editor) *Tri-State Medical Journal* p. 34.

Klenner, F. (February 1956) A new office procedure for the determination of plasma levels for ascorbic acid. *Tri-State Medical Journal* pp. 26-28.

Klenner, F. (September 1956) Poliomyelitis-case histories. *Tri-State Medical Journal* pp. 28-31.

Klenner, F. (June 1957) An "insidious" virus. *Tri-State Medical Journal* pp.10-12.

Klenner, F. (December 1957) The black widow spider: case history. *Tri-State Medical Journal* pp.15-18.

Klenner, F. (October 1958) The clinical evaluation and treatment of a deadly syndrome caused by an insidious virus. *Tri-State Medical Journal* pp. 11-15.

Klenner, F. (February 1959) The folly in the continued use of a killed polio virus vaccine. *Tri-State Medical Journal* pp. 11-19.

Klenner, F. (February 1960) Virus encephalitis as a sequela of the pneumonias. *Tri-State Medical Journal* pp. 7-11.

Klenner, F. (1971) Observations of the dose and administration of ascorbic acid when employed beyond the range of a vitamin in human pathology. *Journal of Applied Nutrition* 23(3&4):61-88.

Klenner, F. (1973) Response of peripheral and central nerve pathology to mega-doses of the vitamin B-complex and other metabolites. *Journal of Applied Nutrition* pp.16-40.

Klenner, F. (1974) Significance of high daily intake of ascorbic acid in preventive medicine. *Journal of the International Academy of Preventive Medicine* 1(1):45-69.

Kligler, I. and H. Bernkopf. (1937) Inactivation of vaccinia virus by ascorbic acid and glutathione. *Nature* 139:965-966.

Kligler, I., L. Leibowitz, and M. Berman. (1937) The effect of ascorbic acid (vitamin C) on toxin production by *C. Diphtheriae* in culture media. *Journal of Pathology* 45:415-429.

Kligler, I., K. Guggenheim, and F. Warburg. (1938) Influence of ascorbic acid on the growth and toxin production of *Cl. tetani* and on the detoxication of tetanus toxin. *Journal of Pathology* 46:619-629.

Knodell, R., M. Tate, B. Akl, and J. Wilson. (1981) Vitamin C prophylaxis for posttransfusion hepatitis: lack of effect in a controlled trial. *American Journal of Clinical Nutrition* 34(1):20-23.

Kodama, T. and T. Kojima. (1939) Studies of the staphylococcal toxin, toxoid and antitoxin; effect of ascorbic acid on staphylococcal lysins and organisms. *Kitasato Archives of Experimental Medicine* 16:36-55.

Komar, V., and V. Vasil'ev. (1992) [The use of water-soluble vitamins in viral hepatitis A]. Article in Russian. *Klinicheskaia Meditsina* 70(1):73-75.

Kotler, D. (1998) Antioxidant therapy and HIV infection: 1998 [editorial]. *The American Journal of Clinical Nutrition* 67:7-9.

Kraut, E., E. Metz, and A. Sagone. (1980) *In vitro* effects of ascorbate on white cell metabolism and the chemiluminescence response. *Journal of the Reticuloendothelial Society* 27(4):359-366.

Krishnan, K. (1938) Calcutta: Annual report of the All-India Institute of Hygiene and Public Health. *Malaria* pp. 27-31. Also cited in: (1940) *Tropical Diseases Bulletin* 37(10):744-745.

Kulacz, R. and T. Levy. (2002) *The Roots of Disease: Connecting Dentistry and Medicine*. Philadelphia, PA: Xlibris Corporation.

Landwehr, R. (1991) The origin of the 42-year stonewall of vitamin C. *Journal of Orthomolecular Medicine* 6(2):99-103.

Ledermann, E. (1962) Vitamin-C deficiency and ulceration of the face. *The Lancet* 2:1382.

Leichtentritt, B. (1924) *Deutsche Medizinische Wochenschrift* 40:672.

Lerner, M. et al. (1972) Detecting herpes encephalitis earlier. *Medical World News* May 26.

Leroy, E., S. Baize, V. Volchkov, S. Fisher-Hoch, M. Georges-Courbot, J. Lansoud-Soukate, M. Capron, P. Debre, J. McCormick, and A. Georges. (2000) Human asymptomatic Ebola infection and strong inflammatory response. *Lancet* 355(9222):2210-2215.

Levander, O. and A. Ager. (1993) Malarial parasites and antioxidant nutrients. *Parasitology* 107 Suppl:S95-S106.

Leveque, J. (1969) Ascorbic acid in treatment of the canine distemper complex. *Veterinary Medicine/Small Animal Clinician* 64(11):997-999, 1001.

Levy, R. and F. Schlaeffer. (1993) Successful treatment of a patient with recurrent furunculosis by vitamin C : improvement of clinical course and of impaired neutrophil functions. *International Journal of Dermatology* 32(11):832-834.

Levy, R., O. Shriker, A. Porath, K. Riesenberg, and F. Schlaeffer. (1996) Vitamin C for the treatment of recurrent furunculosis in patients with impaired neutrophil functions. *The Journal of Infectious Diseases* 173(6):1502-1505.

Li, Y. and T. Lovell. (1985) Elevated levels of dietary ascorbic acid increase immune responses in channel catfish. *The Journal of Nutrition* 115(1):123-131.

Locke, A., R. Locke, R. Bragdon, and R. Mellon. (1937) Fitness, sulfanilamide and pneumococcus infection in the rabbit. *Science* 86(2227):228-229.

Lotze, H. (1938) Klinisch-experimentelle untersuchungen bei malaria tertiana. [Clinical experimental investigations in benign tertian malaria.] *Arch f Schiffs-u Trop-Hyg* 42(7):287-305. Also cited in: (1938) *Tropical Diseases Bulletin* 35:733.

McBroom, J., D. Sunderland, J. Mote, and T. Jones. (1937) Effect of acute scurvy on the guinea-pig heart. *Archives of Pathology* 23: 20-32.

McConkey, M. and D. Smith. (1933) The relation of vitamin C deficiency to intestinal tuberculosis in the guinea pig. *Journal of Experimental Medicine* 58:503-512.

McCormick, W. (1951) Vitamin C in the prophylaxis and therapy of infectious diseases. *Archives of Pediatrics* 68(1):1-9.

McCullough, N. (1938) Vitamin C and resistance of the guinea pig to infection with *Bacterium necrophorum*. *The Journal of Infectious Diseases* 63:34-53.

McKee, R. and Q. Geiman. (1946) Studies on malarial parasites. V. Effects of ascorbic acid on malaria (*Plasmodium knowlesi*) in monkeys. *Proceedings of the Society for Experimental Biology and Medicine* 63:313-315.

McLemore, J., P. Beeley, K. Thornton, K. Morrisroe, W. Blackwell, and A. Dasgupta. (1998) Rapid automated determination of lipid hydroperoxide concentrations and total antioxidant status of serum samples from patients infected with HIV: elevated lipid hydroperoxide concentrations and depleted total antioxidant capacity of serum samples. *American Journal of Clinical Pathology* 109(3):268-273.

Magne, R. Vargas. (1963) Vitamin C in treatment of influenza. *El Dia Medico* 35:1714-1715.

Manders, S. (1998) Toxin-mediated streptococcal and staphylococcal disease. *Journal of the American Academy of Dermatology* 39(3): 383-398.

Martin, G. and F. Heise. (1937) Vitamin C nutrition on pulmonary tuberculosis. *American Journal of Digestive Diseases and Nutrition* 4:368-373.

Marva, E., A. Cohen, P. Saltman, M. Chevion, and J. Golenser. (1989) Deleterious synergistic effects of ascorbate and copper on the development of *Plasmodium falciparum*: an *in vitro* study in normal and in G6PD-deficient erythrocytes. *International Journal of Parasitology* 19(7):779-785.

Marva, E., J. Golenser, A. Cohen, N. Kitrossky, R. Har-el, and M. Chevion. (1992) The effects of ascorbate-induced free radicals on Plasmodium falciparum. *Tropical Medicine and Parasitology* 43(1): 17-23.

Massell, B., J. Warren, P. Patterson, and H. Lehmus. (1950) Antirheumatic activity of ascorbic acid in large doses. Preliminary observations on seven patients with rheumatic fever. *The New England Journal of Medicine* 242(16):614-615.

Matsuo, E., O. Skinsnes, and P. Chang. (1975) Acid mucopolysaccharide metabolism in leprosy. 3. Hyaluronic acid mycobacterial growth enhancement, and growth suppression by saccharic acid and vitamin C as inhibitors of ß-glucuronidase. *International Journal of Leprosy and Other Mycobacterial Diseases* 43(1):1-13.

Meier, K. (1945) Vitamin C treatment of pertussis. *Annales de Pediatrie* (Paris) 164:50-53.

Mick, E. (1955) Brucellosis and its treatment. Observations—preliminary report. *Archives of Pediatrics* 72:119-125.

Miller, T. (1969) Killing and lysis of gram-negative bacteria through the synergistic effect of hydrogen peroxide, ascorbic acid, and lysozyme. *Journal of Bacteriology* 98(3):949-955.

Millet (1940) Paludismo e suprarenaes. Formas suprarenaes do paludismo. Syndrome de fraga. [Malaria and the suprarenal glands.] *Brasil-Medico* 54(3):36-47. Also cited in: (1940) *Tropical Diseases Bulletin* 37(10):744.

Mishra, N., L. Kabilan, and A. Sharma. (1994) Oxidative stress and malaria-infected erythrocytes. *Indian Journal of Malariology* 31(2):77-87.

Mizutani, A., H. Maki, Y. Torii, K. Hitomi, and N. Tsukagoshi. (1998) Ascorbate-dependent enhancement of nitric oxide formation in activated macrophages. *Nitric Oxide: Biology and Chemistry* 2(4): 235-241.

Mizutani, A. and N. Tsukagoshi. (1999) Molecular role of ascorbate in enhancement of NO production in activated macrophage-like cell line, J774.1. *Journal of Nutritional Science and Vitaminology* 45(4):423-435.

Mohr, W. (1941) Vitamin C-stoffwechsel und malaria. [Malaria and assimilation of vitamin C.] *Deut Trop Zeitschrift* 45(13):404-405. Also cited in: (1943) *Tropical Diseases Bulletin* 40(1):13-14.

Moraes-Souza, H. and J. Bordin. (1996) Strategies for prevention of transfusion-associated Chagas' disease. *Transfusion Medicine Reviews* 10(3):161-170.

Morbidity and Mortality Weekly Report (2000) Outbreak of poliomyelitis—Cape Verde, 2000. 49:1070.

Morbidity and Mortality Weekly Report (2001) Outbreak of poliomyelitis—Dominican Republic and Haiti, 2000-2001. 50:147-148.

Morishige, F. and A. Murata. (1978) Vitamin C for prophylaxis of viral hepatitis B in transfused patients. *Journal of the International Academy of Preventive Medicine* 5(1):54-58.

Mouriquand, G., A. Dochaix, and L. Dosdat. (1925) Tuberculose virulente et avitaminose C. *Compt Rend Soc Biol* 93:901.

Muller, R., A. Svardal, I. Nordoy, R. Berge, P. Aukrust, and S. Froland. (2000) Virological and immunological effects of antioxidant treatment in patients with HIV infection. *European Journal of Clinical Investigation* 30(10):905-914.

Murphy, B., J. Krushak, J. Maynard, and D. Bradley. (1974) Ascorbic acid (vitamin C) and its effects on parainfluenza type III virus infection in cotton-topped marmosets. *Laboratory Animal Science* 24(1):229-232.

Myrvik, Q., R. Weiser, B. Houglum, and L. Berger. (1954) Studies on the tuberculoinhibitory properties of ascorbic acid derivatives and their possible role in inhibition of tubercle bacilli by urine. *American Review of Tuberculosis* 69:406-418.

Nakanishi, T. (1992) [A report on a clinical experience of which has successfully made several antibiotics-resistant bacteria (MRSA etc.) negative on a bedsore]. Article in Japanese. *Iqaku Kenkyu, Acta Medica.* 62(1):31-37.

Nakanishi, T. (1993) [A report on the therapeutical experiences of which have successfully made several antibiotics-resistant bacteria (MRSA etc.) negative on bedsores and respiratory organs]. Article in Japanese. *Igaku Kenkyu. Acta Medica.* 63(3):95-100.

Nandi, B., N. Subramanian, A. Majumder, and I. Chatterjee. (1974) Effect of ascorbic acid on detoxification of histamine under stress conditions. *Biochemical Pharmacology* 23(3):643-647.

Naraqi, S., S. Okem, N. Moyia, T. Dutta, B. Zzferio, and D. Lalloo. (1992) Quinine blindness. *Papua and New Guinea Medical Journal* 35(4):308-310.

Nelson, J., J. Alexander, P. Jacobs, R. Ing, and C. Ogle. (1992) Metabolic and immune effects of enteral ascorbic acid after burn trauma. *Burns: Journal of the International Society for Burn Injuries* 18(2):92-97.

Njoku, O., I. Ononogbu, D. Nwachukwu. (1995) Plasma cholesterol, ß-carotene and ascorbic acid changes in human malaria. *The Journal of Communicable Diseases* 27(3):186-190.

Nungester, W. and A. Ames. (1948) The relationship between ascorbic acid and phagocytic activity. *Journal of Infectious Diseases* 83: 50-54.

Oberritter, H., B. Glatthaar, U. Moser, and K. Schmidt. (1986) Effect of functional stimulation on ascorbate content in phagocytes under physiological and pathological conditions. *International Archives of Allergy and Applied Immunology* 81(1):46-50.

Oran, B., E. Atabek, S. Karaaslan, Y. Reisli, F. Gultekin, and Y. Erkul. (2001) Oxygen free radicals in children with acute rheumatic fever. *Cardiology in the Young* 11(3):285-288.

Orens, S. (1983) Hepatitis B—a ten day cure: a personal history. *Bulletin Philadelphia Cty Dental Society* 48(6):4-5.

Ormerod, M. and B. Unkauf. (1937) Ascorbic acid (vitamin C) treatment of whooping cough. *Canadian Medical Association Journal* 37(2):134-136.

Ormerod, M., B. Unkauf, and F. White. (1937) A further report on the ascorbic acid treatment of whooping cough. *Canadian Medical Association Journal* 37(3):268-272.

Osborn, T. and J. Gear. (1940) Possible relation between ability to synthesize vitamin C and reaction to tubercle bacillus. *Nature* 145:974.

Otani, T. (1936) On the vitamin C therapy of pertussis. *Klinische Wochenschrift* 15(51):1884-1885.

Otani, T. (1939) Influence of vitamin C (L-ascorbic acid) upon the whooping cough bacillus and its toxin. *Oriental Journal of Diseases of Infants* 25:1-4.

Paez de la Torre, J. (1945) Ascorbic acid in measles. *Archives Argentinos de Pediatria* 24:225-227.

Pakter, J. and B. Schick. (1938) Influence of vitamin C on diphtheria toxin. *American Journal of Diseases of Children* 55:12-26.

Panush, R., J. Delafuente, P. Katz, and J. Johnson. (1982) Modulation of certain immunologic responses by vitamin C. III. Potentiation of *in vitro* and *in vivo* lymphocyte responses. *International Journal for Vitamin and Nutrition Research*. Supplement 23:35-47.

Patrone, F., F. Dallegri, E. Bonvini, F. Minervini, and C. Sacchetti. (1982) Effects of ascorbic acid on neutrophil function. Studies on normal and chronic granulomatous disease neutrophils. *Acta Vitaminologica et Enzymologica* 4(1-2):163-168.

Pauling, L. (1970) *Vitamin C and the Common Cold*. San Francisco, CA: W.H. Freeman and Company.

Peloux, Y., C. Lofre, A. Cier, and A. Colobert. (1962) Inactivation du virus polio-myelitique par des systemes chimique generateurs du radical libre hydroxide. Mechanism de l'activite virulicide du peroxide d'hydrogene et de l'acide ascorbique. *Annls Inst Pasteur, Paris* 102:6.

Perla, D. (1937) The effect of an excess of vitamin C on the natural resistance of mice and guinea pigs to trypanosome infections. *American Journal of Hygiene* 26:374-381.

Petter, C. (1937) Vitamin C and tuberculosis. *The Journal-Lancet* (Minneapolis) 57:221-224.

Pijoan, M. and B. Sedlacek. (1943) Ascorbic acid in tuberculous Navajo Indians. *American Review of Tuberculosis* 48:342-346.

Pitt, H. and A. Costrini. (1979) Vitamin C prophylaxis in marine recruits. *Journal of the American Medical Association* 241(9): 908-911.

Plit, M., A. Theron, H. Fickl, C. van Rensbury, S. Pendel, and R. Anderson. (1998) Influence of antimicrobial chemotherapy and smoking status on the plasma concentrations of vitamin C, vitamin E, beta-carotene, acute phase reactants, iron and lipid peroxides in patients with pulmonary tuberculosis. *The International Journal of Tuberculosis and Lung Disease* 2(7):590-596.

Povey, R. (1969) Viral respiratory disease. *The Veterinary Record* 84(13):335-338.

Prinz, W., R. Bortz, B. Bregin, and M. Hersch. (1977) The effect of ascorbic acid supplementation on some parameters of the human immunological defence system. *International Journal for Vitamin and Nutrition Research* 47(3):248-257.

Radford, M., E. de Savitsch, and H. Sweany. (1937) Blood changes following continuous daily administration of vitamin C and orange juice to tuberculous patients. *American Review of Tuberculosis* 35:784-793.

Ramirez, L., E. Lages-Silva, G. Pianetti, R. Rabelo, J. Bordin, and H. Moraes-Souza. (1995) Prevention of transfusion-associated Chagas' disease by sterilization of *Trypanosoma cruzi*-infected blood with gentian violet, ascorbic acid, and light. *Transfusion* 35(3):226-230.

Rawal, B. and B. Charles. (1972) Inhibition of *Pseudomonas aeruginosa* by ascorbic acid-sulphamethoxazole-trimethoprim combination. *The Southeast Asian Journal of Tropical Medicine and Public Health* 3(2):225-228.

Rawal, B., G. McKay, and M. Blackhall. (1974) Inhibition of *Pseudomonas aeruginosa* by ascorbic acid acting singly and in combination with antimicrobials: *in-vitro* and *in-vivo* studies. *Medical Journal of Australia* 1(6):169-174.

Rawal, B. (1978) Bactericidal action of ascorbic acid on *Pseudomonas aeruginosa*: alteration of cell surface as a possible mechanism. *Chemotherapy* 24(3):166-171.

Rawal, B., F. Bartolini, and G. Vyas. (1995) *In vitro* inactivation of human immunodeficiency virus by ascorbic acid. *Biologicals* 23(1):75-81.

Rebora, A., F. Crovato, F. Dallegri, and F. Patrone. (1980) Repeated staphylococcal pyoderma in two siblings with defective neutrophil bacterial killing. *Dermatologica* 160(2):106-112.

Rinehart, J. and S. Mettier. (1933) The heart valves in experimental scurvy and in scurvy with superimposed infection. *American Journal of Pathology* 9:923-933;952-955.

Reinhart, J. and S. Mettier. (1934) The heart valves and muscle in experimental scurvy with superimposed infection, with notes on the similarity of the lesions to those of rheumatic fever. *American Journal of Pathology* 10:61-79.

Rinehart, J., C. Connor, and S. Mettier. (1934) Further observations on pathologic similarities between experimental scurvy combined with infection, and rheumatic fever. *Journal of Experimental Medicine* 59:97-114.

Rinehart, J. (1936) An outline of studies relating to vitamin C deficiency in rheumatic fever. *The Journal of Laboratory and Clinical Medicine* 21:597-608.

Rinehart, J., L. Greenberg, and A. Christie. (1936) Reduced ascorbic acid content of blood plasma in rheumatic fever. *Proceedings of the Society for Experimental Biology and Medicine* 35(2):350-353.

Rinehart, J., L. Greenberg, M. Olney, and F. Choy. (1938) Metabolism of vitamin C in rheumatic fever. *Archives of Internal Medicine* 61:552-561.

Rivas, C., J. Vera, V. Guaiquil, F. Velasques, O. Borquez-Ojeda, J. Carcamo, I. Concha, and D. Golde. (1997) Increased uptake and accumulation of vitamin C in human immunodeficiency virus 1-infected hematopoietic cell lines. *Journal of Biological Chemistry* 272(9):5814-5820.

Robertson, W., M. Ropes, and W. Bauer. (1941) The degradation of mucins and polysaccharides by ascorbic acid and hydrogen peroxide. *The Biochemical Journal* 35:903.

Rogers, L. (1927) *Great Britain Rep Public Health and Med Subj, Ministry of Health* 44:26.

Rosenow, E. (1912) Further studies of the toxic substances obtainable from pneumococci. *The Journal of Infectious Diseases* 11:94-108.

Rotman, D. (1978) Sialoresponsin and an antiviral action of ascorbic acid. *Medical Hypotheses* 4(1):40-43.

Rudra, M. and S. Roy. (1946) Haematological study in pulmonary tuberculosis and the effect upon it of large doses of vitamin C. *Tubercle* 27:93-94.

Ruskin, S. (1938) Contribution to the study of grippe otitis, myringitis bullosa hemorrhagica, and its relationship to latent scurvy. *Laryngoscope* 48:327-334.

Sabin, A. (1939) Vitamin C in relation to experimental poliomyelitis with incidental observations on certain manifestations in *Macacus rhesus* monkeys on a scorbutic diet. *Journal of Experimental Medicine* 69:507-515.

Sadun, E., G. Carrera, I. Krupp, and D. Allain. (1950) Effect of single inocula of *Entamoeba histolytica* trophozoites on guinea-pigs. *Proceedings of the Society for Experimental Biology and Medicine* 73:362-366.

Sadun, E., J. Bradin, Jr., and E. Faust. (1951) The effect of ascorbic acid deficiency on the resistance of guinea-pigs to infection with *Entamoeba histolytica* of human origin. *American Journal of Tropical Medicine* 31:426-437.

Sagripanti, J., L. Routson, A. Bonifacino, and C. Lytle. (1997) Mechanism of copper-mediated inactivation of herpes simplex virus. *Antimicrobial Agents and Chemotherapy* 41(4):812-817.

Sahu, K. and R. Das. (1994) Reduction of clastogenic effect of clofazimine, an antileprosy drug, by vitamin A and vitamin C in bone marrow cells of mice. *Food and Chemical Toxicology* 32(10):911-915.

Sakamoto, M., S. Kobayashi, S. Ishii, K. Katoo, and N. Shimazono. (1981) The effect of vitamin C deficiency on complement systems and complement components. *Journal of Nutritional Science and Vitaminology* 27(4):367-378.

Salo, R. and D. Cliver. (1978) Inactivation of enteroviruses by ascorbic acid and sodium bisulfite. *Applied and Environmental Microbiology* 36(1):68-75.

Sandler, J., J. Gallin, and M. Vaughan. (1975) Effects of serotonin, carbamylcholine, and ascorbic acid on leukocyte cyclic GMP and chemotaxis. *The Journal of Cell Biology* 67(2 Pt 1):480-484.

Sarin, K., A. Kumar, A. Prakash, and A. Sharma. (1993) Oxidative stress and antioxidant defence mechanism in *Plasmodium vivax* malaria before and after chloroquine treatment. *Indian Journal of Malariology* 30(3):127-133.

Schwager, J. and J. Schulze. (1997) Influence of ascorbic acid on the response to mitogens and interleukin production of porcine lymphocytes. *International Journal for Vitamin and Nutrition Research* 67(1):10-16.

Scott, J. (1982) On the biochemical similarities of ascorbic acid and interferon. *Journal of Theoretical Biology* 98(2):235-238.

Semba, R., N. Graham, W. Caiaffa, J. Margolick, L. Clement, and D. Vlahov. (1993) Increased mortality associated with vitamin A deficiency during human immunodeficiency virus type 1 infection. *Archives of Internal Medicine* 153(18):2149-2154.

Sennewald, K. (1938) *Fortschrifte der Therapie* 14:139.

Senutaite, J. and S. Biziulevicius. (1986) Influence of vitamin C on the resistance of rats to *Trichinella spiralis* infection. *Wiadomosci Parazytologiczne* 32(3):261-262.

Sessa, T. (1940) Vitamin C therapy of whooping cough. *Riforma Medica* 56:38-43.

Siegel, B. (1974) Enhanced interferon response to murine leukemia virus by ascorbic acid. *Infection and Immunity* 10(2):409-410.

Siegel, B. (1975) Enhancement of interferon production by poly(rI)-poly(rC) in mouse cell cultures by ascorbic acid. *Nature* 254(5500):531-532.

Siegel, B. and J. Morton. (1977) Vitamin C and the immune response. *Experientia* 33(3):393-395.

Siegel, B. and J. Morton. (1984) Vitamin C and immunity: influence of ascorbate on prostaglandin E2 synthesis and implications for natural killer cell activity. *International Journal for Vitamin and Nutrition Research* 54(4):339-342.

Sigal, A. and C. King. (1937) The influence of vitamin C deficiency upon the resistance of guinea pigs to diphtheria toxin: glucose tolerance. *Journal of Pharmacology and Experimental Therapeutics* 61:1-9.

Sinha, S., S. Gupta, A. Bajaj, P. Singh, and P. Kumar. (1984) A study of blood ascorbic acid in leprosy. *International Journal of Leprosy and Other Mycobacterial Diseases* 52(2):159-162.

Skinsnes, O. and E. Matsuo. (1976) Hyaluronic acid, ß-glucuronidase, vitamin C and the immune defect in leprosy. *International Journal of Dermatology* 15(4):286-289.

Skurnick, J., J. Bogden, H. Baker, F. Kemp, A. Sheffet, G. Quattrone, and D. Louria. (1996) Micronutrient profiles in HIV-1-infected heterosexual adults. *Journal of Acquired Immune Deficiency Syndromes and Human Retrovirology* 12(1):75 83.

Slotkin, G. and R. Fletcher. (1944) Ascorbic acid in pulmonary complications following prostatic surgery: a preliminary report. *Journal of Urology* 52:566-569.

Smith, L. (1988) *The Clinical Experiences of Frederick R. Klenner, M.D.: Clinical Guide to the Use of Vitamin C.* Portland, OR: Life Sciences Press.

Smith, T. (1913) Some bacteriological and environmental factors in the pneumonias of lower animals with special reference to the guinea-pig. *The Journal of Medical Research* 29:291-323.

Sokolova, V. (1958) Application of vitamin C in treatment of dysentery. *Terapevticheskii Arkhiv* (Moskva) 30:59-64.

Steinbach, M. and S. Klein. (1936) Effect of crystalline vitamin C (ascorbic acid) on tolerance to tuberculin. *Proceedings of the Society for Experimental Biology and Medicine* 35:151-154.

Steinbach, M. and S. Klein. (1941) Vitamin C in experimental tuberculosis. *American Review of Tuberculosis* 43:403-414.

Stimson, A., O. Hedley, and E. Rose. (1934) Notes on experimental rheumatic fever. *Public Health Reports* 49(11):361-363.

Stone, I. (1972) *The Healing Factor: "Vitamin C" Against Disease.* New York, NY: Grosset & Dunlap.

Stone, I. (1980) The possible role of mega-ascorbate in the endogenous synthesis of interferon. *Medical Hypotheses* 6(3):309-314.

Strangeways, W. (1937) Observations on the trypanocidal action in vitro of solutions of glutathione and ascorbic acid. *Annals of Tropical Medicine and Parasitology* 31:405-416.

Sweany, H., C. Clancy, M. Radford, and V. Hunter. (1941) The body economy of vitamin C in health and disease. With special studies in tuberculosis. *The Journal of the American Medical Association* 116(6):469-474.

Szirmai, F. (1940) Value of vitamin C in treatment of acute infectious diseases. *Deutsches Archive fur Klinische Medizin* 85:434-443.

Tang, A., N. Graham, A. Kirby, L. McCall, W. Willett, and A. Saah. (1993) Dietary micronutrient intake and risk of progression to acquired immunodeficiency syndrome (AIDS) in human immunodeficiency virus type 1 (HIV-1)-infected homosexual men. *American Journal of Epidemiology* 138(11):937-951.

Tappel, A. (1973) Lipid peroxidation damage to cell components. *Federation Proceedings* 32(8):1870-1874.

Terezhalmy, G., W. Bottomley, and G. Pelleu. (1978) The use of water-soluble bioflavonoid-ascorbic acid complex in the treatment of recurrent herpes labialis. *Oral Surgery, Oral Medicine, Oral Pathology* 45(1):56-62.

Thomas, W. and P. Holt. (1978) Vitamin C and immunity: an assessment of the evidence. *Clinical and Experimental Immunology* 32(2):370-379.

Treitinger, A., C. Spada, J. Verdi, A. Miranda, O. Oliveira, M. Silveira, P. Moriel, and D. Abdalla. (2000) Decreased antioxidant defence in individuals infected by the human immunodeficiency virus. *European Journal of Clinical Investigation* 30(5):454-459.

Turner, G. (1964) Inactivation of vaccinia virus by ascorbic acid. *Journal of General Microbiology* 35:75-80.

Umar, I., A. Wuro-Chekke, A. Gidado, and I. Igbokwe. (1999) Effects of combined parenteral vitamins C and E administration on the severity of anaemia, hepatic and renal damage in *Trypanosoma brucei brucei* infected rabbits. *Veterinary Parasitology* 85(1):43-47.

Vallance, S. (1977) Relationships between ascorbic acid and serum proteins of the immune system. *British Medical Journal* 2(6084):437-438.

Vasil'ev, V. and V. Komar. (1988) [Ascorbic acid level and the indicators of cellular immunity in patients with hepatitis A during pathogenetic therapy]. Article in Russian. *Voprosy Pitaniia* July-August;(4):31-34.

Vasil'ev, V., V. Komar, and N. Kisel'. (1989) [Humoral and cellular indices of nonspecific resistance in viral hepatitis A and ascorbic acid]. Russian. *Terapevticheskii Arkhiv* 61(11):44-46.

Vermillion, E. and G. Stafford. (1938) A preliminary report on the use of cevitaminic acid in the treatment of whooping cough. *Journal of the Kansas Medical Society* 39(11):469, 479.

Versteeg, J. (1970) Investigations on the effect of ascorbic acid on antibody production in rabbits after injection of bacterial and viral antigens by different routes. *Proceedings of the Koninklijke Nederlandse Akademie van Wetenschappen. Series C. Biological and Medical Sciences* 73(5):494-501.

Veselovskaia, T. (1957) Effect of vitamin C on the clinical picture of dysentery. *Voenno-Meditsinskii Zhurnal* (Moskva) 3:32-37.

Vitorero, J. and J. Doyle. (1938) Treatment of intestinal tuberculosis with vitamin C. *Medical Weekly* 2:636-640.

Vogl, A. (1937) *Munchener Medizinische Wochenschrift* 84:1569.

von Gagyi, J. (1936) Ueber die bactericide und antitoxische wirkung des vitamin C. *Klinische Wochenschrift* 15:190-195.

Wahli, T., W. Meier, and K. Pfister. (1986) Ascorbic acid induced immune-mediated decrease in mortality in *Ichthyophthirius multifiliis* infected rainbow-trout (*Salmo gairdneri*). *Acta Tropica* 43(3): 287-289.

Ward, B. and B. Carroll. (1966) Spore germination and vegetative growth of *Clostridium botulinum* type E in synthetic media. *Canadian Journal of Microbiology* 12:1146-1156.

Washko, P., Y. Wang, and M. Levine. (1993) Ascorbic acid recycling in human neutrophils. *The Journal of Biological Chemistry* 268(21): 15531-15535.

White, L., C. Freeman, B. Forrester, and W. Chappell. (1986) *In vitro* effect of ascorbic acid on infectivity of herpesviruses and paramyxoviruses. *Journal of Clinical Microbiology* 24(4):527-531.

Winter, R., M. Ignatushchenko, O. Ogundahunsi, K. Cornell, A. Oduola, D. Hinrichs, and M. Riscoe. (1997) Potentiation of an antimalarial oxidant drug. *Antimicrobial Agents and Chemotherapy* 41(7):1449-1454.

Witt, W., G. Hubbard, and J. Fanton. (1988) *Streptococcus pneumoniae* arthritis and osteomyelitis with vitamin C deficiency in guinea pigs. *Laboratory Animal Science* 38(2):192-194.

Woringer, P. and T. Sala. (1928) *Rev Franc de Ped* 4:809.

Wynne, E. (1957) Symposium on bacterial spore germination. *Bacteriological Reviews* 21:259-262.

Wu, C., T. Dorairajan, and T. Lin. (2000) Effect of ascorbic acid supplementation on the immune response of chickens vaccinated and challenged with infectious bursal disease virus. *Veterinary Immunology and Immunopathology* 74(1-2):145-152.

Yamamoto, Y., S. Yamashita, A. Fujisawa, S. Kokura, and T. Yoshikawa. (1998) Oxidative stress in patients with hepatitis, cirrhosis, and hepatoma evaluated by plasma antioxidants. *Biochemical and Biophysical Research Communications* 247(1): 166-170.

Zinsser, H., R. Castaneda, and C. Seastone, Jr. (1931) Studies on typhus fever. VI. Reduction of resistance by diet deficiency. *Journal of Experimental Medicine* 53:333-338.

Zureick, M. (1950) Treatment of shingles and herpes with vitamin C intravenously. *Journal des Praticiens* 64:586.

Chapter Three

The Ultimate Antidote

Science commits suicide when it adopts a creed.

HUXLEY

Overview

Vitamin C has demonstrated the ability to neutralize a wide variety of toxic substances, many of which are completely unrelated chemically. Frequently, vitamin C directly interacts chemically with a given toxin to render it less toxic or nontoxic. This is known as a chemical antidote effect. However, vitamin C can also act as a physiological antidote to a toxin or poison. Such an antidote effect can result when vitamin C helps to undo or repair the damage caused by a certain toxin without having to directly interact with the toxin (Nowak et al., 2000). In Chapter 2 it has already been demonstrated that vitamin C is superbly effective in either neutralizing or negating the effects of a number of chemically different and extremely potent endotoxins and exotoxins, which are produced as by-products of microbial growth. Furthermore, when the toxin is a chemotherapy drug, vitamin C quite often will promote the anticancer actions of that drug without increasing the drug-induced toxic effects. In mice with liver tumors, Taper et al. (1987) showed that the combination

217

of vitamin C with another vitamin was able to increase the therapeutic effectiveness of six different cytotoxic drugs without increasing their undesirable toxic side effects.

Some toxic substances have also been documented to have cancer-causing effects. Many of these toxins can be demonstrated to increase the consumption of vitamin C. This is one important piece of evidence implying that vitamin C plays a role in the neutralization of toxins. Calabrese (1985) published a significant partial list of toxins that lowered vitamin C levels and whose toxicity or cancer-causing effects were modified by vitamin C. While not nearly exhaustive, this list serves to underscore the versatility of vitamin C in lessening or eliminating the toxicity of chemically diverse substances. Calabrese listed the following:

1. Some chlorinated hydrocarbon insecticides and organophosphate insecticides

2. Toxic elements: arsenic, cadmium, chromium, cobalt, copper, cyanide, fluoride, lead, mercury, selenium, silica, and tellurium

3. Industrial hydrocarbons: benzanthrone, benzene, chloroform, glycerol, hydrazine, polychlorinated biphenyls, trinitrotoluene, and vinyl chloride

4. Gaseous pollutants: carbon monoxide and ozone

It is important to supplement vitamin C even if it is only to normalize the body's vitamin C status. However, supplementation is also essential because depletion of vitamin C levels in the face of toxicity indicates that toxins are being neutralized as a result of vitamin C's metabolic breakdown in the body. A given chemical toxin can make the body's ability to cope with other challenges all the more difficult by lowering the vitamin C level in the course of its detoxification. In the extreme, however, large enough doses of such a chemical toxin can rapidly produce a toxin-induced scurvy, which is a state that can kill the patient in short order even if the chemical toxin presence is self-limited and not continuous. In this chapter you will see that a large amount of evidence exists to indicate that the toxin-induced lowering of vitamin C levels actually indicates that available vitamin C is working to neutralize as much toxin as possible. The depleted vitamin C status of the body merits prompt supplementation for no reason other than the fact that it is depleted, reliably weakening the immune system and potentially exposing the body to other medical problems.

Although many toxins have been shown to decrease vitamin C levels in the non-vitamin C-producing human, the opposite effect is typically seen in a vitamin C-producing animal. As long as the amount of toxin is not so large as to immediately overwhelm the vitamin C-producing capacity of the animal, vitamin C levels will reliably rise when toxic challenges present themselves. This allows all toxin challenges of a lesser degree to be "automatically" neutralized by the increased vitamin C production in such an animal. Longenecker et al. (1939) and Longenecker et al. (1940) noted that the vitamin C-producing rat responded with an increased formation of vitamin C to a large number of organic compounds generally considered to be toxic. Conney et al. (1961) also noted a number of drugs "possessing completely unrelated chemical and pharmacological properties" would "stimulate markedly" the excretion of vitamin C in rats, indicating an increased liver production of vitamin C to the toxic challenges posed by these drugs. The list of drugs that Conney et al. found would stimulate vitamin C synthesis, metabolic breakdown, and excretion included the following:

while many toxins decrease vitamin C levels in the non-vitamin C-producing human, the opposite effect is typically seen in a vitamin C-producing animal

1. Hypnotics: chloretone and barbital
2. Analgesics: aminopyrine and antipyrine
3. Muscle relaxants: orphenadrine and meprobamate
4. Antirheumatics: phenylbutazone and oxyphenbutazone
5. Uricosuric agent: sulfinpyrazone
6. Antihistaminics: diphenhydramine and chlorcyclizine
7. Carcinogenic hydrocarbons: 3-methylcholanthrene and 3,4-benzpyrene

It is not really important whether you are familiar with any of the drugs just mentioned above. What is important is that vitamin C appears to be a natural detoxifying agent to neutralize these drugs along with many other toxins, or drugs perceived by the body as toxic. It is also important to realize that vitamin C is effective in detoxifying a wide array of dissimilar and diverse toxins.

In addition to the direct antioxidant effects that vitamin C has on so many toxins, which reduces them to less toxic or nontoxic metabolites, it is important to realize that vitamin C has another important effect in the mechanism of drug detoxification. Vitamin C also appears to stimulate the activity of several drug-metabolizing enzymes in the liver (Zannoni et al., 1987). Schvartsman (1983) asserted that the action of vitamin C in stimulating the enzymatic system of the liver "may thus constitute the main justification for increasing its use in the therapy of intoxications." It has long been known that one of the main functions of the liver is to detoxify toxins, and increased vitamin C appears to directly stimulate this activity in addition to its direct antioxidant action on a given toxin.

This chapter will deal with the documented effects of vitamin C on specific toxic agents. Although vitamin C can often offer complete cures or absolute protection for many different types of poisoning, little of this information has reached any of the medical textbooks, and many people worldwide continue to suffer and die needlessly from such intoxications since modern medicine still has no effective treatment for them. Furthermore, even when a given toxin cannot be neutralized or eliminated by vitamin C, the damage inflicted by such toxins can almost always be significantly repaired by the administration of adequate doses of vitamin C. Almost all toxins precipitate varying amounts of damage by generating large amounts of tissue-damaging and enzyme-damaging free radicals. Antioxidant therapy, headed by vitamin C, remains the best way to deal with an onslaught of free radicals.

Although there are many antioxidants available to help deal with the excess free radicals seen in different medical conditions and intoxications, it is important to understand that all antioxidants are not created equal and do not have equal potency. Challem and Taylor (1998) pointed out that the human body cannot completely compensate for a lack of vitamin C with its own internally produced antioxidants, such as superoxide dismutase and uric acid. To be sure, the antioxidants as a group will attempt to compensate for the lack of some by an increased activity of others. However, vitamin C is probably the only antioxidant that cannot be completely and safely eliminated from the diet by the substitution of any of the other antioxidants, regardless of their doses or the combination used. Frei et al. (1989) and Frei et al. (1990) pointed out that vitamin C is the only antioxidant in the blood plasma that can offer complete protection for circulating blood fats (lipids) from metabolic breakdown (peroxidation). They also asserted that vitamin C is the most effective antioxidant in human blood plasma, offering blood lipoproteins complete protection against the oxidative damage that can be caused by activated white blood cells.

vitamin C is the only antioxidant in the blood plasma that can offer complete protection for circulating blood fats from metabolic breakdown

Specific Toxins and Vitamin C

Alcohol (Ethanol)

As most people know, alcohol in excess is clearly a toxin. The toxicity level of smaller amounts continues to be debated. As with so many other toxins, the liver is the main site of alcohol neutralization/metabolism when a toxic dose of alcohol is encountered.

Susick and Zannoni (1987) looked at the effects of vitamin C on the consequences of acute alcohol consumption in humans. Vitamin C or a placebo was given to 20 male subjects for two weeks prior to alcohol consumption. The subjects who received the vitamin C demonstrated improved motor coordination and color discrimination, which is evidence of a lessened alcohol toxicity. The vitamin C also resulted in a "significant enhancement" in the elimination of alcohol from the

blood. Klenner (1971) asserted that 40,000 mg of vitamin C given intravenously along with vitamin B1 will "neutralize" the effects of alcohol
in an intoxicated person. Klenner also asserted that the same treatment
would "save the life" of a person unfortunate enough to drink a significant amount of alcohol after taking Antibuse (disulfiram). This drug,
used to make alcoholics feel sick after drinking in order to break their
habit, can also kill. It prevents alcohol from being completely metabolized, which results in high concentrations of acetaldehyde in the body.
Vitamin C detoxifies the acetaldehyde (see below, this section).

Meagher et al. (1999) showed that alcohol ingestion in healthy
humans increases oxidative stress as indicated by an increase in the
products of lipid peroxidation (LPO). They also showed that the same
abnormal laboratory indicators of oxidative stress were already significantly elevated in patients with alcohol-induced hepatitis or chronic
liver disease in the absence of additional acute alcohol intake. Finally,
they were able to show that vitamin C was able to reduce abnormal elevations of oxidative stress in patients who already had chronic alcoholic
liver disease. They concluded that oxidative stress, which was significantly lowered by vitamin C, preceded and contributed to the evolution
of alcoholic liver disease.

Zhou and Chen (2001) were able to show that alcohol abusers demonstrated lower blood levels of antioxidant enzymes and antioxidants,
including vitamin C. They suggested that chronic oxidative damage in
alcoholics should be treated chronically with antioxidant supplementation that included vitamin C to minimize long-term oxidative damage
to the body. A similar recommendation was made by Marotta et al.
(2001), who also concluded that an "effective antioxidant supplementation" regimen was able to decrease laboratory evidence of increased
oxidative stress. Furthermore, such supplementation should be especially properly dosed, as the diuretic (increased urine-forming) property of alcohol ingestion is associated with a further substantial loss of
vitamin C in the urine (Faizallah et al., 1986). This means that alcoholics
both metabolize vitamin C more quickly and flush it out more quickly
in the urine, mandating vigilant supplementation in order to minimize
the long-term toxic damage of alcohol.

Lesser consumptions of alcohol appear to be associated with lesser utilizations of vitamin C and other antioxidants. In 11 "apparently healthy" subjects the blood levels of vitamin C were reduced by approximately 12% to 15% after a course of "moderate" alcohol consumption over a total time period of 12 weeks (van der Gaag et al., 2000). Interestingly, at the levels of alcohol ingested, the mild drops in vitamin C levels were seen with beer and "spirits" drinking, but not with red wine. Even the slight drop in vitamin C levels is evidence that alcohol may very well be toxic at any dose.

One of the primary breakdown products of alcohol (ethanol) is acetaldehyde, another toxic substance (Cohen, 1977). Vitamin C appears to play a direct role in both the initial breakdown of any non-excreted ethanol to acetaldehyde (Giles and Meggiorini, 1983; Susick and Zannoni, 1984), and in the improved detoxification of the acetaldehyde through the increased and more stable binding of acetaldehyde to blood proteins (Tuma et al., 1984).

Wickramasinghe and Hasan (1992) looked at the toxic effects that the serum of alcohol drinkers had on lymphocytes outside of the body. They believed the toxicity was due to the presence of unstable acetaldehyde-protein complexes, allowing the acetaldehyde to break free and poison the lymphocytes. Vitamin C was able to reduce this cytotoxic effect, further justifying its use in alcohol toxicity. In seven healthy volunteers Wickramasinghe and Hasan (1994) showed that only 1,000 mg of vitamin C daily for three days prior to an acute alcohol consumption decreased the associated acetaldehyde-mediated toxicity that resulted from that ingestion. Krasner et al. (1974) were able to show that there was a direct correlation between the level of vitamin C in the white blood cells and the rate of clearance of ethanol from the blood.

Sprince et al. (1975) and Sprince et al. (1979) looked at acetaldehyde-induced toxicity in rats. They found that vitamin C could offer significant protection against the toxic symptoms of acetaldehyde and the ultimate lethality of the acetaldehyde. O'Neill and Rahwan (1976) also showed that vitamin C resulted in a "statistically significant reduction in acetaldehyde-induced toxicity" when given to mice exposed to symptom-inducing amounts of acetaldehyde. Moldowan and Acholonu

(1982) found that a dose of vitamin C given to mice 90 minutes before an otherwise fatal injection of acetaldehyde reduced the mortality rate. Also looking at mice, Tamura et al. (1969) demonstrated that vitamin C, along with glucose and cysteine, had a clear antidotal effect in blocking the otherwise lethal effect of acetaldehyde given to mice.

Navasumrit et al. (2000) also showed in mice that alcohol increased the generation of free radicals and the frequency of damage to DNA. A pretreatment regimen with vitamin C lessened the increase in alcohol-induced oxidative stress, and the otherwise increased frequency of DNA damage was prevented.

Suresh et al. (2000) looked at the effects of a large vitamin C dose on alcohol-induced toxicity in rats. The dose was 200 mg per 100 g body weight, which would equate to 140,000 mg of vitamin C for a 150-pound person. The vitamin C clearly reduced alcohol-induced toxicity, as reflected in decreased triglyceride and liver enzyme levels relative to the rats given alcohol (ethanol) alone. In mice, Busnel and Lehmann (1980) examined the motor (muscle) disturbances in swimming behavior induced by alcohol. This was effectively a laboratory test equivalent to a human's drunken walk. They found that fairly large doses of vitamin C (125 and 500 mg/kg body weight) completely prevented alcohol-induced abnormal swimming behavior, while a smaller dose of vitamin C (62.5 mg/kg) had no significant effect. A 500 mg/kg dose would amount to 35,000 mg of vitamin C for a 150-pound person, while the lowest dose would amount to slightly less than 4,400 mg of vitamin C for the same person. This study of Busnel and Lehmann is another clear example of how important the proper dose of vitamin C is in treating any toxic condition, whether in animal or man. It also shows how a suboptimal dose may have little or no effect on a given toxin or toxic clinical effect.

this study reemphasizes how important the proper dose of vitamin C is in treating any toxic condition... a suboptimal dose may have little or no effect

A significant amount of research has also been done regarding the effects of vitamin C on alcohol toxicity in guinea pigs. Yunice et al.

(1984) found that administration of vitamin C was clearly effective in accelerating the clearance of infused ethanol from the blood of guinea pigs. Yunice and Lindeman (1977) were also able to show that vitamin C could completely prevent the lethal effects of an acute alcohol dosage that would otherwise kill 68% of the mice recipients. Ginter and Zloch (1999) were able to demonstrate that guinea pigs receiving the most vitamin C over a 5-week pretreatment period metabolized alcohol much more quickly than guinea pigs on minimal amounts.

Yunice et al. also showed that greater amounts of supplemented vitamin C were able to help ethanol-treated guinea pigs gain weight compared to ethanol-treated animals receiving significantly less vitamin C. The concentrations of vitamin C were noted to be lower in the liver, kidney, and adrenal glands in the ethanol-treated animals relative to control animals, which indicated the increased utilization of vitamin C by the toxicity of the ethanol. Suresh et al. (1999) also found that alcohol administration lowered tissue levels of vitamin C in guinea pigs.

Ginter et al. (1998) gave guinea pigs diets with no added vitamin C, "medium" amounts of vitamin C, or "high" amounts of vitamin C for a five-week period. Just prior to sacrificing the animals, an injection of ethanol calculated to result in short-term acute intoxication was given. As a model of chronic alcohol abuse, several other groups of guinea pigs with differing vitamin C intakes were given lesser alcohol doses every week prior to being sacrificed. Relative to unsupplemented animals, guinea pigs with the highest tissue vitamin C concentrations had "significantly decreased" levels of ethanol and acetaldehyde in the liver and brain. They also had lower liver enzyme levels and lower cholesterol levels. The authors concluded that the administration of "large amounts" of vitamin C appears to accelerate the metabolism of both ethanol and acetaldehyde, while reducing some of their adverse health effects.

Suresh et al. (1999a) looked at the effects of a "mega dose" of vitamin C on increased LPO induced by alcohol in guinea pigs. They found that the supplementation of vitamin C to the alcohol-fed animals decreased laboratory findings of oxidative stress and reduced the levels of increased enzyme activity toxically induced by the alcohol. Susick and Zannoni (1987a) maintained guinea pigs on differing doses of vitamin C. They gave a dose of ethanol that raised the SGOT (a liver enzyme) 12-fold in animals that had liver vitamin C levels below 16 mg/100 g of liver weight. However, the same dose of ethanol given to animals that had liver vitamin C levels above this threshold had a "marked reduction" (60%) in the ethanol-induced increase in SGOT. Suresh et al. (1997) looked at the alcohol-induced increase in blood fats (hyperlipidemia) in guinea pigs and found that vitamin C significantly reduced this increase. Susick et al. (1986) were also able to demonstrate that enough vitamin C had a significant protective effect against the toxic effects of chronic alcohol consumption in guinea pigs.

adequately dosed vitamin C is the best way to detoxify alcohol, prevent future alcohol-induced damage, and repair past alcohol-induced damage

Acute and chronic alcohol consumption in humans takes a serious toll in both morbidity and mortality. Zannoni et al. (1987) wrote a review article clearly demonstrating that adequately dosed vitamin C is the best way to detoxify alcohol, prevent future alcohol-induced damage, and repair past alcohol-induced damage. Pawan (1968) provides an example of a study contesting the ability of vitamin C to accelerate the ethanol clearance rate in man.

As is so often the case, however, the vitamin C dosage is tiny. Pawan reported that 600 mg of vitamin C given acutely had no influence on ethanol clearance rates. It is unlikely that 600 mg of vitamin C could seriously affect the clinical status of virtually any form of significant toxicity in an adult human, unless some of the symptoms related to a toxin-induced scurvy. The cumulative research on ethanol and vitamin C indicates that vitamin C can definitely lessen much of the damage done to the body by alcohol, especially in the liver. Furthermore, studies looking at acute alcohol exposure and vitamin C indicate that a high dosing of vitamin C, rather than hot coffee and forced ambulation, is the best and quickest way to metabolize alcohol and sober someone up. Obviously, the best way to deal with transporting an acutely intoxicated individual is through the use of a designated driver.

Barbiturates

Barbiturates have long been used for hypnotic or anesthesia applications. Phenobarbital is a type of barbiturate that has long been used in the management of epilepsy. Excess barbiturates in the body result in depression of the central nervous system.

Klenner (1971) reported dramatic success in reversing acute barbiturate toxicity with vitamin C. A patient who had ingested 2,640 mg of talbutal, an intermediate-acting oral barbiturate, presented to Klenner in the emergency room with a blood pressure of 60/0. By blood pressure standards, this is barely alive. Klenner gave 12,000 mg of vitamin C with a 50 cc syringe by intravenous push, followed by a slower infusion of vitamin C by vein. Within only 10 minutes the patient's blood pressure was up to 100/60. The patient woke up three hours later and completely recovered, having received a total of 125,000 mg of vitamin C over a 12-hour period.

Klenner also reported on another patient with a secobarbital barbiturate overdose. The patient awoke after 42,000 mg of vitamin C was "given by vein as fast as a 20 gauge needle could carry the flow." Ultimately this patient received 75,000 mg of vitamin C by vein and 30,000 mg by mouth over a 24-hour period.

Klenner asserted that the success of his vitamin C protocol "in no less than 15 cases of barbiturate poisoning" indicated that "no death should occur" in this condition. Klenner (1974), in discussing the dramatic effects of vitamin C on barbiturate poisoning (and carbon monoxide poisoning), commented that "the results are so dramatic that it borders on malpractice to deny this therapy."

the success of Klenner's vitamin C protocol "in no less than 15 cases of barbiturate poisoning" is "so dramatic that it borders on malpractice to deny this therapy"

In dogs and mice, Kao et al. (1965) were able to show that a "large dosage" of injected vitamin C helped to reverse the barbiturate-induced depression of the central nervous system. They found that the vitamin C in this situation improved the blood pressure and breathing in acutely intoxicated animals.

Carbon Monoxide

Carbon monoxide poisoning operates by a similar mechanism to methemoglobinemia, which is discussed in a later section. Carbon monoxide binds much more tightly to hemoglobin than oxygen, resulting in a loss of oxygen-carrying capacity for all of the hemoglobin bound to carbon monoxide rather than oxygen. When enough carbon monoxide is bound in the blood, the rapidly increasing oxygen debt in all of the body's tissues ultimately causes death.

Klenner (1971) reported a dramatic success in a case of probable carbon monoxide poisoning. On a cold day an unconscious patient was brought to Klenner's office, and the history was that the person had been found in the cab of his truck with the engine running and the windows closed. Assuming carbon monoxide poisoning, Klenner promptly gave 12,000 mg of vitamin C in a 50 cc syringe by intravenous push through a 20 gauge needle. The patient was awake within 10 minutes and wondering why he was at the doctor's office. He returned to work within 45 minutes.

Klenner (1974) made a further suggestion regarding carbon monoxide poisoning. He noted that victims of house fires, particularly children, frequently die as a result of carbon monoxide poisoning. He suggested that treating patients with any form of smoke inhalation with vitamin C at a dose of 500 mg/kg body weight will immediately negate the toxic effects of the carbon monoxide. Klenner stated that this is an especially desirable intervention to apply early after smoke exposure since some symptoms of "smoke poisoning" can be delayed up to 48 hours.

Although Klenner's observations on the effects of vitamin C on carbon monoxide poisoning are the only ones that I found in the literature, they are still quite dramatic. The clinician should have no doubt that intravenous vitamin C should be generously administered in the treatment of carbon monoxide poisoning, as vitamin C appears to be the clear treatment of choice for this condition.

Endotoxin

An endotoxin is one of the toxins associated with the outer membranes of certain bacteria and is released only when the bacteria are disrupted or killed. Endotoxins are not secreted and are generally less toxic than exotoxins, which are secreted as a consequence of microbial metabolism rather than microbial death.

De la Fuente and Victor (2001) showed that vitamin C was one of the antioxidants that could protect mouse lymphocytes from endotoxin-induced oxidative stress. Cadenas et al. (1998) showed that increased dietary vitamin C could protect against the endotoxin-induced oxidative injury to guinea pig liver proteins. They also showed that vitamin C inhibited the endotoxin-induced increase in markers of oxidative stress outside of the guinea pig. Rojas et al. (1996) found that endotoxic shock in guinea pigs totally depleted the heart tissue of vitamin C, although vitamin E levels were not affected. They found that vitamin C supplementation completely blocked the elevation of a certain laboratory indicator of increased oxidative stress in the heart. These authors concluded that vitamin C in the heart is a target substance metabolized by enough endotoxin, and vitamin C can have a protective effect against endotoxin-induced free radical damage in the heart tissue. This is especially interesting in light of data linking heart disease to periodontal (gum) disease (Katz et al., 2001; Abou-Raya et al., 2002; Teng et al., 2002), periodontal disease with the presence of endotoxin (Aleo et al., 1974), and increased levels of vitamin C with a lessened incidence of heart disease (Khaw et al., 2001; Simon et al., 2001).

LaLonde et al. (1997) studied rats subjected to excessive liver oxidant stress resulting from third-degree burns. Although a 20% burn did not produce animal death, the addition of endotoxin caused many of the burned animals to die. This was associated with a further decline in laboratory evidence of liver antioxidant defenses. Vitamin C was the antioxidant most depleted in the liver, and its administration along with several other antioxidants prevented animal death.

Endotoxin can have other significant toxic effects. Dwenger et al. (1994) administered endotoxin intravenously to sheep while monitoring a number of laboratory parameters. The administration of vitamin C intravenously before endotoxin was given helped to protect against the elevated lung blood pressures seen with endotoxin alone. Benito and Bosch (1997) found that guinea pigs maintained on low dietary vitamin C were very sensitive to endotoxin. These guinea pigs had no detectable vitamin C in their lungs, and their levels of vitamin E were significantly decreased as well. The researchers concluded that supplemental vitamin C was important in the protection of the lungs against oxidative injury associated with the presence of endotoxin. Similarly, Fuller et al. (1971) were able to show that guinea pigs maintained on minimal vitamin C were very susceptible to shock induced by endotoxin. In the animals that died, the tissue damage was most pronounced in the lungs and heart.

Victor et al. (2002) found that immune cells challenged with endotoxin had lower levels of vitamin C. Victor et al. (2000) looked at the effects of giving vitamin C to mice with endotoxin-induced shock on the function of macrophages, important immune cells. They found that enough vitamin C could essentially normalize macrophage function in the face of substantial endotoxin. Aleo and Padh (1985) looked at fibroblasts, a specialized cell type known to be especially sensitive to the toxicity of endotoxin. They found that endotoxin directly inhibited the uptake of vitamin C by the fibroblasts in a dose-dependent manner. The more endotoxin was present, the less vitamin C ended up inside the cells, where it is needed. This inhibition of vitamin C uptake by endotoxin was similarly demonstrated in adrenal gland cells (Garcia and Municio, 1990).

This vitamin C uptake inhibition is particularly significant since it suggests that one of the especially negative effects of endotoxin is to keep adequate amounts of vitamin C from getting into the cells. Such a finding also indicates that achieving a certain level of vitamin C in the blood does not assure its delivery in adequate amounts to some of the tissues when enough endotoxin is already present. In fact, Shaw et al. (1966) found that vitamin C at a dose of only 200 mg/kg body weight did not reduce the lethal effects of a certain dose of endotoxin given to rats. As with so many other toxins and infections, an inadequate or suboptimal dose of vitamin C often has no discernible effect on the clinical outcome. Aleo (1980) also concluded that vitamin C was able to help protect against the endotoxin-induced depression of cell growth. This is a function that is vital to "the recovery and regeneration of connective tissues subjected to the disease process."

The details in the above studies documenting the effectiveness of vitamin C in treating illnesses provoked by bacteria-generated endotoxins serve to demonstrate once again why vitamin C is the ideal agent to be used in nearly all infectious diseases. Vitamin C has already been shown to be highly effective in the treatment of nearly every infectious disease investigated (see Chapter 2). Many advanced infections have their own related toxins and/or toxic effects, and vitamin C appears to be the ideal agent for treating both the infection and associated toxin.

many advanced infections have their own related toxins... vitamin C appears to be the ideal agent for treating both the infection and associated toxin

Methemoglobinemia

Methemoglobinemia might not be a familiar term, but it is a potentially fatal condition that is characterized by increased amounts of methemoglobin in the blood. Methemoglobin is incapable of binding and transporting oxygen, which accounts for the toxicity associated with this type of hemoglobin in the blood. A higher methemoglobin level in the body means a greater amount of oxygen starvation throughout the body. This condition can be one of several significant types of damage caused by a variety of different toxins. However, depending upon a number of factors, a given toxin that can cause methemoglobinemia in one situation can also be fatal by other mechanisms in a different clinical setting without provoking methemoglobinemia.

Prchal and Jenkins (2000) listed a number of drugs and other chemicals that can cause or be associated with methemoglobinemia. Studies that have advocated the use of vitamin C in the treatment or prevention of the associated methemoglobinemias are noted in parentheses after the drug or chemical:

Drugs:
- Acetaminophen (Cullison, 1984; Savides et al., 1985; Hjelle and Grauer, 1986)
- Dapsone (Nair and Philip, 1984; Diwan et al., 1991)
- Flutamide (Schott et al., 1991)
- Metoclopramide
- Nitroglycerin
- Paraquat
- Phenacetin
- Phenazopyridine (pyridium)
- Primaquine
- Sulfamethoxazole

Chemicals:
- Acetanilide (Cuthbert, 1971)
- Aniline dyes (Magos and Sziza, 1962; Nomura, 1980)
- Nitric oxide (Dotsch et al., 1998)
- Nitrites (Stoewsand et al., 1973; Blanco and Meade, 1980; Doyle et al., 1985)
- Amyl nitrite
- Isobutyl nitrite
- Sodium nitrite (Bolyai et al., 1972; Calabrese et al., 1983; Kaplan et al., 1990)
- Nitrates (Hirneth and Classen, 1984)
- Nitrobenzenes/nitrobenzoates (Chongtham et al., 1999)
- Nitroethane (nail polish remover)
- Nitrofurans
- 4-Amino-biphenyl

Van Dijk et al. (1983) reported on a case of deliberate nitrate intoxication in a cow. The authors declared vitamin C to be ineffective in treating the resulting methemoglobinemia, but the dose of vitamin C for the cow was roughly the equivalent of slightly more than 1,000 mg of vitamin C for a 150-pound man. Using relatively larger doses of vitamin C, McConnico and Brownie (1992) reported excellent results in the treatment of marked methemoglobinemia in two horses that became acutely toxic as a result of eating wilted red maple leaves. Outside of blood transfusions and hydration, vitamin C was the only significant therapy for these horses. The authors specifically decided against using methylene blue in their treatment protocol. When reviewing the vitamin C literature, always try to determine what the approximate equivalent human dosage of vitamin C would be for the condition treated. Many millions of patients world-wide have never benefited from vitamin C because of hasty and scientifically invalid conclusions based on small, and sometimes ridiculously small, doses of vitamin C when a higher dose would readily cure the condition.

millions world-wide have never benefited from vitamin C because of hasty and scientifically invalid conclusions based on small, and sometimes ridiculously small, doses of vitamin C

Prchal and Jenkins (2000) also noted that methylene blue, the agent commonly used to treat methemoglobinemia, should not be given to patients with a condition known as G6PD deficiency. However, they added that vitamin C can be used as an effective substitute.

It should also be remembered that methemoglobinemia can occur unpredictably even when an individual is genetically intact and without any known hereditary defects. Hrgovic (1990) used intravenous vitamin C to successfully treat a newborn who demonstrated methemoglobinemia that was felt to have resulted from the local prilocaine anesthesia given the mother for delivery. Considering the safe clinical profile of vitamin C, it is probably a good idea to treat any cyanotic (purple-lipped, oxygen-starved) patient with vitamin C while further pursuing the diagnosis. This can be especially important when cyanosis occurs during surgery, indicating the possible presence of an anesthesia-induced methemoglobinemia that can readily be treated with intravenous vitamin C (Tao et al., 1994).

Methemoglobin is normally found in the blood at a level of 1% or less (Kueh et al., 1986). The iron in methemoglobin is in the oxidized ferric form, and vitamin C is one of the agents that can reduce the ferric form back to the ferrous state, which restores the hemoglobin to its normal, oxygen-carrying state.

Methylene blue is still the most common treatment for methemoglobinemia. However, vitamin C has been used as the sole treatment, and it has also proved to be very effective (Nair and Philip, 1984). Indeed, the effective doses of vitamin C that have been reported for the treatment of human methemoglobinemia are still much lower than the doses of vitamin C used so effectively by Klenner for a wide variety of poisonings and infections. As with so many other conditions, the true effectiveness of optimally dosed vitamin C for the treatment of methemoglobinemia is likely yet to be determined. Also, vitamin C therapy can be used to help control some of the hereditary forms of methemoglobinemia (Jaffe, 1982; Svecova and Bohmer, 1998; Prchal and Jenkins, 2000).

Fifty-One Miscellaneous Toxins

Acetaminophen is a common over-the-counter analgesic, which can be fatal if overdosed. Acute toxicity can manifest as various degrees of liver toxicity, including acute liver failure. In mice, Peterson and Knodell (1984) found that a 1,000 mg/kg body size dose of vitamin C given either one hour before or one hour after a dose of acetaminophen that would kill a large number of liver cells had a pronounced protective (or reparative) effect. Romero-Ferret et al. (1983), using a maximal vitamin C dose of only 200 mg/kg body weight, did not increase the survival rate of mice given potentially lethal doses of acetaminophen. A 600 mg/kg body weight dose of ascorbyl palmitate, a vitamin C derivative, was able to significantly protect mice from acetaminophen-induced liver damage, while regular vitamin C did not have that protective effect at the same dose (Jonker et al., 1988; Mitra et al., 1991). These studies clearly support Klenner's finding that enough vitamin C must be used for a given condition, or the beneficial effect may be completely missed.

In cats, acetaminophen can be potentially fatal. Ilkiw and Ratcliffe (1987) reported on a cat that had ingested acetaminophen 14 hours earlier. The cat was described as being already "moribund and cyanotic." Treatment with vitamin C, N-acetyl cysteine, and DL-methionine allowed the cat to clinically recover over the next 12 days.

Acetanilide, aniline, and **antipyrine** are three aromatic chemicals with structural similarities to benzene (discussed below). One important metabolic detoxification pathway for a substantial number of toxic chemicals is by hydroxylation, which is a process that adds a hydroxide ion (OH-). Vitamin C is required for the optimal performance of this detoxifying process. Axelrod et al (1954) showed that vitamin C-depleted guinea pigs took substantially longer to hydroxylate acetanilide, aniline, and antipyrine. In other words, the half-life of each of these chemicals was longer in the vitamin C-depleted guinea pig, because vitamin C repletion increased the hydroxylation rate for each chemical.

Acrolein is extremely toxic to humans and is commonly formed from the breakdown of certain air pollutants, burning gasoline, or burning tobacco,. Nardini et al. (2002) looked at acrolein-induced toxicity in human bronchial cells. Acrolein induces cellular death by a mechanism (apoptosis) that is strongly inhibited by supplemented vitamin C. Vitamin C also serves to accelerate the restoration of important cellular glutathione stores that have been acutely depleted by acrolein exposure.

Arumugam et al. (1997) and Arumugam et al. (1999) showed that acrolein was another toxin that promotes the metabolic consumption of vitamin C in animals. Rats acutely exposed to acrolein demonstrated reduced levels of vitamin C, vitamin E, and glutathione and the expected increases in oxidative stress and lipid peroxidation so commonly seen in toxic exposure. These studies indicate that vitamin C is ideal for preventing and undoing damage inflicted by acrolein.

In survival studies, Sprince et al. (1979) showed that vitamin C in combination with L-cysteine and thiamine provided a high degree of protection for rats given lethal doses of acrolein. Although the control group showed only a 5% survival rate, the combination therapy noted above resulted in treated rats showing a 90% survival.

Aflatoxin, which is toxic to the liver and known to cause cancer, is a toxic factor that comes from molds contaminating ground nut seedlings. Netke et al. (1997) showed that vitamin C protects guinea pigs from acute aflatoxin toxicity. Salem et al. (2001) showed that vitamin C reduced the negative effects of aflatoxin on the reproductive system of the rabbit. Verma et al. (1999) showed that vitamin C afforded significant protection against aflatoxin-induced rupture of red blood cells in the test tube. Bose and Sinha (1991) showed that vitamin C given to mice decreased the incidence of aflatoxin-induced chromosomal abnormalities in the bone marrow cells. Finally, Raina and Gurtoo (1985) and Bhattacharya et al. (1987) were able to demonstrate that vitamin C could lessen the ability of aflatoxin to induce mutations in some bacteria.

Allyl alcohol is an organic compound that is corrosive and can be fatal if enough is swallowed or inhaled. A chronic exposure can damage the liver or kidneys. Glascott et al. (1996) examined liver cells in culture exposed to toxic amounts of allyl alcohol. They found that both vitamins C and E had protective and independent effects against the lethal effects of allyl alcohol on these cells.

Amphetamine is a chemical that has a stimulant effect on the nervous system. Beyers (2001) reported on a case of Ecstasy overdose treated with vitamin C. Ecstasy is an amphetamine derivative. The patient, a 17-year-old boy, presented in a coma and had a grand mal seizure before reaching the hospital. The author gave only 1,000 mg of vitamin C intravenously over 30 minutes, and within 20 minutes the patient was "wide awake and talking." The vitamin C lowered urine pH from 7.5 to 5.0 within the same period, which probably accelerated the urinary excretion of amphetamine. However, it seems unlikely that increased urinary excretion of the Ecstasy alone would have resulted in such a prompt and dramatic clinical recovery.

In rats, White et al. (1988) were able to show that vitamin C lessened the behavioral effects associated with amphetamine administration. Desole et al. (1987) reached similar conclusions. Miquel et al. (1999) suggested that vitamin C appears to have anti-dopamine effects in the brain, while Mueller and Kunko (1990) noted that amphetamine enhances the release of dopamine. Wagner et al. (1985) showed that pretreatment with vitamin C clinically lessened the neurotoxic effects of methamphetamine in rats. De Vito and Wagner (1989) also noted that pretreatment with vitamin C and other antioxidants appeared to lessen the long-lasting depletions of dopamine in the brain resulting from methamphetamine administration to rats. Perry and Juhl (1977) recommended vitamin C, along with haloperidol, for the treatment of a 16-year-old girl who presented with a picture of psychosis secondary to amphetamine excess. Rebec et al. (1985) reported that vitamin C was able to substantially enhance the anti-amphetamine effects of haloperidol. These authors suggested that vitamin C has an "important role in modulating the behavioral effects of haloperidol" and other related drugs.

Overall, the evidence seems to indicate that vitamin C is of benefit in controlling the symptoms of amphetamine excess, perhaps by opposing the effects of increased dopamine released by the amphetamine while accelerating the urinary elimination of amphetamine from the body. It would also appear that vitamin C may well play an important role in keeping dopamine levels stable in the brain.

Aromatic hydrocarbons (anthracene and 3,4-benzpyrene) are likely detoxified more readily in the presence of vitamin C, becoming less carcinogenic and more readily excreted (Warren, 1943).

Benzanthrone is a chemical encountered in the industrial manufacture of dyes. Consistent with a toxic effect, Dwivedi et al. (2001) noted that its presence consumed vitamin C as well as glutathione, another antioxidant. Das et al. (1994) looked at the toxicity of benzanthrone in guinea pigs and found that a relatively small amount of vitamin C (50 mg/kg body weight) "resulted in marked improvement" in the microscopic appearance and biochemical changes seen in the liver, testis, kidney, and bladder of animals exposed to benzanthrone. Pandya et al. (1970) found that benzanthrone administration to guinea pigs caused a "significant decrease" of vitamin C levels in the blood, adrenal glands, and liver. These researchers also found that a vitamin C dose of only 25 mg/kg body weight/day caused a 40% lowering of the rate of benzanthrone-induced death in supplemented guinea pigs compared to the vitamin C-depleted group.

Dwivedi et al. (1993) also looked at the toxicity of benzanthrone applied to the skin of mice. They found that vitamin C taken orally or applied to the skin "resulted in substantial protection" against benzanthrone-induced toxic effects on both the skin and liver.

Vitamin C also has favorable effects on decreasing the organ deposition of benzanthrone and increasing its urinary and fecal elimination. In guinea pigs, Garg et al. (1992) showed that pretreating these animals with vitamin C caused a 32% increase in the excretion of benzanthrone, while organ retention of this toxin was reduced by approximately 50%. Das et al. (1991) also found that vitamin C enhanced excretion and decreased retention of benzanthrone in guinea pigs. Garg et al. suggested giving vitamin C to industrial workers exposed to benzanthrone could prevent symptoms of toxicity.

Benzene is a volatile liquid hydrocarbon, which is generated as a by-product of coal distillation. It is frequently used as a solvent in chemical laboratories, and it is a known cancer-causing agent. Meyer (1937) observed that severe chronic benzene poisoning in a benzene plant worker resulted in "symptoms like those of scurvy." Meyer reported being quite amazed when it took a total of 11,500 mg of vitamin C (6,300 mg of it intravenous) before this patient started spilling significant amounts in the urine. Meyer also noted that after this saturation was reached and then maintained with a daily dosage of vitamin C, "the objective and subjective state of the patient had been greatly improved."

A similar scurvy-like state that was benzene-induced and successfully treated with vitamin C was reported by Cathala et al. (1936). Castrovilli (1937) published evidence supportive of the conclusions of Cathala et al. Bormann (1937) also noted that workers exposed to benzene had lower vitamin C levels in the urine. In a study on rabbits, Bormann found that supplemental vitamin C appeared to delay the onset of symptoms associated with benzene poisoning. Libowitsky and Seyfried (1940) associated increased capillary fragility, a symptom seen in vitamin C deficiency, with benzene exposure in the workers they studied. They found that vitamin C administration eliminated this symptom. Forssman and Frykholm (1947) compared workers with and without environmental benzene exposure, finding that workers exposed to the benzene "display a definitely delayed saturation of vitamin C as compared with the control group." This finding is consistent with the greater consumption of vitamin C by the benzene-exposed workers.

As noted earlier, an increased requirement of vitamin C indicates an increased consumption of vitamin C, which is a typical indicator of vitamin C exerting a neutralizing effect on the toxin. Gontea et al. (1969) showed that benzene intoxication lowered the blood levels of vitamin C in guinea pigs, and it also lowered the vitamin C concentrations in the liver and adrenal glands. Browning (1952), in discussing the signs and symptoms of chronic benzene poisoning, outlined a number of findings that she, like Meyer, noted as being scurvy-like in appearance. Such an observation is consistent with a chronic exposure to benzene resulting in a significant toxic consumption of vitamin C stores. Lurie (1965) recommended that "the administration of vitamin C as a further aid in the prevention of benzene poisoning" was "a justifiable practice."

Aldashev et al. (1980) found that compared to workers without toxic exposures, greater amounts of vitamin C were needed for workers exposed to benzene fumes and the fumes of other aromatic hydrocarbons to achieve target blood levels. The authors argued that these results, along with additional data gathered on guinea pigs, indicated that higher amounts of vitamin C should be given to workers exposed to "an elevated content of benzene and vapours of its methyl derivatives."

Calabrese (1980) hypothesized that inadequate amounts of several nutrients including vitamin C could enhance the toxic effect of benzene, including benzene-induced leukemia. This is especially important because different workers with similar exposures and different levels of nutrients had highly variable evidences of clinical toxicity. Rao and Snyder (1995) also reported that vitamin C lessens benzene toxicity. These authors found that a number of different benzene metabolites appeared to cause an accumulation of free radicals in studies on human leukemia cells. Such an accumulation of free radicals would logically be an easy target for a strong antioxidant such as vitamin C.

In rat liver cell preparations, Wu et al. (1996) found that vitamin C, in a dose-dependent fashion, afforded protection from the toxic effects of bromobenzene, a benzene-related chemical. They also found that the protective effects were seen during both short-tem and long-term incubations with the bromobenzene. In guinea pigs exposed to benzene and variable amounts of vitamin C, more vitamin C was able to lessen the amount of benzene-protein binding that took place. This effect was felt to be consistent with lessened toxicity (Sawahata and Neal, 1983; Smart and Zannoni, 1984; Smart and Zannoni, 1985; Smart and Zannoni, 1986). Also studying guinea pigs, Gontea et al. (1969) showed that an increased dose of vitamin C in one experimental system lessened the toxic symptoms of benzene and lowered the mortality rate by 57%.

Carbon tetrachloride (CCl4) is a clear, volatile liquid used as a solvent in pharmaceutical preparations. Inhalation of its vapors can depress the central nervous system, and carbon tetrachloride commonly has toxic effects on the liver and kidneys.

In experiments on rats, Sheweita et al. (2001) and Shewaita et al. (2001a) concluded that repeated doses of vitamins C and E could reduce the toxic effects of carbon tetrachloride on the liver. They were able to show objective normalization of toxin-induced liver enzyme elevations with these two antioxidants. Ademuyiwa et al. (1994) also demonstrated that vitamin C prevented carbon tetrachloride-induced liver damage in rats.

Sun et al. (2001) showed that carbon tetrachloride is a toxin which consumes vitamin C, especially in the liver. They found that the liver concentration of vitamin C in rats was decreased significantly within 24 hours after carbon tetrachloride administration, although the level of vitamin C in the plasma was not yet influenced significantly. Gonskii et al. (1996) also found that carbon tetrachloride administration to rats decreased the vitamin C concentration in the liver. Furthermore, they found that "the total antioxidative activity" of the rat liver was lowered by this toxic substance.

Several research teams have reported that much of carbon tetrachloride-induced liver injury may be due to increased oxidative stress and the appearance of increased free radicals. As with many other toxicities, this is a condition ideally suited for treatment by vitamin C (Maellaro et al., 1994; Ohta et al., 1997; Zhang et al., 2001; Sun et al., 2001). Soliman et al. (1965) experimented with mice and found that an intravenous injection of 30 mg of vitamin C prior to the administration of an LD10 (a lethal dose for 10% of the test group) of carbon tetrachloride completely prevented death in the 30 mice given both agents. The authors also noted that this vitamin C dose minimized the carbon tetrachloride-induced abnormal tissue changes as seen under the microscope.

Chatterjee (1967) was able to demonstrate that vitamin C could prevent another toxic manifestation of carbon tetrachloride poisoning in rats. Chatterjee noted that carbon tetrachloride induced gonadal degeneration in rats, and he was able to prevent this toxin-induced degeneration with vitamin C and normalize the gonadal rhythm.

Chloramphenicol is a broad-spectrum antibiotic that also has a significant toxic profile. Farombi (2001) looked at rats that were given chloramphenicol and found that the levels of vitamin C, vitamin A, and beta carotene were all "significantly decreased" following this administration. Consistent with these decreases in antioxidant levels, Farombi also showed that chloramphenicol significantly increased oxidative stress in rats. Working with mice, Banerjee and Basu (1975) reported that chloramphenicol significantly lowered tissue levels of vitamin C, especially in the liver. Alabi et al. (1994) looked at the effects of chloramphenicol on human plasma vitamin C levels outside of the body. Increasing amounts of chloramphenicol significantly reduced these vitamin C levels.

In addition to the above evidence that chloramphenicol consumes vitamin C stores like other toxins, Rawal (1978) showed that the addition of vitamin C to a solution of bacteria increased the effectiveness of chloramphenicol as an antibiotic against the bacteria. It would seem that routine administration of vitamin C with chloramphenicol can increase the antimicrobial effectiveness of chloramphenicol while decreasing its toxicity.

Chloroform was once widely used as an inhalation anesthetic agent. It is readily toxic to the liver and kidneys when ingested. Tamura et al. (1970) looked at the antidotal effect of vitamin C on chloroform toxicity in mice. They found that higher vitamin C doses had a better ability to protect mice from a dose of chloroform that would otherwise kill 50% of the mice. A vitamin C dose of 400 mg/kg body weight reduced the death rate to 40%, and a vitamin C dose of 600 mg/kg body weight reduced the death rate to only 10%. Finally, a vitamin C dose of 1,000 mg/kg body weight allowed 100% survival of all chloroform-exposed mice. In the words of the authors, at this dosage level "the toxicity of chloroform was rendered nil."

Cisplatin is an antitumor drug used against a wide variety of cancers. It also has significant toxic side effects, including inducing genetic abnormalities that can result in new or secondary cancers. Vitamin C lessened the ability of a cisplatin drug complex to cause DNA damage in human lymphocyte cultures (Blasiak and Kowalik, 2001) and in endometrial cancer cells (Blasiak et al., 2002). Nefic (2001) also showed that vitamin C reduced the ability of cisplatin to induce chromosomal damage in human lymphocyte cultures. Giri (1998) demonstrated that vitamin C could protect against cisplatin-induced chromosomal damage in mouse bone marrow cells.

Cisplatin can also induce kidney damage, hearing damage, and other nonspecific oxidative damage. Greggi Antunes et al. (2000) showed that vitamin C protected rat kidneys from the toxic effects of cisplatin in a dose-dependent manner. Appenroth (1997) also showed that vitamin C when administered with vitamin E did an even better job in protecting the rat kidney from cisplatin-induced toxicity. Rybak et al. (1999) concluded that hearing damage in rats caused by cisplatin was initiated by the production of more free radicals (increased oxidative stress). Lopez-Gonzalez et al. (2000) were able to lessen this hearing damage in rats with an antioxidant treatment that included vitamin C. Finally, Olas et al. (2000) showed that vitamin C could protect against cisplatin-induced LPO and other indicators of oxidative stress in blood platelets.

Cyanides are all extremely potent and rapidly-acting toxins that effectively reduce oxygen availability to cells. Consistent with the vitamin C-depleting effects of other toxins, Koshiishi et al. (1997) were able to show that a specific plant soaked in sodium cyanate solution demonstrated a significant depletion of its vitamin C content. Such a solution is used as a herbicide. These authors suggested that this data indicated that at least one mechanism of cyanide toxicity comes through the induction of oxidative stress, which consumes vitamin C.

In cultures of rat cells, Kanthasamy et al. (1997) were able to show that cyanide induces toxicity by generating reactive oxygen species and overall increased oxidative stress. Consistent with the potent antioxidant properties of vitamin C, these authors showed that vitamin C lessened this oxidative stress and blocked the cell death induced by cyanide. Using the same cell line, Mills et al. (1996) were also able to show that vitamin C helped protect against cyanide-induced cell death. Nakao (1961) showed that cyanide accelerated the metabolic consumption (oxidation) of vitamin C in rat tissue (intestine) preparations.

Cyclophosphamide is a chemotherapeutic agent used in a wide variety of cancers. It is also a common part of the treatment used to suppress the immune systems in patients with transplanted organs. Interestingly, cyclophosphamide itself is pharmacologically inert, but several active metabolites are produced by enzyme systems in the liver.

Lee et al. (1996) reported data on cases of fatal cyclophosphamide-induced cardiac toxicity. Of 10 patients treated with "conventional therapy," nine died and the other went into chronic congestive heart failure. However, one of three other patients who received an "antioxidant therapy" of vitamin C and theophylline was reported to have survived the acute cyclophosphamide toxicity.

As with many other potent toxins, cyclophosphamide increases oxidative stress and generates excess free radicals (Venkatesan and

Chandrakasan, 1995). Consistent with this finding, Venkatesan and Chandrakasan showed that rats with cyclophosphamide intoxication demonstrated increased levels of lipid peroxidation in blood and lung tissue. Correspondingly, the levels of vitamin C and glutathione were lowered. In a similar animal model, Venkatesan and Chandrakasan (1994, 1994a) also showed lower vitamin C and glutathione levels in the lung washings of cyclophosphamide-toxic rats.

Some indicators of liver toxicity from cyclophosphamide can be restored to normal by vitamin C. Ghosh et al. (1999) found that cyclophosphamide significantly elevated two common liver enzymes (SGOT and SGPT), and vitamin C supplementation could normalize these test values. Vasavi et al. (1998) found that rats treated with cyclophosphamide developed significant lipid abnormalities, including substantial increases in total cholesterol and triglycerides. Also, they found that the "good" cholesterol (HDL-cholesterol) was lowered by treatment with this toxin. All of these toxin-induced abnormalities, however, were "corrected by the co-administration" of vitamin C.

A number of investigators have looked at the effects of vitamin C on cyclophosphamide-induced chromosomal damage. Vijayalaxmi and Venu (1999) found that relatively low doses of vitamin C (10 to 60 mg/kg body weight) given to mice were effective in reducing the microscopic evidence of this chromosomal damage. Also in mice, Ghaskadbi et al. (1992) showed that a wider dosing range of vitamin C (1.56 to 200 mg/kg body weight) "exhibited a significant antimutagenic effect" against the toxicity of cyclophosphamide. They also noted that the "dose-response relationship was highly significant," indicating larger doses of vitamin C had the most pronounced antitoxic effects.

Other investigators have looked at the ability of vitamin C to protect against cyclophosphamide-induced chromosomal damage and to protect animal fetuses from birth defects. In pregnant mice, Kola et al. (1989) found a vitamin C dose of 800 mg/kg body weight significantly lowered the cyclophosphamide-induced chromosomal abnormalities and resulted in a "significantly higher number of viable fetuses." Also in pregnant mice, Vogel and Spielmann (1989) found a vitamin C dosage range of 25 to 1,600 mg/kg body weight reduced chromosomal damage from cyclophosphamide. They suggested that vitamin C "seems to protect early embryos against damage induced by genotoxic agents" such as cyclophosphamide. Pillans et al. (1990) looked at the effects of much higher vitamin C dosing in cyclophosphamide-toxic pregnant mice. Administration of vitamin C at doses of 3,340 mg/kg body weight was "not associated with demonstrable toxic effects" and had "a protective effect against the toxic manifestations of cyclophosphamide." Furthermore, at this vitamin C dose level "all fetuses were morphologically normal and there was no reduction in fetal weight."

In non-pregnant toxic mice, Krishna et al. (1986) showed that this large vitamin C dose level provided a very good protection against chromosomal damage. Interestingly, Pillans et al. gave a maximal vitamin C dose of 6,680 mg/kg body weight in their pregnant mice. This is roughly equivalent to a vitamin C dose of 607,000 mg in a 200-pound person. At this dose they found a 46% incidence in fetal mortality, even though the lower doses were clearly protective of the fetus. Although it is highly unusual, these researchers may have inadvertently defined a dose beyond which vitamin C should not be acutely dosed, at least for pregnant mice. It points out the fact that too much of a good thing, even vitamin C, might be harmful. However, as has been shown in numerous studies, the highest vitamin C dosage levels that consistently produce positive results are rarely approached.

Cyclosporine is a drug commonly used to suppress the immune system in order to prevent rejection in organ transplant recipients. In rabbits treated with cyclosporine, Durak et al. (1998) demonstrated that cyclosporine induced damage in the kidney cells. They showed that vitamins C and E lessened this damage as well as the increase in oxidative stress also resulting from the cyclosporine. Wolf et al. (1997) showed a similar toxic effect of cyclosporine on rat liver cells in culture and a similar protective effect by vitamins C and E. The authors concluded that cyclosporine causes toxicity in rat liver cells at least partially by an increase in oxidative stress. Benito et al. (1995) found that cyclosporine caused certain changes in the electrophoresis patterns of rat liver and kidney samples. The researchers also showed that, in the doses used, vitamins C and E were "able to prevent around 30% of the effects caused by cyclosporine" in these patterns.

In human lymphocyte cultures Rojas et al. (2002) observed that cyclosporine induced cell death, and that vitamin C and N-acetyl cysteine could lessen this toxic effect.

In lung transplant patients, Williams et al. (1999) found that there existed persistent oxidative stress as well as a compromised antioxidant status. These findings strongly indicate that vitamin C therapy may be of benefit in decreasing organ rejection. Slakey et al. (1993) and Slakey et al. (1993a) also felt that increased free radicals, or increased oxidative stress, were likely an important part of the process of organ transplant rejection. They worked with rats that had undergone heart transplants. The rats given both cyclosporine and vitamins C and E demonstrated a prolonged survival of the transplanted organs. The doses of vitamin C were also quite substantial, equating to about 100,000 mg daily for a 200-pound person.

Digoxin is a heart drug commonly used for the treatment of heart failure or certain abnormal heart rhythms, even though digoxin can have toxic effects when too much is given. De et al. (2001) studied the effect of digoxin in a goat liver tissue preparation. The drug caused a measurable increase in oxidative stress while reducing the levels of glutathione, an important antioxidant. Vitamin C was able to significantly suppress these manifestations of digoxin-induced toxicity, and the authors suggested that digoxin toxicity may be the result of increased free radicals.

Dopamine is an essential neurotransmitter in the central nervous system. However, when out of balance in the body, dopamine is also a "known neurotoxin" that may play a role in the development of several neurodegenerative diseases (Stokes et al., 2000). Stokes et al. showed that dopamine can increase oxidative stress and cell death in a culture of cells from nervous tissue. Vitamin C exerted a protective effect against the dopamine-induced toxicity.

Levodopa, a drug used in the treatment of Parkinson's disease, is a precursor to dopamine. Levodopa has also been shown to cause toxicity in nervous tissue. Pardo et al. (1993) have shown that the toxic effect of levodopa in cultures of human nervous tissue is prevented by the administration of vitamin C. Furthermore, the toxicity of levodopa in this system is associated with increasing levels of quinone, which are also prevented by vitamin C. In cultures of rat nervous tissue, Mena et al. (1993) and Pardo et al. (1995) showed that vitamin C completely blocked the levodopa-induced production of quinone, thereby lessening the observed toxic effects of levodopa on these cultures.

Doxorubicin is the chemical name for an anthracycline antibiotic best known by its trademark name Adriamycin. Doxorubicin is considered to have one of the widest spectrums of antitumor activity among the commonly used chemotherapy agents. However, it is also an exceptionally toxic agent as the cumulative dose increases. Fukuda et al. (1992) reported that increased oxidative stress, as manifested by increased lipid peroxidation, is known to be a mechanism for the toxicity of this drug. Geetha et al. (1989) showed that vitamin C and vitamin E could lessen the amount of lipid peroxidation initiated by doxorubicin in rats. Fujita et al. (1982) also showed that vitamin C significantly prolonged the lifespans of mice and guinea pigs treated with doxorubicin, while preserving the antitumor effect of the drug. They also noted that vitamin C was able to block the increased lipid peroxidation seen in the blood and liver after doxorubicin administration.

Outside of the body (*in vitro*) Kurbacher et al. (1996) examined the interaction between vitamin C and doxorubicin in cultured human breast cancer cells. They found vitamin C had its own cell-killing ability against the cancer cells and also significantly improved the cell-killing ability of the doxorubicin in this system. Even when the vitamin C was given at a dosage that was not directly cytotoxic, it was still able to improve the cell-killing ability of the doxorubicin.

Doxorubicin is well-known to cause a severe cardiac toxicity when used long enough. Dalloz et al. (1999) showed in rats that doxorubicin decreased vitamin C and E levels in the heart, while increasing the levels of lipid peroxidation. The authors suggested that these effects support the idea of using high-dose antioxidants to combat this toxicity. Kojima et al. (1994) looked at doxorubicin-induced heart toxicity in a mouse model. They found that benzylideneascorbate, a derivative of vitamin C, was very effective in decreasing heart enzyme elevations associated with doxorubicin-induced toxicity. In mice and guinea pigs, Shimpo et al. (1991) reported that vitamin C significantly prolonged the lifespan of animals given doxorubicin even though it did not diminish the antitumor activity of this drug in their research setting. Furthermore, these authors asserted that the significant prevention of doxorubicin-induced cardiac toxicity was "proved by electron microscopy," demonstrating that the microscopic picture agreed with the positive clinical effects afforded by vitamin C.

When intravenous doxorubicin accidentally gets under the skin rather than in the vein, severe local skin damage can result. Hajarizadeh et al. (1994) were able to show that when a 1 mg/ml concentration of vitamin C was delivered along with the doxorubicin, direct injections of this combination under the skin in pigs decreased the resulting ulcer incidence from 87% to 27%. The authors suggested that such a regimen would likely be useful in people receiving doxorubicin infusions.

Finally, doxorubicin has been shown to induce chromosome damage that can be blocked or lessened by vitamin C. Tavares et al. (1998) showed that vitamin C "significantly decreased the frequency" of doxorubicin-induced chromosome damage in rat bone marrow cells. In the same type of cells, Antunes and Takahaski (1998) also demonstrated the protective ability of vitamin C against such damage. They also showed that the efficiency of vitamin C in protecting against doxorubicin-induced chromosome damage was "dependent on the dose used."

Halogenated ethers are known toxins capable of causing cancer. Sram et al. (1983) looked at a group of 77 workers occupationally exposed to bis (chloromethyl) ether and chloromethyl methyl ether. Blood samples were drawn at the beginning and end of a five-month period of vitamin C administration (1,000 mg daily). Workers without any occupational exposure to the toxins were used as controls. By looking at the lymphocytes in the blood specimens, Sram et al. were able to determine that this relatively low dose of vitamin C significantly reduced the "risk of genetic injury," as indicated by the decreased frequency of chromosomal abnormalities seen in the supplemented workers.

Hydrazine sulfate is a chemical agent used as a germicide. Beyer (1943) used this agent to experimentally induce liver damage in vitamin C-depleted guinea pigs. Known as fatty degeneration, this type of injury is associated with an increased accumulation of fat in the liver. Beyer was able to show that the vitamin C-deficient guinea pigs given the hydrazine demonstrated "an average of 50.3 per cent more fat in their livers" than did the guinea pigs given "adequate" vitamin C along with the hydrazine. Beyer was also able to show that the microscopic changes of fatty degeneration were far less and "relatively mild" in the livers of guinea pigs given more vitamin C.

Iproniazid is a monoamine oxidase inhibitor originally developed for the treatment of tuberculosis. Although no longer used because of liver toxicity, iproniazid was also used as an antidepressant after it was found to lessen depression in some tuberculosis patients.

In rats, Matsuki et al. (1992) found that vitamin C significantly inhibited the iproniazid-induced increase in free radicals. Matsuki et al. (1994) later reported that iproniazid-induced cell death in the liver of rats was "remarkably lowered both quantitatively and qualitatively" by the administration of vitamin C.

Isoniazid, a related drug to iproniazid that is still used to treat tuberculosis, was also found to be a free radical generator. Matsuki et al. (1991) found that vitamin C was also able to significantly inhibit this increase in oxidative stress. Isoniazid can cause a drug-induced hepatitis like iproniazid, and Matsuki et al. suggested that vitamin C may lessen or suppress this toxic effect of isoniazid on the liver.

Isoproterenol is a drug used as an airway relaxant and cardiac stimulant. The cardiac stimulant effect of isoproterenol can quickly become toxic. In rats, Bloom and Davis (1972) noted that isoproterenol resulted in increased heart contraction strength when given in microgram doses, but killed heart cells when given in milligram doses. In a heart attack heart cells die, and there is a substantial increase in the products of lipid peroxidation as the cells break down (Nirmala and Puvanakrishnan, 1996). In cultured rat heart cells, vitamin C lessened isoproterenol-induced damage (Ramos and Acosta, 1983; Acosta et al., 1984; Persoon-Rothert et al., 1989; Mohan and Bloom, 1999). Persoon-Rothert et al. also showed that the formation of free radicals was the likely reason for isoproterenol-induced toxicity to heart cells.

Ramos et al. (1984) were able to show that isoproterenol toxicity resulted in the gradual accumulation of calcium inside rat heart cells and vitamin C blocked much of this intracellular increase in calcium. Laky et al. (1984) demonstrated the protective effects of magnesium ascorbate, a mineral salt of vitamin C, on isoproterenol-induced cardiac toxicity in rats.

Methanol, also known as methyl or wood alcohol, is a component of many commercially available solvents. Although methanol itself is almost completely nontoxic, its immediate breakdown products are very toxic, and accidental ingestion of enough methanol can be fatal.

The immediate oxidation product of methanol is formaldehyde. Vitamin C has been shown to accelerate this oxidative transformation in bovine tissue extracts (Sippel and Forsander, 1974) and guinea pig liver preparations (Susick and Zannoni, 1984). Formaldehyde, used for embalming, is highly toxic. Sprince et al. (1979) showed that vitamin C could substantially lessen the lethal effect of a formaldehyde dose that would otherwise kill approximately 90% of rats given this toxin. Even though a fairly small dose of vitamin C was used (about 50 mg/kg body weight), about 55% of the rats survived the formaldehyde dose. It seems likely that a Klenner-sized vitamin C dose would have a more dramatic protective effect.

In mice, Miquel et al. (1999) demonstrated that vitamin C lessened the abnormalities of body movement after a dose of methanol. Skrzydlewska and Farbiszewski (1996, 1997, 1998) showed that methanol intoxication in rats led to impaired liver, red blood cell, and blood serum antioxidant mechanisms, along with laboratory abnormalities indicating an increase in lipid peroxidation and antioxidant stress. It would be expected that vitamin C should reliably lessen or block these types of changes.

Poon et al. (1998) found that rats exposed to a chronic inhalation exposure to methanol had a dose-related increase in urinary vitamin C after two, four, and eight weeks of exposure. Poon et al. (1997) also looked at the toxicity of tris(4-chlorophenyl)methanol, a methanol derivative, in rats. As with methanol exposure, they observed an increased excretion of vitamin C in the urine, which is an anticipated response of rats to any toxin that is not immediately overwhelming in amount. They also saw a direct toxic effect on the liver, with many cells sustaining a lethal effect. Farbiszewski et al. (2000) were able to show that other antioxidants could also improve the defenses of rat brains against methanol toxicity.

N-methyl-D-aspartate (NMDA) is a neurotoxic substance that can induce cell death in rat neuron cultures. Majewska and Bell (1990) showed that vitamin C "completely protected" against NMDA-induced injury at a lower NMDA dose. They also showed that vitamin C "markedly reduced cell death" caused by a higher dose of NMDA. Bell et al. (1996) later showed a similar protective effect of vitamin C against NMDA-induced injury in neuron cultures.

Methylmalonic acid is sometimes an indicator of vitamin B12 deficiency when found elevated in the blood. When enough methylmalonic acid is given to rats, seizures result. Fighera et al. (1999) showed that vitamin C and vitamin E pretreatment decreased the duration of these toxin-induced seizures.

In a seven-year-old boy with excess methylmalonic acid in the blood due to an inborn error of metabolism, Treacy et al. (1996) demonstrated that vitamin C therapy was of significant benefit. Specifically, vitamin C therapy resulted in the resolution of the boy's skin lesions (eczema), the excess lactic acid in his blood, and his jaundice.

Morphine is a well-known opiate pain reliever that can readily kill when overdosed. Dunlap and Leslie (1985) found that a vitamin C dose of 1,000 mg/kg body weight in mice provided "significant protection against mortality due to respiratory depression." Willette et al.

(1983), also working with mice, found that a much lower dose of vitamin C (8 mg/kg) could still produce a decrease in the analgesic effect of morphine. Furthermore, they showed that larger doses of vitamin C produced a greater inhibition of this effect in a dose-dependent manner.

Nicotine is a very poisonous substance commonly known to the public because of its presence in cigarettes. However, nicotine has also served as an insecticide and a parasiticide.

Tamura et al. (1969) studied the toxicity of nicotine in mice. They were able to show that a vitamin C dose of 400 mg/kg body weight helped to protect mice against the lethal effects of a nicotine solution injection.

Halimi and Mimran (2000) looked at the effects of vitamin C on nicotine toxicity in nonsmoking human volunteers. Even though a small dose of vitamin C was given (about 200 mg), it was able to block the nicotine-induced lowering of cyclic GMP. Cyclic GMP is an important substance in regulating normal cellular function in all cells, and it appears that increased oxidative stress will lower its levels.

In pregnant rats, Maritz (1993) was able to show that a tiny dose of vitamin C (1 mg/kg body weight) prevented the toxic effects of the mother's nicotine exposure on several of the neonate's lung chemistries. Maritz also showed that the toxic effect of nicotine reduced the vitamin C content in the mother's lungs by 76%.

Nitrates and **nitrites**, along with their associated compounds, can exert significant toxicity when ingested in high enough amounts. In rats, Garcia-Roche et al. (1987) showed that a daily dose of vitamin C had an apparent protective effect against the toxic effects of nitrates and nitrites on the liver, as reflected in multiple liver laboratory tests, and in microscopic examination of the liver.

When the body establishes a tolerance to nitrate compounds used in the treatment of heart disease, a lessening of the nitrate effectiveness is known to occur. This tolerance appears to result, at least partially, from enhanced oxidant stress with an impairment of nitrate-induced relaxation of the blood vessels that improves blood flow. In dogs, Fink et al. (1999) found that vitamin C suppressed this nitrate-induced oxidant stress, lessening the clinical picture of nitrate tolerance.

The effect of vitamin C on nitrates and nitrites is also seen in studies on stomach cancer. One of the reasons favoring stomach cancer development is the dietary presence of excess nitrates and nitrites, which can produce nitrosamine, a cancer-causing agent. Cummings (1978), Schmahl and Eisenbrand (1982), Ohshima and Bartsch (1984), and Bartsch (1991) noted that the reaction converting nitrates and nitrites to nitrosamine and other cancer-causing N-nitroso compounds in the stomach is inhibited by vitamin C. Forman (1991) also noted that the protective effect of eating fruit and vegetables is probably due largely to increased dietary vitamin C. Sierra et al. (1991) and Srivatanakul et al. (1991) showed in humans that the ingestion of additional vitamin C lessened the appearance of a monitored nitrosamine in the urine. Shi et al. (1991) looked at patients who already had stomach cancer, finding that such patients had higher nitrate and lower vitamin C levels in the urine compared to normal controls. Walker (1990) recommended that vitamin C be used to reduce the conversion of nitrites in the diet to cancer-causing compounds. Wawrzyniak et al. (1997) were able to demonstrate in "simulated stomach content" outside the body that vitamin C appeared capable of decreasing the level of measurable nitrite added to the system.

A similar inhibition of nitrate conversion into cancer-causing compounds has also been demonstrated in mice. Perez et al. (1990) showed that vitamin C helped to block the formation of a N-nitroso compound when the mice were also fed high doses of nitrate.

A nitrite derivative, peroxynitrite, appears to be an important tissue-damaging compound that substantially increases oxidative stress in the affected tissue. Whiteman and Halliwell (1996) showed that both vitamin C and glutathione "protected efficiently" against several of the measurable toxic effects of this compound. Sandoval et al. (1997) looked at human and mouse cells in culture, finding that vitamin C decreased the peroxynitrite-induced cell death in these cultures.

Kok (1997) hypothesized that vitamin C may prevent the formation of peroxynitrite in the brain, and that lowered brain levels of vitamin C may play a role in the development of amyotrophic lateral sclerosis (ALS, Lou Gehrig's disease). The protective role of vitamin C against peroxynitrite-induced brain damage has also been advanced by Vatassery (1996).

Van der Vliet et al. (1994) have found that the presence of peroxynitrite in human blood plasma rapidly depletes the vitamin C present, an observation consistent with the toxicity of peroxynitrite and its metabolic breakdown when enough vitamin C is present. They also observed that peroxynitrite leads to lipid peroxidation, concluding that it likely causes a general depletion of antioxidants and an increase in oxidative stress and damage. Bohm et al. (1998) have also observed that vitamin C works very well with other antioxidants (vitamin E, beta carotene) in protecting cells from the toxicity of peroxynitrite. Shi et al. (1994) concluded that vitamin C probably provides "a detoxification pathway" for peroxynitrite. Kirsch and Groot (2000) observed that vitamin C has a potent antidote effect against several different peroxynitrite-induced oxidation reactions.

Peroxynitrite appears to have some interesting toxic effects on the heart, and vitamin C has been observed to counteract these toxic effects. Carnes et al. (2001) have demonstrated that an abnormal heart rhythm, atrial fibrillation (AF), "is associated with increased atrial oxidative stress and peroxynitrite formation." They also showed that supplemented vitamin C given to 43 patients prior to cardiac bypass surgery and for five subsequent days significantly reduced the incidence of postoperative AF. Vitamin C-supplemented patients had a 16.3% incidence of AF after surgery, and control patients without the vitamin C had a 34.9% incidence of AF. In rat hearts, Gao et al. (2002a) were able to show that vitamin C along with a glutathione derivative could reduce the amount of heart tissue injury after the experimental termination of blood flow to a part of the heart. The authors felt that this effect was at least partially due to a lessening of toxic peroxynitrite formation in the heart tissue.

The scientific evidence indicates that vitamin C is very effective in blocking the conversion of nitrates and nitrites into compounds of known toxicity and cancer-causing ability. At the same time vitamin C also serves to directly lessen the toxicity of a related nitrite compound.

Nitrogen dioxide is a gas that is primarily toxic to the lungs. Once in the airways, it converts locally to nitric and nitrous acid, which exert a direct toxic effect on the cells that they contact. Human exposure to nitrogen dioxide commonly occurs in arc welders, firefighters, and those working with explosives. Nitrogen dioxide can also be generated as a by-product of the anaerobic fermentation of crops.

Tu et al. (1995) looked at the direct toxicity of nitrogen dioxide to cultured human blood vessel cells. They found that vitamin C played an important role in protecting the cells from these toxic effects. Also, they found that glutathione worked well with vitamin C in providing this protection. Cooney et al. (1986) showed that both vitamin C and glutathione were able to inhibit the ability of nitrogen dioxide to form cancer-causing compounds by its chemical reaction with another compound, morpholine. Miyanishi et al. (1996) also showed that vitamin C could lessen the mutagenic (mutation-causing) effects of nitrogen dioxide in mice.

In keeping with its profile as a toxin, nitrogen dioxide was shown by Halliwell et al. (1992) to rapidly deplete vitamin C levels in human blood plasma. Similarly, Leung and Morrow (1981) showed that nitrogen dioxide exposure substantially lowered vitamin C concentrations in guinea pig lungs. The importance of vitamin C in the detoxification of nitrogen dioxide is also suggested by the work of Hatch et al. (1986). These researchers showed that vitamin C deficiency in guinea pigs enhanced the lung toxicity of nitrogen dioxide. Bohm et al. (1998) showed that vitamin C, vitamin E, and beta carotene all worked together to protect against nitrogen dioxide toxicity.

Ochratoxin is a mycotoxin, which is a toxin derived from fungus. Ochratoxin has no known commercial use, but its experimental use can cause cancer and promote genetic damage. It is a naturally occurring mycotoxin, and is found as a contaminant on corn, peanuts, storage grains, cottonseed, animal feeds, and decaying vegetation. Pfohl-Leszkowicz (1994) showed that vitamin C can lessen ochratoxin-induced tumors in the kidneys and livers of rats. Grosse et al. (1997) also showed this vitamin C anticancer effect in ochratoxin-exposed mouse kidneys. Marquardt and Frohlich (1992) showed that vitamin C could lessen the toxicity of ochratoxin in laying hens.

Rahimtula et al. (1988) showed that ochratoxin enhanced lipid peroxidation and oxidative stress in both rats and chicks, suggesting this effect as a reason for the toxicity of ochratoxin. Hoehler and Marquardt (1996) also demonstrated that ochratoxin increased lipid peroxidation in chicks. They showed that vitamin E lessened this increase, even though a small dose of vitamin C was ineffective.

In mice, Bose and Sinha (1994) showed that a relatively small vitamin C dose was quite effective in lessening sperm abnormalities caused by ochrotoxin.

Ofloxacin is an antibiotic observed to promote mutations in the microorganism *Euglena gracilis*. Ebringer et al. (1996) showed that vitamin C could "significantly decrease" this "genotoxic effect" of ofloxacin.

Ozone is a gas and potent oxidant capable of damaging the lungs when inhaled in a high enough concentration. The cornea of the eye can also be an oxidation target. Weber et al. (1999) showed that acute exposure of mice to ozone decreased the concentration of vitamin C in the outer layer of skin, "providing further evidence that ozone induces oxidative stress in this outer skin layer," while demonstrating the typical consumption of vitamin C by the presence of a toxin.

Kari et al. (1997) showed in the lungs of rats that protection against ozone-induced toxicity was "mediated partially by increases in ascorbate in the fluid bathing the lung surface." Wiester et al. (1996) demonstrated that vitamin C levels were elevated in the fluids used to irrigate the lungs of rats that had adapted to ozone. They also found that the extent of adaptation was related to vitamin C concentration in this irrigation fluid.

In guinea pigs, Kodavanti et al. (1995) and Kodavanti et al. (1995a) asserted that acute ozone toxicity seen in the lungs was increased by a vitamin C deficiency. In human subjects exposed to inhaled ozone,

Mudway et al. (1996) found that greater amounts of inhaled ozone consumed more vitamin C. These researchers also showed that vitamin C was depleted more rapidly than glutathione by the toxic effects of ozone. In mice, Kratzing and Willis (1980) were also able to show that ozone exposure decreased lung vitamin C levels.

Ichinose and Sagai (1989) found in guinea pigs that a combined chronic exposure of ozone and nitrogen dioxide resulted in a substantial increase in oxidative stress, as measured by increased lipid peroxides. Also in a guinea pig model, Yeadon and Payne (1989) showed that vitamin C could prevent ozone-induced bronchial hyperreactivity. In another experimental system, Cotovio et al. (2001) were able to demonstrate increased oxidative stress in cultured human skin cells due to ozone exposure. They also showed that vitamin C was efficient in preventing this ozone-induced oxidative damage to the cells. Acknowledging this ozone-induced increase in oxidative stress, Menzel (1994) suggested a regular supplementation with both vitamin C and vitamin E, adding that such supplementation is especially important for protecting the developing lungs of children.

In plants, it has also been shown that vitamin C is a likely protector against oxidative stress such as that induced by ozone exposure. Vitamin C levels in leaves were noted to fluctuate during the day, showing the highest levels at those times when environmental ozone exposure was highest and indicating a probable adaptive response.

Paraquat is used primarily as a herbicide. In addition to being capable of inducing methemoglobinemia, paraquat can cause substantial liver, kidney, and lung damage. Schvartsman et al. (1984) were able to show that vitamin C could delay death and even cause a slight increase in the survival rate of rats given fatal doses of paraquat. Similarly, Matkovics et al. (1980) were able to show that vitamin C improved survival in paraquat-exposed mice. Hong et al. (2002) suggested that injected vitamin C was very important in maintaining a high enough total antioxidant status in the blood of paraquat-poisoned patients to facilitate their recoveries. In keeping with paraquat's role as a toxin, Minakata et al. (1993) were able to show that the presence of paraquat in human serum clearly accelerated the destruction (utilization) of vitamin C that was already in the serum.

Cappelletti et al. (1998) looked at the protective effects of vitamin C and N-acetyl cysteine, both potent antioxidants, on cultured human lung cells from the toxicity of paraquat. They found that these two antioxidants reduced paraquat-induced death of these cells.

An additional example of vitamin C's importance in dealing with paraquat toxicity comes from Minakata et al. (1996), who studied a rat mutant that was unable to synthesize vitamin C. The mutant readily showed toxicity after being given paraquat, while a normal rat given paraquat resembled a normal rat given none. The difference in this experiment was the rat's ability to make vitamin C in response to a toxic stress.

Paraquat is also felt to cause significant oxidative damage. Vismara et al. (2001) showed that vitamin C was able to "drastically reduce" the toxicity of paraquat which resulted from toxin-induced oxidative damage on frog embryos.

An additional potential benefit of vitamin C in the treatment of paraquat intoxications comes from the work of Fujimoto et al. (1989). In preparations of rabbit kidney they were able to show that vitamin C exerted a dose-dependent inhibition of paraquat accumulation. The authors suggested that this effect supported the choice of vitamin C as an antidote for paraquat toxicity.

Phencyclidine is the hallucination-inducing anesthetic agent commonly known as PCP or Angel Dust. It is a commonly abused street drug that is most often smoked rather than swallowed to allow better control of the drug's effects by the user. Rappolt et al. (1979) described the effects of a low, moderate, or heavy overdose of PCP. The heavy overdose is usually ingested, while the low overdose is usually smoked. In all three stages of PCP overdose, the authors have used vitamin C as part of a successful treatment protocol. Intravenous vitamin C was recommended by the authors for moderate and heavy overdoses.

Part of the positive effect that vitamin C has on PCP intoxication relates to accelerated urinary excretion of PCP by acidifying the urine

(Rappolt et al., 1979a; Hamilton and Garnett, 1980). Vitamin C as ascorbic acid is one of the agents that has been used in this manner (Simpson and Khajawall, 1983). In fact, vitamin C can be administered to patients suspected of PCP intoxication in order to confirm the diagnosis when the PCP subsequently appears in the urine (Kaul and Davidow, 1980).

Giannini et al. (1987) reported that vitamin C was effective as an antipsychotic agent when given to men with PCP intoxication. They also found that haloperidol and vitamin C together had an even better antipsychotic effect than either one alone. Aronow et al. (1980) advocated giving 2,000 mg of vitamin C intravenously every six hours to comatose patients intoxicated with PCP. Even though the researchers apparently thought vitamin C was helping only by promoting the acidity of the urine to better excrete the PCP, undoubtedly a much broader antidotal effect was taking place. Welch and Correa (1980) reported success in treating a PCP-toxic 11-day-old baby with a regimen that included 250 mg of vitamin C every six hours.

Phenol is an extremely toxic compound that typically poisons by ingestion or skin absorption. Phenol is also known as hydroxybenzene since it is the major metabolite of benzene (Smart and Zannoni, 1984). Benzene was shown earlier to be at least partially detoxified by vitamin C.

Skvortsova et al. (1981) looked at rats chronically exposed to phenol. They identified phenol-induced abnormalities in laboratory tests looking at carbohydrate and fat metabolism. They were able to show that vitamin C, along with thiamine and calcium pantothenate, normalized these phenol-induced laboratory abnormalities. They suggested that supplementing industrial workers exposed to phenol with these nutrients could "prevent phenol poisonings more effectively."

A phenol derivative, 2-amino-4,5-dichlorophenol, is directly toxic to rat kidney tissue *in vitro*. Valentovic et al. (2002) showed that pretreatment of the tissue with vitamin C or glutathione reduced toxicity. Valentovic et al. (1999) also showed that pretreatment with vitamin C reduced the toxicity of 2-amino-5-chlorophenol in rat kidney tissue preparations. Hong et al. (1997) looked at the toxicity of a closely related compound, 4-amino-2,6-dichlorophenol, in the rat kidney. In this experiment, the toxin was given directly to the rat, and kidney toxicity was pronounced. Vitamin C "afforded complete prevention" from several of the measured toxic effects of this agent, and the authors felt that oxidation of the toxin appeared to be essential for its toxicity in the kidney.

Nagyova and Ginter (1995) studied the toxic effects of 2,4-dichlorophenol in guinea pigs. They found that the administration of this toxin to guinea pigs with a low vitamin C intake significantly reduced the activity of important liver detoxification enzymes. They were also able to show that such an enzyme reduction did not occur in guinea pigs that were given the toxin along with a higher vitamin C dose.

Eugenol is a phenol derivative used as a dental analgesic. Satoh et al. (1998) showed that vitamin C "completely scavenged" the eugenol in solution, and it reduced the toxicity that eugenol exerted against some cell lines in culture.

Aminophenol compounds have also been shown to be toxic to the kidneys. Song et al. (1999) showed that vitamin C prevented the toxicity of p-aminophenol when it was given to mice. In rats, Lock et al. (1993) showed that vitamin C "completely protected against the cell death" induced by 4-aminophenol in a suspension of rabbit kidney cells.

Polychlorinated biphenyl compounds (PCBs) are a group of substances used as heat-transfer agents and insulators in electrical equipment. They tend to accumulate in animal tissues, causing a number of different toxic effects including cancer.

Multiple researchers have established that chronic exposure of PCBs to rats will result in increased vitamin C blood levels, increased urinary excretion of vitamin C, and increased liver vitamin C levels. This is the classic reaction to a toxin by an animal capable of neutralizing a toxin by synthesizing its own vitamin C. Where measured, the researchers also found that PCB exposure resulted in elevations of blood cholesterol, which is another nonspecific but consistent response to the presence of a toxin such as PCB (Chow et al., 1979; Chow et al., 1981; Horio and Yoshida, 1982; Horio et al., 1983; Oda et al., 1987; Kawai-

Kobayashi and Yoshida, 1988; Nagaoka et al., 1991; Pelissier et al., 1992; Poon et al., 1994; Chu et al., 1996; Mochizuki et al., 2000). Fujiwara and Kuriyama (1977) also showed that the elevated levels of vitamin C seen in rats after a PCB challenge were due to expected increased synthesis rather than some mechanism slowing vitamin C breakdown. Dvorak (1989) showed a similar rise in vitamin C blood and urine levels in PCB-fed pigs. Like rats, pigs can also synthesize vitamin C in response to toxic challenges.

The work of Kawai-Kobayashi and Yoshida (1986) and Saito (1990) also demonstrated that increased vitamin C is useful in counteracting PCB toxicity. These researchers showed that PCB-fed rats had increased lipid peroxidation and oxidative stress. Other researchers (Horio et al., 1986; Suzuki et al., 1993; Matsushita et al., 1993), in studying a mutant rat unable to make vitamin C, found that vitamin C is needed for the general support and maximum induction of several liver enzyme systems needed to detoxify PCB and other toxins.

Chakraborty et al. (1978a) also demonstrated that PCB toxicity "drastically disturbed" the normal microscopic pattern of rat liver cells. However, these researchers also showed that supplementing these animals with vitamin C "could afford a definite protection" against the toxin-induced changes in the microscopic appearance of the liver cells.

Porphyrins are found in the hemoglobin of the red blood cell. Some porphyrins can generate free radicals by absorbing energy from light, and are considered phototoxic. Bohm et al. (2001) described two types of phototoxic porphyrins. They showed that vitamin C, especially when combined with beta carotene and vitamin E, could help protect against the toxicity of these porphyrins in cell cultures.

Quinone compounds are known to have toxic effects. Vamvakas et al. (1992) showed that 2-bromo-3-(N-acetylcystein-S-yl)hydroquinone induced a decrease in the viability of cultured rat kidney cells. This decrease in viability was dependent on exposure time and concentration of toxin used, and vitamin C afforded some protection from the toxic effect.

Liehr (1991) showed that vitamin C reduced the incidence and severity of kidney tumors induced in hamsters by estrogens. This researcher hypothesized that the estrogens were oxidized to quinone metabolites, which then exerted the tumor-promoting effect. Liehr felt that the antitumor effect of vitamin C in this system was likely due to the inhibitory effect that vitamin C had on the formation of quinone metabolites.

Tayama and Nakagawa (1994) showed that chromosomal defects caused by phenylhydroquinone in cultured hamster ovary cells could be inhibited by vitamin C. Lambert and Eastmond (1994) also found that vitamin C could "significantly inhibit" the chromosomal damage inflicted by phenylhydroquinone on hamster lung cells.

Rubidium is a rare metallic element with derivative compounds that can pose significant health hazards. Rubidium compounds are used widely throughout industry, including the pharmaceutical, photographic, and electronic fields. Johnson et al. (1975) reported that significant ingestion of these compounds can result in acute toxicity. In rats, Chatterjee et al. (1979) studied the effects of "subacute rubidium chloride toxicity" in relation to vitamin C metabolism and certain enzymes in the liver, kidney, and brain tissues. Although the supplemented rats received a fairly low daily vitamin C dose (100 mg/kg body weight), "some protection against the alterations of certain liver enzymes" and against the microscopic changes in the liver and kidney "as caused by rubidium toxicity" was noted.

Selenium is a nonmetallic element and an essential mineral that is a component of the important enzyme glutathione peroxidase. However, excessive exposures to selenium and selenium-related compounds can be highly toxic. Civil and McDonald (1978) reported a case of acute selenium poisoning where a 15-year-old girl intentionally swallowed 400 ml of sheep drench labeled "sodium selenate 5 mg/ml." The authors calculated her dose to be "many times the minimum lethal dose" of sodium selenate for animals. Furthermore, her blood levels were found to be "at least" 20 times higher than the normal range. She was treated with intramuscular and oral vitamin C along with dimercaprol, an agent used for heavy metal chelation. She was noted to be well six months after the incident.

In studies on rats, Svirbely (1938) noted that selenium poisoning lowered vitamin C levels in spite of the rat's ability to make vitamin C. Apparently the dose was large enough in this study to overwhelm the ability of the rat's liver to compensate for the toxic insult. Svirbely also found that the levels of selenides (selenium compounds) in these animals could be reduced by vitamin C supplementation.

The addition of enough sodium selenate will induce subsequent congenital malformations in rat embryo cultures. Usami et al. (1999) were able to show that vitamin C could reduce the incidence of such malformations. The authors concluded that the oxidation-reduction state was critical in the development of selenium-induced congenital defects.

Terada et al. (1997) showed that selenious acid, another selenium compound, was able to induce significant damage to cultures of cells that line the blood vessels. However, when vitamin C was given with selenious acid, this damage was not observed.

Hill (1979) found that high levels of selenium were able to significantly retard growth in chicks. Hill also found that an increase in dietary vitamin C was able to lessen this growth retardation.

In mice, Jacques-Silva et al. (2001) found that diphenyl diselenide reduced blood hemoglobin levels. They showed that when mice given this form of selenium were also given vitamin C, the hemoglobin content was "significantly higher." Consistent with the presence of a toxin, the liver vitamin C content of exposed mice increased. Furthermore, these researchers showed that vitamin C "decreased significantly" the deposition of selenium in the livers and brains of rats receiving diphenyl diselenide. They suggested their results indicated "that vitamin C may have a protective role in organoselenide intoxication."

The existing literature justifies the use of vitamin C as at least one of the treating agents in cases of selenium poisoning.

Strontium is a metallic element. While not especially toxic, when taken in excess it can replace calcium in the bone and eventually lessen bone strength. Ortega et al. (1989) looked at vitamin C along with a number of chelating agents in a mouse experimental system. After strontium injections into the abdomens of the mice, vitamin C was the only agent that significantly increased the fecal excretion of strontium. Furthermore, they also showed that vitamin C was among the most effective chelators in reducing the concentrations of strontium in various tissues.

Sulfa drugs are antibacterial compounds that have been largely replaced by more effective and less toxic antibiotics. Schropp (1943) reported probable toxic side effects of sulfapyridine in a five-year-old boy. The boy presented with pneumonia documented by X-ray. Eight hours after his first dose of sulfapyridine, he developed a fever blister and his gums became red and swollen, bleeding easily. The gum deterioration was consistent with the gums of a scurvy patient. Sulfapyridine was not discontinued, but a mere 50 mg of vitamin C was given with each subsequent dose of sulfapyridine. Schropp termed the clinical results "astounding." By 10 hours after the first vitamin C dose, the soreness of the mouth and gums had completely disappeared, and the swelling of the tongue had resolved. One interpretation of this case is that sulfapyridine toxicity further consumed vitamin C in a body already significantly depleted of vitamin C by advanced infection. However, the small doses of vitamin C were nevertheless very effective in resolving the acute manifestations of scurvy.

McCormick (1945) noted that sulfa drugs were frequently associated with toxic effects. McCormick reported a case of "sulfonamide poisoning" successfully treated with vitamin C. The patient was "a middle-aged female" who developed a rash over her entire body and "mucous membranes." This occurred after the use of a "sulfa ointment" for a sore on her hand. Her urine showed "a pronounced C-avitaminosis," and she was given 500 mg of vitamin C daily for a week, making "a rapid and uneventful recovery." McCormick made the very insightful observation that a sensitivity, allergy, or idiosyncrasy to an agent like a sulfa drug may actually be an acute manifestation of severe vitamin C deficiency. The deficiency may be precipitated by the metabolic demands of the infection and the vitamin C-consuming toxic effects of the drug. McCormick recommended that whenever vitamin C levels are found to be low, which should be the case in all acute infections, vitamin C should always be included with whatever other "chemotherapy" is being given to the patient.

Landauer and Sopher (1970) reported on the effects of vitamin C on sulfanilamide toxicity on chicken embryos. Sulfanilamide alone significantly increases birth defects when injected into fertilized eggs. When vitamin C was added to the sulfanilamide, these authors noted that "the frequency of grossly normal embryos was much increased."

Tetracycline is an antibiotic capable of causing kidney damage. Polec et al. (1971) studied the kidney damage induced by intravenous administration of tetracycline in both rats and dogs. They found that a vitamin C injection prevented this damage. Furthermore, they showed that preceding the tetracycline injection by five to ten minutes with the vitamin C injection was much more effective in its protection than when the injection order was reversed.

Thallium is a metallic element with poisonous salts. Thallium toxicity is characterized by a variety of neurologic and psychic symptoms, and it can also cause liver and kidney damage. Appenroth and Winnefeld (1998) showed that vitamin C in rats had a protective effect against thallium toxicity in the kidney, even though the metal concentration in the kidney was not affected.

Thioacetamide is a known liver toxin and cancer-causing agent. Sun et al. (2000) showed that when rats were exposed to thioacetamide, the damage to the liver was accompanied by increased evidence of oxidative stress. Also, the liver concentrations of vitamins C and E showed significant decreases. This evidence is like that seen with many other toxins, and it suggests that vitamin C administration would likely lessen the damage caused by thioacetamide.

Valproic acid is a drug used to treat epilepsy. It has been known to cause a drug-induced hepatitis, which sometimes results in liver failure and death. In cultures of rat liver cells, Jurima-Romet et al. (1996)

demonstrated that valproic acid and its metabolites have a "dose-dependent cytotoxicity," as evidenced by increased levels of LDH, an enzyme found in the liver. Vitamins C and E demonstrated a protective effect against the cellular damage induced by a valproic acid metabolite.

Mushroom Poisoning

Even today, fatal poisoning continues to occur as mushrooms are misidentified in the wild and consumed. Eating the poisonous variety initiates a very vicious and relentless form of poisoning. *Amanita phalloides*, also known as the "death cap," is the species of mushroom that is especially toxic, generally causing irreversible damage in heart, liver, and kidney cells after 24 hours. The likelihood of death from this type of poisoning ranges from 50% to 90%. Consumption of these mushrooms results in the exposure to multiple toxins (Faulstich and Wieland, 1996), and ingestion of as little as one quarter mushroom cap, approximately 20 grams, is usually fatal.

Laing (1984) reported a highly successful treatment protocol for mushroom poisoning. The protocol consisted of giving 3,000 mg of intravenous vitamin C daily, along with nifuroxazide and dihydrostreptomycin, for three days. Laing noted that a Dr. Bastien had discovered this method in the 1950s and successfully treated 15 patients by 1969. Laing also commented that Dr. Bastien twice publicly consumed what would have easily been fatal doses of mushrooms (about 70 grams), only to give himself the treatment and demonstrate its incredible effectiveness. Laing asserted that this method became the treatment of choice at a number of medical centers in France.

> **Dr. Bastien twice publicly consumed what would have easily been fatal doses of mushrooms only to give himself the treatment (including 3,000 mg of intravenous vitamin C) and demonstrate its incredible effectiveness**

Another potent antioxidant, alpha lipoic acid, has also been shown to be highly effective in facilitating the recovery from mushroom poisoning. Berkson (1979) reported on the successful treatment of six patients suffering from liver damage that resulted from mushroom poisoning. Still another potent antioxidant, N-acetyl cysteine, has been shown to be highly effective in the treatment of mushroom poisoning. Montanini et al. (1999) reported on the treatment of 11 patients in their intensive care unit. Ten recovered successfully even though one patient who had already had preexisting liver disease required liver transplantation.

Currently, there is still no official acknowledgment of the important role that vitamin C and other antioxidants should be playing in the consistent and effective reversal of mushroom poisoning. As with so many other conditions, relatively small doses of vitamin C have generally been used for this condition even though the work of Laing, noted above, still demonstrates that such doses can be highly effective.

Once again, studies using Klenner-sized doses of vitamin C could not be found in the literature for the treatment of mushroom poisoning. Like so many other diseases, there are compelling reasons to believe that the reversal of this condition would be even more complete in a higher percentage of cases if such doses were used. As with numerous other conditions covered in this book, authors currently reporting on the treatment of mushroom poisoning do not even report or indicate a knowledge of the effects of vitamin C, while just dismissing the benefits of an antioxidant like alpha lipoic acid without further explanation (Gussow, 2000; *Conn's Current Therapy*, 2001).

In America and many other areas of the world mushroom poisoning regularly continues to needlessly kill adults and many children. Considering the ruthless and progressive nature of mushroom poisoning, all therapies that have any documentation or chance of being clinically effective should be included in the treatment protocol.

Six Types of Pesticides

Pesticides are substances used to deliberately poison rodents, insects, certain plants, and some undesired fungi. Pesticides are diverse in chemical structure, but they are usually susceptible to neutralization by vitamin C. Vitamin C also tends to readily repair the damage done by many pesticides. As will become apparent, many pesticides cause great damage by increasing lipid peroxidation, free radicals, and oxidative stress in general in the body. As has been mentioned, dealing with increased oxidative stress is a job easily accomplished by enough vitamin C.

Klenner (1971) reported on three young boys who were heavily exposed to the pesticide spray of a crop-dusting airplane. The youngest boy, aged seven years, ended up being covered by the older boys and received little exposure. The oldest boy, aged 12 years, was treated by Klenner and given 10,000 mg of vitamin C with a 50 cc syringe every eight hours. This child was discharged to home on the second hospital day. The other child did not receive any vitamin C but only received "supportive care." This child developed a chemical burn and dermatitis, and he died on the fifth day of hospitalization. This clinical response is very consistent with all of the following data on vitamin C and the detoxification of various pesticides. Each pesticide discussed is italicized when first mentioned.

Methylviologen compounds such as diquat and paraquat are herbicides that cause an overproduction of free radicals in the target plants, resulting in severe oxidative stress. They induce a loss of chlorophyll in the course of killing the plant, which is an effect that vitamin C can play a role in blocking (Beligni and Lamattina, 1999). Diquat also induces a potentially lethal increase in free radicals in rat liver cells. Nakagawa et al. (1991) showed that this increase did not occur as long as cellular levels of vitamin C were maintained.

Endosulfan, phosphamidon, and **mancozeb** are three pesticides that are significantly toxic to the sperm of mice fed these agents. Toxic effects included decreased sperm count and increased abnormalities of appearance. Khan and Sinha (1996) showed that this effect was lessened by vitamin C administration, even though the maximal dose given was quite low (40 mg/kg body weight) compared to a Klenner-sized dose. Khan and Sinha (1994) were also able to show in mice that even a very low dose of vitamin C had a lessening effect on the increased chromosomal abnormalities induced by the above three pesticides. Such abnormalities can lead to mutations and possible birth defects or cancer.

Organophosphorus pesticide toxicity is generally lessened, blocked, and/or repaired by vitamin C therapy. Geetanjali et al. (1993) showed that vitamin C could protect mice quite adequately from chromosomal abnormalities induced in bone marrow cells by the insecticide dimethoate. Hoda and Sinha (1991) and Hoda and Sinha (1993) also showed that vitamin C could significantly lessen both malathion-induced and dimethoate-induced chromosomal abnormalities in mice and lethal mutations in *Drosophila,* a genus of flies. Parathion and malathion are two organophosphorus insecticides known to retard the growth rate of rats and induce microscopic evidence of toxicity in the liver and kidney tissues. Chakraborty et al. (1978) showed that vitamin C was "very effective in counteracting the growth retardation" as well the microscopic tissue abnormalities in those exposed rats. Hoda et al. (1993) were able to show that vitamin C blocks the malathion-induced and dimethoate-induced depression of cell division rate in mouse sperm cells.

The effect of vitamin C on the toxicity of another organophosphorus pesticide, chlorpyrifos-ethyl (CE), has been studied. Gultekin et al. (2001) looked at the protective role of vitamins C and E against the oxidative damage inflicted by CE in the red blood cells of rats. They found that CE administered directly to the rat increased lipid peroxidation and antioxidant stress in the red blood cells, while vitamins C and E reduced this manifestation of toxicity. A relatively low dose of vitamin C (200 mg/kg body weight) was given.

Organochlorine pesticide toxicity is also generally lessened, blocked, and/or repaired by vitamin C therapy. Street and Chadwick (1975) reported that DDT, dieldrin, and lindane "are profound inducers" of the liver enzyme systems in rats that detoxify toxins. Furthermore, they reported that the exposure to such toxic pesticides induces increases in vitamin C formation and excretion, which are the expected responses of a vitamin C-producing animal to the introduction of a toxin. These authors also found that the detoxification of these pesticides was lessened in the vitamin C-deficient guinea pig, and greater amounts of pesticide residues would accumulate in the tissues. Street and Chadwick concluded that the liver's vitamin C status was of "central significance" in the effective metabolic breakdown and detoxification of these pesticides.

Lindane intoxication in rats was also studied by Tiwari et al. (1982). They found that supplementation of vitamin C by separate oral administration to lindane-toxic rats "neutralized the growth retardation and maintained almost normal values" of all liver enzymes studied. Koner et al. (1998) looked at lindane and DDT intoxication in rats. They found that the simultaneous administration of a relatively small dose of vitamin C (100 mg/kg body weight) markedly lessened the ability of these pesticides to induce oxidative stress or to suppress the immune system in red blood cells.

Additional studies documenting the effectiveness of vitamin C in preventing, lessening, and/or repairing the damage of pesticide-induced toxicity comes from the following authors:

1. Verma et al. (1982): malathion and thiotox in fish

2. Samanta et al. (1999); Sahoo et al. (2000): hexachlorocyclohexane in rats

3. Chatterjee et al. (1981): chlordane in rats

4. Agrawal et al. (1978): aldrin in fish

5. Bandyopadhyay et al. (1982): dieldrin in rats

6. Hassan et al. (1991): endrin and rats

7. Rajini and Krishnakumari (1985): pirimiphos-methyl in rats

8. Ram and Singh (1988): carbofuran and fish

9. Grabarczyk et al. (1991): fenarimol and human white blood cells

10. Wagstaff and Street (1971): dieldrin, DDT, and lindane in guinea pigs

Overall, pesticides are a chemically diverse group of compounds that generally demonstrate substantial toxicity to most animals and other biological systems in high enough doses. It appears that a substantial degree of pesticide toxicity comes from the induction of oxidative stress, with an increase in intracellular and extracellular free radical content and increased laboratory evidence of lipid peroxidation.

Such a mechanism of toxicity is ideally suited to treatment by a powerful and widely distributed antioxidant like vitamin C. Furthermore, vitamin C is of major importance in the induction and potency of the liver's detoxification enzyme pathways that operate to neutralize pesticides and many other toxins (Wagstaff and Street, 1971; Zannoni et al., 1972).

Virtually all of the research studies that have determined vitamin C to be of limited or no value in the detoxification of pesticides utilized very low doses of vitamin C. In acute toxic states with death becoming clinically imminent, Klenner (1971) would use as much as 1,200 mg of vitamin C/kg body weight by intravenous application. This equates to more than 100,000 mg of vitamin C in a 200-pound man. Furthermore, Klenner advocated repeating a given dose only an hour later if the clinical picture was not clearly improving. As Klenner liked to point out, whatever toxicity is present in the body, especially after a defined (versus ongoing) exposure such as in a snake bite, the patient must have enough vitamin C to completely neutralize it. Otherwise, a positive clinical response can be severely limited or may not occur at all. It is truly remarkable that so many animal studies showed such effective detoxification against a variety of poisons when the vitamin C dosing schedule was so much lower than that so successfully used by Klenner.

in acute toxic states with death becoming clinically imminent, Klenner would use as much as 100,000 mg vitamin C doses for a 200-pound man by intravenous application

Radiation

While not a physical substance in the sense of other toxins discussed, radiation is very much a toxic agent that has very clear and pronounced toxic effects. Like the other toxins discussed, the evidence shows clearly that vitamin C can help to prevent the damage induced by radiation and repair the damage that had already occurred from a previous radiation exposure. The specific type of radiation being addressed here is "ionizing radiation," as distinguished from "non-ionizing radiation." The nonionizing type includes radiation such as light, radio waves, and radar waves. This kind of radiation is generally considered harmless because the effects of such radiation are not pronounced and immediately measurable with current technology. On the other hand, ionizing radiation produces destructive effects, usually measurable as a flood of free radicals including other indicators of oxidative stress and immediate cellular damage. Typical examples of ionizing radiation include X-rays, gamma rays, and particle bombardments from neutrons, electrons, protons, or mesons.

Radiation toxicity will commonly damage the body in a number of different ways. Radiation injury can cause mutations, cause cancer, and lead to increased birth defects. Also, bone marrow is readily suppressed by a significant ionizing radiation exposure. All of the tissues can be affected, and the associated symptoms will generally be consistent with the effects of a large increase in free radicals and oxidant stress in the affected tissues. A potent antioxidant like vitamin C is ideally suited for coping with the onslaught of oxidant stress unleashed by a significant radiation exposure.

Ala-Ketola et al. (1974) studied whether vitamin C could prevent death caused by whole body ionizing radiation. These researchers found that a relatively small dose of vitamin C given to rats after exposure to gamma radiation caused a significant increase in survival. A maximal vitamin C dose of only 80 mg/kg body weight was given daily for a week before the radiation and then for a month after the radiation. Only one rat died out of 25 in this treatment group, while nine rats out of 25 in the control group died. It seems logical that larger doses of vitamin C would have produced more dramatic results, especially if the radiation dose was increased to a level where 100% of the rats would be expected to die without vitamin C intervention.

Klenner (1974) asserted that vitamin C will "prevent radiation burns." Furthermore, in addressing the issue of radiation therapy for cancer patients, Klenner also asserted that "massive employment of vi-

tamin C will make possible prolonged radiation therapy in late cases."
In mice, Blumenthal et al. (2000) found that vitamins C, E, and A were
able to reduce the "normal" tissue toxicity induced by the radio-immunotherapy used in the treatment of cancer. Specifically, the antioxidant
combination significantly reduced the ionizing radiation damage to
bone marrow. The antioxidants also increased what is known as the
"maximal tolerated dose" of ionizing radiation. Okunieff (1991) studied
mouse cancer cells and found evidence that after enough vitamin C is
given "the radiation dose given to cancer patients could be increased
without increasing acute complications but with an expected increase
in tumor-control probability."

Kennedy et al. (2001) recently found that vitamins C and E could
successfully treat the symptoms of chronic radiation proctitis following courses of pelvic irradiation for cancer in that area of the body.
Symptoms such as bleeding, diarrhea, and pain all improved, and
seven of twenty patients reported a "return to normal." All ten patients
who were reinterviewed a year later "reported a sustained improvement in their symptoms." Very significantly, this positive effect was
achieved with a dose of vitamin C that was quite small (500 mg three
times a day). Kretzschmar and Ellis (1974), in commenting on patients
receiving radiation therapy, asserted that "a sufficiently large daily dose
of ascorbic acid, given either intravenously or by mouth, can prevent or
minimise the fall of white blood cells which follows X-ray exposure."
They further noted that vitamin C therapy "also improves considerably
the general condition of the patient, and X-ray sickness is very slight or
entirely absent."

As with other toxins, ionizing radiation readily depletes vitamin C
levels because the free radical load produced by any radiation injury
readily increases the metabolic breakdown of whatever vitamin C is
present. Chevion et al. (1999) showed that the total body irradiation
given to essentially destroy patient bone marrow prior to bone marrow
transplantation "caused a pronounced decrease in antioxidant capacity and an excessive increase in oxidant stress." Mukundan et al. (1999)
looked at patients with uterine cancer who received radiation therapy.
They found that plasma and red blood cell levels of glutathione, another

important antioxidant that supports the physiological role of vitamin C, were lower in all of the irradiated patients compared to normal control women. Spirichev et al. (1994) examined the vitamin and trace element status of personnel at the Chernobyl, Russia, nuclear power station and of preschool children in a nearby city. Although the Chernobyl nuclear reactor explosion occurred in 1986, the authors found that most of the people they examined still had significant deficiencies of vitamin C, folic acid, and vitamins B1, B2, and B6. These deficiencies indicate a probable ongoing accelerated breakdown of vitamin C and other nutrients by residual radiation effects. Umegaki et al. (1995) showed that whole body X-ray irradiation in mice significantly decreased vitamin C levels in the bone marrow. Because of its rapidly multiplying cells, bone marrow is always especially sensitive to the toxic effects of radiation.

Koyama et al. (1998) were able to show in cultured irradiated cells that vitamin C could lessen the free radical load when given prior to irradiation. Furthermore, vitamin C given after irradiation still effectively reduced the free radical load. Finally, these researchers showed that vitamin C given 20 hours after irradiation was still able to reduce the mutation frequency in human cell studies.

Sarma and Kesavan (1993) were able to show that vitamins C and E were able to reduce the amount of damage in bone marrow chromosomes from mice exposed to whole body gamma irradiation. Furthermore, these researchers showed that the two vitamins afforded as much protection when given two hours after the irradiation as when given before. Similar results were obtained by Konopacka et al. (1998), who gave an antioxidant combination of vitamin C, vitamin E, and beta carotene to mice for lessening gamma ray-induced chromosomal damage. Fomenko et al. (1997) found that an antioxidant mixture containing vitamin C, vitamin E, and beta carotene "reliably decreased" the evidence of chromosomal damage in the bone marrow cells of X-ray exposed mice. They also showed that this antioxidant mixture "significantly decreased" the mutation rate of mouse spleen cells after chronic irradiation.

Narra et al. (1993) have looked at the ability of vitamin C to possibly protect against the toxicity of deliberate exposure to a radioactive material. The radionuclide I^{131}, a radioactive form of iodine sometimes used to treat hyperthyroidism, was injected along with vitamin C into mice. Looking at the effects on mouse sperm cells, the authors found that the addition of vitamin C significantly increased the survival of these cells. The authors suggested that **vitamin C serves to protect against the radiation damage of either accidental exposures or intentional medical exposures** vitamin C serves to protect against the radiation damage of either accidental exposures or intentional medical exposures, "especially when radionuclides are incorporated in the body and deliver the dose in a chronic fashion."

As might be expected from the data cited above showing the ability of vitamin C to protect against radiation-induced chromosomal damage, multiple studies also indicate that vitamin C protects against radiation-induced DNA damage and increased chance of cancer. Konopacka and Rzeszowska-Wolny (2001) showed that the combination of vitamin C, vitamin E, and beta carotene reduced DNA damage to human lymphocytes in culture. This effect was observed when the vitamins were added to the cells before and after irradiation. Riabchenko et al. (1996) showed that the same combination of antioxidants could increase "the efficiency of DNA repair" in the spleen of irradiated mice. Yasukawa et al. (1989) were able to demonstrate that vitamin C could significantly suppress the X-ray induced transformation of cultured mouse cells into cancer cells. The authors suggested that their data might "be useful as a guide for chemopreventive efforts against radiation carcinogenesis."

Ionizing radiation has also been reported to decrease the production of prostacyclin by intact blood vessels. Prostacyclin is the most potent known inhibitor of blood platelets sticking together, an event that usually initiates blood clotting. Prostacyclin also has a relaxing effect on the muscle in the blood vessel wall (vasodilatation), which tends to keep blood vessels more open. Eldor et al. (1987) found that vitamin C could improve the ability of irradiated bovine endothelial cells (cells lining the blood vessel wall) to produce prostacyclin. On et al. (2001)

also looked at the damaging effects that irradiation had on the endothelial lining cells in rat aortas. They found that vitamin C pretreatment could prevent the irradiation from blocking the ability of blood vessels to vasodilate.

Shapiro et al. (1965) looked at the ability of vitamin C to protect important enzyme systems concentrated in solution from ionizing radiation. They concluded that vitamin C "in low concentrations can protect enzymes in highly concentrated solutions." Because of low toxicity, they asserted that vitamin C had significant promise as a protectant against radiation.

Although not technically classified as a form of ionizing radiation, ultraviolet (UV) light appears to cause a similar type of tissue damage. However, the wavelength of UV light does not allow for great tissue penetration, and the damage inflicted is largely limited to the skin or eyes. Vitamin C appears to play a significant role in lessening this type of radiation damage as well.

Mireles-Rocha et al. (2002) noted that UV radiation absorption is responsible for the production of free radicals in damaged cells. These are the skin cells that become sunburned when exposed to excessive UV radiation. In a trial on healthy human volunteers, the authors looked at the minimal UV dose needed to cause skin reddening (the early stage of sunburn). They found that vitamin C and vitamin E taken orally offered significant protection against this form of radiation damage. Eberlein-Konig et al. (1998) performed a similar study in a double-blind, placebo-controlled manner. They also found that a vitamin C and vitamin E combination taken orally reduced the free radical-induced sunburn reaction.

Similar research has been conducted on the protective effects of vitamin C against UV-induced skin damage in animals. Moison and Beijersbergen van Henegouwen (2002) found that a topical (versus ingested) application of vitamins C and E provided complete protection against the increase in lipid peroxidation (oxidative stress or free radicals) induced by the exposure of pig skin to UVB (ultraviolet light, type B) exposure. Kobayashi et al. (1996) examined the UVB-induced increase in free radicals and inflammation in mouse skin. They found that injecting a vitamin C derivative prior to UVB exposure significantly reduced a number of laboratory indices of increased oxidative stress. Neumann et al. (1999) utilized a new biological model for determining the toxicity of ultraviolet light using the embryonic yolk sacs of incubated hen eggs. Although UVB alone induced "severe phototoxic damage," vitamin C "led to a significant and remarkable reduction of the UVB-induced damage." Interestingly, other anti-inflammatory agents were also tested. Aspirin was less effective than vitamin C, and indomethacin, a strong prescription anti-inflammatory drug, showed no protection at all against the UVB-induced toxic effects.

In studies of the protective effect of vitamin C against UVB toxicity on cells or bacteria in culture, the results were similar to those noted above. In human skin cells, Miyai et al. (1996) looked at a "stable derivative" of vitamin C, finding the derivative improved cell survival significantly after UVB exposure. There were also less large DNA fragments in the debris of cells that were killed. In a species of photosynthetic bacteria exposed to UVB, He and Hader (2002) found that vitamin C "exhibited a significant protective effect on lipid peroxidation and DNA strand breaks." They also found that the presence of vitamin C resulted "in a considerably higher survival rate" among the irradiated bacteria.

UV light, like ionizing radiation, can also induce genetic damage and ultimately cause cancer. Dreosti and McGown (1992) observed that vitamin C pretreatment significantly lessened the microscopic evidence of chromosomal damage in irradiated mice and irradiated mouse spleen cells (*in vivo* and *in vitro*). Dunham et al. (1982) looked at the effects of supplemented vitamin C on the incidence of UV light-induced skin cancers in mice. They found that vitamin C afforded "a pronounced effect" in "decreasing the incidence and delaying the onset of the malignant lesions" in the mice studied.

Raziq and Jafarey (1987) also reported some research on the effects of vitamin C given to guinea pigs after exposure to radiation. They gave a mere 5 mg daily to each exposed guinea pig. No significant difference between the vitamin C-treated and control guinea pigs was seen. In their discussion these authors acknowledged that the doses of vitamin C to the guinea pigs would be the approximate equivalent of

500 mg in a 150-pound human. This amounts to an incredibly small dose of vitamin C when dealing with the toxicity of a whole body exposure to radiation.

It is very significant to note that even though the authors acknowledge the smallness of the vitamin C dose in their discussion, they have no problem in concluding without qualification that their research "therefore, showed that *vitamin C when given after exposure has no influence on the effects of radiation.*" (emphasis added) Unfortunately, this does not represent an appropriate or straightforward summarization of the research data. The true effectiveness of vitamin C against radiation toxicity remains unrecognized by many who see such an article since literature researchers often read only the authors' abstract, trusting that the authors will honestly and competently summarize their results.

a ridiculous conclusion that vitamin C is ineffective in repairing radiation damage can always be reached when a small enough dose is used

It appears that vitamin C is clearly an effective agent in preventing and treating radiation injury. Vitamin C should always be included in the treatment of this condition due to its nontoxic nature and documented efficacy. Indeed, Mothersill et al. (1978) asserted that "regardless of the detail of the mechanism, the evidence presently available demonstrates that vitamin C is a radioprotective agent." It is also important to note that the types of injury described in the above literature are very much like the types of injury one would see with nuclear bomb fallout, or after contamination from a nuclear power plant leakage or exposure. Based on Klenner's work with very high vitamin C dosages, it would seem prudent for anyone with a significant radiation exposure, regardless of cause, to dose with intravenous vitamin C as soon as possible. Chronic lower oral vitamin C dosing should be maintained only after there is evidence indicating control of the radiation-induced free radical overload.

Strychnine and Tetanus Toxin

Strychnine and tetanus toxin poisonings are being grouped together since it appears that their modes of action and sites of action in the nervous system are very comparable. Indeed, the clinical pictures of advanced toxicity with these agents are similar, and the protective effect of vitamin C against these two toxins is similar as well.

In mice, Dey (1967) was able to show that vitamin C "completely counteracted the convulsive and lethal actions of strychnine." Furthermore, Dey demonstrated that the protective action of vitamin C was "directly dependent on the plasma ascorbic acid level." Dey (1965) had shown earlier that vitamin C

Dey demonstrated that vitamin C "completely counteracted the convulsive and lethal actions of strychnine"

was likely to be very effective in directly neutralizing the toxic abilities of strychnine outside of the body. Dey demonstrated this by incubating strychnine with vitamin C-rich lemon juice. Furthermore, Dey showed that the detoxifying effect was lost when the juice was heated to 50°C, a temperature that would destroy much of the vitamin C content. Dey concluded that vitamin C "in very high doses shows protection against strychnine." Dey (1967) also cited earlier work that indicated strychnine toxicity was greatly increased in scurvy-stricken guinea pigs, an observation consistent with the strychnine-neutralizing abilities of vitamin C already noted. Jahan et al. (1984) were also able to show that vitamin C significantly lessened the ability of strychnine to produce a tetanus-like condition in young chicks.

The studies on the neutralization of tetanus toxin by vitamin C were already discussed in some detail in Chapter 2. To briefly recap, Klenner (1954) discussed the successful treatment of a tetanus infection in a six-year-old boy who was already demonstrating advanced symptoms from the production of tetanus toxin. Klenner felt the clinical course of the boy strongly suggested that the toxicity of the tetanus antitoxin worked against the boy's recovery, and the vitamin C injections were needed to also neutralize this toxicity. Jahan et al. (1984) were also able to show that vitamin C therapy, at a dose much lower than advocated by Klenner, was able to save all 31 tetanus patients aged from one to 12 years. Older patients, however, showed less protection from the lethal effects of the tetanus infection and toxin, as the same fixed dosage of vitamin C had less effect on the larger adult bodies.

Dey (1966) studied the ability of vitamin C to protect rats from doses of tetanus toxin that were known to be twice the minimal lethal amounts. Dey was able to clearly demonstrate that enough vitamin C could be given to completely neutralize otherwise fatal amounts of tetanus toxin. This is without the assistance of tetanus antitoxin, which can have its own significant toxicity.

Vitamin C had also been shown to neutralize tetanus toxin in the test tube by Jungeblut (1937). Overall, the clinical and laboratory research findings reviewed make it quite clear that vitamin C is the optimal agent for neutralizing the toxic effect of tetanus toxin. Although less research exists on the interactions of vitamin C and strychnine, it would appear that vitamin C is likely the optimal agent for neutralizing this toxin as well.

Nine Toxic Elements

Mercury has three primary chemical forms, all of which are toxic to man. Mercury can be present in its uncombined elemental form, as an inorganic mercuric salt, and as an organic mercurial compound. Mercury poisoning, especially when low-grade and chronic, can precipitate a wide range of clinical findings in man. In fact, because the findings are typically so subtle and nonspecific enough, a diagnosis of chronic mercury poisoning is rarely ever considered. These clinical findings, often written off as just being the result of an overactive imagination, include insomnia, nervousness, tremor, impaired judgment and coordination, decreased clarity and efficiency of thought, emotional instability, headache, fatigue, loss of sex drive, and depression. Low-grade mercury exposure commonly results from the continual vaporization of mercury in dental amalgam fillings, which increases dramatically with chewing. Vimy and Lorscheider (1985) showed that the amount of mercury released from such amalgam fillings either comprised or exceeded "a major percentage" of the suggested threshold limits for environmental mercury exposure in different countries.

Another common source of significant and chronic mercury exposure comes from the ingestion of seafood. Virtually all seafood has some methylmercury, which is an especially toxic form of mercury. Mahaffey (1999) pointed out that large predatory fish species have the highest concentrations. Furthermore, it is now being recognized that the development of the fetus in a pregnant woman is especially sensitive to this form of mercury in the mother's diet. Steuerwald et al. (2000) showed that eating such seafood by the pregnant mother was associated with an "increased risk of neurodevelopmental deficit" in the baby.

In spite of its known enormous toxicity to humans and other animals, mercury continues to be used in a wide array of industrial applications. Large accidental industrial exposures can result in acute mercury toxicity. However, both acute and chronic exposures to mercury can be effectively treated with vitamin C, and typically most of the damage from such poisonings can be prevented and/or promptly repaired.

Huggins and Levy (1999) repeatedly observed the ability of vitamin C infusions ranging from 35,000 to 50,000 mg to lessen and often completely block any of the acute toxic effects of mercury when amalgam fillings were being removed. However, lower doses of infused vitamin C (25,000 mg) would occasionally allow some symptoms of acute mercury toxicity to emerge. The

vitamin C infusions ranging from 35,000 mg to 50,000 mg can lessen and often completely block any of the acute toxic effects of mercury when amalgam fillings are removed

higher doses of vitamin C appeared to be essential for complete protection during the actual drilling on an amalgam filling, which enormously increases the amount of mercury vapor in and around the patient's mouth. When the vitamin C infusion was started before the dental work, maintained during the dental work, and continued for a time following the dental work, even the sickest of patients often ended up feeling better than when the dental work was started. This was in spite of the additional acute mercury exposure faced and the unavoidable trauma of the dental work itself.

The empirical observations of Huggins and Levy noted above should come as no surprise in light of the significant research already performed on mercury toxicity and vitamin C. Chapman and Shaffer (1947) looked at the ability of vitamin C to lessen the toxicity of mercurial diuretic drugs administered to dogs. At that time, diuretic (urine volume-increasing) drugs given to humans were often mercury-based compounds, and fatalities were known to occur suddenly after the administration of such a diuretic. It was of great significance for Chapman and Shaffer to evaluate agents that could possibly make such fatal reactions less likely. They found that one of the commonly used mercurial diuretics of the day, meralluride (Mercuhydrin), exerted clearly lessened toxicity in the face of vitamin C. Specifically, they found that the lethal dose of meralluride given to dogs was significantly increased by the addition of vitamin C to the drug administration. In other words, as more vitamin C was given, more meralluride was needed to exert a fatal effect.

Ruskin and Johnson (1949), also noting the occasional immediate fatalities in the use of mercurial diuretics, examined the protective effects of vitamin C on the toxic effects of meralluride and other mercurial diuretics in isolated rabbit heart preparations. By looking at the previously well-defined cardiac toxicity of such toxic diuretics, they were able to determine that vitamin C in even higher doses than used by Chapman and Shaffer had even more pronounced protective effects against such toxicity. Ruskin and Ruskin (1952) later looked at the toxicity of meralluride on rat heart and kidney preparations. They found that vitamin C could prevent the lowering of oxygen uptake caused by meralluride, which they considered to be a protective effect that directly facilitated tissue respiration. They felt that this facilitation of tissue respiration was completely consistent with the ability of vitamin C to clinically protect the entire animal from mercury as noted above in the work of Chapman and Shaffer.

The guinea pig has also been used by a number of investigators to examine the relationship between mercury and vitamin C. Blackstone et al. (1974) studied guinea pigs that were given variable doses of both vitamin C and mercury as mercuric chloride. They found that dosing with vitamin C resulted in an increased deposition of mercury in the liver and kidney.

As these are organs of detoxification and excretion, this is not necessarily an undesirable effect. Somewhat conversely, they also found that mercury significantly reduced the concentration of vitamin C in the brains, adrenals, and spleens of guinea pigs kept on maintenance doses of vitamin C.

In following up the work of Blackstone et al., Murray and Hughes (1976) found that a dosing regimen of vitamin C appeared to increase the tissue levels of an orally administered form of either organic mercury (methylmercuric iodide) or inorganic mercury (mercuric chloride). These investigators interpreted this information as a warning against taking large doses of vitamin C. However, the practical clinical protective effect of specific doses of vitamin C was not examined in this study. Furthermore, increased mercury in storage forms may well be the way in which the clinical toxicity of mercury can be lessened.

Earlier investigators established that vitamin C was highly clinically protective against the toxicity of mercury. Carroll et al. (1965) were able to show in rats that vitamin C could prevent the damage sustained by the kidneys from mercuric chloride when given beforehand. Vauthey (1951), working with guinea pigs, found a certain dose of mercury cyanide that killed 100% of the guinea pigs within one hour of injection. However, when he kept the guinea pigs on a large dose of vitamin C prior to mercury injection, 40% of them survived. The dose was moderately large, equivalent to 35,000 mg per day for a human being weighing about 150 pounds. However, this was still substantially less than a Klenner-sized dose, and it was not a repeated dose. For what would otherwise be a fatal injection, then, a suboptimal dose of vitamin C by Klenner's standards was still able to offer significant protection. Mavin (1941) had earlier found a similar protective effect against mercury chloride. Mokranjac and Petrovic (1964) found that continuing vitamin C dosing after the mercury poisoning was critical in determining the chances of survival. They gave guinea pigs 200 mg of vitamin C daily prior to the administration of a mercury chloride dose that had already been determined to be 100% fatal when left untreated. When the 200 mg dose of vitamin C continued to be given daily for 20 days after the mercury chloride was given, all animals survived. When no vitamin C was continued after the mercury chloride was given, a few animals still died. When vitamin C was given daily only after the mercury chloride was given, nine of 25 animals died. When vitamin C was given only as a single large injection after mercury chloride was given, eight of 25 animals died. Just as Klenner had demonstrated with so many different infectious diseases, the optimal effects of vitamin C in mercury poisoning depended on both the size of the dose as well as the duration of the administration.

The antioxidant activity of vitamin C probably plays a role in the protection of the host against mercury-induced toxicity. Grunert (1960) was able to show that another potent antioxidant, alpha lipoic acid, was also able to prevent mercury intoxication in mice as long as a sufficiently large dose was utilized. However, alpha lipoic acid also appears to significantly enhance the excretion of mercury into the feces via the bile (Gregus et al., 1992). This would make alpha lipoic acid a good agent to combine with vitamin C in treating mercury toxicity.

Panda et al. (1995) looked at mercury-induced evidence of chromosome damage in a plant model. They found that antioxidants, including vitamin C, "conferred protection against the genotoxicity" of mercuric chloride.

An increased level of mercury in the tissues is not nearly as important as whether the stored mercury is rendered relatively nontoxic in the process. Part of vitamin C's effective clinical neutralization of mercury may well involve mercury's storage in a much less toxic form due to its interaction with vitamin C. Indeed, this is one very good reason why a great deal of caution must be exerted when embarking upon a brisk detoxification program. Mercury and a host of other stored toxins can be readily mobilized from storage sites with a number of different detoxification agents. A significant deterioration in one's clinical status can result if there is no protection against the reappearance of highly potent toxins in the lymph and bloodstream as they proceed on their way to excretion. Safe detoxification must generally be slow and controlled, and nontoxic chelators and toxin neutralizers must be intelligently used while the process takes place.

Because vitamin C has been so effective in clinically reducing the toxicity of mercury, many have just assumed that vitamin C chelates (binds) the mercury and hastens its urinary excretion from the body. However, this does not appear to be the case. Dirks et al. (1994) examined the urinary excretion of mercury from the body after the intravenous administration of vitamin C. They found that infusions of as much as 60,000 mg of vitamin C did not result in any significant increase of mercury excretion in the urine, although there was a small, statistically insignificant increase. Both mercuric ion (inorganic mercury) and methylmercury (organic mercury) are excreted preferentially into the bile rather than the urine (Gregus and Klaassen, 1986), and a significant portion of bile excretion eventually ends up in the feces. In healthy volunteers, Aberg et al. (1969) reported that methylmercury is primarily excreted in the feces, even though a smaller amount of elimination does take place in the urine. A similar conclusion was reached by Gage (1964), who studied the excretion of organic mercury forms in rats. It would appear that the study of the effects of different agents on mercury excretion should best be focused on fecal excretion testing.

Gage (1975) later reported on different mechanisms by which vitamin C biodegrades organic mercury compounds in a rat liver preparation. He found that the antioxidant properties of vitamin C were responsible for the reduction of organic mercury forms to inorganic and elemental forms. This mechanism represents a relative detoxification of mercury since organic mercury forms are much more clinically toxic than the reduced forms. This biodegradation of mercury by vitamin C also relates to the fact that vitamin C does not appear to significantly promote mercury excretion, but it does unequivocally lessen the mercury toxicity in the body.

Just as with infectious diseases, toxins also play a direct role in accelerating the utilization and metabolism of vitamin C, resulting in lower blood, tissue, and urine levels of vitamin C. This is also the case with mercury, which was noted earlier in the work of Blackstone et al. (1974) when their guinea pigs were noted to have lowered levels of vitamin C in some of their tissues after being given mercury. Chatterjee and Pal (1975) were also able to demonstrate that mercury administered to rats decreased vitamin C levels in the urine and in the liver. Ficek (1994) was able to show that mercuric chloride, along with cadmium chloride and lead chloride, caused a substantial decrease in the content of vitamin C in the rat thymus gland. This not only supports the fact that toxins use up vitamin C stores, but it also implies one additional mechanism by which toxins such as mercury can impair immune function. The thymus gland is a very important player in the production and regulation of important immune cells (T lymphocytes). It is very likely the depletion of vitamin C concentration in the thymus gland has a significant negative impact on its contribution to host immune defense.

Over a century and a half ago, Budd (1840) observed that "mercury in every form should be religiously avoided" by scurvy patients. He added that he had noted "instances in which the scorbutic symptoms seemed to have been much aggravated by mercury, taken before the scurvy made its appearance." The presence of any mercury would rapidly complete the depletion of vitamin C stores in these patients so that scurvy would quickly and clearly manifest itself. Clearly, vitamin C administration is indicated in any case of mercury toxicity, even if it is only aimed at trying to restore the acute depletion of vitamin C caused by the mercury.

the totality of the evidence cited from the literature strongly supports the ability of vitamin C to be highly effective in neutralizing the toxicity of different mercurial compounds

The totality of the evidence cited from the literature strongly supports the ability of vitamin C to be highly effective in neutralizing the toxicity of different mercurial compounds. The ability of vitamin C to protect against the negative clinical effects of mercury toxicity is clear and straightforward. The evidence also suggests that vitamin C does not play a significant role in the accelerated excretion of these compounds even though it makes their storage forms far less toxic. However, proper care must be taken when the exposed individual undertakes a subsequent detoxification regimen since the stored forms of mercury can once again poison the detoxifying patient as mobilization and excretion of these toxins take place.

Lead poisoning is typically a chronic process, with long-term, low-grade exposure to this toxic metal producing a variety of symptoms. The systems of the body most commonly affected are the gastrointestinal tract, blood, and nervous system. The kidneys are also commonly involved. A number of chelating agents, which bind to lead and promote both its inactivation and excretion, comprise the primary traditional ways to treat this form of toxicity.

No studies employing Klenner-sized doses of vitamin C for the treatment of lead poisoning could be found. However, there does exist a number of studies documenting the benefit of significantly smaller doses of vitamin C on lead toxicity. As with so many of the infectious diseases discussed in Chapter 2, it still remains to be clearly established what much larger doses of vitamin C could do for this form of toxicity.

Holmes et al. (1939) examined a population of workers at an industrial plant where lead exposure was significant. In a group of 17 people felt to have chronic lead poisoning, a mere 100 mg of vitamin C was given daily. Within a week or less, most of the treated workers were sleeping normally, eating better, and no longer afflicted with tremors.

Holmes et al. had already observed that the symptoms of chronic lead exposure resembled early scurvy. A 100 mg daily dose of vitamin C is usually enough to rapidly resolve impending symptoms of scurvy, which will always be clinically impressive. Lead and many other toxins rapidly metabolize vitamin C and deplete its stores. A significant part of the clinical toxicity of many potent toxins is the appearance of symptoms associated with early scurvy, which will nearly always respond dramatically to a very small dose of vitamin C. Even when vitamin C does not necessarily directly neutralize or eliminate the toxin in question, the resolution of the induced scurvy symptoms with vitamin C can relieve much suffering for many such poisoned patients. Using the same small dose of vitamin C in 400 male workers with industrial exposure to lead, however, Evans et al. (1943) did not report the same success as Holmes et al. Certainly, responses to such a small dose of vitamin C can vary widely depending upon the preexisting body stores of vitamin C in the treated workers and the size of the toxin exposure. If the workers treated by Evans et al. had much more toxin exposure on the job than the workers treated by Holmes et al., the 100 mg of daily vitamin C would not be expected to result in any well-defined improvements since the vitamin C would be metabolized so quickly that even mild scurvy symptoms would not have a chance to respond positively.

Gontzea et al. (1963) studied workers who had been long employed at a lead-storage battery plant. They found that blood levels of vitamin C were below normal. Anetor and Adeniyi (1998) also found that Nigerian lead workers who had significantly higher mean blood lead levels than those found in non-exposed controls had substantially lower amounts of vitamin C excretion. A low excretion amount of vitamin C is generally a direct reflection of a low blood level of vitamin C. In order to prevent the development of lead-induced scurvy symptoms or to lessen the consequences of the vitamin C deficiency invariably caused by the presence of the excess lead, it would seem advisable that at least some dose of vitamin C should be administered to any person chronically exposed to lead. Marchmont-Robinson (1941) stated that beneficial effects were clearly seen when only 50 mg of vitamin C daily was given to automobile workers exposed to the toxicity of lead fumes and lead dust.

Utilizing a small, yet substantially larger dose of vitamin C than administered in the studies noted above, Tandon et al. (2001) achieved very positive results in Indian silver refiners with relatively high blood lead levels. A 250 mg daily dose of vitamin C was able to significantly lower blood lead levels and reverse an enzyme inhibition typically associated with lead toxicity.

Altmann et al. (1981) studied pregnant women known to have an increased lead burden. These researchers found that a therapy combining vitamin C and calcium phosphate was able to decrease the lead content of the mother's milk by 15%, relative to untreated mothers. Much more remarkably, this therapy was found to decrease the lead content of the placenta by 90%.

Goyer and Cherian (1979) addressed the treatment of lead toxicity in rats. They found that orally administered vitamin C had a comparable ability to that of injected EDTA in the removal of lead from the animals, with equivalent amounts of lead being excreted in the urine. EDTA is a well-known chelating agent that binds to lead, and it is one of the primary medical treatments for removing lead from the body. Perhaps even more interestingly, Goyer and Cherian established that the combination of vitamin C and EDTA was more than twice as effective as either agent alone in the removal of lead. Furthermore, they found that the vitamin C-EDTA combination was especially effective in removing lead from the central nervous system, which is one of the typical target tissues of ingested lead. Unlike the situation with mercury noted above, vitamin C promotes the elimination of lead and does not just clinically detoxify it as it accumulates in storage forms.

orally administered vitamin C had a comparable ability to that of injected EDTA in the removal of lead from animals, with equivalent amounts of lead being excreted in the urine

Flora and Tandon (1986), also studying rats, found that vitamin C was effective in chelating lead already absorbed into the body as well as preventing lead from being absorbed in the gastrointestinal tract in the first place. Morton et al. (1985) also demonstrated that vitamin C was able to decrease the intestinal absorption of lead in rats. Further, Niazi et al. (1982) were able to show that vitamin C was able to enhance the elimination of lead in rat kidneys.

Additionally, Dhawan et al. (1988) were able to show that vitamin C could enhance the effects of traditional chelating drugs in removing lead from the liver and kidneys of rats. They also showed that such combination therapy with vitamin C further enhanced the elimination of lead in the urine and reversed the toxic effect that lead had on a measurable blood enzyme activity. Vij et al. (1998) were able to demonstrate that vitamin C markedly reduced the blood and liver lead concentration in poisoned rats and was effective in restoring specific lead-induced abnormalities in blood synthesis and activity levels of certain drug-metabolizing enzymes. Clearly, there are multiple benefits of vitamin C on lead toxicity in experimental rat studies.

Undoubtedly, the antioxidant activity of vitamin C plays at least some role in the effects that it has on tissue levels and the toxic activity of lead in the body. It should be noted that other antioxidants have also been shown to reduce the degree of lead toxicity. Dhawan et al. (1989) were able to show that vitamin E, an important antioxidant, was able to reduce the severity of lead toxicity when given along with lead to rats. Blood and liver lead concentrations were significantly reduced.

Upasani et al. (2001) showed that the antioxidant ability of either vitamin E or vitamin C was able to decrease some specific oxidation products seen in lead-treated rats, thereby protecting the animals from lead-induced toxicity. Gurer et al. (1999) found that alpha lipoic acid, also a potent antioxidant, was able to increase the survival of cells in culture that were exposed to lead. Hsu et al. (1998) found that both vitamins C and E were able to protect rat sperm from specific lead-induced toxic effects. They suggested that these two vitamins inhibited the generation of free radicals by lead, thereby offering some protection against oxidative damage.

Much more recent human studies have reached similar conclusions to those reached in the rat studies of Goyer and Cherian. All these studies have concluded that vitamin C promotes the excretion of lead from the body. Simon and Hudes (1999) examined the relationship of vitamin C blood levels to lead blood levels in 19,578 subjects between the ages of six and 90 years. They found that high serum levels of vitamin C are independently associated with a decreased prevalence of elevated blood lead levels. Houston and Johnson (2000) were able to demonstrate the same association. They suggested

multiple recent human studies have concluded that vitamin C promotes the excretion of lead from the body

that their data might indicate that vitamin C protects against excess lead in the body. Consistent with this assertion, Cheng et al. (1998) concluded in their epidemiological study among 747 men that a lower dietary intake of vitamin C may increase blood lead levels.

Sohler et al. (1977) looked at the blood lead levels of 1,113 psychiatric outpatients, finding lead levels ranging from 3.8 to 53 mcg%. They gave 2,000 mg of vitamin C and 30 mg zinc daily to 47 of these outpatients. Over a several month period of treatment, blood lead levels showed a significant decline. This outcome certainly implies that vitamin C probably played a direct role in the lowering of the blood lead levels, and it was not merely associated with lower levels after the fact. Flanagan et al. (1982) were able to show that the retention of lead in the body was directly reduced by the administration of vitamin C. They worked with 85 volunteers who agreed to drink a lead-containing drink in order to conduct the study. They also found that both vitamin C and EDTA lowered lead retention, further supporting the results of the animal study conducted by Goyer and Cherian, noted above.

Dawson et al. (1999) looked at the blood lead levels of 75 adult male smokers who had no history of industrial lead exposure. Although 200 mg of vitamin C had no effect on their blood or urine lead levels, a week-long course of 1,000 mg of vitamin C daily resulted in a very striking 81% decrease in the blood lead levels. Interestingly, both dosage groups demonstrated significant increases in their serum vitamin C levels, indicating that relying solely on blood vitamin C levels to assess the clinical adequacy of a certain vitamin C dosage can be very misleading.

In another study (Lauwerys et al., 1983) 1,000 mg of vitamin C given only five days a week rather than daily resulted in a less pronounced lowering of blood lead levels. These declines ranged from 11% to 23%. It would seem that 1,000 mg of vitamin C supplementation daily is really the very minimal dose at which some favorable response in lowering blood lead levels can be expected. Of course, different individuals with different chronic diseases can vary widely in their daily requirements of vitamin C. It is very likely that the chronic daily dosing of vitamin C well in excess of the 1,000 mg level would produce more consistent and dramatic reductions of blood lead levels.

Pillemer et al. (1940) reported that vitamin C was quite effective in protecting guinea pigs from developing the neurological symptoms associated with large doses of lead carbonate, which include muscular spasms and even paralysis. In guinea pigs getting significant supplemental vitamin C, only two of 26 developed any neurological symptoms, and none of the 26 died. In the other group, 18 of 24 guinea pigs given much less vitamin C developed neurological symptoms, and 12 ended up dying of lead poisoning. For some reference to dosage, assuming the average guinea pig weighs approximately 400 grams, the "high" dose of vitamin C was roughly equivalent to a daily dose of 3,500 mg for a normal adult human, versus a lower daily dose equivalency of about 155 mg (still much more than the daily recommended dietary allowance). Nevertheless, a dramatic protection by vitamin C against the toxic properties of lead was achieved with vastly lower doses than Klenner would have used. It is even likely that the protection against clinical toxicity would have been complete at such higher doses.

In rats, which are vitamin C-synthesizing animals, Rudra et al. (1975) showed that the toxic presence of lead induced the liver to increase its synthesis of vitamin C as a protective and compensatory response. Furthermore, they were able to show that the severe anemia seen in lead intoxicated rats could be "recovered to a considerable extent by simultaneous supplementation" of vitamin C. In another rat study, Dalley et al. (1989) found that an earlier administration of vitamin C significantly lowered the concentrations of lead in the femur (bone), kidney, liver, and blood plasma.

Vitamin C has also been shown to be protective against lead toxicity in animal cell cultures. Fischer et al. (1998) found that vitamin C reduced the lead-caused cellular toxic effects and inhibited the uptake of lead by the cultured cells.

Vitamin C has also been shown to exert unmistakable protective effects against lead toxicity in another experimental animal model. Han-Wen et al. (1959) looked at the effects of vitamin C in preventing tadpoles that were exposed to high levels of lead from dying. Initially, they kept a hundred tadpoles in water with a high lead level for 24 hours, finding that eight of them died. Then the surviving tadpoles were divided into water tanks with and without vitamin C. After six more days, 88% of the tadpoles in the water without vitamin C had died, while there were no casualties among the tadpoles in the vitamin C-treated water. At least in this experiment the protective abilities of vitamin C against lead toxicity appeared to be absolute with regard to premature death.

Other investigators have asserted that vitamin C is ineffective in the treatment of lead poisoning. Dannenberg et al. (1940), claiming they were using "extremely large doses" of vitamin C in the treatment of a 27-month-old child felt to have significant chronic lead poisoning, reported that vitamin C was "without effect" in treating this child. However, their "extremely large" doses of vitamin C were actually quite small and almost inconsequential in size by Klenner's dosing standards.

The child was receiving a total of 350 mg of vitamin C daily (100 mg by mouth, 250 mg intravenously), which is equivalent to only about 1,500 mg daily for a 150-pound adult. Furthermore, their small doses were continued for only 17 days, even though the blood lead level was approximately 12 times higher than normal. Klenner (1974) himself commented on the study by the Dannenberg group, asserting that had Dannenberg "administered 350 mg/kg body weight every two hours, he would have seen the other side of the coin." By conservative calculations, such a vitamin C dose would have been roughly 100 times greater than the dose administered by the Dannenberg group. Even though clinicians such as Dannenberg and his co-researchers are undoubtedly sincere, many doctors read only their conclusions in the published article, and an enormously beneficial therapy for a severe form of poisoning effectively never reaches untold numbers of patients, especially children. If a high enough dosage of vitamin C is administered in just about any form of poisoning, clinical success will almost always be achieved.

In lead toxicity vitamin C should *always* be administered. At the very least, toxin-induced depletion of vitamin C in the body can be lessened, and acute expressions of scurvy can be avoided. However, it appears that high enough doses of vitamin C should be very effective in reversing the clinical symptoms in most cases of lead toxicity. Furthermore, it is also clear that vitamin C can serve as a valuable adjunct in improving the efficacy of other lead-chelating agents, even if only suboptimal doses of vitamin C are added.

Chromium is a metal considered to be an important human nutrient in trace amounts. However, larger exposures are highly toxic to humans. Chromium and its derivative chromate compounds have a wide variety of industrial applications. More than 50 occupations permit enough chromate exposure to regularly cause dermatitis, a reactive skin inflammation. Although chromium is well-known as an alloy that is used in the electroplating of other metals, it is also commonly found in cement and printing inks. This exposes a large number of people who work regularly with such substances, making chromium the most common contact allergen in industry throughout the world (Milner, 1980). Low levels of vitamin C and other vitamins in the blood and urine have been reported in chrome industry workers (Karimov, 1988). This is likely a reflection that vitamins are used up at an accelerated rate whenever toxins are present.

Milner reported on the case of a 33-year-old male printing company foreman who had suffered with what was diagnosed as chromium dermatitis of his hands for seven years, treating it adequately with antihistamines and steroids. However, the disease finally progressed to the point where his hands and wrists gave him severe discomfort due to the increasing "swelling, oozing, weeping, and fissuring." These worsening symptoms were no longer controlled by steroids, either oral or injectable. Gloves and barrier creams were not acceptable for him, since his sense of touch was important in determining whether the printing was being performed correctly.

A solution of 10% vitamin C (as ascorbic acid) was prepared for the foreman. While at work he would dip his hands in this solution once each hour and then blot them dry. The solution was changed daily. His symptoms were dramatically reduced after a week of this therapy, and within one month he was completely off of his steroid and antihistamine therapy. His control of this condition with continued use of the vitamin C solution was effective for years.

The response of chromium dermatitis to vitamin C therapy described above by Milner has also been observed in studies on rats. Samitz et al. (1962) concluded that vitamin C can be used as an effective antidote for chromium poisoning in these animals, including both internal and external exposures. Pirozzi et al. (1968) showed that the topical use of vitamin C clearly shortened the time needed for the healing of chrome skin ulcers in guinea pigs. Samitz et al. (1968) hypothesized it was the reducing power of vitamin C that was the primary mechanism involved in the detoxification of chromium and the prevention of chrome dermatitis. Samitz and Katz (1965) found that vitamin C could also protect against the toxicity of inhaling chromic acid mist. Also, Samitz and Shrager (1966) demonstrated that vitamin C can prevent the allergic response seen in chromate-sensitive subjects.

Little et al. (1996) examined the ability of vitamin C to protect against the toxicity of chromium on human skin cells in culture. They found that of the five agents tested, which included cysteine and glutathione, vitamin C was the only agent that "offered complete protection." This is a good example of the fact that all antioxidants do not offer the same degrees of protection from oxidant-induced damage, and even though antioxidants are not interchangeable, they will bolster the effects of one another.

of the five agents tested, which included cysteine and glutathione, vitamin C was the only agent that "offered complete protection" against chromium toxicity on human skin cells in culture

Walpole et al. (1985) reported on the successful treatment of acute oral chromium poisoning in a 2-year-old child with a protocol including vitamin C. The authors considered the early administration of vitamin C as the most important part of their protocol. In fact, the authors wrote that "theoretically and experimentally, ascorbic acid is a very satisfactory antidote" to the most toxic forms of chromium. However, the authors gave only 1,000 mg orally to this child daily. Although the child ultimately recovered (that is, did not die) from the acute poisoning, he began to have seizures about two months after the accidental drinking of a sodium dichromate solution. In recalling the results Klenner achieved in so many toxic conditions using much higher doses of vitamin C, given intravenously or intramuscularly rather than orally, it is very possible this child could have made a more complete and rapid recovery had higher doses of vitamin C been given by needle.

Korallus et al. (1984) reported on the treatment of chromium toxicity (hexavalent chromium) with vitamin C. They concluded that vitamin C "is a true antidote" for this type of poisoning and the "therapy of choice." They further suggested that intravenous vitamin C therapy be initiated at the "earliest possible time" in order to prevent and/or lessen the kidney damage that is so commonly seen with this kind of poisoning. In mice,

Susa et al. (1989) reported that kidney damage caused by hexavalent chromium was inhibited by the simultaneous injection of vitamin C. Samitz (1970) reported that vitamin C was "an effective antidote when administered promptly to rats poisoned with chromate." Samitz also reported that a 10% aqueous vitamin C solution significantly shortened the healing time for chromate-induced ulcers in guinea pigs. Finally, Samitz noted that the same 10% vitamin C solution "proved effective" in the protection of chromate-sensitive workers in the printing and lithographing industries. Samitz asserted that the mechanism for the inactivation of the toxic hexavalent chromium by the vitamin C "involved reduction to trivalent chromium and subsequent complex formation of the trivalent species."

Dey et al. (2001) recently examined the protective role of vitamin C in preventing and/or reversing the cellular membrane damage induced by chromium. They noted it is the stepwise reduction of the toxic hexavalent chromium species by vitamin C and other cellular reductants that reduces toxicity. Although Dey used a daily dose of vitamin C in rats that was not even the equivalent of 500 mg in a 150-pound person, they found that this dose afforded significant although incomplete restoration of specific chromium-induced enzymatic defects in the kidneys and liver. Na et al. (1992) also showed that vitamin C afforded protection against sodium chromate-induced kidney toxicity. It is unknown whether a much larger dose of vitamin C would have proven even more effective in reversing the toxic effects seen in this experiment.

In cellular studies, Blankenship et al. (1997) showed that vitamin C, but not vitamin E, was able to protect cells from breaking down and dying after exposure to sodium chromate. They further noted that both vitamins "markedly inhibited" the chromosomal defects associated with exposure to sodium chromate. Wise et al. (1993) were also able to demonstrate that vitamin C could block the chromosome-damaging effects of lead chromate in animal cell cultures. Rai and Raizada (1988) showed that vitamin C and glutathione "appreciably counteracted" the toxicity of chromium in bacterial cultures. Ginter et al. (1989) were able to demonstrate in guinea pigs that vitamin C could offer definite protection against both the toxic and mutation-causing effects of chromium.

Vitamin C is also considered to be a chelator (binder) of chromium. Tandon and Gaur (1977) compared the ability of vitamin C to remove chromium from the tissues of laboratory animals as well as from preparations of animal cells in the test tube. Vitamin C proved to be the most effective in taking chromium out of the test tube preparations.

In spite of all the data and evidence noted above, for unclear reasons some investigators continue to offer "caution" in the use of vitamin C for chromium toxicity. Bradberry and Vale (1999) maintain that there is no confirmed clinical evidence that vitamin C lessens morbidity or mortality in "systemic chromium poisoning." Perhaps the authors did not make an exhaustive review of the world medical literature, or perhaps they chose to ignore or dismiss the validity of the report of Walpole et al. cited and discussed above. If vitamin C clearly helps just one person with chromium poisoning who was otherwise destined to die or go into kidney failure, that information cannot be ignored or even minimized. This is especially true when there are no really good alternatives for this form of toxicity. Furthermore, the nontoxic profile of vitamin C therapy simply does not allow any clinician aware of its benefits to be vindicated from not always using it, even if it were used only as an adjunct to the much less beneficial and more traditional therapies. Such a recommendation was made by Meert et al. (1994), who reported on the futility of exchange transfusion and hemodialysis in saving a child from the ingestion of ammonium chromate, a very toxic form of chromium. The authors apparently want to help prevent future children from dying under similar circumstances since they suggest that "immediate, large doses" of vitamin C would acutely reduce the toxicity of chromium and result in "less cellular toxicity."

It would appear that prompt intravenous administration of vitamin C would be the treatment of choice for the various forms of chromium poisoning. The optimal dose has yet to be worked out, and the effects of Klenner-sized doses of vitamin C on this form of toxicity remain unknown. However, it is very logical to predict a highly favorable clinical response from such dosing.

Since the reducing ability of vitamin C appears to play a prominent role in the neutralization of toxic chromium compounds, it would also seem logical to add other potent antioxidants such as alpha lipoic acid to the treatment regimen. Finally, it should be kept in mind that all these therapeutic interventions can be implemented in addition to whatever more "traditional" types of treatment are being given. With only the rarest of exceptions, vitamin C and antioxidant therapy will enhance the effectiveness of whatever other treatments are being given for just about any given toxic and/or infectious condition.

Arsenicals are arsenic-containing compounds, which are toxic to humans and capable of causing cancer in some cases. Chronic exposure to an arsenical will commonly cause variable degrees of muscle weakness in the extremities, sometimes progressing to an objective wasting of the muscle mass. A degenerative condition of the brain can result as well. Characteristic rashes occur, and many other nonspecific signs and symptoms can also result from this type of poisoning, including nausea, vomiting, diarrhea or constipation, enlarged liver, kidney dysfunction, and impairment of the blood-forming elements of the body.

Presently, only a few chemical chelating agents are all that can be offered for therapy. Dialysis has also been reported to remove some arsenic from the body (Vaziri et al., 1980).

One of the most important ways to detoxify arsenic and its related compounds, as well as many other toxic chemicals, is by chemical reduction (Ehrlich, 1909). Chemical reduction is a primary function of antioxidants such as vitamin C.

Friend and Marquis (1936) noted that vitamin C levels were quite low in five patients who had developed signs of arsenic intoxication. These were patients who had been given arsphenamine, an early treatment for syphilis that contained arsenic. The authors were able to conclude that the vitamin C levels dropped because of the toxic treatment, which was in agreement with the consistent observation that any significant toxin consumes or excessively utilizes vitamin C, depleting its stores.

In animals such as rats that can make vitamin C in their livers, a challenge with arsenic will raise liver and plasma vitamin C levels (Schinella et al., 1996). These levels will eventually drop and stay low if large enough doses of arsenic (or any other significant toxin) are administered to the vitamin C-producing test animal.

In guinea pigs, Sulzberger and Oser (1935) were able to show that a toxic reaction to an arsphenamine compound (neoarsphenamine) was inhibited by a diet rich in vitamin C. Another researcher, Cormia (1937), demonstrated that guinea pigs on a low vitamin C diet had a dramatic toxic response to neoarsphenamine, and guinea pigs given much larger amounts of vitamin C were protected from such toxicity. McChesney et al. (1942) also found that vitamin C significantly reduced the toxicity of neoarsphenamine in the rats they tested. McChesney (1945) later asserted that his experiments demonstrated a high blood concentration of vitamin C was necessary when neoarsphenamine was in circulation for a detoxifying effect to take place.

Dainow (1935) found that intravenous vitamin C shortened the recovery time of three patients with arsphenamine-related dermatitis. Vitamin C has also been used effectively in the past to help clinicians avoid the occasional severe reactions demonstrated by some syphilis

patients to the administration of neoarsphenamine. Bundesen et al.
(1941) did neoarsphenamine patch testing on the skin to help determine
which patients had the highest risk of severe reaction to neoarsphenamine therapy for syphilis. They were able to demonstrate that even
in severe reactors, the addition of vitamin C to the patch before testing could usually completely eliminate the skin reaction. The authors
used these results to support their contention that if enough vitamin C
was given along with the neoarsphenamine in treating most of their
syphilis patients, most of the toxic reactions that might otherwise occur
could be greatly lessened or prevented. Lahiri (1943) was also able to
conclude from his own observations and those of others that giving
enough vitamin C was the "safest way of avoiding arsenical intolerance
in antisyphylitic therapy."

Much more recently, Chattopadhyay et al. (2001) showed that rats
were protected from the toxic effects of sodium arsenite on specific
ovarian and brain functions by vitamin C. This was an especially significant finding for these researchers since they gave a dosage of arsenic to rats that approximated arsenic contamination levels of some
drinking water in India.

In addition to its direct ability to neutralize the toxicity of arsenic-containing compounds, vitamin C has also been shown to possibly enhance the effectiveness of arsenic in the treatment of syphilis,
which was an important way to treat this disease before the discovery
of penicillin. Ruskin and Silberstein (1938) treated 14 patients who all
had positive serologic testing (Wasserman) for syphilis. Furthermore,
all 14 had their syphilis diagnoses for extended periods ranging from
eight months to twenty years in duration. All had already received
courses of neoarsphenamine, with or without bismuth. After vitamin C
was added to the treatment, 10 of the 14 patients had their Wasserman
testing go from positive to negative, indicating an effective control and
possibly eradication of the infection. The typical course of treatment
involved about 20 injections, one given every two weeks. It is possible
that the vitamin C by itself could have eradicated the infection. The
doses given were not revealed in the short article.

While it might appear obvious that the vitamin C worked alone in treating the syphilis cases discussed above, it should also be noted that vitamin C has recently been shown to work well with another arsenic compound in helping to control a certain form of cancer. Grad et al. (2001) found that vitamin C enhanced the ability of arsenic trioxide to kill certain malignant cells (multiple myeloma). Gao et al. (2002) have also shown a similar interaction between vitamin C and arsenic trioxide in killing a certain type of leukemic cell. Similar results were reported by Bachleitner-Hofmann et al. (2001).

No straightforward studies of arsenic poisoning in humans treated with optimally high doses of vitamin C could be found. However, as with so many other toxins, there is more than ample evidence in the scientific literature on the interactions of vitamin C with arsenic to suggest that prompt treatment of acute arsenic poisoning with enough intravenous vitamin C should be very clinically effective. How effective similar doses of vitamin C would be in reversing the changes induced by chronic arsenic or arsenical poisoning is less clear. Certainly, there appears to be every good reason to try similarly high doses of vitamin C in chronic poisoning as well.

Cadmium is a metal used in great quantity by industry. In the United States alone over 10 million pounds of cadmium are used every year. Cadmium is a component of alloys, and it is present in electrical conductors, electroplating, ceramics, pigments, dental prosthetics, plastic stabilizers, and storage batteries. Cadmium is also used in the photographic, rubber, motor, and airline industries. Airborne cadmium pollution is a result of smelters, metal-processing furnaces, and the burning of coal and oil (Robertson, 2000).

An acute cadmium intoxication is accompanied by lung symptoms. If the exposure is survived, long-term pulmonary defects can emerge. Kidney insufficiency and/or failure can result. Chronic cadmium intoxication features damage especially to the lungs and the kidneys. As a result, chronic exposures can eventually result in emphysema. Although progressive kidney failure is rare, the kidneys often show damage, with chronic spilling of protein in the urine.

No studies directly addressing the effects of vitamin C on acute or chronic toxicity of cadmium on humans could be found. However, there are a number of animal studies that support the likelihood that vitamin C would be a very useful therapy for human cadmium toxicity, just as it is with so many other toxins and toxic elements.

There have been a number of studies on vitamin C and cadmium in the guinea pig, which like humans cannot produce its own vitamin C. Nagyova et al. (1994) administered cadmium (1 mg per animal per day) in the drinking of water of guinea pigs for 12 weeks. One group of animals was maintained on "low" amounts of vitamin C (2 mg per animal per day), while another group received "high" amounts of vitamin C (100 mg per animal per day). Kidney damage, as reflected by direct examination under the microscope, was significantly reduced in the guinea pigs given the higher dose of vitamin C.

Also, blood tests of kidney function (creatinine, blood urea nitrogen) were not significantly affected by cadmium in the "high" vitamin C group, even though the same tests were significantly worsened in the "low" vitamin C group of animals. It should be emphasized, however, that the "high" dosage of vitamin C given in this experiment was approximately equal to only about 5,000 mg for a 150-pound (70-kilogram) person. However, the authors appreciated the effects of these lower doses of vitamin C and concluded that vitamin C "can be effective in the protection" against cadmium-induced liver damage in guinea pigs.

Kubova et al. (1993) examined the toxic effects of cadmium in the face of "low" and "high" vitamin C dosing on guinea pig immune function. The cadmium and vitamin C doses were the same as noted in the study of Nagyova et al. These researchers concluded that the higher dose of vitamin C was able to reduce the toxic effects of cadmium on the immune system. The immune parameters examined included the ability of special white blood cells to consume microbes and other particulate matter as well as the level of activity of T-lymphocytes in the blood.

Hudecova and Ginter (1992) examined the toxic effects of cadmium and the protective effects of vitamin C on lipid peroxidation (LPO) in guinea pigs. LPO is a direct laboratory indicator of oxidative stress, which is one of the primary ways by which many toxins do much of their damage. Just as an iron bar will oxidize to form rust, important fats (lipids) in the body can oxidize, or "rust," to form lipid peroxides. A lipid peroxide can also be considered a breakdown product of a degenerative disease. Using the same doses of cadmium and vitamin C as used by Nagyova et al. and Kubova et al. noted above, Hudecova and Ginter showed that guinea pigs given the "high" doses of vitamin C had clearly lower levels of LPO than the animals given the "low" vitamin C doses. This is further laboratory evidence of the beneficial effects afforded the guinea pig against cadmium-induced damage. As cadmium-induced tissue damage is lessened, as was seen in the kidney by Nagyova et al., LPO will also generally be lessened. Gupta and Kar (1998) were able to show in mice that vitamin C would reduce certain laboratory indicators of LPO that were otherwise increased by cadmium administration.

Cadmium accumulation in the organs of guinea pigs receiving vitamin C supplementation was also examined. Kadrabova et al. (1992) found that vitamin C appeared to be especially effective in preventing greater accumulation of cadmium in the brain, heart, and testes of test animals. Calabrese et al. (1987) studied the effects of vitamin C on cadmium accumulation in the blood and hair. Even though small doses of vitamin C, 500 or 1,000 mg, were used in the study, they nevertheless concluded that vitamin C did not significantly affect cadmium levels in the blood or the hair.

Guinea pig studies on cadmium toxicity and vitamin C indicate several levels of protection. Vitamin C clearly protects against cadmium-induced liver damage. It lessens the laboratory evidence (increased LPO) of cadmium-induced oxidative damage to the tissues. Also, vitamin C reduces the toxic effects of cadmium on the immune system. Finally, vitamin C reduces cadmium accumulation in several vital organs of the guinea pig.

Multiple investigators have also examined cadmium toxicity and the beneficial effects of vitamin C in rats. In a straightforward survival study, Shiraishi et al. (1993) gave rats a dose of cadmium that caused a 93% mortality rate. Another group of rats pretreated with vitamin C were given the same dose of cadmium but demonstrated little lethal effect. Furthermore, the direct toxicity of the cadmium on the liver was significantly decreased by the pretreatment with vitamin C. Lyall et al. (1982) found that increasing doses of cadmium to rats produced progressive amounts of kidney damage. They also found that lower vitamin C tissue levels correlated with the severity of kidney damage. Chatterjee et al. (1973) showed that cadmium intoxication in rats caused a severe anemia, and that vitamin C administration could reverse this abnormality. In cultured mouse cells, Fahmy and Aly (2000) were able to demonstrate that vitamin C offered a significant protection against chromosomal damage induced by cadmium chloride exposure.

Fox and Fry (1970) and Fox (1975) investigated the effects of dietary vitamin C supplementation on the toxic effects of cadmium in young Japanese quail. This bird is known to have a very rapid rate of growth, and it is very sensitive to both dietary deficits and toxins. The dose of cadmium induced severe anemia and growth retardation in these quail. The addition of vitamin C to the cadmium administration had a "marked protective effect on the anemia," with a less pronounced protective effect on growth retardation. It was also concluded that the protective effect of vitamin C against the toxicity of cadmium did not involve the prevention of cadmium absorption.

Vitamin C does appear to affect the absorption and/or bioavailability of dietary cadmium in some animal models. In broiler chickens, Rambeck and Guillot (1996) found that the addition of 1,000 mg of vitamin C to every kilogram of feed lowered cadmium accumulation in the kidney and liver by as much as 40%. In the commercial feeding of pigs, Rothe et al. (1994) found that the addition of 1,000 mg of vitamin C to every kilogram of pig feed reduced cadmium content in the kidney, liver, and muscle tissues by 35% to 40%.

It would seem reasonable to conclude from these studies that cadmium is another toxin in humans that would likely be effectively treated by adequate doses of vitamin C. However, hard data to support this specific conclusion is lacking.

Vanadium is a metal used in the steel and chemical industries. It is also used in alloys. In humans, abdominal cramping and diarrhea can result from chronic toxicity. The kidneys and blood are also targets of chronic vanadium exposure, resulting in compromised kidney function and anemia. There is also an inhalation toxicity that affects chiefly the lungs. Larger, acute oral exposures can also result in liver toxicity.

Domingo et al. (1985) found that vitamin C had a significant protective, antidote effect against what was otherwise a lethal dose of a vanadium-containing compound for mice. Jones and Basinger (1983) also found vitamin C to be an effective antidote in mice against two vanadium compounds. These authors looked at the effectiveness of 18 different antidotes, many of them effective metal chelators, for the treatment of vanadium intoxication, and they concluded that vitamin C "appeared to be the most promising." Domingo et al. (1986) also found that vitamin C was very effective in preventing vanadium intoxication in mice when administered immediately after the vanadium.

Chakraborty et al. (1977) found that vanadium intoxication in rats lowered liver levels of vitamin C and decreased its excretion in the urine. Zaporowska (1994) also demonstrated that vanadium toxicity reduces vitamin C levels in the liver, kidneys, spleen, and adrenal glands of rats. These findings indicate that vanadium was acting as a toxin in using up vitamin C stores in rats.

Chakraborty et al. also found that microscopic evidence of liver and kidney damage from vanadium in rats "showed marked signs of restoration" after vitamin C was given. These findings are also consistent with the observations of Donaldson et al. (1985), who found that the administration of vitamin C to mice before they were given vanadium resulted in a significant reduction of LPO in the liver, indicating a lessened degree of oxidative stress. These investigators also found that pretreatment with vitamin C significantly reduced the clinical toxicity of vanadium in mice, as evidenced by less respiratory depression and limb paralysis.

In chicks Hill (1979) was able to demonstrate that vitamin C reduced the growth retardation that was related to the administration of vanadium. Ousterhout and Berg (1981) also found that vitamin C could protect the hen from the toxic effects of vanadium in decreasing egg production and body weight. Toussant and Latshaw (1994) came to similar conclusions. Benabdeljelil and Jensen (1990) also found that vitamin C could protect the eggs of laying hens from the decreased albumen (egg white) quality associated with excess dietary vanadium.

Gomez et al. (1991) found that vitamin C was not able to significantly increase the urinary excretion of vanadium or decrease its tissue concentrations in rats given vanadium. In mice, however, Domingo et al. (1990) showed that vitamin C was able to increase the urinary elimination of administered vanadium. The ability of vitamin C to help eliminate vanadium appears to be uncertain, even though it clearly decreases its toxicity in multiple animal studies.

In vanadium intoxication, as with many other metal poisonings, vitamin C exerts a significant portion of its positive effects by being a potent reducing agent (antioxidant). Ferrer and Baran (2001) suggested that vitamin C is one of the possible natural reducing agents of vanadium. Song et al. (2002) have also demonstrated the potent ability of vitamin C to reduce vanadium compounds while further demonstrating its vast superiority over the reducing ability of glutathione, another important antioxidant, for the same vanadium compounds.

The ability of vitamin C to reduce vanadium has also been of practical value in the treatment of manic depressive psychosis. Naylor (1984) reported that vanadium levels were elevated in both mania and depression. This indicates the possibility that both conditions are, at least in part, caused by the toxic effects of excessive vanadium.

The established therapies for manic depression, such as phenothiazines and monoamine oxidase inhibitors, have been shown to help reduce vanadium to a less active form. Naylor also added that vitamin C has been reported to be effective in the treatment of depression and mania, probably secondary largely to its ability to reduce vanadium. Adam-Vizi et al. (1981) were able to show that vanadium could inhibit an important enzyme that helped neurons communicate in the brain. They also showed that vitamin C could partially reverse this vanadium inhibition. Even if not directly related to depression and mania, this work strongly suggests that vanadium plays a toxic role in some neurologic diseases and vitamin C can act to block or reverse some toxic effects of the vanadium.

Overall, the scientific literature does not directly address the effects of vitamin C administration on acute or chronic human vanadium toxicity. However, certain animal studies are compelling, and the data on manic depression also suggests an important role for vitamin C in the treatment of vanadium toxicity in humans. The safety of vitamin C, even in large intravenous doses, should justify treating acute or chronic vanadium intoxication along with whatever other traditional treatments are given. The scientific literature on vanadium toxicity definitely suggests that adequate vitamin C given soon enough may negate the clinical toxicity of vanadium. This would hold true even if the vitamin C does not reduce tissue stores or increase urinary elimination of vanadium, which is a situation somewhat similar to the published literature on mercury toxicity and vitamin C.

Nickel is another metal used in various alloys. It is known to cause significant lung toxicity when a large enough industrial exposure occurs. It is also known to be a potent cancer-causing agent, especially in the tissues of the respiratory tract.

Chen and Lin (2001) looked at the effects of nickel chloride on human platelets (the sticky elements in the blood that initiate blood clotting). They found that LPO, an index of oxidative stress, was increased in the nickel-exposed platelets, while vitamin E and glutathione levels were decreased. They also showed that nickel depressed the ability of platelets to stick together. Vitamin C in this system significantly increased platelet clumping, reduced LPO levels, and increased the levels of vitamin E and glutathione. The authors concluded that vitamin C was able to offer protection to human platelets from nickel-induced toxicity. Chen and Lin (1998) also found that vitamin C could reduce the LPO activity in human placental tissue exposed to nickel.

In human lymphocyte cultures, Wozniak and Blasiak (2002) were able to demonstrate that nickel induced an activity associated with increased DNA damage. The study went on to show that pretreatment with vitamin C could decrease this activity, implying that vitamin C could provide some degree of protection against the genetic toxicity of nickel, which leads to mutations or cancer. Dhir et al. (1991) were able to show that feeding a plant with a high concentration of vitamin C to mice decreased clear microscopic evidence of chromosomal damage in the bone marrow cells. Osipova et al. (1998) also found that pretreatment with vitamin C increased the viability (percent living) of human lymphocytes exposed to nickel sulfate.

In a study more directly pertinent to the lessening of clinical nickel toxicity in humans by vitamin C, Perminova et al. (2001) looked at lymphocytes from smelting shop workers in a copper-nickel sulfide processing plant. The body content of nickel was approximated by hair analysis. A microscopic finding in the lymphocytes (number of micronuclei) was found to be significantly decreased in workers after they had been given 1,000 mg daily of vitamin C for a month. Greater numbers of micronuclei indicate greater amounts of chromosome damage. Therefore, these microscopic findings indicate that a fairly minimal vitamin C supplementation was able to decrease the level of chromosome damage to workers occupationally exposed to nickel.

Chatterjee et al. (1979) demonstrated that vitamin C could restore impaired growth rates of rats that had received toxic doses of nickel. Furthermore, they showed vitamin C restored the activities of multiple enzymes in the liver and kidney "to a significant extent." Das et al. (2001) looked at the ability of nickel to induce increased LPO activity in rats. LPO activity is a direct indicator of toxin-induced oxidative stress in a test animal. Nickel significantly increased LPO activity, while the simultaneous administration of vitamin C significantly lessened this LPO activity increase. Furthermore, Das et al. measured the levels of three important antioxidant enzymes along with another important antioxidant, glutathione, in the liver. Nickel reliably lowered the levels of these enzymes and glutathione, while a simultaneous administration of vitamin C offered a "relative protection" against this nickel-induced liver toxicity.

Chen et al. (1998) found the administration of vitamin C to rats that received nickel chloride showed a lesser degree of LPO (oxidative stress) and lower levels of two liver enzymes that were directly reflecting nickel-induced liver toxicity. Chen et al. (1998a) were able to show in mice that vitamin C with glutathione was able to lower nickel-induced LPO and decrease the concentration of nickel in the liver.

Like chromium, nickel will induce a toxic contact dermatitis in some people. Memon et al. (1994) tested a number of agents on nickel-sensitive people. A 20% preparation of vitamin C clearly helped some of the subjects, while the commonly used 1% hydrocortisone preparation had no significant effect.

The cumulative research on nickel toxicity and vitamin C strongly suggests that even higher doses of vitamin C than those cited in the research could have even more dramatic effects, both clinically and in laboratory tests. As with the other toxic elements, there appears to be no good reason offered in the scientific literature to prohibit or even be wary of using large doses of vitamin C in human cases of nickel toxicity.

Aluminum, the most abundant metal in the earth's crust, has no clearly useful biological function. Aluminum exposure can come through drinking water, aluminum containers and cookware, multiple aluminum-containing medications, and even many antiperspirants. Toxicity can be seen especially in the brain, liver, kidneys, and bone. Deferoxamine, a chelating agent, is the common therapy for aluminum toxicity.

In human skin cell cultures, Anane and Creppy (2001) showed that LPO, an important manifestation of oxidative damage in the blood, is induced by the presence of aluminum. These researchers were able to show that an antioxidant treatment protocol including vitamin C was able to largely block the ability of aluminum to increase LPO activity. The authors felt that LPO activity was a significant factor in the facilitation of aluminum's cytotoxic effect. Swain and Chainy (2000) were also able to show that vitamin C could prevent increased LPO activity induced by aluminum in chick brain preparations.

In contrast to some other toxic elements discussed so far, there is evidence that vitamin C can promote the elimination of aluminum from the body. Fulton and Jeffery (1990) gave rabbits drinking water with aluminum chloride and vitamin C. Compared to rabbits receiving only the aluminum chloride, the rabbits that also received vitamin C demonstrated enhanced excretion of aluminum. Furthermore, the vitamin C did not enhance aluminum accumulation in any of the tissues studied, and it even prevented accumulation of aluminum in the bone.

Vitamin C has also been demonstrated to offer protection against the chromosome-damaging abilities of aluminum. Dhir et al. (1990) showed that vitamin C could protect against some of the chromosome breakage induced by aluminum in mouse bone marrow cells. Roy et al. (1992) also showed that vitamin C could reduce the formation of micronuclei, an index of chromosome damage, in mouse bone marrow cells exposed to aluminum. Both of these studies indicate that vitamin C can probably offer at least partial protection against the ability of aluminum to toxically induce mutations and cause cancer.

Although there are relatively few studies dealing with vitamin C and aluminum toxicity, a similar pattern of protection against toxic effects compared to other more studied toxic elements emerges. Furthermore, it appears likely that in addition to neutralizing the toxicity of aluminum, vitamin C also helps to promote its elimination from the body. Since vitamin C has little or no toxicity in most people, it would appear very reasonable to at least include vitamin C in the treatment regimen of a patient felt to be suffering from aluminum toxicity.

Fluorine (fluoride) is a toxic inhibitor of several enzyme systems in the body, and it is known to diminish tissue respiration. Although fluoride has long been promoted as an agent that can decrease the incidence of tooth decay, it is an uncontested fact that fluoride is always toxic when enough of it has been ingested for a long enough period of time. One of its salt forms, sodium fluoride, was long used as insect poison. This same form is commonly used in toothpastes with the aim of preventing tooth decay.

One of the most common forms of fluoride toxicity is seen in dental fluorosis. This is largely due to the fact that the cosmetic appearance of this condition, involving a progressive deterioration of tooth enamel, makes diagnosis ultimately unavoidable. There is general agreement, even among those who promote water fluoridation, that children with evidence of dental fluorosis have ingested too much fluoride over time, and further fluoride exposure should in no way be encouraged.

The incidence of dental caries (decaying teeth) is associated with higher levels of lead in the blood (Moss et al., 1999). Although a study directly looking at blood levels of vitamin C and degrees of dental decay could not be found, the totality of the data summarized in the section on vitamin C and lead makes it appear quite likely that enough daily vitamin C supplementation would have some protective effect against dental decay. Vitamin C would reduce the blood lead level, which would then result in a lower rate of dental decay.

Certainly, the nontoxic nature of vitamin C, along with its many other documented benefits, makes it vastly more desirable for reducing dental decay than ingested forms of fluoride. Fluoride will always be toxic when enough of it accumulates in the body, and few individuals can be expected to end up with what is considered an "optimal" amount of fluoride in their teeth. Accumulation will continue, and some degree of fluoride toxicity can be anticipated in most people with significant exposures, especially those consuming fluoridated water. Vitamin C supplementation would be an excellent alternative to the existing water fluoridation programs already in place in so many communities.

Gupta et al. (1994) showed that dental fluorosis, long considered to be an irreversible condition, could be very effectively treated with a protocol that included vitamin C, vitamin D, and calcium. The earliest grade of fluorosis proved to be completely reversible in nearly all children treated. The more advanced cases of dental fluorosis did not resolve completely, but did show significant improvement. Especially noteworthy was that the vitamin C protocol "markedly reduced" the fluoride levels in the blood, serum, and urine. Gupta et al. (1996) were able to show that a similar vitamin C protocol as used above was also able to reverse early skeletal fluorosis as well as dental fluorosis.

Reddy and Srikantia (1971) induced experimental skeletal fluorosis in monkeys. They were able to demonstrate that "adequate calcium and vitamin C" in the diet lessened the toxic effects of fluoride on bones.

These toxic effects included a thinning of bone density on X-ray and an abnormal elevation of alkaline phosphatase, an enzyme especially active in bones.

Other toxic effects of fluoride and their effective treatment with vitamin C have been discussed in the literature. Guna Sherlin and Verma (2000) showed that the sodium fluoride-induced lowering of calcium and phosphorus levels in rats could be appreciably blocked by the simultaneous administration of antioxidants including vitamin C. Narayana and Chinoy (1994) observed that sodium fluoride could induce several different types of damage in rat sperm cells. Vitamin C was found to bring about a significant recovery from these fluoride-induced toxic effects.

It would appear that vitamin C can offer a significant protection against many of the toxic effects of fluoride if taken in adequate daily amounts. It would also seem reasonable to include large doses of intravenous vitamin C in the treatment of any significant acute fluoride toxicity, such as would be seen with the oral ingestion of an insecticide fluoride compound like sodium fluoride.

Venoms

Klenner (1957) reported on the successful treatment of acute poisoning secondary to a Black Widow spider bite in a girl aged three and one-half years. She recalled "knocking a big black bug off her stomach" while playing during the day she fell ill. Her onset of illness was sudden, with a loss of appetite and a "severe gripping pain" in her stomach. She had nausea almost immediately and began vomiting about six hours later. The vomiting became intermittent throughout the night, and after 12 hours she developed a fever. Her mother also noted a redness around the child's navel, "associated with considerable swelling and rigidity," and touching the area elicited severe pain. Over the next few hours the child's condition deteriorated dramatically. Her "speech became incoherent" as she became progressively "stuporous." When Klenner first saw the little girl about 18 hours after onset, with a magnifying glass he was able to identify the "obvious" fang marks of the spider bite. Klenner noted that the child was non-responsive to his questions, near-comatose, and had developed labored breathing. Her abdomen was described as "board-like." Klenner was confident in his diagnosis, and he first gave the child an intravenous injection of calcium gluconate. This was followed within 15 minutes by 4,000 mg of vitamin C intravenously.

Even though Klenner acknowledged that the little girl was "critically ill," he was confident of the success of his treatment, allowing the parents to manage the child's condition at home rather than at the hospital. Six hours later he was able to apply pressure to the abdomen, and the little girl's fever had dropped from 103.5°F to 101°F. Klenner gave another 4,000 mg of vitamin C intravenously, and fluids by mouth were now encouraged. After another six hours the fever was down to 100°F, the child was "listless but awake," and she was readily taking small amounts of fluid. On the next morning, 12 hours later, the child was "awake, relatively active, not so tender and about 50 per cent of the swelling and discoloration about the umbilicus gone."

Klenner then administered another 4,000 mg of vitamin C intravenously along with 3,000 mg intramuscularly. Over the next three days the child steadily improved, taking 1,000 mg of vitamin C every three to four hours. The child passed a large tarry stool on the fourth day with a small enema. Such a stool usually indicates bleeding in the stomach and/or intestines. Furthermore, the toxin of the spider may have depleted the little girl's body stores of vitamin C so rapidly that this bleeding represented an acute scurvy syndrome with scurvy-induced bleeding. After this stool was passed the child's appetite returned, and her return to complete normalcy was rapid. Klenner reported that he had successfully treated "eight proven cases of Black Widow bite" during his medical practice. In addition to a single dose of calcium gluconate, Klenner recommended intravenous vitamin C at a minimum dosage of 350 mg/kg of body weight, to be repeated as the patient's clinical condition dictated.

Klenner reported that he had successfully treated "eight proven cases of Black Widow bite" with vitamin C during his medical practice

Klenner (1971) described the cure of another dramatic case of venom poisoning with intravenous vitamin C. An adult male presented to Klenner's office after having been bitten by a Puss Caterpillar only 10 minutes earlier. Klenner initially assumed it was a Black Widow spider bite, and gave the man 1,000 mg of calcium gluconate intravenously. The man felt no improvement, and started telling Klenner that "he was dying." Klenner noted that the patient was becoming cyanotic (blue), meaning the venom was literally robbing him of the oxygen necessary for survival. Klenner, realizing that his patient was near death, drew up 12,000 mg of vitamin C into a 50 cc syringe. He pushed the vitamin C intravenously through a 20 gauge needle "as fast as the plunger could be pushed."

Before the injection was even completed, the patient exclaimed, "Thank God," as his clinical condition improved just as rapidly as it had deteriorated. Clinically, Klenner was certain the patient would have died quickly from shock and oxygen starvation. Klenner has suggested that the very rapid administration of 12 to 50 grams of vitamin C produces a "flash oxidation" effect that quickly restores the oxygen content in the blood.

Klenner (1971) also noted that when a "quick reversal" of toxic, infective, and/or allergic "insults" is needed, doses of vitamin C "must range from 350 mg to 1,200 per kg body weight," and "must be given by needle." Generally, such an approach should be reserved for clinical situations when the physician literally feels death is imminent; otherwise, preparing a bottle with vitamin C for intravenous infusion is the optimal approach.

Klenner (1954a) also reported on the successful treatment of a four-year-old child who received a "full strike" from a mature Highland moccasin. Klenner used a total of 12,000 mg of vitamin C to effectively neutralize the snake venom that had been released into the child. Smith (1988), in reporting on Klenner's results, noted that the young girl presented with severe pain in her leg, and was "already vomiting within twenty minutes after the bite." Klenner first gave 4,000 mg of vitamin C intravenously. The child stopped crying within 30 minutes, took fluids by mouth, and even had occasion to laugh. She commented while sitting on the emergency room table: "Come on daddy, I'm all right now, let's go home." Because of slight fever and persistent tenderness in the leg, Klenner gave her another 4,000 mg of vitamin C intravenously, and finally another 4,000 mg late in the day. No antibiotics and no antiserum were ever given. In Klenner's words, "38 hours after being bitten, she was completely normal."

Klenner compared the case of the little girl described above to that of a 16-year-old girl who also received a moccasin bite. Judging from the appearance of the fang marks, Klenner figured the moccasin was roughly the same size as the one that had bitten the little girl. This older patient did not receive any vitamin C but was given three doses of antivenom. Her arm swelled to four times the size of the opposite arm, she needed morphine for pain control, and she required three weeks of hospitalization.

Smith quoted Klenner describing his approach to the patient dealing with the toxicity of venom:

> All the venom that will be encountered exists as you see the patient. It is important to give sufficient sodium ascorbate to neutralize the bite. The more you give; the faster will be the cure. We now routinely give 10 to 15 grams sodium ascorbate depending on the weight of the victim. Then as much of the drug as can be tolerated by mouth is given, usually 5 grams, every four hours.

Smith also related Klenner's encounter with a snake bite victim who had already been treated at another emergency room. The bite area had become badly infected after a doctor had tried to cut out the area, and the patient had a 104°F fever. Klenner started the patient on 15,000 mg of vitamin C intravenously twice daily, along with 5,000 mg of oral vitamin C every four hours. Penicillin was given as well, and the patient was back to work in seven days.

Although Klenner did not report a large experience in treating snake bites with vitamin C, he was confident that properly dosed vitamin C would cure any type of snake bite. He asserted that larger doses of vitamin C, in the range of 40,000 to 60,000 mg, would have to be used to neutralize the venom of a bite from a snake such as a large diamond-back or cottonmouth (Klenner, 1974).

Certainly, it would appear that vitamin C should be added to the treatment of any serpent, animal, or insect bite. Cilento et al. (1980) have written that since vitamin C "is a non toxic, non specific antitoxin it may be used for any type of venomous bite without having to await identification of the culprit."

since vitamin C "is a non toxic, non specific antitoxin it may be used for any type of venomous bite without having to await identification of the culprit"

Klenner made two more important observations in this area. He felt that the various antitoxin preparations often made patients worse. Furthermore, Klenner (1974) has noted that the amount of vitamin C administered to a patient "is the all important factor" in assuring a positive clinical response, regardless of the condition being treated. Klenner went on to say that 30,000 mg of vitamin C each day seemed to be critical in terms of obtaining a positive clinical response, regardless of age and weight. This was a general rule although small infants and toddlers could require less vitamin C to produce a positive clinical response. Klenner added that in some "pathological conditions like barbiturate intoxication, snake bite or virus encephalitis," larger doses may be needed for some individuals.

Indeed, for some of the acute viral syndromes that so quickly metabolize body stores of vitamin C, Klenner advised to "never give less than 350 mg/kg body weight," repeated every hour for six to twelve doses. Depending upon clinical improvement, the doses could be spaced from two to four hours until the patient recovered. Furthermore, Klenner (1971) has found that the *initial* dose of vitamin C should be as high as 1,200 mg/kg body weight for the critically ill person, such as a patient comatose with viral encephalitis. This can translate to a 100,000 mg first dose of vitamin C. Frequently, the vitamin C doses in the literature, for either treating toxins and/or infectious diseases, are less than 1% of the typical doses used by Klenner to achieve his incredible clinical successes.

Summary

In light of the information cited in this chapter it is absolutely amazing that vitamin C is still so little used in the treatment of different toxic states and acute poisonings. There never seems to be enough information available for a traditional physician to "jump on board" and start applying the incredible healing and curative properties of vitamin C. Calabrese (1979), who has done a sizeable amount of primary research on vitamin C, wrote an article examining whether the Recommended Dietary Allowance (RDA) of vitamin C should be increased in light of the effects of so many pollutants on human health and vitamin C metabolism.

Calabrese noted that it is "widely accepted" that vitamin C "markedly affects the toxicity and/or carcinogenicity of greater than 50 pollutants, many of which are ubiquitous in the air, water, and food environments." Incredibly, after making such an assertion, Calabrese still concluded that "the data do not warrant changing" the vitamin C RDA "in light of the knowledge of pollutant interactions."

The statements of Calabrese and others like him beg a significant question: how much data is required to routinely recommend higher daily intakes of vitamin C? Klenner's data is compelling enough to routinely use vitamin C in any toxic patient, and the very many research studies cited in this chapter only serve to underscore that Klenner was scientifically correct in prescribing high doses of vitamin C in so many different situations. However, to my knowledge, since Klenner's death no physician has systematically and consistently used vitamin C in sufficiently high dosages in as many situations. Obviously, however, there are no good reasons not to do so.

It is also important to point out once again the importance of dosage level whenever using vitamin C. When adequate vitamin C is not given in a particular clinical situation, the desired recovery simply will not occur no matter how appropriate optimally dosed vitamin C might have otherwise been for that situation. If you review a significant number of the scientific articles cited in this chapter, you will see that vitamin C researchers have looked at the effects of vitamin C doses ranging from 1 mg/kg body weight to over 6,000 mg/kg body weight in their toxic experimental subjects. Not surprisingly, a 6,000-fold range in vitamin C dosing will have a wide range of clinical responses. Unfortunately, in reading some of these research papers, there are a number of researchers who readily conclude that vitamin C is of no use for certain types of poisoning even though very small doses were used. As soon as *any* amount of vitamin C fails to improve a given clinical situation, the conclusion is frequently made that vitamin C is of "no benefit" for that form of toxicity. A much more honest and scientific conclusion would be that vitamin C in the dosage used is of no benefit, but the benefits of using much larger doses remain unknown. Ironically, vitamin C has often been shown to have positive effects even in very tiny doses. Perhaps this is one reason why so many researchers never even consider using vastly higher doses.

In reviewing the literature, it would appear that vitamin C should be used in virtually all forms of toxicity, whether acute or chronic. All toxins examined accelerate the consumption of vitamin C, which rapidly causes its own significant problems if not promptly and aggressively treated. Indeed, the acute manifestations of scurvy are often the last symptoms of a poisoned person before death.

Although very important as an antioxidant, vitamin C has other positive effects in the effective treatment of a toxic condition. Its ability to directly reduce so many different toxins to less toxic or nontoxic metabolites is not its only important effect. Other antioxidants help to support the positive effects of vitamin C and should be freely administered as well, but they should never serve as complete substitutes for vitamin C.

In addition to the importance of dose, the importance of the route of administration cannot be overstated. Oral vitamin C is always self-limited by the induction of the diarrhea (C-flush) effect. Furthermore, in critically ill patients a rapid intravenous push or intravenous drip administration of vitamin C may be the only way to save the patient or gain the upper hand on the toxin. Intramuscular vitamin C should only be used when intravenous access is not available and oral vitamin C is not likely to elevate blood concentrations quickly enough. However, if possible, oral vitamin C should always be given in addition to intravenous or intramuscular doses. Vigorous hydration should always be maintained as well.

Even though the use of Klenner-sized doses of vitamin C alone would often be curative for a wide variety of chemical intoxications, there should never be any reluctance to add vitamin C to whatever standard regimen is being used to treat an acute or chronic toxic state. The reluctant physician who finally relents and adds even a few grams of vitamin C to a poison treatment protocol will quickly realize that the standard treatment somehow became more effective.

References

Aberg, B., L. Ekman, R. Falk, U. Greitz, G. Persson, and J. Snihs. (1969) Metabolism of methyl mercury (^{203}Hg) compounds in man. *Archives of Environmental Health* 19(4):478-484.

Abou-Raya, S., A. Naeem, K. Abou-El, and B. El. (2002) Coronary artery disease and periodontal disease: is there a link? *Angiology* 53(2):141-148.

Acosta, D., A. Combs, and K. Ramos. (1984) Attenuation by antioxidants of Na+/K+ ATPase inhibition by toxic concentrations of isoproterenol in cultured rat myocardial cells. *Journal of Molecular and Cellular Cardiology* 16(3):281-284.

Adam-Vizi, V., G. Varadi, and P. Simon. (1981) Reduction of vanadate by ascorbic acid and noradrenaline in synaptosomes. *Journal of Neurochemistry* 36(5):1616-1620.

Ademuyiwa, O., O. Adesanya, and O. Ajuwon. (1994) Vitamin C in CCl4 hepatotoxicity—a preliminary report. *Human & Experimental Toxicology* 13(2):107-109.

Agrawal, N., C. Juneja, and C. Mahajan. (1978) Protective role of ascorbic acid in fishes exposed to organochlorine pollution. *Toxicology* 11(4):369-375.

Alabi, Z., K. Thomas, O. Ogunbona, and I. Elegbe. (1994) The effect of antibacterial agents on plasma vitamin C levels. *African Journal of Medicine and Medical Sciences* 23(2):143-146.

Ala-Ketola, L., R. Varis, and K. Kiviniitty. (1974) Effect of ascorbic acid on the survival of rats after whole body irradiation. *Strahlentherapie* 148(6):643-644.

Aldashev, A., T. Igumnova, and G. Servetnik-Chalaia. (1980) [Effect of benzene and its homologues on body ascorbic acid allowance under prolonged C vitaminization]. Article in Russian. *Voprosy Pitaniia* 1:38-41.

Aleo, J., F. De Renzis, P. Farber, and A. Varboncoeur. (1974) The presence and biologic activity of cementum-bound endotoxin. *Journal of Periodontology* 45(9):672-675.

Aleo, J. (1980) Inhibition of endotoxin-induced depression of cellular proliferation by ascorbic acid. *Proceedings of the Society for Experimental Biology and Medicine* 164(3):248-251.

Aleo, J. and H. Padh. (1985) Inhibition of ascorbic acid uptake by endotoxin: evidence of mediation by serum factor(s). *Proceedings of the Society for Experimental Biology and Medicine* 179(1):128-131.

Altmann, P., R. Maruna, H. Maruna, W. Michalica, and G. Wagner. (1981) [Lead detoxication effect of a combined calcium phosphate and ascorbic acid therapy in pregnant women with increased lead burden]. German. *Wiener Medizinische Wochenschrift* 131(12): 311-314.

Anane, R. and E. Creppy. (2001) Lipid peroxidation as pathway of aluminium cytotoxicity in human skin fibroblast cultures: prevention by superoxide dismutase+catalase and vitamins E and C. *Human & Experimental Toxicology* 20(9):477-481.

Anetor, J. and F. Adeniyi. (1998) Decreased immune status in Nigerian workers occupationally exposed to lead. *African Journal of Medicine and Medical Sciences* 27(3-4):169-172.

Antunes, L. and C. Takahashi. (1998) Effects of high doses of vitamins C and E against doxorubicin-induced chromosomal damage in Wistar rat bone marrow cells. *Mutation Research* 419(1-3): 137-143.

Appenroth, D., S. Frob, L. Kersten, F. Splinter, and K. Winnefeld. (1997) Protective effects of vitamin E and C on cisplatin nephrotoxicity in developing rats. *Archives of Toxicology* 71(11):677-683.

Appenroth, D. and K. Winnefeld. (1998) Vitamin E and C in the prevention of metal nephrotoxicity in developing rats. *Experimental and Toxicologic Pathology* 50(4-6):391-396.

Aronow, R., J. Miceli, and A. Done. (1980) A therapeutic approach to the acutely overdosed PCP patient. *Journal of Psychedelic Drugs* 12(3-4):259-267.

Arumugam, N., V. Sivakumar, J. Thanislass, and H. Devaraj. (1997) Effects of acrolein on rat liver antioxidant defense system. *Indian Journal of Experimental Biology* 35(12):1373-1374.

Arumugam, N., V. Sivakumar, J. Thanislass, K. Pillai, S. Devaraj, and H. Devaraj. (1999) Acute pulmonary toxicity of acrolein in rats—underlying mechanism. *Toxicology Letters* 104(3):189-194.

Axelrod, J., S. Udenfriend, and B. Brodie. (1954) Ascorbic acid in aromatic hydroxylation. III. Effect of ascorbic acid on hydroxylation of acetanilide, aniline and antipyrine *in vivo*. *The Journal of Pharmacology and Experimental Therapeutics* 111:176-181.

Bachleitner-Hofmann, T., B. Gisslinger, E. Grumbeck, and H. Gisslinger. (2001) Arsenic trioxide and ascorbic acid: synergy with potential implications for the treatment of acute myeloid leukaemia? *British Journal of Haematology* 112(3):783-786.

Bandyopadhyay, S., R. Tiwari, A. Mitra, B. Mukherjee, A. Banerjee, and G. Chatterjee. (1982) Effects of L-ascorbic acid supplementation on dieldrin toxicity in rats. *Archives of Toxicology* 50(3-4): 227-232.

Banerjee, S. and P. Basu. (1975) Ascorbic acid metabolism in mice treated with tetracyclines & chloramphenicol. *Indian Journal of Experimental Biology* 13(6):567-569.

Bartsch, H. (1991) N-nitroso compounds and human cancer: where do we stand? *IARC Scientific Publications* 105:1-10.

Beligni, M. and L. Lamattina. (1999) Nitric oxide protects against cellular damage produced by methylviologen herbicides in potato plants. *Nitric Oxide: Biology and Chemistry* 3(3):199-208.

Bell, J., C. Beglan, and E. London. (1996) Interaction of ascorbic acid with the neurotoxic effects of NMDA and sodium nitroprusside. *Life Sciences* 58(4):367-371.

Benabdeljelil, K. and L. Jensen. (1990) Effectiveness of ascorbic acid and chromium in counteracting the negative effects of dietary vanadium on interior egg quality. *Poultry Science* 69(5):781-786.

Benito, B., D. Wahl, N. Steudel, A. Cordier, and S. Steiner. (1995) Effects of cyclosporine A on the rat liver and kidney protein pattern, and the influence of vitamin E and C coadministration. *Electrophoresis* 16(7):1273-1283.

Benito, E. and M. Bosch. (1997) Impaired phosphatidylcholine biosynthesis and ascorbic acid depletion in lung during lipopolysaccharide-induced endotoxaemia in guinea pigs. *Molecular and Cellular Biochemistry* 175(1-2):117-123.

Berkson, B. (1979) Thioctic acid in treatment of hepatotoxic mushroom (phalloides) poisoning. *The New England Journal of Medicine* 300(7):371.

Beyer, C. (2001) Rapid recovery from Ecstasy intoxication. *South African Medical Journal* 91(9):708-709.

Beyer, K. (1943) Protective action of vitamin C against experimental hepatic damage. *Archives of Internal Medicine* 71:315-324.

Bhattacharya, R., A. Francis, and T. Shetty. (1987) Modifying role of dietary factors on the mutagenicity of aflatoxin B1: *in vitro* effect of vitamins. *Mutation Research* 188(2):121-128.

Blackstone, S., R. Hurley, and R. Hughes. (1974) Some inter-relationships between vitamin C (L-ascorbic acid) and mercury in the guinea-pig. *Food and Cosmetics Toxicology* 12(4):511-516.

Blanco, O. and T. Meade. (1980) Effect of dietary ascorbic acid on the susceptibility of steelhead trout (*Salmo gairdneri*) to nitrite toxicity. *Revista de Biologia Tropical* 28(1):91-107.

Blankenship, L., D. Carlisle, J. Wise, J. Orenstein, L. Dye, and S. Patierno. (1997) Induction of apoptotic cell death by particulate lead chromate: differential effects of vitamins C and E on genotoxicity and survival. *Toxicology and Applied Pharmacology* 146(2):270-280.

Blasiak, J. and J. Kowalik. (2001) Protective action of vitamin C against DNA damage induced by selenium-cisplatin conjugate. *Acta Biochimica Polonica* 48(1):233-240.

Blasiak, J., M. Kadlubek, J. Kowalik, H. Romanowicz-Makowska, and T. Pertynski. (2002) Inhibition of telomerase activity in endometrial cancer cells by selenium-cisplatin conjugate despite suppression of its DNA-damaging activity by sodium ascorbate. *Teratogenesis, Carcinogenesis, and Mutagenesis* 22(1):73-82.

Bloom, S. and D. Davis. (1972) Calcium as mediator of isoproter-enol-induced myocardial necrosis. *American Journal of Pathology* 69(3):459-470.

Blumenthal, R., W. Lew, A. Reising, D. Soyne, L. Osorio, Z. Ying, and D. Goldenberg. (2000) Anti-oxidant vitamins reduce normal tissue toxicity induced by radio-immunotherapy. *International Journal of Cancer* 86(2):276-280.

Bohm, F., R. Edge, D. McGarvey, and T. Truscott. (1998) Beta-carotene with vitamins E and C offers synergistic cell protections against NOx. *FEBS Letters* 436(3):387-389.

Bohm, F., R. Edge, S. Foley, L. Lange, and T. Truscott. (2001) Antioxidant inhibition of porphyrin-induced cellular phototoxicity. *Journal of Photochemistry and Photobiology. B, Biology* 65(2-3): 177-183.

Bolyai, J., R. Smith, and C. Gray. (1972) Ascorbic acid and chemically induced methemoglobinemias. *Toxicology and Applied Pharmacology* 21(2):176-185.

Borman, G. (1937) Zur diagnose und therepe der chronischen ben-zolvergiftung. *Arch fur Gewerbepath und Gewerbehyg* 8:194.

Bose, S. and S. Sinha. (1991) Aflatoxin-induced structural chromosomal changes and mitotic disruption in mouse bone marrow. *Mutation Research* 261(1):15-19.

Bose, S. and S. Sinha. (1994) Modulation of ochratoxin-produced genotoxicity in mice by vitamin C. *Food and Chemical Toxicology* 32(6):533-537.

Bradberry, S. and J. Vale. (1999) Therapeutic review: is ascorbic acid of value in chromium poisoning and chromium dermatitis? *Journal of Toxicology. Clinical Toxicology* 37(2):195-200.

Browning, E. (1953) *Toxicity of Industrial Organic Solvents.* Industrial Health Research Board. M.R.C. Report No. 80. London H.M.S.O.

Budd, G. (1840) Scurvy. In *The Library of Medicine.* Vol. 5. Edited by A. Tweedie. Whittaker & Co., London.

Bundesen, H., H. Aron, R. Greenebaum, C. Farmer, and A. Abt. (1941) The detoxifying action of vitamin C (ascorbic acid) in arsenical therapy. I. Ascorbic acid as a preventive of reactions of human skin to neoarsphenamine. *The Journal of the American Medical Association* 117(20):1692-1695.

Busnel, R. and A. Lehmann. (1980) Antagonistic effect of sodium ascorbate on ethanol-induced changes in swimming of mice. *Behavioural Brain Research* 1(4):351-356.

Cadenas, S., C. Rojas, and G. Barja. (1998) Endotoxin increases oxidative injury to proteins in guinea pig liver: protection by dietary vitamin C. *Pharmacology & Toxicology* 82(1):11-18.

Calabrese, E. (1979) Should the concept of the recommended dietary allowance be altered to incorporate interactive effects of ubiquitous pollutants? *Medical Hypotheses* 5(12):1273-1285.

Calabrese, E. (1980) Does nutritional status affect benzene induced toxicity and/or leukemia? *Medical Hypotheses* 6(5):535-544.

Calabrese, E., G. Moore, and M. McCarthy. (1983) The effect of ascorbic acid on nitrite-induced methemoglobin formation in rats, sheep, and normal human erythrocytes. *Regulatory Toxicology and Pharmacology* 3(3):184-188.

Calabrese, E. (1985) Does exposure to environmental pollutants increase the need for vitamin C? *Journal of Environmental Pathology, Toxicology and Oncology* 5(6):81-90.

Calabrese, E., A. Stoddard, D. Leonard, and S. Dinardi. (1987) The effects of vitamin C supplementation on blood and hair levels of cadmium, lead, and mercury. *Annals of the New York Academy of Sciences* 498:347-353.

Cappelletti, G., M. Maggioni, and R. Maci. (1998) Apoptosis in human lung epithelial cells: triggering by paraquat and modulation by antioxidants. *Cell Biology International* 22(9-10):671-678.

Carnes, C., M. Chung, T. Nakayama, H. Nakayama, R. Baliga, S. Piao, A. Kanderian, S. Pavia, R. Hamlin, P. McCarthy, J. Bauer, and D. Van Wagoner. (2001) Ascorbate attenuates atrial pacing-induced peroxynitrite formation and electrical remodeling and decreases the incidence of postoperative atrial fibrillation. *Circulation Research* 89(6):E32-E38.

Carroll, R., K. Kovacs, and E. Tapp. (1965) Protection against mercuric chloride poisoning of the rat kidney. *Arzneimittelforschung* 15(11):1361-1363.

Castrovilli, G. (1937) Contributo all terapia della intossicazione da benzolo (la vitamina C nel benzolismo sperimentale). *Med del Lavoro* 28:106.

Cathala, J., M. Bolgert, and P. Grenet. (1936) Scorbut chez un sujet soumis a une intoxication benzolique professionelle. *Bull et Mem Soc d Hop de Paris* 52:1648.

Chakraborty, D., A. Bhattacharyya, K. Majumdar, and G. Chatterjee. (1977) Effects of chronic vanadium pentoxide administration on L-ascorbic acid metabolism in rats: influence of L-ascorbic acid supplementation. *International Journal for Vitamin and Nutrition Research* 47(1):81-87.

Chakraborty, D., A. Bhattacharyya, K. Majumdar, K. Chatterjee, S. Chatterjee, A. Sen, and G. Chatterjee. (1978) Studies on L-ascor bic acid metabolism in rats under chronic toxicity due to organo-phosphorus insecticides: effects of supplementation of L-ascorbic acid in high doses. *The Journal of Nutrition* 108(6):973-980.

Chakraborty, D., A. Bhattacharyya, J. Chatterjee, K. Chatterjee, A. Sen, S. Chatterjee, K. Majumdar, and G. Chatterjee. (1978a) Biochemical studies on polychlorinated biphenyl toxicity in rats: manipulation by vitamin C. *International Journal for Vitamin and Nutrition Research* 48(1):22-31.

Challem, J. and E. Taylor. (1998) Retroviruses, ascorbate, and muta-tions, in the evolution of *Homo sapiens*. *Free Radical Biology & Medicine* 25(1):130-132.

Chapman, D. and C. Shaffer. (1947) Mercurial diuretics. A comparison of acute cardiac toxicity in animals and the effect of ascorbic acid on detoxification in their intravenous administration. *Archives of Internal Medicine* 79:449-456.

Chatterjee, A. (1967) Role of ascorbic acid in the prevention of gonadal inhibition by carbon tetrachloride. *Endokrinologie* 51(5-6):319-322.

Chatterjee, G., S. Banerjee, and D. Pal. (1973) Cadmium administra-tion and L-ascorbic acid metabolism in rats: effect of L-ascorbic acid supplementation. *International Journal for Vitamin and Nutrition Research* 43(3):370-377.

Chatterjee, G. and D. Pal. (1975) Metabolism of L-ascorbic acid in rats under *in vivo* administration of mercury: effect of L-ascorbic acid supplementation. *International Journal for Vitamin and Nutrition Research* 45(3):284-292.

Chatterjee, G., S. Chatterjee, K. Chatterjee, A. Sahu, A. Bhattacharyya, D. Chakraborty, and P. Das. (1979) Studies on the protective effects of ascorbic acid in rubidium toxicity. *Toxicology and Applied Pharmacology* 51(1):47-58.

Chatterjee, K., D. Chakraborty, K. Majumdar, A. Bhattacharyya, and G. Chatterjee. (1979) Biochemical studies on nickel toxicity in weanling rats—influence of vitamin C supplementation. *International Journal for Vitamin and Nutrition Research* 49(3): 264-275.

Chatterjee, K., S. Banerjee, R. Tiwari, K. Mazumdar, A. Bhattacharyya, and G. Chatterjee. (1981) Studies on the protective effects of L-ascorbic acid in chronic chlordane toxicity. *International Journal for Vitamin and Nutrition Research* 51(3):254-265.

Chattopadhyay, S., S. Ghosh, J. Debnath, and D. Ghosh. (2001) Protection of sodium arsenite-induced ovarian toxicity by coadministration of L-ascorbate (vitamin C) in mature Wistar strain rat. *Archives of Environmental Contamination and Toxicology* 41(1):83-89.

Chen, C. and T. Lin. (1998) Nickel toxicity to human term placenta: *in vitro* study on lipid peroxidation. *Journal of Toxicology and Environmental Health. Part A* 54(1):37-47.

Chen, C., Y. Huang, and T. Lin. (1998) Association between oxidative stress and cytokine production in nickel-treated rats. *Archives of Biochemistry and Biophysics* 356(2):127-132.

Chen, C., Y. Huang, and T. Lin. (1998a) Lipid peroxidation in liver of mice administered with nickel chloride: with special reference to trace elements and antioxidants. *Biological Trace Element Research* 61(2):193-205.

Chen, C. and T. Lin. (2001) Effects of nickel chloride on human platelets: enhancement of lipid peroxidation, inhibition of aggregation and interaction with ascorbic acid. *Journal of Toxicology and Environmental Health. Part A* 62(6):431-438.

Cheng, Y., W. Willett, J. Schwartz, D. Sparrow, S. Weiss, and H. Hu. (1998) Relation of nutrition to bone lead and blood lead levels in middle-aged to elderly men. The Normative Aging Study. *American Journal of Epidemiology* 147(12):1162-1174.

Chevion, S., R. Or, and E. Berry. (1999) The antioxidant status of patients subjected to total body irradiation. *Biochemistry and Molecular Biology International* 47(6):1019-1027.

Chow, C., R. Thacker, and C. Gairola. (1979) Increased level of L-ascorbic acid in the plasma of polychlorobiphenyls-treated rats and its inhibition by dietary vitamin E. *Research Communications in Chemical Pathology and Pharmacology* 26(3):605-608.

Chow, C., R. Thacker, and C. Gairola. (1981) Dietary selenium and levels of L-ascorbic acid in the plasma, livers, and lungs of polychlorinated biphenyls-treated rats. *International Journal for Vitamin and Nutrition Research* 51(3):279-283.

Chu, I., D. Villenueve, A. Yagminas, P. Lecavalier, R. Poon, H. Hakansson, U. Ahlborg, V. Valli, S. Kennedy, A. Bergman, F. Seegal, and M. Feeley. (1996) Toxicity of 2,4,4'-trichlorobiphenyl in rats following 90-day dietary exposure. *Journal of Toxicology and Environmental Health* 49(3):301-318.

Cilento, P., A. Kalokerinos, I. Dettman, and G. Dettman. (1980) Venomous bites and vitamin C status. *The Australasian Nurses Journal* 9(6):19.

Civil, I. and M. McDonald. (1978) Acute selenium poisoning: case report. *New Zealand Medical Journal* 87(612):354-356.

Chongthan, D., J. Phurailatpam, M. Singh, and T. Singh. (1999) Methaemoglobinaemia in nitrobenzene poisoning—a case report. *Journal of the Indian Medical Association* 97(11):469-470.

Cohen, G. (1977) An acetaldehyde artifact in studies of the interaction of ethanol with biogenic amine systems: the oxidation of ethanol by ascorbic acid. *Journal of Neurochemistry* 29(4):761-762.

Conney, A., G. Bray, C. Evans, and J. Burns. (1961) Metabolic interactions between L-ascorbic acid and drugs. *Annals of the New York Academy of Sciences* 92(1):115-126.

Conn's Current Therapy. (2001) Edited by Rakel, R. and E. Bope. Philadelphia, PA: W.A. Saunders Company.

Cooney, R., P. Ross, and G. Bartolini. (1986) N-nitrosation and N-nitration of morpholine by nitrogen dioxide: inhibition by ascorbate, glutathione and alpha-tocopherol. *Cancer Letters* 32(1): 83-90.

Cormia, F. (1937) Experimental arsphenamine dermatitis: the influence of vitamin C in the production of arsphenamine sensitiveness. *Canadian Medical Association Journal* 36:392.

Cotovio, J., L. Onno, P. Justine, S. Lamure, and P. Catroux. (2001) Generation of oxidative stress in human cutaneous models following *in vitro* ozone exposure. *Toxicology In Vitro* 15(4-5):357-362.

Cullison, R. (1984) Acetaminophen toxicosis in small animals: clinical signs, mode of action, and treatment. *Compend Continu Educ Pract Vet* 6:315-320.

Cummings, J. (1978) Dietary factors in the aetiology of gastrointestinal cancer. *Journal of Human Nutrition* 32(6):455-465.

Cuthbert, J. (1971) Hazards of acetanilide production. *The Practitioner* 207(242):807-808.

Dainow, I. (1935) Desensitizing action of L-ascorbic acid. *Ann Dermat et Syph.* 6:830.

Dalley, J., P. Gupta, F. Lam, and C. Hung. (1989) Interaction of L-ascorbic acid on the disposition of lead in rats. *Pharmacology & Toxicology* 64(4):360-364.

Dalloz, F., P. Maingon, Y. Cottin, F. Briot, J. Horiot, and L. Rochette. (1999) Effects of combined irradiation and doxorubicin treatment on cardiac function and antioxidant defenses in the rat. *Free Radical Biology & Medicine* 26(7-8):785-800.

Dannenberg, A., A. Widerman, and P. Friedman. (1940) Ascorbic acid in the treatment of chronic lead poisoning. Report of a case of clinical failure. *The Journal of the American Medical Association* 114(15):1439-1440.

Das, K., S. Das, and S. DasGupta. (2001) The influence of ascorbic acid on nickel-induced hepatic lipid peroxidation in rats. *Journal of Basic and Clinical Physiology and Pharmacology* 12(3):187-195.

Das, M., K. Garg, G. Singh, and S. Khanna. (1991) Bio-elimination and organ retention profile of benzanthrone in scorbutic and non-scorbutic guinea pigs. *Biochemical and Biophysical Research Communications* 178(3):1405-1412.

Das, M., K. Garg, G. Singh, and S. Khanna. (1994) Attenuation of benzanthrone toxicity by ascorbic acid in guinea pigs. *Fundamental and Applied Toxicology* 22(3):447-456.

Dawson, E., D. Evans, W. Harris, M. Teter, and W. McGanity. (1999) The effect of ascorbic acid supplementation on the blood lead levels of smokers. *Journal of the American College of Nutrition* 18(2):166-170.

De, K., K. Roy, A. Saha, and C. Sengupta. (2001) Evaluation of alpha-tocopherol, probucol and ascorbic acid as suppressors of digoxin induced lipid peroxidation. *Acta Poloniae Pharmaceutica* 58(5): 391-400.

De la Fuente, M. and V. Victor. (2001) Ascorbic acid and N-acetylcysteine improve *in vitro* the function of lymphocytes from mice with endotoxin-induced oxidative stress. *Free Radical Research* 35(1): 73-84.

De Vito, M. and G. Wagner. (1989) Methamphetamine-induced neuronal damage: a possible role for free radicals. *Neuropharmacology* 28(10):1145-1150.

Desole, M., V. Anania, G. Esposito, F. Carboni, A. Senini, and E. Miele. (1987) Neurochemical and behavioural changes induced by ascorbic acid and d-amphetamine in the rat. *Pharmacological Research Communications* 19(6):441-450.

Dey, P. (1965) Protective action of lemon juice and ascorbic acid against lethality and convulsive property of strychnine. *Die Naturwissenschaften* 52:164.

Dey, P. (1966) Efficacy of vitamin C in counteracting tetanus toxicity. *Die Naturwissenschaften* 53(12):310.

Dey, P. (1967) Protective action of ascorbic acid & its precursors on the convulsive & lethal actions of strychnine. *Indian Journal of Experimental Biology* 5(2):110-112.

Dey, S., P. Nayak, and S. Roy. (2001) Chromium-induced membrane damage: protective role of ascorbic acid. *Journal of Environmental Sciences (China)* 13(3):272-275.

Dhawan, M., D. Kachru, and S. Tandon. (1988) Influence of thiamine and ascorbic acid supplementation on the antidotal efficacy of thiol chelators in experimental lead intoxication. *Archives of Toxicology* 62(4):301-304.

Dhawan, M., S. Flora, and S. Tandon. (1989) Preventive and therapeutic role of vitamin E in chronic plumbism. *Biomedical and Environmental Sciences* 2(4):335-340.

Dhir, H., A. Roy, A. Sharma, and G. Talukder. (1990) Modification of clastogenicity of lead and aluminium in mouse bone marrow cells by dietary ingestion of *Phyllanthus emblica* fruit extract. *Mutation Research* 241(3):305-312.

Dhir, H., K. Agarwal, A. Sharma, and G. Talukder. (1991) Modifying role of *Phyllanthus emblica* and ascorbic acid against nickel clastogenicity in mice. *Cancer Letters* 59(1):9-18.

Dirks, M., D. Davis, E. Cheraskin, and J. Jackson. (1994) Mercury excretion and intravenous ascorbic acid. *Archives of Environmental Health* 49(1):49-52.

Diwan, S., A. Sharma, A. Jain, O. Gupta, and U. Jajoo. (1991) Dapsone induced methaemoglobinaemia. *Indian Journal of Leprosy* 63(1):103-105.

Domingo, J., J. Llobet, and J. Corbella. (1985) Protection of mice against the lethal effects of sodium metavanadate: a quantitative comparison of a number of chelating agents. *Toxicology Letters* 26(2-3):95-99.

Domingo, J., J. Llobet, J. Tomas, and J. Corbella. (1986) Influence of chelating agents on the toxicity, distribution and excretion of vanadium in mice. *Journal of Applied Toxicology* 6(5):337-341.

Domingo, J., M. Gomez, J. Llobet, and J. Corbella. (1990) Chelating agents in the treatment of acute vanadyl sulphate intoxication in mice. *Toxicology* 62(2):203-211.

Donaldson, J., R. Hemming, and F. LaBella. (1985) Vanadium exposure enhances lipid peroxidation in the kidney of rats and mice. *Canadian Journal of Physiology and Pharmacology* 63(3):196-199.

Dotsch, J., S. Demirakca, A. Cryer, J. Hanze, P. Kuhl, and W. Rascher. (1998) Reduction of NO-induced methemoglobinemia requires extremely high doses of ascorbic acid *in vitro*. *Intensive Care Medicine* 24(6):612-615.

Doyle, M., J. Herman, and R. Dykstra. (1985) Autocatalytic oxidation of hemoglobin induced by nitrite: activation and chemical inhibition. *Journal of Free Radicals in Biology & Medicine* 1(2):145-153.

Dunlap, C. and F. Leslie. (1985) Effect of ascorbate on the toxicity of morphine in mice. *Neuropharmacology* 24(8):797-804.

Dreosti, I. and M. McGown. (1992) Antioxidants and UV-induced genotoxicity. *Research Communications in Chemical Pathology and Pharmacology* 75(2):251-254.

Dunham, W., E. Zuckerkandl, R. Reynolds, R. Willoughby, R. Marcuson, R. Barth, and L. Pauling. (1982) Effects of intake of L-ascorbic acid on the incidence of dermal neoplasms induced in mice by ultraviolet light. *Proceedings of the National Academy of Sciences of the United States of America* 79(23):7532-7536.

Durak, I., H. Karabacak, S. Buyukkocak, M. Cimen, M. Kacmaz, E. Omeroglu, and H. Ozturk. (1998) Impaired antioxidant defense system in the kidney tissues from rabbits treated with cyclosporine. Protective effects of vitamins E and C. *Nephron* 78(2): 207-211.

Dvorak, M. (1989) [The effect of polychlorinated biphenyls on the vitamin A, vitamin E, and ascorbic acid status in young pigs]. Article in German. *Archiv fur Experimentelle Veterinarmedizin* 43(1):51-60.

Dwenger, A., H. Pape, C. Bantel, G. Schweitzer, K. Krumm, M. Grotz, B. Lueken, M. Funck, and G. Regel. (1994) Ascorbic acid reduces the endotoxin-induced lung injury in awake sheep. *European Journal of Clinical Investigation* 24(4):229-235.

Dwivedi, N., M. Das, A. Joshi, G. Singh, and S. Khanna. (1993) Modulation by ascorbic acid of the cutaneous and hepatic biochemical effects induced by topically applied benzanthrone in mice. *Food and Chemical Toxicology* 31(7):503-508.

Dwivedi, N., M. Das, and S. Khanna. (2001) Role of biological antioxidants in benzanthrone toxicity. *Archives of Toxicology* 75(4): 221-226.

Eberlein-Konig, B., M. Placzek, and R. Przybilla. (1998) Protective effect against sunburn of combined systemic ascorbic acid (vitamin C) and d-alpha-tocopherol (vitamin E). *Journal of the American Academy of Dermatology* 38(1):45-48.

Ebringer, L., J. Dobias, J. Krajcvoic, J. Polonyi, L. Krizkova, and N. Lahitova. (1996) Antimutagens reduce ofloxacin-induced bleaching in *Euglena gracilis*. *Mutation Research* 359(2):85-93.

Ehrlich, P. (1909) Ueber den jetzigen stand der chemotherapie. *Ber d deutsch chem Gesellsch* 42:1-31.

Eldor, A., I. Vlodavsky, E. Riklis, and Z. Fuks. (1987) Recovery of prostacyclin capacity of irradiated endothelial cells and the protective effect of vitamin C. *Prostaglandins* 34(2):241-255.

Evans, E., W. Norwood, R. Kehoe, and W. Machle. (1943) The effects of ascorbic acid in relation to lead absorption. *The Journal of the American Medical Association* 121(7):501-504.

Fahmy, M. and F. Aly. (2000) *In vivo* and *in vitro* studies on the genotoxicity of cadmium chloride in mice. *Journal of Applied Toxicology* 20(3):231-238.

Faizallah, R., A. Morris, N. Krasner, and R. Walker. (1986) Alcohol enhances vitamin C excretion in the urine. *Alcohol and Alcoholism* 21(1):81-84.

Farbiszewski, R., A. Witek, and E. Skrzydlewska. (2000) N-acetylcysteine or trolox derivative mitigate the toxic effects of methanol on the antioxidant system of rat brain. *Toxicology* 156(1):47-55.

Farombi, E. (2001) Antioxidant status and hepatic lipid peroxidation in chloramphenicol-treated rats. *The Tokohu Journal of Experimental Medicine* 194(2):91-98.

Faulstich, H. and T. Wieland. (1996) New aspects of amanitin and phalloidin poisoning. *Advances in Experimental Medicine and Biology* 391:309-314.

Ferrer, E. and E. Baran. (2001) Reduction of vanadium(V) with ascorbic acid and isolation of the generated oxovanadium(IV) species. *Biological Trace Element Research* 83(2):111-119.

Ficek, W. (1994) Heavy metals and the mammalian thymus: *in vivo* and *in vitro* investigations. *Toxicology and Industrial Health* 10(3):191-201.

Fighera, M., C. Queiroz, M. Stracke, M. Brauer, L. Gonzalez-Rodriguez, R. Frussa-Filho, M. Wajner, and C. de Mello. (1999) Ascorbic acid and alpha-tocopherol attenuate methylmalonic acid-induced convulsions. *Neuroreport* 10(10):2039-2043.

Fink, B., M. Schwemmer, N. Fink, and E. Bassenge. (1999) Tolerance to nitrates with enhanced radical formation suppressed by carvedilol. *Journal of Cardiovascular Pharmacology* 34(6):800-805.

Fischer, A., C. Hess, T. Neubauer, and T. Eikmann. (1998) Testing of chelating agents and vitamins against lead toxicity using mammalian cell cultures. *Analyst* 123(1):55-58.

Flanagan, P., M. Chamberlain, and L. Valberg. (1982) The relationship between iron and lead absorption in humans. *The American Journal of Clinical Nutrition* 36(5):823-829.

Flora, S. and S. Tandon. (1986) Preventive and therapeutic effects of thiamine, ascorbic acid and their combination in lead intoxication. *Acta Pharmacologica et Toxicologica* (Copenh) 58(5):374-378.

Fomenko, L., T. Bezlepkina, A. Anoshkin, and A. Gaziev. (1997) [A vitamin-antioxidant diet decreases the level of chromosomal damages and the frequency of gene mutations in irradiated mice]. Article in Russian. *Izvestiia Akademii Nauk. Seriia Biologicheskaia* 4:419-424.

Forman, D. (1991) The etiology of gastric cancer. *IARC Scientific Publications* 105:22-32.

Forssman, S. and K. Frykholm. (1947) Benzene poisoning. II. Examination of workers exposed to benzene with reference to the presence of ester sulfate, muconic acid, urochrome A and polyphenols in the urine together with vitamin C deficiency. Prophylactic measures. *Acta Medica Scandinavica* 128(3):256-280.

Fox, M. and B. Fry. (1970) Cadmium toxicity decreased by dietary ascorbic acid supplements. *Science* 169(949):989-991.

Fox, M. (1975) Protective effects of ascorbic acid against toxicity of heavy metals. *Annals of the New York Academy of Sciences* 258: 144-150.

Frei, B., L. England, and B. Ames. (1989) Ascorbate is an outstanding antioxidant in human blood plasma. *Proceedings of the National Academy of Sciences of the United States of America* 86(16): 6377-6381.

Frei, B., R. Stocker, L. England, and B. Ames. (1990) Ascorbate: the most effective antioxidant in human blood plasma. *Advances in Experimental Medicine and Biology* 264:155-163.

Friend, D. and H. Marquis. (1936) Arsphenamine sensitivity and vitamin C. *American Journal of Syphilis, Gonorrhea and Venereal Diseases* 22:239-242.

Fujimoto, Y., E. Nakatani, M. Horinouchi, K. Okamoto, S. Sakuma, and T. Fujita. (1989) Inhibition of paraquat accumulation in rabbit kidney cortex slices by ascorbic acid. *Research Communications in Clinical Pathology and Pharmacology* 65(2):245-248.

Fujita, K., K. Shinpo, K. Yamada, T. Sato, N. Niimi, M. Shamoto, T. Nagatsu, T. Takeuchi, and H. Umezawa. (1982) Reduction of adriamycin toxicity by ascorbate in mice and guinea pigs. *Cancer Research* 42(1):309-316.

Fujiwara, M. and K. Kuriyama. (1977) Effect of PCB (polychlorobiphe-
nyls) on L-ascorbic acid, pyridoxal phosphate and riboflavin contents in various organs and on hepatic metabolism of L-ascorbic
acid in the rat. *Japanese Journal of Pharmacology* 27(5):621-627.

Fukuda, F., M. Kitada, T. Horie, and S. Awazu. (1992) Evaluation of
adriamycin-induced lipid peroxidation. *Biochemical Pharmacology*
44(4):755-760.

Fuller, R., E. Henson, E. Shannon, A. Collins, and J. Brunson. (1971)
Vitamin C deficiency and susceptibility to endotoxin shock in
guinea pigs. *Archives of Pathology* 92(4):239-243.

Fulton, B. and E. Jeffery. (1990) Absorption and retention of aluminum from drinking water. 1. Effect of citric and ascorbic acids
on aluminum tissue levels in rabbits. *Fundamental and Applied
Toxicology* 14(4):788-796.

Gage, J. (1964) Distribution and excretion of methyl and phenyl mercury salts. *British Journal of Industrial Medicine* 21:197-202.

Gage, J. (1975) Mechanisms for the biodegradation of organic mercury compounds: the actions of ascorbate and of soluble proteins.
Toxicology and Applied Pharmacology 32(2):225-238.

Gao, F., J. Yi, G. Shi, H. Li, X. Shi, Z. Wang, and X. Tang. (2002)
[Ascorbic acid enhances the apoptosis of U937 cells induced by
arsenic trioxide in combination with DMNQ and its mechanism].
Article in Chinese. *Zhonghua Xueyexue Zazhi* 23(1):9-11.

Gao, F., C. Yao, E. Gao, Q. Mo, W. Yan, R. McLaughlin, B. Lopez, T.
Christopher, and X. Ma. (2002a) Enhancement of glutathione
cardioprotection by ascorbic acid in myocardial reperfusion injury.
The Journal of Pharmacology and Experimental Therapeutics
301(2):543-550.

Garcia, R. and A. Municio. (1990) Effect of *Escherichia coli* endotoxin on ascorbic acid transport in isolated adrenocortical cells.
Proceedings of the Society for Experimental Biology and Medicine
193(4):280-284.

Garcia-Roche, M., A. Castillo, T. Gonzalez, M. Grillo, J. Rios, and N.
Rodriguez. (1987) Effect of ascorbic acid on the hepatoxicity
due to the daily intake of nitrate, nitrite and dimethylamine. *Die
Nahrung* 31(2):99-104.

Garg, K., S. Khanna, M. Das, and G. Singh. (1992) Effect of extraneous supplementation of ascorbic acid on the bio-disposition of benzanthrone in guinea pigs. *Food and Chemical Toxicology* 30(11):967-971.

Geetanjali, D., P. Rita, and P. Reddy. (1993) Effect of ascorbic acid in the detoxification of the insecticide dimethoate in the bone marrow erythrocytes of mice. *Food and Chemical Toxicology* 31(6): 435-437.

Geetha, A., J. Catherine, and C. Shyamala Devi. (1989) Effect of alpha-tocopherol on the microsomal lipid peroxidation induced by doxorubicin: influence of ascorbic acid. *Indian Journal of Physiology and Pharmacology* 33(1):53-58.

Ghaskadbi, S., S. Rajmachikar, C. Agate, A. Kapadi, and V. Vaidya. (1992) Modulation of cyclophosphamide mutagenicity by vitamin C in the *in vivo* rodent micronucleus assay. *Teratogenesis, Carcinogenesis, and Mutagenesis* 12(1):11-17.

Ghosh, S., D. Ghosh, S. Chattopadhyay, and J. Debnath. (1999) Effect of ascorbic acid supplementation on liver and kidney toxicity in cyclophosphamide-treated female albino rats. *The Journal of Toxicological Sciences* 24(3):141-144.

Giannini, A., R. Loiselle, L. DiMarzio, and M. Giannini. (1987) Augmentation of haloperidol by ascorbic acid in phencyclidine intoxication. *The American Journal of Psychiatry* 144(9):1207-1209.

Giles, H. and S. Meggiorini. (1983) Artifactual production and recovery of acetaldehyde from ethanol in urine. *Canadian Journal of Physiology and Pharmacology* 61(7):717-721.

Ginter, E., D. Chorvatovicova, and A. Kosinova. (1989) Vitamin C lowers mutagenic and toxic effect of hexavalent chromium in guinea pigs. *International Journal for Vitamin and Nutrition Research* 59(2):161-166.

Ginter, E., Z. Zloch, and R. Ondreicka. (1998) Influence of vitamin C status on ethanol metabolism in guinea-pigs. *Physiological Research* 47(2):137-141.

Ginter, E. and Z. Zloch. (1999) Influence of vitamin C status on the metabolic rate of a single dose of ethanol-1-(14)C in guinea pigs. *Physiological Research* 48(5):369-373.

Giri, A., D. Khynriam, and S. Prasad. (1998) Vitamin C mediated protection on cisplatin induced mutagenicity in mice. *Mutation Research* 421(2):139-148.

Glascott, P., E. Gilfor, A. Serroni, and J. Farber. (1996) Independent antioxidant action of vitamins E and C in cultured rat hepatocytes intoxicated with allyl alcohol. *Biochemical Pharmacology* 52(8): 1245-1252.

Gomez, M., J. Domingo, J. Llobet, and J. Corbella. (1991) Effectiveness of some chelating agents on distribution and excretion of vanadium in rats after prolonged oral administration. *Journal of Applied Toxicology* 11(3):195-198.

Gonskii, I., M. Korda, I. Klishch, and L. Fira. (1996) [Role of the antioxidant system in the pathogenesis of toxic hepatitis]. Article in Russian. *Patologicheskaia Fiziologiia i Eksperimental'naia Terapiia* 2:43-45.

Gontea, I., S. Dumitrache, A. Rujinski, and M. Draghicescu. (1969) Influence of chronic benzene intoxication on vitamin C in the guinea pig and rat. *Igiena* 18:1-11.

Gontzea, J. et al. (1963) The vitamin C requirements of lead workers. *Internationale Zeitschrift fur Augenwardte Phisiologie Einschliesslich Arbeits Physiologie* (Berlin) 20:20-33.

Goyer, R. and M. Cherian. (1979) Ascorbic acid and EDTA treatment of lead toxicity in rats. *Life Sciences* 24(5):433-438.

Grabarczyk, M., U. Podstawka, and J. Kopec-Szlezak. (1991) [Protection of human peripheral blood leukocytes with vitamin E and C from toxic effects of fenarimol *in vitro*]. Article in Polish. *Acta Haematologica Polonica* 22(1):136-144.

Grad, J., N. Bahlis, I. Reis, M. Oshiro, W. Dalton, and L. Boise. (2001) Ascorbic acid enhances arsenic trioxide-induced cytotoxicity in multiple myeloma cells. *Blood* 98(3):805-813.

Greggi Antunes, L., J. Darin, and M. Bianchi. (2000) Protective effects of vitamin C against cisplatin-induced nephrotoxicity and lipid peroxidation in adult rats: a dose-dependent study. *Pharmacological Research* 41(4):405-411.

Gregus, Z. and C. Klaassen. (1986) Disposition of metals in rats: a comparative study of fecal, urinary, and biliary excretion and tissue distribution of eighteen metals. *Toxicology and Applied Pharmacology* 85(1):24-38.

Gregus, Z., A. Stein, F. Varga, and C. Klaassen. (1992) Effect of lipoic acid on biliary excretion of glutathione and metals. *Toxicology and Applied Pharmacology* 114(1):88-96.

Grosse, Y., L. Chekir-Ghedira, A. Huc, S. Obrecht-Pflumio, G. Dirheimer, H. Bacha, and A. Pfohl-Leszkowicz. (1997) Retinol, ascorbic acid and alpha-tocopherol prevent DNA adduct formation in mice treated with the mycotoxins ochratoxin A and zearalenone. *Cancer Letters* 114(1-2):225-229.

Grunert, R. (1960) The effect of DL-alpha-lipoic acid on heavy-metal intoxication in mice and dogs. *Archives of Biochemistry and Biophysics* 86:190-194.

Gultekin, F., N. Delibas, S. Yasar, and I. Kilinc. (2001) *In vivo* changes in antioxidant systems and protective role of melatonin and a combination of vitamin C and vitamin E on oxidative damage in erythrocytes induced by chlorpyrifos-ethyl in rats. *Archives of Toxicology* 75(2):88-96.

Guna Sherlin, D. and R. Verma. (2000) Amelioration of fluoride-induced hypocalcaemia by vitamins. *Human & Experimental Toxicology* 19(11):632-634.

Gupta, S., R. Gupta, and A. Seth. (1994) Reversal of clinical and dental fluorosis. *Indian Pediatrics* 31(4):439-443.

Gupta, S., R. Gupta, A. Seth, and A. Gupta. (1996) Reversal of fluorosis in children. *Acta Paediatrica Japonica* 38(5):513-519.

Gupta, P. and A. Kar. (1998) Role of ascorbic acid in cadmium-induced thyroid dysfunction and lipid peroxidation. *Journal of Applied Toxicology* 18(5):317-320.

Gurer, H., H. Ozgunes, S. Oztezcan, and N. Ercal. (1999) Antioxidant role of alpha-lipoic acid in lead toxicity. *Free Radical Biology & Medicine* 27(1-2):75-81.

Gussow, L. (2000) The optimal management of mushroom poisoning remains undetermined. *The Western Journal of Medicine* 173(5): 317-318.

Hajarizadeh, H., L. Lebredo, R. Barrie, and E. Woltering. (1994) Protective effect of doxorubicin in vitamin C or dimethyl sulfoxide against skin ulceration in the pig. *Annals of Surgical Oncology* 1(5):411-414.

Halimi, J. and A. Mimran. (2000) Systemic and renal effect of nicotine in non-smokers: influence of vitamin C. *Journal of Hypertension* 18(11):1665-1669.

Halliwell, B., M. Hu, S. Louie, T. Duvall, B. Tarkington, P. Motchnik, and C. Cross. (1992) Interaction of nitrogen dioxide with human plasma. Antioxidant depletion and oxidative damage. *FEBS Letters* 313(1):62-66.

Hamilton, R. and W. Garnett. (1980) Phencyclidine overdose. *Annals of Emergency Medicine* 9(3):173-174.

Han-Wen, H. et al. (1959) Treatment of lead poisoning. II. Experiments on the effect of vitamin C and rutin. *Chinese Journal Internal Medicine* 7:19-20.

Hassan, M., I. Numan, N. al-Nasiri, and S. Stohs. (1991) Endrin-induced histopathological changes and lipid peroxidation in livers and kidneys of rats, mice, guinea pigs and hamsters. *Toxicologic Pathology* 19(2):108-114.

Hatch, G., R. Slade, M. Selgrade, and A. Stead. (1986) Nitrogen dioxide exposure and lung antioxidants in ascorbic acid-deficient guinea pigs. *Toxicology and Applied Pharmacology* 82(2):351-359.

He, Y. and D. Hader. (2002) UV-B-induced formation of reactive oxygen species and oxidative damage of the cyanobacterium *Anabaena* sp.: protective effects of ascorbic acid and N-acetyl-L-cysteine. *Journal of Photochemistry and Photobiology. B, Biology* 66(2):115-124.

Hill, C. (1979) Studies on the ameliorating effect of ascorbic acid on mineral toxicities in the chick. *The Journal of Nutrition* 109(1): 84-90.

Hirneth, H. and H. Classen. (1984) Inhibition of nitrate-induced increase of plasma nitrite and methemoglobinemia in rats by simultaneous feeding of ascorbic acid or tocopherol. *Arzneimittelforschung* 34(9):988-991.

Hjelle, J. and G. Grauer. (1986) Acetaminophen-induced toxicosis in dogs and cats. *Journal of the American Veterinary Medical Association* 188(7):742-746.

Hoda, Q. and S. Sinha. (1991) Minimization of cytogenetic toxicity of malathion by vitamin C. *Journal of Nutritional Science and Vitaminology* 37(4):329-339.

Hoda, Q. and S. Sinha. (1993) Vitamin C-mediated minimisation of Rogor-induced genotoxicity. *Mutation Research* 299(1):29-36.

Hoda, Q., M. Azfer, and S. Sinha. (1993) Modificatory effect of vitamin C and vitamin B-complex on meiotic inhibition induced by organophosphorus pesticide in mice *Mus musculus*. *International Journal for Vitamin and Nutrition Research* 63(1):48-51.

Hoehler, D. and R. Marquardt. (1996) Influence of vitamins E and C on the toxic effects of ochratoxin A and T-2 toxin in chicks. *Poultry Science* 75(12):1508-1515.

Holmes, H., K. Campbell, and E. Amberg. (1939) Effect of vitamin C on lead poisoning. *Journal of Laboratory and Clinical Medicine* 24: 1119-1127.

Hong, S., D. Anestis, J. Ball, M. Valentovic, P. Brown, and G. Rankin. (1997) 4-Amino-2,6-dichlorophenol nephrotoxicity in the Fisher 344 rat: protection by ascorbic acid, AT-125, and aminooxyacetic acid. *Toxicology and Applied Pharmacology* 147(1):115-125.

Hong, S., K. Hwang, E. Lee, S. Eun, S. Cho, C. Han, Y. Park, and S. Chang. (2002) Effect of vitamin C on plasma total antioxidant status in patients with paraquat intoxication. *Toxicology Letters* 126(1):51-59.

Horio, F. and A. Yoshida. (1982) Effects of some xenobiotics on ascorbic acid metabolism in rats. *The Journal of Nutrition* 112(3):416-425.

Horio, F., M. Kimura, and A. Yoshida. (1983) Effects of several xenobiotics on the activities of enzymes affecting ascorbic acid synthesis in rats. *Journal of Nutritional Science and Vitaminology* 29(3): 233-247.

Horio, F., K. Ozaki, M. Kohmura, A. Yoshida, S. Makino, and Y. Hayashi. (1986) Ascorbic acid requirement for the induction of microsomal drug-metabolizing enzymes in a rat mutant unable to synthesize ascorbic acid. *The Journal of Nutrition* 116(11):2278-2289.

Houston, D. and M. Johnson. (2000) Does vitamin C intake protect against lead toxicity? *Nutrition Reviews* 58(3 Pt 1):73-75.

Hrgovic, Z. (1990) [Methemoglobinemia in a newborn infant following pudendal anesthesia in labor with prilocaine. A case report]. Article in German. *Anasthesie, Intensivtherapie, Notfallmedizin* 25(2):172-174.

Hsu, P., M. Liu, C. Hsu, L. Chen, and Y. Guo. (1998) Effects of vitamin E and/or C on reactive oxygen species-related lead toxicity in the rat sperm. *Toxicology* 128(3):169-179.

Hudecova, A. and E. Ginter. (1992) The influence of ascorbic acid on lipid peroxidation in guinea pigs intoxicated with cadmium. *Food and Chemical Toxicology* 30(12):1011-1013.

Huggins, H. and T. Levy. (1999) *Uninformed Consent: The Hidden Dangers in Dental Care.* Charlottesville, VA: Hampton Roads Publishing Company, Inc.

Ichinose, T. and M. Sagai. (1989) Biochemical effects of combined gases of nitrogen dioxide and ozone. III. Synergistic effects on lipid peroxidation and antioxidative protective systems in the lungs of rats and guinea pigs. *Toxicology* 59(3):259-270.

Ilkiw, J. and R. Ratcliffe. (1987) Paracetamol toxicity in a cat. *Australian Veterinary Journal* 64(8):245-247.

Jacques-Silva, M., C. Nogueira, L. Broch, E. Flores, and J. Rocha. (2001) Diphenyl diselenide and ascorbic acid changes deposition of selenium and ascorbic acid in liver and brain of mice. *Pharmacology & Toxicology* 88(3):119-125.

Jaffe, E. (1982) Enzymopenic hereditary methemoglobinemia. *Haematologia* 15(4):389-399.

Jahan, K., K. Ahmad, and M. Ali. (1984) Effect of ascorbic acid in the treatment of tetanus. *Bangladesh Medical Research Council Bulletin* 10(1):24-28.

Johnson, G., T. Lewis, and W. Wagner. (1975) Acute toxicity of cesium and rubidium compounds. *Toxicology and Applied Pharmacology* 32(2):239-245.

Jones, M. and M. Basinger. (1983) Chelate antidotes for sodium vanadate and vanadyl sulfate intoxication in mice. *Journal of Toxicology and Environmental Health* 12(4-6):749-756.

Jonker, D., V. Lee, R. Hargreaves, and B. Lake. (1988) Comparison of the effects of ascorbyl palmitate and L-ascorbic acid on paracetamol-induced hepatotoxicity in the mouse. *Toxicology* 52(3):287-295.

Jungeblut, C. (1937) Inactivation of tetanus toxin by crystalline vitamin C (L-ascorbic acid). *Journal of Immunology* 33:203-214.

Jurima-Romet, M., F. Abbott, W. Tang, H. Huang, and L. Whitehouse. (1996) Cytotoxicity of unsaturated metabolites of valproic acid and protection by vitamins C and E in glutathione-depleted rat hepatocytes. *Toxicology* 112(1):69-85.

Kadrabova, J., A. Madaric, and E. Ginter. (1992) The effect of ascorbic acid on cadmium accumulation in guinea pig tissues. *Experientia* 48(10):989-991.

Kanthasamy, A., B. Ardelt, A. Malave, E. Mills, T. Powley, J. Borowitz, and G. Isom. (1997) Reactive oxygen species generated by cyanide mediate toxicity in rat pheochromocytoma cells. *Toxicology Letters* 93(1):47-54.

Kao, H., S. Jai, and Y. Young. (1965) [A study of the therapeutic effect of large dosage of injection ascorbici acidi on the depression of the central nervous system as in acute poisoning due to barbiturates]. Article in Chinese. *Acta Pharmaceutica Sinica* 12(11): 764-765.

Kaplan, A., C. Smith, D. Promnitz, B. Joffe, and H. Seftel. (1990) Methaemoglobinaemia due to accidental sodium nitrite poisoning. Report of 10 cases. *South African Medical Journal* 77(6):300-301.

Kari, F., G. Hatch, R. Slade, K. Crissman, P. Simeonova, and M. Luster. (1997) Dietary restriction mitigates ozone-induced lung inflammation in rats: a role for endogenous antioxidants. *American Journal of Respiratory Cell and Molecular Biology* 17(6):740-747.

Karimov, T. (1988) [Vitamin status of workers in the chromium industry]. Article in Russian. *Voprosy Pitaniia* May-June (3):20-22.

Katz, J., G. Chaushu, and Y. Sharabi. (2001) On the association between hypercholesterolemia, cardiovascular disease and severe periodontal disease. *Journal of Clinical Periodontology* 28(9):865-868.

Kaul, B. and B. Davidow. (1980) Application of a radioimmunoassay screening test for detection and management of phencyclidine intoxication. *Journal of Clinical Pharmacology* 20(8-9):500-505.

Kawai-Kobayashi, K. and A. Yoshida. (1986) Effect of dietary ascorbic acid and vitamin E on metabolic changes in rats and guinea pigs exposed to PCB. *The Journal of Nutrition* 116(1):98-106.

Kawai-Kobayashi, K. and A. Yoshida. (1988) Effect of polychlorinated biphenyls on lipids and ascorbic acid metabolism in streptozotocin-induced diabetic rats. *Journal of Nutritional Science and Vitaminology* 34(3):281-291.

Kennedy, M., K. Bruninga, E. Mutlu, J. Losurdo, S. Choudhary, and A. Keshavarzian. (2001) Successful and sustained treatment of chronic radiation proctitis with antioxidant vitamins E and C. *The American Journal of Gastroenterology* 96(4):1080-1084.

Khan, P. and S. Sinha. (1994) Impact of higher doses of vitamin C in modulating pesticide genotoxicity. *Teratogenesis, Carcinogenesis, and Mutagenesis* 14(4):175-181.

Khan, P. and S. Sinha. (1996) Ameliorating effect of vitamin C on murine sperm toxicity induced by three pesticides (endosulfan, phosphamidon and mancozeb). *Mutagenesis* 11(1):33-36.

Khaw, K., S. Bingham, A. Welch, R. Luben, N. Wareham, S. Oakes, and N. Day. (2001) Relation between plasma ascorbic acid and mortality in men and women in EPIC-Norfolk prospective study: a prospective population study. European Prospective Investigation into Cancer and Nutrition. *Lancet* 357(9257):657-663.

Kirsch, M. and H. de Groot. (2000) Ascorbate is a potent antioxidant against peroxynitrite-induced oxidation reactions. Evidence that ascorbate acts by re-reducing substrate radicals produced by peroxynitrite. *The Journal of Biological Chemistry* 275(22):16702-16708.

Klenner, F. (1954) Recent discoveries in the treatment of lockjaw with vitamin C and Tolserol. *Tri-State Medical Journal* July; pp. 7-11.

Klenner, F. (1954a) Case history cure of a 4-year-old child bitten by a mature Highland moccasin. *Tri-State Medical Journal* July.

Klenner, F. (1957) The Black Widow spider. Case History. *Tri-State Medical Journal* December; pp. 15-18.

Klenner, F. (1971) Observations on the dose and administration of ascorbic acid when employed beyond the range of a vitamin in human pathology. *Journal of Applied Nutrition* 23(3&4):61-88.

Klenner, F. (1974) Significance of high daily intake of ascorbic acid in preventive medicine. *Journal of the International Academy of Preventive Medicine* 1(1):45-69.

Kobayashi, S., M. Takehana, S. Itoh, and E. Ogata. (1996) Protective effect of magnesium-L-ascorbyl-2 phosphate against skin damage induced by UVB irradiation. *Photochemistry and Photobiology* 64(1):224-228.

Kodavanti, U., G. Hatch, B. Starcher, S. Giri, D. Winsett, and D. Costa. (1995) Ozone-induced pulmonary functional, pathological, and biochemical changes in normal and vitamin C-deficient guinea pigs. *Fundamental and Applied Toxicology* 24(2):154-164.

Kodavanti, U., D. Costa, K. Dreher, K. Crissman, and G. Hatch. (1995a) Ozone-induced tissue injury and changes in antioxidant homeostasis in normal and ascorbate-deficient guinea pigs. *Biochemical Pharmacology* 50(2):243-251.

Kojima, S., H. Iizuka, H. Yamaguchi, S. Tanuma, M. Kochi, and Y. Ueno. (1994) Antioxidative activity of benzylideneascorbate and its effect on adriamycin-induced cardiotoxicity. *Anticancer Research* 14(5A):1875-1880.

Kok, A. (1997) Ascorbate availability and neurodegeneration in amyotrophic lateral sclerosis. *Medical Hypotheses* 48(4):281-296.

Kola, I., R. Vogel, and H. Spielmann. (1989) Co-administration of ascorbic acid with cyclophosphamide (CPA) to pregnant mice inhibits the clastogenic activity of CPA in preimplantation murine blastocysts. *Mutagenesis* 4(4):297-301.

Koner, B., B. Banerjee, and A. Ray. (1998) Organochlorine pesticide-induced oxidative stress and immune suppression in rats. *Indian Journal of Experimental Biology* 36(4):395-398.

Konopacka, M., M. Widel, and J. Rzeszowska-Wolny. (1998) Modifying effect of vitamins C, E and beta-carotene against gamma-ray-induced DNA damage in mouse cells. *Mutation Research* 417(2-3):85-94.

Konopacka, M. and J. Rzeszowska-Wolny. (2001) Antioxidant vitamins C, E and beta-carotene reduce DNA damage before as well as after gamma-ray irradiation of human lymphocytes *in vitro*. *Mutation Research* 491(1-2):1-7.

Korallus, U., C. Harzdorf, and J. Lewalter. (1984) Experimental bases for ascorbic acid therapy of poisoning by hexavalent chromium compounds. *International Archives of Occupational and Environmental Health* 53(3):247-256.

Koshiisi, I., Y. Mamura, and T. Imanari. (1997) Cyanate causes depletion of ascorbate in organisms. *Biochimica et Biophysica Acta* 1336(3):566-574.

Koyama, S., S. Kodama, K. Suzuki, T. Matsumoto, T. Miyazaki, and M. Watanabe. (1998) Radiation-induced long-lived radicals which cause mutation and transformation. *Mutation Research* 421(1): 45-54.

Krasner, N., J. Dow, M. Moore, and A. Goldberg. (1974) Ascorbic-acid saturation and ethanol metabolism. *Lancet* 2(7882):693-695.

Kratzing, C. and R. Willis. (1980) Decreased levels of ascorbic acid in lung following exposure to ozone. *Chemico-Biological Interactions* 30(1):53-56.

Kretzschmar, C. and F. Ellis. (1974) The effect of x rays on ascorbic acid concentration in plasma and in tissues. *The British Journal of Radiology* 20(231):94-99.

Krishna, G., J. Nath, and T. Ong. (1986) Inhibition of cyclophosphamide and mitomycin C-induced sister chromatid exchanges in mice by vitamin C. *Cancer Research* 46(6):2670-2674.

Kubova, J., J. Tulinska, E. Stolcova, A. Mosat'ova, and E. Ginter. (1993) The influence of ascorbic acid on selected parameters of cell immunity in guinea pigs exposed to cadmium. *Zeitschrift fur Ernahrungswissenschaft* 32(2):113-120.

Kueh, Y., L. Chio, and R. Guan. (1986) Congenital enzymopenic methaemoglobinaemia. *Annals of the Academy of Medicine, Singapore* 15(2):250-254.

Kurbacher, C., U. Wagner, B. Kolster, P. Andreotti, D. Krebs, and H. Bruckner. (1996) Ascorbic acid (vitamin C) improves the antineoplastic activity of doxorubicin, cisplatin, and paclitaxel in human breast carcinoma cells *in vitro*. *Cancer Letters* 103(2):183-189.

Lahiri, K. (1943) Advancement in the treatment of arsenical intolerance. *Indian Journal of Venereal Diseases and Dermatology* 9(1): 115-117.

Laing, M. (1984) A cure for mushroom poisoning. *South African Medical Journal* 65(15):590.

Laky, D., S. Constantinescu, G. Filipescu, E. Ratea, and C. Zeana. (1984) Morphophysiological studies in experimental myocardial stress induced by isoproterenol. Note II. The myocardioprotector effect of magnesium ascorbate. *Morphologie et Embryologie* 30(1):55-59.

LaLonde, C., U. Nayak, J. Hennigan, and R. Demling. (1997) Excessive liver oxidant stress causes mortality in response to burn injury combined with endotoxin and is prevented with antioxidants. *The Journal of Burn Care & Rehabilitation* 18(3):187-192.

Lambert, A. and D. Eastmond. (1994) Genotoxic effects of the o-phenylphenol metabolites phenylhydroquinone and phenylbenzoquinone in V79 cells. *Mutation Research* 322(4):243-256.

Landauer, W. and D. Sopher. (1970) Succinate, glycerophosphate and ascorbate as sources of cellular energy and as antiteratogens. *Journal of Embryology and Experimental Morpholoqy* 24(1):187-202.

Lauwerys, R., H. Roels, J. Buchet, A. Bernard, L. Verhoeven, and J. Konings. (1983) The influence of orally-administered vitamin C or zinc on the absorption of and the biological response to lead. *Journal of Occupational Medicine* 25(9):668-678.

Lee, C., G. Harman, R. Hohl, and R. Gingrich. (1996) Fatal cyclophosphamide cardiomyopathy: its clinical course and treatment. *Bone Marrow Transplantation* 18(3):573-577.

Lee, E. (1991) Plant resistance mechanisms to air pollutants: rhythms in ascorbic acid production during growth under ozone stress. *Chronobiology International* 8(2):93-102.

Leung, H. and P. Morrow. (1981) Interaction of glutathione and ascorbic acid in guinea pig lungs exposed to nitrogen dioxide. *Research Communications in Chemical Pathology and Pharmacology* 31(1): 111-118.

Libowitkzy, O. and H. Seyfried. (1940) Bedeutung des vitamin C fur benzolarbeiter. *Wein Klinische Wochenschrift* 53:543.

Liehr, J. (1991) Vitamin C reduces the incidence and severity of renal tumors induced by estradiol or diethylstilbestrol. *The American Journal of Clinical Nutrition* 54(6 Suppl):1256S-1260S.

Little, M., D. Gawkrodger, and S. MacNeil. (1996) Chromium- and nickel-induced cytotoxicity in normal and transformed human keratinocytes: an investigation of pharmacological approaches to the prevention of Cr(VI)-induced cytotoxicity. *The British Journal of Dermatology* 134(2):199-207.

Lock, E., T. Cross, and R. Schnellmann. (1993) Studies on the mechanism of 4-aminophenol-induced toxicity to renal proximal tubules. *Human & Experimental Toxicology* 12(5):383-388.

Longenecker, H., R. Musulin, R. Tully, and C. King. (1939) An acceleration of vitamin C synthesis and excretion by feeding known organic compounds to rats. *The Journal of Biological Chemistry* 129:445-453.

Longenecker, H., H. Fricke, and C. King. (1940) The effect of organic compounds upon vitamin C synthesis in the rat. *The Journal of Biological Chemistry* 135:492-510.

Lopez-Gonzalez, M., J. Guerrero, F. Rojas, and F. Delgado. (2000) Ototoxicity caused by cisplatin is ameliorated by melatonin and other antioxidants. *Journal of Pineal Research* 28(2):73-80.

Lurie, J. (1965) Benzene intoxication and vitamin C. *The Transactions of the Association of Industrial Medical Officers* 15:78-79.

Lyall, V., V. Chauhan, R. Prasad, A. Sarkar, and R. Nath. (1982) Effect of chronic chromium treatment on the ascorbic acid status of the rat. *Toxicology Letters* 12(2-3):131-135.

McChesney, E., O. Barlow, and G. Klinck, Jr. (1942) The detoxication of neoarsphenamine by means of various organic acids. *The Journal of Pharmacology and Experimental Therapeutics* 80: 81-92.

McChesney, E. (1945) Further studies on the detoxication of the arsphenamines by ascorbic acid. *The Journal of Pharmacology and Experimental Therapeutics* 84:222-235.

McConnico, R. and C. Brownie. (1992) The use of ascorbic acid in the treatment of 2 cases of red maple *(Acer rubrum)*—poisoned horses. *The Cornell Veterinarian* 82(3):293-300.

McCormick, W. (1945) Sulfonamide sensitivity and C-avitaminosis. *Canadian Medical Association Journal* 52:68-70.

Maellaro, E., B. Del Bello, L. Sugherini, A. Pompella, A. Casini, and M. Comporti. (1994) Protection by ascorbic acid against oxidative injury of isolated hepatocytes. *Xenobiotica* 24(3):281-289.

Magos, L. and M. Sziza. (1962) Effect of ascorbic acid in aniline poisoning. *Nature* 194(4833):1084.

Mahaffey, K. (1999) Methylmercury: a new look at the risks. *Public Health Reports* 114(5):396-399.

Majewska, M. and J. Bell. (1990) Ascorbic acid protects neurons from injury induced by glutamate and NMDA. *Neuroreport* 1(3-4):194-196.

Marchmont-Robinson, S. (1941) Effect of vitamin C on workers exposed to lead dust. *Journal of Laboratory and Clinical Medicine* 26:1478-1481.

Maritz, G. (1993) The influence of maternal nicotine exposure on neonatal lung metabolism. Protective effect of ascorbic acid. *Cell Biology International* 17(6):579-585.

Marotta, F., P. Safran, H. Tajiri, G. Princess, H. Anzulovic, G.M. Ideo, A. Rouge, M. Seal, and G. Ideo. (2001) Improvement of hemorheological abnormalities in alcoholics by an oral antioxidant. *Hepatogastroenterology* 48(38):511-517.

Marquardt, R. and A. Frohlich. (1992) A review of recent advances in understanding ochratoxicosis. *Journal of Animal Science* 70(12): 3968-3988.

Matkovics, B., K. Barabas, L. Szabo, and G. Berencsi. (1980) *In vivo* study of the mechanism of protective effects of ascorbic acid and reduced glutathione in paraquat poisoning. *General Pharmacology* 11(5):455-461.

Matsuki, Y., M. Akazawa, K. Tsuchiya, H. Sakurai, H. Kiwada, and T. Goromaru. (1991) [Effects of ascorbic acid on the free radical formations of isoniazid and its metabolites]. Article in Japanese. *Yakugaku Zasshi. Journal of the Pharmaceutical Society of Japan* 111(10):600-605.

Matsuki, Y., Y. Hongu, Y. Noda, H. Kiwada, H. Sakurai, and T. Goromaru. (1992) [Effects of ascorbic acid on the metabolic fate and the free radical formation of iproniazid]. Article in Japanese. *Yakugaku Zasshi. Journal of the Pharmaceutical Society of Japan.* 112(12):926-933.

Matsuki, Y., R. Bandou, H. Kiwada, H. Maeda, and T. Goromaru. (1994) Effects of ascorbic acid on iproniazid-induced hepatitis in phenobarbital-treated rats. *Biological & Pharmaceutical Bulletin* 17(8):1078-1082.

Matsushita, N., T. Kobayashi, H. Oda, F. Horio, and A. Yoshida. (1993) Ascorbic acid deficiency reduces the level of mRNA for cytochrome P-450 on the induction of polychlorinated biphenyls. *Journal of Nutritional Science and Vitaminology* 39(4):289-302.

Mavin, J. (1941) Experimental treatment of acute mercury poisoning of guinea pigs with ascorbic acid. *Revista de la Sociedad Argentina de Biologia* (Buenos Aires) 17:581-586.

Meagher, E., O. Barry, A. Burke, M. Lucey, J. Lawson, J. Rokach, and G. FitzGerald. (1999) Alcohol-induced generation of lipid peroxidation products in humans. *The Journal of Clinical Investigation* 104(6):805-813.

Meert, K., J. Ellis, R. Aronow, and E. Perrin. (1994) Acute ammonium dichromate poisoning. *Annals of Emergency Medicine* 24(4):748-750.

Memon, A., M. Molokhia, and P. Friedmann. (1994) The inhibitory effects of topical chelating agents and antioxidants on nickel-induced hypersensitivity reactions. *Journal of the American Academy of Dermatology* 30(4):560-565.

Mena, M., B. Pardo, C. Paino, and J. de Yebenes. (1993) Levodopa toxicity in foetal rat midbrain neurons in culture: modulation by ascorbic acid. *Neuroreport* 4(4):438-440.

Menzel, D. (1994) The toxicity of air pollution in experimental animals and humans: the role of oxidative stress. *Toxicology Letters* 72(1-3):269-277.

Meyer, A. (1937) Benzene poisoning. *The Journal of the American Medical Association* 108(11):911.

Mills, E., P. Gunasekar, G. Pavlakovic, and G. Isom. (1996) Cyanide-induced apoptosis and oxidative stress in differentiated PC12 cells. *Journal of Neurochemistry* 67(3):1039-1046.

Milner, J. (1980) Ascorbic acid in the prevention of chromium dermatitis. *Journal of Occupational Medicine* 22(1):51-52.

Minakata, K., O. Suzuki, S. Saito, and N. Harada. (1993) Ascorbate radical levels in human sera and rat plasma intoxicated with paraquat and diquat. *Archives of Toxicology* 67(2):126-130.

Minakata, K., O. Suzuki, S. Saito, and N. Harada. (1996) Effect of dietary paraquat on a rat mutant unable to synthesize ascorbic acid. *Archives of Toxicology* 70(3-4):256-258.

Miquel, M., M. Aguilar, and C. Aragon. (1999) Ascorbic acid antagonizes ethanol-induced locomotor activity in the open-field. *Pharmacology, Biochemistry, and Behavior* 62(2):361-366.

Mireles-Rocha, H., I. Galindo, M. Huerta, B. Trujillo-Hernandez, A. Elizalde, and R. Cortes-Franco. (2002) UVB photoprotection with antioxidants: effects of oral therapy with d-alpha-tocopherol and ascorbic acid on the minimal erythema dose. *Acta Dermato-Venereologica* 82(1):21-24.

Mitra, A., A. Kulkarni, V. Ravikumar, and D. Bourcier. (1991) Effect of ascorbic acid esters on hepatic glutathione levels in mice treated with a hepatotoxic dose of acetaminophen. *Journal of Biochemical Toxicology* 6(2):93-100.

Miyai, E., M. Yanagida, J. Akiyama, and I. Yamamoto. (1996) Ascorbic acid 2-O-alpha-glucoside, a stable form of ascorbic acid, rescues human keratinocyte cell line, SCC, from cytotoxicity of ultraviolet light B. *Biological & Pharmaceutical Bulletin* 19(7):984-987.

Miyanishi, K., T. Kinouchi, K. Kataoka, T. Kanoh, and Y. Ohnishi. (1996) *In vivo* formation of mutagens by intraperitoneal administration of polycyclic aromatic hydrocarbons in animals during exposure to nitrogen dioxide. *Carcinogenesis* 17(7):1483-1490.

Mochizuki, H., H. Oda, and H. Yokogoshi. (2000) Dietary taurine alters ascorbic acid metabolism in rats fed diets containing polychlorinated biphenyls. *The Journal of Nutrition* 130(4):873-876.

Mohan, P. and S. Bloom. (1999) Lipolysis is an important determinant of isoproterenol-induced myocardial necrosis. *Cardiovascular Pathology* 8(5):255-261.

Moison, R. and G. Beijersbergen van Henegouwen. (2002) Topical antioxidant vitamins C and E prevent UVB-radiation-induced peroxidation of eicosapentaenoic acid in pig skin. *Radiation Research* 157(4):402-409.

Mokranjac, M. and C. Petrovic. (1964) Vitamin C as an antidote in poisoning by fatal doses of mercury. *Comptes Rendus Hebdomadaires des Seances de l'Academie des Sciences* 258: 1341-1342.

Moldowan, M. and W. Acholonu. (1982) Effect of ascorbic acid or thiamine on acetaldehyde, disulfiram-ethanol- or disulfiram-acetaldehyde-induced mortality. *Agents and Actions* 12(5-6):731-736.

Montanini, S., D. Sinardi, C. Pratico, A. Sinardi, and G. Trimarchi. (1999) Use of acetylcysteine as the life-saving antidote in *Amanita phalloides* (death cap) poisoning. Case report on 11 patients. *Arzneimittelforschung* 49(12):1044-1047.

Morton, A., S. Partridge, and J. Blair. (1985) The intestinal uptake of lead. *Chemistry in Britain* 15:923-927.

Moss, M., B. Lanphear, and P. Auinger. (1999) Association of dental caries and blood lead levels. *The Journal of the American Medical Association* 281(24):2294-2298.

Mothersill, C., J. Malone, and M. O'Connor. (1978) Vitamin C and radioprotection. *British Journal of Radiology* 51(606):474.

Mudway, I., D. Housley, R. Eccles, R. Richards, A. Datta, T. Tetley, and F. Kelly. (1996) Differential depletion of human respiratory tract antioxidants in response to ozone challenge. *Free Radical Research* 25(6):499-513.

Mueller, K. and P. Kunko. (1990) The effects of amphetamine and pilocarpine on the release of ascorbic and uric acid in several rat brain areas. *Pharmacology, Biochemistry, and Behavior* 35(4): 871-876.

Mukundan, H., A. Bahadur, A. Kumar, S. Sardana, S. Niak, A. Ray, and B. Sharma. (1999) Glutathione level and its relation to radiation therapy in patients with cancer of uterine cervix. *Indian Journal of Experimental Biology* 37(9):859-864.

Murray, D. and R. Hughes. (1976) The influence of dietary ascorbic acid on the concentration of mercury in guinea-pig tissues. *The Proceedings of the Nutrition Society* 35(3):118A-119A.

Na, K., S. Jeong, and C. Lim. (1992) The role of glutathione in the acute nephrotoxicity of sodium dichromate. *Archives of Toxicology* 66(9):646-651.

Nagaoka, S., H. Kamuro, H. Oda, and A. Yashida. (1991) Effects of polychlorinated biphenyls on cholesterol and ascorbic acid metabolism in primary cultured rat hepatocytes. *Biochemical Pharmacology* 41(8):1259-1261.

Nagyova, A., S. Galbavy, and E. Ginter. (1994) Histopathological evidence of vitamin C protection against Cd-nephrotoxicity in guinea pigs. *Experimental and Toxicologic Pathology* 46(1):11-14.

Nagyova, A. and E. Ginter. (1995) The influence of ascorbic acid on the hepatic cytochrome P-450, and glutathione in guinea-pigs exposed to 2,4-dichlorophenol. *Physiological Research* 44(5): 301-305.

Nair, P. and E. Philip. (1984) Accidental dapsone poisoning in children. *Annals of Tropical Paediatrics* 4(4):241-242.

Nakagawa, Y., I. Cotgreave, and P. Moldeus. (1991) Relationships between ascorbic acid and alpha-tocopherol during diquat-induced redox cycling in isolated rat hepatocytes. *Biochemical Pharmacology* 42(4):883-888.

Nakao, S. (1961) Studies on the accelerating effect of cyanide on ascorbic acid oxidation by intestinal homogenate of rats. *Japanese Journal of Pharmacology* 10:101-108.

Narayana, M. and N. Chinoy. (1994) Reversible effects of sodium fluoride ingestion on spermatozoa of the rat. *International Journal of Fertility and Menopausal Studies* 39(6):337-346.

Nardini, M., E. Finkelstein, S. Reddy, G. Valacchi, M. Traber, C. Cross, and A. van der Vliet. (2002) Acrolein-induced cytotoxicity in cultured human bronchial epithelial cells. Modulation by alpha-tocopherol and ascorbic acid. *Toxicology* 170(3):173-185.

Narra, V., R. Howell, K. Sastry, and D. Rao. (1993) Vitamin C as a radioprotector against iodine-131 *in vivo*. *Journal of Nuclear Medicine* 34(4):637-640.

Navasumrit, P., T. Ward, N. Dodd, and P. O'Connor. (2000) Ethanol-induced free radicals and hepatic DNA strand breaks are prevented *in vivo* by antioxidants: effects of acute and chronic ethanol exposure. *Carcinogenesis* 21(1):93-99.

Naylor, G. (1984) Vanadium and manic depressive psychosis. *Nutrition and Health* 3(1-2):79-85.

Nefic, H. (2001) Anticlastogenic effect of vitamin C on cisplatin induced chromosome aberrations in human lymphocyte cultures. *Mutation Research* 498(1-2):89-98.

Netke, S., M. Roomi, C. Tsao, and A. Niedzwiecki. (1997) Ascorbic acid protects guinea pigs from acute aflatoxin toxicity. *Toxicology and Applied Pharmacology* 143(2):429-435.

Neumann, N., E. Holzle, M. Wallerand, S. Vierbaum, T. Ruzicka, and P. Lehmann. (1999) The photoprotective effect of ascorbic acid, acetylsalicylic acid, and indomethacin evaluated by the photo hen's egg test. *Photodermatology, Photoimmunology & Photomedicine* 15(5):166-170.

Niazi, S., J. Lim, and J. Bederka. (1982) Effect of ascorbic acid on renal excretion of lead in the rat. *Journal of Pharmaceutical Sciences* 71(10):1189-1190.

Nirmala, C. and R. Puvanakrishnan. (1996) Protective role of curcumin against isoproterenol induced myocardial infarction in rats. *Molecular and Cellular Biochemistry* 159(2):85-93.

Nomura, A. (1980) [Studies of sulfhemoglobin formation by various drugs (4). Influences of various antidotes on chemically induced methemoglobinemia and sulfhemoglobinemia (author's transl)]. Article in Japanese. *Nippon Yakurigaku Zasshi. Japanese Journal of Pharmacology* 76(6):435-446.

Nowak, G., C. Carter, and R. Schnellmann. (2000) Ascorbic acid promotes recovery of cellular functions following toxicant-induced injury. *Toxicology and Applied Pharmacology* 167(1):37-45.

Oda, H., K. Yamashita, S. Sasaki, F. Horio, and A. Yoshida. (1987) Long-term effects of dietary polychlorinated biphenyl and high level of vitamin E on ascorbic acid and lipid metabolism in rats. *The Journal of Nutrition* 117(7):1217-1223.

Ohshima, H. and H. Bartsch. (1984) Monitoring endogenous nitrosamine formation in man. *IARC Scientific Publications* 59:233-246.

Ohta, Y., K. Nishida, E. Sasaki, M. Kongo, and I. Ishiguro. (1997) Attenuation of disrupted hepatic active oxygen metabolism with the recovery of acute liver injury in rats intoxicated with carbon tetrachloride. *Research Communications in Molecular Pathology and Pharmacology* 95(2):191-207.

Okunieff, P. (1991) Interactions between ascorbic acid and the radiation of bone marrow, skin, and tumor. *The American Journal of Clinical Nutrition* 54(6 Suppl):1281S-1283S.

Olas, B., B. Wachowicz, and A. Buczynski. (2000) Vitamin C suppresses the cisplatin toxicity on blood platelets. *Anti-cancer Drugs* 11(6):487-493.

On, Y., H. Kim, S. Kim, I. Chae, B. Oh, M. Lee, Y. Park, Y. Choi, and M. Chung. (2001) Vitamin C prevents radiation-induced endothelium-dependent vasomotor dysfunction and de-endothelialization by inhibiting oxidative damage in the rat. *Clinical and Experimental Pharmacology & Physiology* 28(10):816-821.

O'Neill, P. and R. Rahwan. (1976) Protection against acute toxicity of acetaldehyde in mice. *Research Communications in Chemical Pathology and Pharmacology* 13(1):125-128.

Ortega, A., M. Gomez, J. Domingo, and J. Corbella. (1989) The removal of strontium from the mouse by chelating agents. *Archives of Environmental Contamination and Toxicology* 18(4): 612-616.

Osipova, T., T. Sinel'shchikova, I. Perminova, and G. Zasukhina. (1998) [Repair processes in human cultured cells upon exposure to nickel salts and their modification]. Article in Russian. *Genetika* 34(6):852-856.

Ousterhout, L. and L. Berg. (1981) Effects of diet composition on vanadium toxicity in laying hens. *Poultry Science* 60(6):1152-1159.

Panda, B., A. Subhadra, and K. Panda. (1995) Prophylaxis of anti-oxidants against the genotoxicity of methyl mercuric chloride and maleic hydrazide in *Allium* micronucleus assay. *Mutation Research* 343(2-3):75-84.

Pandya, K., G. Singh, and N. Joshi. (1970) Effect of benzan-throne on the body level of ascorbic acid in guinea pigs. *Acta Pharmacologica et Toxicologica* 28(6):499-506.

Pardo, B., M. Mena, S. Fahn, and J. de Yebenes. (1993) Ascorbic acid protects against levodopa-induced neurotoxicity on a catecholine-rich human neuroblastoma cell line. *Movement Disorders* 8(3): 278-284.

Pardo, B., M. Mena, M. Casarejos, C. Paino, and J. de Yebenes. (1995) Toxic effects of L-DOPA on mesencephalic cell cultures: protection with antioxidants. *Brain Research* 682(1-2):133-143.

Pawan, G. (1968) Vitamins, sugars and ethanol metabolism in man. *Nature* 220(165):374-376.

Pelissier, M., M. Siess, M. Lhuissier, P. Grolier, M. Suschetet, J. Narbonne, R. Albrecht, and L. Robertson. (1992) Effect of pro-totypic polychlorinated biphenyls on hepatic and renal vitamin contents and on drug-metabolizing enzymes in rats fed diets con-taining low or high levels of retinyl palmitate. *Food and Chemical Toxicology* 30(8):723-729.

Perez, A., S. Fernandez, M. Garcia-Roche, A. de las Cagigas, A. Castillo, G. Fonseca, and M. Herrera. (1990) Mutagenicity of N-nitrosomorpholine biosynthesized from morpholine in the pres-ence of nitrate and its inhibition by ascorbic acid. *Die Nahrung* 34(7):661-664.

Perminova, I., T. Sinel'shchikova, N. Alekhina, E. Perminova, and G. Zasukhina. (2001) Individual sensitivity to genotoxic effects of nickel and antimutagenic activity of ascorbic acid. *Bulletin of Experimental Biology and Medicine* 131(4):367-370.

Perry, P. and R. Juhl. (1977) Amphetamine psychosis. *American Journal of Hospital Pharmacy* 34(8):883-885.

Persoon-Rothert, M., E. van der Valk-Kokshoorn, J. Egas-Kenniphaas, I. Mauve, and A. van der Laarse. (1989) Isoproterenol-induced cytotoxicity in neonatal rat heart cell cultures is mediated by free radical formation. *Journal of Molecular and Cellular Cardiology* 21(12):1285-1291.

Peterson, F. and R. Knodell. (1984) Ascorbic acid protects against acetaminophen- and cocaine-induced hepatic damage in mice. *Drug-Nutrient Interactions* 3(1):33-41.

Pfohl-Leszkowicz, A. (1994) [Ochratoxin A, ubiquitous mycotoxin contaminating human food]. Article in French. *Comptes Rendus des Seances de la Societe de Biologie et de Ses Filiales* 188(4): 335-353.

Pillans, P., S. Ponzi, and M. Parker. (1990) Effects of ascorbic acid on the mouse embryo and on cyclophosphamide-induced cephalic DNA strand breaks *in vivo*. *Archives of Toxicology* 64(5):423-425.

Pillemer, L., J. Seifter, A. Kuehn, and E. Ecker. (1940) Vitamin C in chronic lead poisoning. An experimental study. *The American Journal of the Medical Sciences* 200:322-327.

Pirozzi, D., P. Gross, and M. Samitz. (1968) The effect of ascorbic acid on chrome ulcers in guinea pigs. *Archives of Environmental Health* 17(2):178-180.

Polec, R., S. Yeh, and M. Shils. (1971) Protective effect of ascorbic acid, isoascorbic acid and mannitol against tetracycline-induced nephrotoxicity. *The Journal of Pharmacology and Experimental Therapeutics* 178(1):152-158.

Poon, R., I. Chu, P. Lecavalier, A. Bergman, and D. Villeneuve. (1994) Urinary ascorbic acid—HPLC determination and application as a noninvasive biomarker of hepatic response. *Journal of Biochemical Toxicology* 9(6):297-304.

Poon, R., P. Lecavalier, A. Bergman, A. Yagminas, I. Chu, and V. Valli. (1997) Effects of tris(4-chlorophenyl)methanol on the rat following short-term oral exposure. *Chemosphere* 34(1):1-12.

Poon, R., G. Park, C. Viau, I. Chu, M. Potvin, R. Vincent, and V. Valli. (1998) Inhalation toxicity of methanol/gasoline in rats: effects of 13-week exposure. *Toxicology and Industrial Health* 14(4):501-520.

Prchal, J. and M. Jenkins. (2000) Hemoglobinopathies: methemoglobinemias, polycythemias, and unstable hemoglobins. *Cecil Textbook of Medicine*, 21st ed. Edited by Goldman, L. and J. Bennett, Philadelphia, PA: W.B. Saunders Company.

Rahimtula, A., J. Bereziat, V. Bussacchini-Griot, and H. Bartsch. (1988) Lipid peroxidation as a possible cause of ochratoxin A toxicity. *Biochemical Pharmacology* 37(23):4469-4477.

Rai, L. and M. Raizada. (1988) Impact of chromium and lead on *Nostoc muscorum*: regulation of toxicity by ascorbic acid, glutathione, and sulfur-containing amino acids. *Ecotoxicology and Environmental Safety* 15(2):195-205.

Raina, V. and H. Gurtoo. (1985) Effects of vitamins A, C, and E on aflatoxin B1-induced mutagenesis in *Salmonella typhimurium* TA-98 and TA-100. *Teratogenesis, Carcinogenesis, and Mutagenesis* 5(1):29-40.

Rajini, P. and M. Krishnakumari. (1985) Effect of L-ascorbic acid supplementation on the toxicity of pirimiphos-methyl to albino rats. *International Journal for Vitamin and Nutrition Research* 55(4): 421-424.

Ram, R. and S. Singh. (1988) Carbofuran-induced histopathological and biochemical changes in liver of the teleost fish, *Channa punctatus* (Bloch). *Ecotoxicology and Environmental Safety* 16(3): 194-201.

Rambeck, W. and I. Guillot. (1996) [Bioavailability of cadmium: effect of vitamin C and phytase in broiler chickens]. Article in German. *Tierarztliche Praxis* 24(5):467-470.

Ramos, K. and D. Acosta. (1983) Prevention by L(-)ascorbic acid of isoproterenol-induced cardiotoxicity in primary cultures of rat myocytes. *Toxicology* 26(1):81-90.

Ramos, K., A. Combs, and D. Acosta. (1984) Role of calcium in isoproterenol cytotoxicity to cultured myocardial cells. *Biochemical Pharmacology* 33(12):1989-1992.

Rao, N. and R. Snyder. (1995) Oxidative modifications produced in HL-60 cells on exposure to benzene metabolites. *Journal of Applied Toxicology* 15(5):403-409.

Rappolt, R., G. Gay, R. Farris. (1979) Emergency management of acute phencyclidine intoxication. *JACEP* 8(2):68-76.

Rappolt, R., G. Gay, M. Soman, and M. Kobernick. (1979a) Treatment plan for acute and chronic adrenergic poisoning crisis utilizing sympatholytic effects of the B1-B2 receptor site blocker propranolol (Inderal) in concert with diazepam and urine acidification. *Clinical Toxicology* 14(1):55-69.

Rawal, B. (1978) Bactericidal action of ascorbic acid on *Pseudomonas aeruginosa*: alteration of cell surface as a possible mechanism. *Chemotherapy* 24(3):166-171.

Raziq, F. and N. Jafarey. (1987) Influence of vitamin C administered after radiation. *The Journal of the Pakistan Medical Association* 37(3):70-72.

Rebec, G., J. Centore, L. White, and K. Alloway. (1985) Ascorbic acid and the behavioral response to haloperidol: implications for the action of antipsychotic drugs. *Science* 227(4685):438-440.

Reddy, G. and S. Srikantia. (1971) Effect of dietary calcium, vitamin C and protein in development of experimental skeletal fluorosis. I. Growth, serum chemistry, and changes in composition, and radiological appearance of bones. *Metabolism* 20(7):642-656.

Riabchenko, N., B. Ivannik, V. Khorokhorina, V. Riabchanko, R. Sin'kova, I. Grosheva, and L. Dzikovskaia. (1996) [The molecular, cellular and systemic mechanisms of the radioprotective action of multivitamin antioxidant complexes]. Article in Russian. *Radiatsionnaia Biologiia, Radioecologiia* 36(6):895-899.

Robertson, W. (2000) Chronic poisoning: trace metals and others. *Cecil Textbook of Medicine*, 21st ed. Edited by Goldman, L. and J. Bennett, Philadelphia, PA: W.B. Saunders Company.

Rojas, C., S. Cadenas, A. Herrero, J. Mendez, and G. Barja. (1996) Endotoxin depletes ascorbate in the guinea pig heart. Protective effects of vitamins C and E against oxidative stress. *Life Sciences* 59(8):649-657.

Rojas, M., M. Rugeles, D. Gil, and P. Patino. (2002) Differential modulation of apoptosis and necrosis by antioxidants in immunosuppressed human lymphocytes. *Toxicology and Applied Pharmacology* 180(2):67-73.

Romero-Ferret, C., G. Mottot, J. Legros, and G. Margetts. (1983) Effect of vitamin C on acute paracetamol poisoning. *Toxicology Letters* 18(1-2):153-156.

Rothe, S., J. Gropp, H. Weiser, and W. Rambeck. (1994) [The effect of vitamin C and zinc on the copper-induced increase of cadmium residues in swine]. Article in German. *Zeitschrift fur Ernahrungswissenshaft* 33(1):61-67.

Roy, A., H. Dhir, and A. Sharma. (1992) Modification of metal-induced micronuclei formation in mouse bone marrow erythrocytes by *Phyllanthus* fruit extract and ascorbic acid. *Toxicology Letters* 62(1):9-17.

Rudra, P., J. Chatterjee, and G. Chatterjee. (1975) Influence of lead administration on L-ascorbic acid metabolism in rats: effect of L-ascorbic acid supplementation. *International Journal for Vitamin and Nutrition Research* 45(4):429-437.

Ruskin, S. and R. Silberstein. (1938) Practical therapeutics. The influence of vitamin C on the therapeutic activity of bismuth, antimony and the arsenic group of metals. *Medical Record* 153:327-330.

Ruskin, A. and J. Johnson. (1949) Cardiodepressive effects of mercurial diuretics. Cardioprotective value of BAL, ascorbic acid and thiamin. *Proceedings of the Society for Experimental Biology and Medicine* 72:577-583.

Ruskin, A. and B. Ruskin. (1952) Effect of mercurial diuretics upon the respiration of the rat heart and kidney. III. The protective action of ascorbic acid against Mercuhydrin *in vitro. Texas Reports on Biology and Medicine* 10:429-438.

Rybak, L., C. Whitworth, and S. Somani. (1999) Application of antioxidants and other agents to prevent cisplatin ototoxicity. *The Laryngoscope* 109(11):1740-1744.

Sahoo, A., L. Samanta, and G. Chainy. (2000) Mediation of oxidative stress in HCH-induced neurotoxicity in rat. *Archives of Environmental Contamination and Toxicology* 39(1):7-12.

Saito, M. (1990) Polychlorinated biphenyls-induced lipid peroxidation as measured by thiobarbituric acid-reactive substances in liver subcellular fractions of rats. *Biochimica et Biophysica Acta* 1046(3):301-308.

Salem, M., K. Kamel, M. Yousef, G. Hassan, and F. El-Nouty. (2001) Protective role of ascorbic acid to enhance semen quality of rabbits treated with sublethal doses of aflatoxin B(1). *Toxicology* 162(3):209-218.

Samanta, L., A. Sahoo, and G. Chainy. (1999) Age-related changes in rat testicular oxidative stress parameters by hexachlorocyclohexane. *Archives of Toxicology* 73(2):96-107.

Samitz, M., J. Shrager, and S. Katz. (1962) Studies on the prevention of injurious effects of chromates in industry. *Industrial Medicine and Surgery* 31:427-432.

Samitz, M. and S. Katz. (1965) Protection against inhalation of chromic acid mist. Use of filters impregnated with ascorbic acid. *Archives of Environmental Health* 11(6):770-772.

Samitz, M. and J. Shrager. (1966) Prevention of dermatitis in the printing and lithographing industries. *Archives of Dermatology* 94(3):307-309.

Samitz, M., D. Scheiner, and S. Katz. (1968) Ascorbic acid in the prevention of chrome dermatitis. Mechanism of inactivation of chromium. *Archives of Environmental Health* 17(1):44-45.

Samitz, M. (1970) Ascorbic acid in the prevention and treatment of toxic effects from chromates. *Acta Dermato-Venereologica* 50(1): 59-64.

Sandoval, M., X. Zhang, X. Liu, E. Mannick, D. Clark, and M. Miller. (1997) Peroxynitrite-induced apoptosis in T84 and RAW 264.7 cells: attenuation by L-ascorbic acid. *Free Radical Biology & Medicine* 22(3):489-495.

Sarma, L. and P. Kesavan. (1993) Protective effects of vitamins C and E against gamma-ray-induced chromosomal damage in mice. *International Journal of Radiation Biology* 63(6):759-764.

Satoh, K., Y. Ida, H. Sakagami, T. Tanaka, and S. Fujisawa. (1998) Effect of antioxidants on radical intensity and cytotoxic activity of eugenol. *Anticancer Research* 18(3A):1549-1552.

Sawahata, T. and R. Neal. (1983) Biotransformation of phenol to hydroquinone and catechol by rat liver microsomes. *Molecular Pharmacology* 23(2):453-460.

Savides, M., F. Oehme, and H. Leipold. (1985) Effects of various antidotal treatments on acetaminophen toxicosis and biotransformation in cats. *American Journal of Veterinary Research* 46(7): 1485-1489.

Schinella, G., H. Tournier, H. Buschiazzo, and P. de Buschiazzo. (1996) Effect of arsenic (V) on the antioxidant defense system: *in vitro* oxidation of rat plasma lipoprotein. *Pharmacology & Toxicology* 79(6):293-296.

Schmahl, D. and G. Eisenbrand. (1982) Influence of ascorbic acid on the endogenous (intragastral) formation of N-nitroso compounds. *International Journal for Vitamin and Nutrition Research. Supplement.* 23:91-102.

Schott, A., T. Vial, I. Gozzo, S. Chareyre, and P. Delmas. (1991) Flutamide-induced methemoglobinemia. *DICP: the Annals of Pharmacotherapy* 25(6):600-601.

Schropp, J. (1943) Case reports: sulfapyridine sensitivity checked by ascorbic acid. *Canadian Medical Association Journal* 49:515.

Schvartsman, S. (1983) Vitamin C in the treatment of paediatric intoxications. *International Journal for Vitamin and Nutrition Research. Supplement* 24:125-129.

Schvartsman, S., S. Zyngier, and C. Schvartsman. (1984) Ascorbic acid and riboflavin in the treatment of acute intoxication by paraquat. *Veterinary and Human Toxicology* 26(6):473-475.

Shapiro, B., G. Kollman, and J. Asnen. (1965) Ascorbic acid protection against inactivation of lysozyme and aldolase by ionizing radiation. *[Technical Report] SAM-TR. USAF School of Aerospace Medicine* August, pp. 1-3.

Shaw, R., M. Holzer, D. Venson, R. Ullman, H. Butcher, and C. Moyer. (1966) A bioassay of treatment of hemorrhagic shock. III. Effects of a saline solution, ascorbic acid, and nicotinamide upon the toxicity of endotoxin for rats. *Archives of Surgery* 93(4):562-566.

Sheweita, S., M. El-Gabar, and M. Bastawy. (2001) Carbon tetrachloride changes the activity of cytochrome P450 system in the liver of male rats: role of antioxidants. *Toxicology* 169(2):83-92.

Sheweita, S., M. El-Gabar, and M. Bastawy. (2001a) Carbon tetrachloride-induced changes in the activity of phase II drug-metabolizing enzyme in the liver of male rats: role of antioxidants. *Toxicology* 165(2-3):217-224.

Shi, K., D. Mao, W. Cheng, Y. Ji, and L. Xu. (1991) An approach to establishing N-nitroso compounds as the cause of gastric cancer. *IARC Scientific Publications* 105:143-145.

Shi, X., Y. Rojanasakul, P. Gannett, K. Liu, Y. Mao, L. Daniel, N. Ahmed, and U. Saffiotti. (1994) Generation of thiyl and ascorbyl radicals in the reaction of peroxynitrite with thiols and ascorbate at physiological pH. *Journal of Inorganic Biochemistry* 56(2):77-86.

Shimpo, K., T. Nagatsu, K. Yamada, T. Sato, H. Niimi, M. Shamoto, T. Takeuchi, H. Umezawa, and K. Fujita. (1991) Ascorbic acid and adriamycin toxicity. *The American Journal of Clinical Nutrition* 54(6 Suppl):1298S-1301S.

Shiraishi, N., H. Uno, and M. Waalkes. (1993) Effect of L-ascorbic acid pretreatment on cadmium toxicity in the male Fischer (F344/NCr) rat. *Toxicology* 85(2-3):85-100.

Sierra, R., H. Ohshima, N. Munoz, S. Teuchmann, A. Pena, C. Malaveille, B. Pignatelli, A. Chinnock, F. el Ghissassi, C. Chen, et al. (1991) Exposure to N-nitrosamines and other risk factors for gastric cancer in Costa Rican children. *IARC Scientific Publications* 105:162-167.

Simon, J. and E. Hudes. (1999) Relationship of ascorbic acid to blood lead levels. *The Journal of the American Medical Association* 281(24):2289-2293.

Simon, J., E. Hudes, and J. Tice. (2001) Relation of serum ascorbic acid to mortality among US adults. *Journal of the American College of Nutrition* 20(3):255-263.

Simpson, G. and A. Khajawall. (1983) Urinary acidifiers in phencyclidine detoxification. *The Hillside Journal of Clinical Psychiatry* 5(2): 161-168.

Sippel, H. and O. Forsander. (1974) Non-enzymic oxidation of lower aliphatic alcohols by ascorbic acid in tissue extracts. *Acta Chemica Scandinavica. Series B. Organic Chemistry and Biochemistry* 28(10):1243-1245.

Skrzydlewska, E. and R. Farbiszewski. (1996) Diminished antioxidant defense potential of liver, erythrocytes and serum from rats with subacute methanol intoxication. *Veterinary and Human Toxicology* 38(6):429-433.

Skrzydlewska, E. and R. Farbiszewski. (1997) Antioxidant status of liver, erythrocytes, and blood serum of rats in acute methanol intoxication. *Alcohol* 14(5):431-437.

Skrzydlewska, E. and R. Farbiszewski. (1998) Lipid peroxidation and antioxidant status in the liver, erythrocytes, and serum of rats after methanol intoxication. *Journal of Toxicology and Environmental Health. Part A.* 53(8):637-649.

Skvortsova, R., V. Pozniakovskii, and I. Agarkova. (1981) [Role of the vitamin factor in preventing phenol poisoning]. Article in Russian. *Voprosy Pitaniia* 2:32-35.

Slakey, D., A. Roza, G. Pieper, C. Johnson, and M. Adams. (1993) Delayed cardiac allograft rejection due to combined cyclosporine and antioxidant therapy. *Transplantation* 56(6):1305-1309.

Slakey, D., A. Roza, G. Pieper, C. Johnson, and M. Adams. (1993a) Ascorbic acid and alpha-tocopherol prolong rat cardiac allograft survival. *Transplantation Proceedings* 25(1):610-611.

Smart, R. and V. Zannoni. (1984) DT-diaphorase and peroxidase influence the covalent binding of the metabolites of phenol, the major metabolite of benzene. *Molecular Pharmacology* 26(1):105-111.

Smart, R. and V. Zannoni. (1985) Effect of ascorbate on covalent binding of benzene and phenol metabolites to isolated tissue preparations. *Toxicology and Applied Pharmacology* 77(2):334-343.

Smart, R. and V. Zannoni. (1986) Effect of dietary ascorbate on covalent binding of benzene to bone marrow and hepatic tissue *in vivo*. *Biochemical Pharmacology* 35(18):3180-3182.

Smith, L. (1988) *The Clinical Experiences of Frederick R. Klenner, M.D.: Clinical Guide to the Use of Vitamin C.* Portland, OR: Life Sciences Press.

Sohler, A., M. Kruesi, and C. Pfeiffer. (1977) Blood lead levels in psychiatric outpatients reduced by zinc and vitamin C. *Journal of Orthomolecular Psychiatry* 6(3):272-276.

Soliman, M., A. Elwi, H. El-Kateb, and S. Kamel. (1965) Vitamin C as prophylactic drug against experimental hepatotoxicity. *The Journal of the Egyptian Medical Association* 48(11):806-812.

Song, B., N. Aebischer, and C. Orvig. (2002) Reduction of [VO2(ma)2]- and [VO2(ema)2]- by ascorbic acid and glutathione: kinetic studies of pro-drugs for the enhancement of insulin action. *Inorganic Chemistry* 41(6):1357-1364.

Song, H., C. Lang, and T. Chen. (1999) The role glutathione in p-aminophenol-induced nephrotoxicity in the mouse. *Drug and Chemical Toxicology* 22(3):529-544.

Spirichev, V., V. Kodentsova, N. Blazheevich, S. Aleinik, A. Sokol'nikov, O. Vrzhesinskaia, V. Isaev, A. Alekseeva, O. Pereverzeva, N. Golubkina, et al. (1994) [The vitamin and trace element status of the personnel of the Chernobyl Atomic Electric Power Station and of preschool children in the city of Slavutich]. Article in Russian. *Fiziol Zhurnal* 40(3-4):38-48.

Sprince, H., C. Parker, G. Smith, and L. Gonzales. (1975) Protective action of ascorbic acid and sulfur compounds against acetalde-hyde toxicity: implications in alcoholism and smoking. *Agents and Actions* 5(2):164-173.

Sprince, H., C. Parker, and G. Smith. (1979) Comparison of protection by L-ascorbic acid, L-cysteine, and adrenergic-blocking agents against acetaldehyde, acrolein, and formaldehyde toxicity: implications in smoking. *Agents and Actions* 9(4):407-414.

Sram, R., I. Samkova, and N. Hola. (1983) High-dose ascorbic acid prophylaxis in workers occupationally exposed to halogenated ethers. *Journal of Hygiene, Epidemiology, Microbiology, and Immunology* 27(3):305-318.

Srivatanakul, P., H. Ohshima, M. Khlat, M. Parkin, S. Sukarayodhin, I. Brouet, and H. Bartsch. (1991) Endogenous nitrosamines and liver fluke as risk factors for cholangiocarcinoma in Thailand. *IARC Scientific Publications* 105:88-95.

Steuerwald, U., P. Weihe, P. Jorgensen, K. Bjerve, J. Brock, B. Heinzow, E. Budtz-Jorgensen, and P. Grandjean. (2000) Maternal seafood diet, methylmercury exposure, and neonatal neurologic function. *Journal of Pediatrics* 136(5):599-605.

Stoewsand, G., J. Anderson, and C. Lee. (1973) Nitrite-induced methemoglobinemia in guinea pigs: influence of diets concerning beets with varying amounts of nitrate, and the effect of ascorbic acid, and methionine. *The Journal of Nutrition* 103(3):419-424.

Stokes, A., D. Lewis, L. Lash, W. Jerome, K. Grant, M. Aschner, and K. Vrana. (2000) Dopamine toxicity in neuroblastoma cells: role of glutathione depletion by L-BSO and apoptosis. *Brain Research* 858(1):1-8.

Street, J. and R. Chadwick. (1975) Ascorbic acid requirements and metabolism in relation to organochloride pesticides. *Annals of the New York Academy of Sciences* 258:132-143.

Sulzberger, M. and B. Oser. (1935) The influence of ascorbic acid in diet on sensitization of guinea pigs to neoarsphenamine. *Proceedings of the Society for Experimental Biology and Medicine* 32:716.

Sun, F., S. Hayami, Y. Ogiri, S. Haruna, K. Tanaka, Y. Yamada, S. Tokumaru, and S. Kojo. (2000) Evaluation of oxidative stress based on lipid hydroperoxide, vitamin C and vitamin E during apoptosis and necrosis caused by thioacetamide in rat liver. *Biochimica et Biophysica Acta* 1500(2):181-185.

Sun, F., E. Hamagawa, C. Tsutsui, Y. Ono, Y. Ogiri, and S. Kojo. (2001) Evaluation of oxidative stress during apoptosis and necrosis caused by carbon tetrachloride in rat liver. *Biochimica et Biophysica Acta* 1535(2):186-191.

Suresh, M., J. Lal, S. Kumar, and M. Indira. (1997) Interaction of ethanol and ascorbic acid on lipid metabolism in guinea pigs. *Indian Journal of Experimental Biology* 35(10):1065-1069.

Suresh, M., J. Lal, C. Sreeranjit Kumar, and M. Indira. (1999) Ascorbic acid metabolism in rats and guinea pigs after the administration of ethanol. *Comparative Biochemistry and Physiology. Part C, Pharmacology, Toxicology & Endocrinology* 124(2):175-179.

Suresh, M., C. Sreeranjit Kumar, J. Lal, and M. Indira. (1999a) Impact of massive ascorbic acid supplementation on alcohol induced oxidative stress in guinea pigs. *Toxicology Letters* 104(3):221-229.

Suresh, M., B. Menon, and M. Indira. (2000) Effects of exogenous vitamin C on ethanol toxicity in rats. *Indian Journal of Physiology and Pharmacology* 44(4):401-410.

Susa, N., S. Ueno, Y. Furukawa, N. Michiba, and S. Minoura. (1989) Induction of lipid peroxidation in mice by hexavalent chromium and its relation to the toxicity. *Nippon Juigaku Zasshi. The Japanese Journal of Veterinary Science* 51(6):1103-1110.

Susick, Jr., R. and V. Zannoni. (1984) Ascorbic acid and alcohol oxidation. *Biochemical Pharmacology* 33(24):3963-3969.

Susick, Jr., R., G. Abrams, C. Zurawski, and V. Zannoni. (1986) Ascorbic acid chronic alcohol consumption in the guinea pig. *Toxicology and Applied Pharmacology* 84(2):329-335.

Susick, Jr., R. and V. Zannoni. (1987) Effect of ascorbic acid on the consequences of acute alcohol consumption in humans. *Clinical Pharmacology and Therapeutics* 41(5):502-509.

Susick, Jr., R. and V. Zannoni. (1987a) Ascorbic acid and elevated SGOT levels after an acute dose of ethanol in the guinea pig. *Alcoholism, Clinical and Experimental Research* 11(3):265-268.

Suzuki, H., Y. Torii, K. Hitomi, and N. Tsukagoshi. (1993) Ascorbate-dependent elevation of mRNA levels for cytochrome P450s induced by polychlorinated biphenyls. *Biochemical Pharmacology* 46(1):186-189.

Svecova, D. and D. Bohmer. (1998) [Congenital and acquired methemoglobinemia and its therapy]. Article in Slovak. *Casopis Lekaru Ceskych* 137(6):168-170.

Svirbely, J. (1938) Vitamin C studies in the rat. The effect of selenium dioxide, sodium selenate and tellurate. *The Biochemical Journal* 32:467-473.

Swain, C. and G. Chainy. (2000) *In vitro* stimulation of chick brain lipid peroxidation by aluminium, and effects of Tiron, EDTA and some antioxidants. *Indian Journal of Experimental* Biology 38(12):1231-1235.

Tamura, T., H. Inoue, T. Iida, and H. Ono. (1969) Studies on the antidotal action of drugs. Part 1. Vitamin C and its antidotal effect against alcoholic and nicotine poisoning. *The Journal of Nihon University School of Dentistry* 11(4):149-151.

Tamura, T., A. Umezawa, T. Iida, and H. Ono. (1970) Studies on the antidotal action of drugs. Part 2. Vitamin C and its antidotal effect against chloroform and carbon tetrachloridum. *The Journal of Nihon University School of Dentistry* 12(1):25-28.

Tandon, S. and J. Gaur. (1977) Chelation in metal intoxication. IV. Removal of chromium from organs of experimentally poisoned animals. *Clinical Toxicology* 11(2):257-264.

Tandon, S., M. Chatterjee, A. Bhargava, V. Shukla, and V. Bihari. (2001) Lead poisoning in Indian silver refiners. *The Science of the Total Environment* 281(1-3):177-182.

Tao, A., E. Chuah, and J. Tung. (1994) [Another reason for cyanosis—methemoglobinemia]. Article in Chinese. *Acta Anaesthesiologica Sinica* 32(2):133-136.

Taper, H., J. de Gerlache, M. Lans, and M. Roberfroid. (1987) Non-toxic potentiation of cancer chemotherapy by combined C and K3 vitamin pre-treatment. *International Journal of Cancer* 40(4): 575-579.

Tavares, D., A. Cecchi, L. Antunes, and C. Takahashi. (1998) Protective effects of the amino acid glutamine and of ascorbic acid against chromosomal damage induced by doxorubicin in mammalian cells. *Teratogenesis, Carcinogenesis, and Mutagenesis* 18(4): 153-161.

Tayama, S. and Y. Nakagawa. (1994) Effect of scavengers of active oxygen species on cell damage caused in CHO-K1 cells by phenyl-hydroquinone, an o-phenylphenol metabolite. *Mutation Research* 324(3):121-131.

Teng, Y., G. Taylor, F. Scannapieco, D. Kinane, M. Curtis, J. Beck, and S. Kogon. (2002) Periodontal health and systemic disorders. *Journal of the Canadian Dental Association* 68(3):188-192.

Terada, A., M. Yoshida, M. Nakada, K. Nakada, N. Yamate, T. Kobayashi, and K. Yoshida. (1997) Influence of combined use of selenious acid and SH compounds in parenteral preparations. *Journal of Trace Elements in Medicine and Biology* 11(2):105-109.

Tiwari, R., S. Bandyopadhyay, and G. Chatterjee. (1982) Protective effect of L-ascorbic acid in lindane intoxicated rats. *Acta Vitaminologica et Enzymologica* 4(3):215-220.

Toussant, M. and J. Latshaw. (1994) Evidence of multiple metabolic routes in vanadium's effects on layers. Ascorbic acid differential effects on prepeak egg production parameters following prolonged vanadium feeding. *Poultry Science* 73(10):1572-1580.

Treacy, E., L. Arbour, P. Chessex, G. Graham, L. Kasprzak, K. Casey, L. Bell, O. Mamer, and C. Scriver. (1996) Glutathione deficiency as a complication of methylmalonic acidemia: response to high doses of ascorbate. *The Journal of Pediatrics* 129(3):445-448.

Tu, B., A. Wallin, P. Moldeus, and I. Cotgreave. (1995) The cytoprotective roles of ascorbate and glutathione against nitrogen dioxide toxicity in human endothelial cells. *Toxicology* 98(1-3):125-136.

Tuma, D., T. Donohue, Jr., V. Medina, and M. Sorrell. (1984) Enhancement of acetaldehyde-protein adduct formation by L-ascorbate. *Archives of Biochemistry and Biophysics* 234(2):377-381.

Umegaki, K., S. Aoki, and T. Esashi. (1995) Whole body x-ray irradiation to mice decreases ascorbic acid concentration in bone marrow: comparison between ascorbic acid and vitamin E. *Free Radical Biology & Medicine* 19(4):493-497.

Upasani, C., A. Khera, and R. Balaraman. (2001) Effect of lead with vitamin E, C, or spirulina on malondialdehyde, conjugated dienes and hydroperoxides in rats. *Indian Journal of Experimental Biology* 39(1):70-74.

Usami, M., H. Tabata, and Y. Ohno. (1999) Effects of ascorbic acid on selenium teratogenicity in cultured rat embryos. *Toxicology Letters* 105(2):123-128.

Valentovic, M., M. Meadows, R. Harmon, J. Ball, S. Hong, and G. Rankin. (1999) 2-Amino-5-chlorophenol toxicity in renal cortical slices from Fisher 344 rats: effect of antioxidants and sulfhydryl agents. *Toxicology and Applied Pharmacology* 161(1):1-9.

Valentovic, M., J. Ball, H. Sun, and G. Rankin. (2002) Characterization of 2-amino-4,5-dichlorophenol (2A45CP) *in vitro* toxicity in renal cortical slices from male Fisher 344 rats. *Toxicology* 172(2):113-123.

Vamvakas, S., D. Bittner, M. Koob, S. Gluck, and W. Dekant. (1992) Glutathione depletion, lipid peroxidation, DNA double-strand breaks and the cytotoxicity of 2-bromo-3-(N-acetylcystein-S-yl)hydroquinone in rat renal cortical cells. *Chemico-Biological Interactions* 83(2):183-199.

van der Gaag, M., R. van den Berg, H. van den Berg, G. Schaafsma, and H. Hendriks. (2000) Moderate consumption of beer, red wine and spirits has counteracting effects on plasma antioxidants in middle-aged men. *European Journal of Clinical Nutrition* 54(7): 586-591.

Van der Vliet, A., D. Smith, C. O'Neill, H. Kaur, V. Darley-Usmar, C. Cross, and B. Halliwell. (1994) Interactions of peroxynitrite with human plasma and its constituents: oxidative damage and antioxidant depletion. *The Biochemical Journal* 303(Pt 1):295-301.

van Dijk, S., A. Lobsteyn, T. Wensing, and H. Breukink. (1983) Treatment of nitrate intoxication in a cow. *The Veterinary Record* 112(12):272-274.

Vasavi, H., M. Thangaraju, J. Babu, and P. Sachdanandam. (1998) The salubrious effects of ascorbic acid on cyclophosphamide instigated lipid abnormalities in fibrosarcoma bearing rats. *Cancer Biochemistry Biophysics* 16(1-2):71-83.

Vatassery, G. (1996) Oxidation of vitamin E, vitamin C, and thiols in rat brain synaptosomes by peroxynitrite. *Biochemical Pharmacology* 52(4):579-586.

Vauthey, M. (1951) Protective effect of vitamin C against poisons. *Praxis* (Bern) 40:284-286.

Vaziri, N., T. Upham, and C. Barton. (1980) Hemodialysis clearance of arsenic. *Clinical Toxicology* 17(3):451-456.

Venkatesan, N. and G. Chandrakasan. (1994) Cyclophosphamide-induced early biochemical changes in lung lavage fluid and alterations in lavage cell function. *Lung* 172(3):147-158.

Venkatesan, N. and G. Chandrakasan. (1994a) *In vivo* administration of taurine and niacin modulate cyclophosphamide-induced lung injury. *European Journal of Pharmacology* 292(1):75-80.

Venkatesan, N. and G. Chandrakasan. (1995) Modulation of cyclophosphamide-induced early lung injury by curcumin, and anti-inflammatory antioxidant. *Molecular and Cellular Biochemistry* 142(1):79-87.

Verma, R., R. Shukla, and D. Mehta. (1999) Interaction of aflatoxin with L-ascorbic acid: a kinetic and mechanistic approach. *Natural Toxins* 7(1):25-29.

Verma, S., I. Tonk, and R. Dalela. (1982) Effects of a few xenobiots on three phosphatases of *Saccobranchus fossilis* and the role of ascorbic acid in their toxicity. *Toxicology Letters* 10(2-3):287-292.

Victor, V., N. Guayerbas, M. Puerto, S. Medina, and M. De la Fuente. (2000) Ascorbic acid modulates *in vitro* the function of macrophages from mice with endotoxic shock. *Immunopharmacology* 46(1):89-101.

Victor, V., N. Guayerbas, and F. De. (2002) Changes in the antioxidant content of mononuclear leukocytes from mice with endotoxin-induced oxidative stress. *Molecular and Cellular Biochemistry* 229(1-2):107-111.

Vij, A., N. Satija, and S. Flora. (1998) Lead induced disorders in hematopoietic and drug metabolizing enzyme system and their protection by ascorbic acid supplementation. *Biomedical and Environmental Sciences* 11(1):7-14.

Vijayalaxmi, K. and R. Venu. (1999) *In vivo* anticlastogenic effects of L-ascorbic acid in mice. *Mutation Research* 438(1):47-51.

Vimy, M. and F. Lorscheider. (1985) Serial measurements of intra-oral air mercury: estimation of daily dose from dental amalgam. *Journal of Dental Research* 64(8):1072-1075.

Vismara, C., G. Vailati, and R. Bacchetta. (2001) Reduction in para-quat embryotoxicity by ascorbic acid in *Xenopus laevis*. *Aquatic Toxicology* 51(3):293-303.

Vogel, R. and H. Spielmann. (1989) Beneficial effects of ascorbic acid on preimplantation mouse embryos after exposure to cyclophos-phamide *in vivo*. *Teratogenesis, Carcinogenesis, and Mutagenesis* 9(1):51-59.

Wagner, G., R. Carelli, and M. Jarvis. (1985) Pretreatment with ascor-bic acid attenuates the neurotoxic effects of methamphetamine in rats. *Research Communications in Chemical Pathology and Pharmacology* 47(2):221-228.

Wagstaff, D. and J. Street. (1971) Ascorbic acid deficiency and induc-tion of hepatic microsomal hydroxylative enzymes by organo-chlorine pesticides. *Toxicology and Applied Pharmacology* 19(1):10-19.

Walker, R. (1990) Nitrates, nitrites and N-nitrosocompounds: a review of the occurrence in food and diet and the toxicological implica-tions. *Food Additives and Contaminants* 7(6):717-768.

Walpole, I., K. Johnston, R. Clarkson, G. Wilson, and G. Bowers. (1985) Acute chromium poisoning in a 2 year old child. *Australian Paediatric Journal* 21(1):65-67.

Warren, F. (1943) Aerobic oxidation of aromatic hydrocarbons in the presence of ascorbic acid. The reaction with anthracene and 3:4-benzpyrene. *Biochemical Journal* 37:338-341.

Wawrzyniak, A., R. Kieres, and A. Gronowska-Senger. (1997) [The *in vitro* effect of ascorbic acid on sodium nitrite intoxication]. Article in Polish. *Roczniki Panstwowego Zakladu Higieny* 48(3):245-252.

Weber, S., J. Thiele, C. Cross, and L. Packer. (1999) Vitamin C, uric acid, and glutathione gradients in murine stratum corneum and their susceptibility to ozone exposure. *The Journal of Investigative Dermatology* 113(6):1128-1132.

Welch, M. and G. Correa. (1980) PCP intoxication in young children and infants. *Clinical Pediatrics* 19(8):510-514.

White, L., M. Carpenter, M. Block, A. Basse-Tomusk, T. Gardiner, and G. Rebec. (1988) Ascorbate antagonizes the behavioral effects of amphetamine by a central mechanism. *Psychopharmacology* 94(2):284-287.

Whiteman, M. and B. Halliwell. (1996) Protection against peroxynitrite-dependent tyrosine nitration and alpha 1-antiproteinase inactivation by ascorbic acid. A comparison with other biological antioxidants. *Free Radical Research* 25(3):275-283.

Wickramasinghe, S. and R. Hasan. (1992) *In vitro* effects of vitamin C, thioctic acid and dihydrolipoic acid on the cytotoxicity of post-ethanol serum. *Biochemical Pharmacology* 43(3):407-411.

Wickramasinghe, S. and R. Hasan. (1994) *In vivo* effects of vitamin C on the cytotoxicity of post-ethanol serum. *Biochemical Pharmacology* 48(3):621-624.

Wiester, M., J. Tepper, D. Winsett, K. Crissman, J. Richards, and D. Costa. (1996) Adaptation to ozone in rats and its association with ascorbic acid in the lung. *Fundamental and Applied Toxicology* 31(1):56-64.

Willette, R., B. Thomas, and G. Barnett. (1983) Inhibition of morphine analgesia by ascorbate. *Research Communications in Chemical Pathology and Pharmacology* 42(3):485-491.

Williams, A., G. Riise, B. Anderson, C. Kjellstrom, H. Schersten, and F. Kelly. (1999) Compromised antioxidant status and persistent oxidative stress in lung transplant recipients. *Free Radical Research* 30(5):383-393.

Wise, J., J. Orenstein, and S. Patierno. (1993) Inhibition of lead chromate clastogenesis by ascorbate: relationship to particle dissolution and uptake. *Carcinogenesis* 14(3):429-434.

Wolf, A., C. Trendelenburg, C. Diez-Fernandez, P. Prieto, S. Houy, W. Trommer, and A. Cordier. (1997) Cyclosporine A-induced oxidative stress in rat hepatocytes. *The Journal of Pharmacology and Experimental Therapeutics* 280(3):1328-1334.

Wozniak, K. and J. Blasiak. (2002) Free radicals-mediated induction of oxidized DNA bases and DNA-protein cross-links by nickel chloride. *Mutation Research* 514(1-2):233-243.

Wu, J., K. Karlsson, and A. Danielsson. (1996) Protective effects of trolox C, vitamin C, and catalase on bromobenzene-induced damage to rat hepatocytes. *Scandinavian Journal of Gastroenterology* 31(8):797-803.

Yasukawa, M., T. Terasima, and M. Seki. (1989) Radiation-induced neoplastic transformation of C3H10T1/2 cells is suppressed by ascorbic acid. *Radiation Research* 120(3):456-467.

Yeadon, M. and A. Payne. (1989) Ascorbic acid prevents ozone-induced bronchial hyperreactivity in guinea-pigs. *British Journal of Pharmacology* 98 Suppl:790P.

Yunice, A. and R. Lindeman. (1977) Effect of ascorbic acid and zinc sulfate on ethanol toxicity and metabolism. *Proceedings of the Society for Experimental Biology and Medicine* 154(1):146-150.

Yunice, A., J. Hsu, A. Fahmy, and S. Henry. (1984) Ethanol-ascorbate interrelationship in acute and chronic alcoholism in the guinea pig. *Proceedings of the Society for Experimental Biology and Medicine* 177(2):262-271.

Zannoni, V., E. Flynn, and M. Lynch. (1972) Ascorbic acid and drug metabolism. *Biochemical Pharmacology* 21(10):1377-1392.

Zannoni, V., I Brodfuehrer, R. Smart, and R. Susick, Jr. (1987) Ascorbic acid, alcohol, and environmental chemicals. *Annals of the New York Academy of Sciences* 498:364-388.

Zaporowska, H. (1994) Effect of vanadium on L-ascorbic acid concentration in rat tissues. *General Pharmacology* 25(3):467-470.

Zhang, Q., T. Li, H. Zhan, and Y. Xin. (2001) [Inhibitory effects of tea polyphenols and vitamin C on lipid peroxidation induced by FeSO4-cysteine in isolated human plasma and carbon tetrachloride-induced liver free radical injury in mice]. Article in Chinese. *Space Medicine & Medical Engineering* 14(1):50-53.

Zhou, J. and P. Chen. (2001) Studies on the oxidative stress in alcohol abusers in China. *Biomedical and Environmental Sciences* 14(3):180-188.

Chapter Four

The Safety of High Doses
of Vitamin C

*Opinions are caught like an infection, and put
into practice without examination.*

Balzac 1799-1850

Overview

Along with its numerous and substantial clinical benefits, vitamin C is also one of the safest and least toxic therapies that can be administered to a patient, regardless of diagnosis. Everybody needs some vitamin C on a regular basis, and the only potential problems with vitamin C administration arise in a very limited number of clinical situations. Some researchers have voiced their concerns about the proper dosing of vitamin C in these situations, and the validity of these concerns will be addressed in some detail.

Long-Term and High-Dose Supplementation

Intravenous vitamin C has already been demonstrated as a very safe form of vitamin C supplementation. Casciari et al. (2001) reported that "terminal cancer patients" were given 50,000 mg of intravenous vitamin C daily for up to eight weeks. The "blood count and chemistry parameters" revealed no evidence of toxicity or side effects from this administration. Kalokerinos et al. (1982) also reported on the safety of intravenous vitamin C, noting that "in Australia alone, some 100 physicians" have administered as much as 300,000 mg of vitamin C per day to their patients. These authors go on to mention that "in most cases the results have been spectacular, the only side effect is 'chronic good health.'"

some 100 physicians have administered as much as 300,000 mg of vitamin C per day to their patients... "in most cases the results have been spectacular, the only side effect is 'chronic good health'"

Cathcart (1981), using his method of dosing patients with vitamin C up to "bowel tolerance" (see Chapter 3, in the treatment of AIDS), often gave individual patients more than 200,000 mg of oral vitamin C daily as ascorbic acid. Cathcart (1985) asserted that he had treated over 11,000 patients in the prior 14 years with vitamin C. Regarding doses ranging from 4,000 mg to over 200,000 mg in a 24-hour period, he commented that there was "a remarkable lack of systemic difficulties" with these doses of vitamin C. By 1993, Cathcart's patient count had exceeded 20,000, and no remarkable difficulties with these dosage levels had emerged (Cathcart, 1993). Some of his AIDS patients (Cathcart, 1984) would take anywhere from 25,000 to 125,000 mg of vitamin C daily on a regular basis, only varying the dose depending upon fluctuating bowel tolerance, which generally reflected the activity level of the disease. Cathcart noted that occasional minor complaints of gas, diarrhea, or acid stomach were seen *more* often in well patients, appearing only rarely in the "very sick" patients. He asserted that even with these high daily doses of vitamin C, he "cannot recall any patient who has been damaged by large doses of ascorbate," except for some dissolving effect on tooth enamel in a few people who swished the vitamin C in their mouths before swallowing.

Cathcart also commented on the incidence of a few possible side effects that some authors feel may be associated with vitamin C therapy. Cathcart noted in the doses of vitamin C that he administered, oxalate kidney stones *did not* occur, and patients who had them previously tended not to get them again. Cathcart's extensive clinical experience directly contradicts the widespread but mistaken belief that large doses of vitamin C will result in kidney stone formation.

Cathcart also noted that "three out of thousands" developed a "light rash" that cleared without discontinuing the vitamin C. Regarding the urinary tract, he noted that "six patients have had mild pain on urination," but that "acute and chronic urinary tract infections" were often eradicated with the vitamin C. A few patients had "discoloration of the skin" under some types of jewelry, possibly because of a detoxification effect of the vitamin C. Cathcart reported that a few patients had small sores in their mouth on lower doses of vitamin C that subsequently cleared when dosing was increased to the bowel tolerance levels. He noted that a few patients with "hidden peptic ulcers" might have had pain, but that others were benefited. Cathcart also commented that he has seen only benefit and no aggravation of gouty arthritis with high doses of vitamin C.

Moertel et al. (1985) conducted a prospective, double-blind study of the effects of 10,000 mg vitamin C daily versus placebo on 100 patients with advanced colorectal cancer. Except for a few patients having slightly more heartburn with vitamin C than placebo (a difference the authors determined to be "not statistically significant"), no "clear evidence of a specific toxicity of vitamin C" was detected in any of the patients. However, ascorbic acid was likely the form of vitamin C administered. Had the vitamin C been given as sodium ascorbate, no heartburn at all would be anticipated.

The median time of vitamin C administration was 2.5 months, with the longest duration being 15.6 months. Even though the subjects were sick patients who would be expected to be especially sensitive to any agent with even mild toxicity, the daily 10,000 mg dose was very well-tolerated with no significant side effects observed. Earlier, Creagan et al. (1979) had administered either 10,000 mg daily of vitamin C as ascorbic acid or placebo to 123 advanced cancer patients who were felt to be "unsuitable" for chemotherapy. These patients were very ill, with a median survival time of seven weeks. Nevertheless, the vitamin C was very well-tolerated, producing only mild nausea and vomiting with the same frequency as the lactose placebo pills. The authors also specifically noted that no kidney stones were produced by this therapy, even though some patients received the vitamin C for over six months.

Bendich and Langseth (1995) compiled a good review article that also addressed the safety of chronic vitamin C supplementation. In addition to the reports noted above, a host of other therapeutic trials with vitamin C have also reported no adverse effects with dosages of vitamin C considered by most researchers and clinicians to be in the "mega-dose" range. In five double-blind studies giving either vitamin C or placebo, the doses of vitamin C ranged from 400 to 4,000 mg daily, and the durations of therapy ranged from one to 24 months (Ludvigsson et al., 1979; Bussey et al., 1982; McKeown-Eyssen et al., 1988; Taylor et al., 1991; Osilesi et al., 1991).

In six other clinical trials that were not double-blinded and had no placebo given, long-term vitamin C administration did not result in any side effects. The vitamin C doses ranged from 500 to 5,000 mg daily, and the durations of thera-

a double-blind study found that vitamin C administration was very safe even for premature infants

py ranged from one to 30 months (Lux and May, 1983; Melethil et al., 1986; Brox et al., 1988; Godeau and Bierling, 1990; Reaven et al., 1993; Sharma and Mathur, 1995). In an article reviewing a large number of vitamin C studies, Hanck (1982) also confirmed the remarkable safety of long-term supplementation. Bass et al. (1998), in a double-blind study, found that vitamin C administration was very safe even for premature infants.

It can certainly be concluded that vitamin C is an exceptionally safe supplement, which has already been given in very large doses for extended periods of time with no significant problems occurring. There are few, if any, prescription or non-prescription medicines or supplements that are as free of side effects as vitamin C. This is in spite of the fact that vitamin C has one of the widest flexibilities in dose amount of any ingestible substance. The mild gastrointestinal effect of slight heartburn or stomach upset is limited to the ascorbic acid form of vitamin C.

Vitamin C is equally effective in its sodium ascorbate form, and there is no stomach upset with this preparation.

Does Vitamin C Cause Kidney Stones?

Vitamin C as ascorbic acid is first metabolized to oxidized ascorbic acid, or dehydroascorbic acid (DHAA). Whenever vitamin C first contributes two electrons to another compound while performing its major responsibility as an antioxidant, DHAA is immediately produced. Other antioxidants and some enzymes can promptly regenerate DHAA back to the potent, unoxidized ascorbic acid (Long and Carson, 1961; Basu et al., 1979; Rose and Bode, 1992; Bode et al., 1993). However, when this regeneration does not occur, further metabolic breakdown of vitamin C can take place. The primary metabolic pathway of vitamin C is as follows (Davies et al., 1991):

1. Vitamin C (ascorbic acid) to DHAA

2. DHAA to diketogulonic acid

3. Diketogulonic acid to lyxonic acid, xylose, threonic acid, or oxalic acid (oxalate)

Oxalate, or oxalic acid, is a major metabolite of vitamin C after it is utilized and fully broken down in the body. Oxalate is considered a true metabolic "end product" because there is no evidence that mammalian tissues further utilize it or break it down any further (Hagler and Herman, 1973). Since the primary constituent in most kidney stones is calcium oxalate (Jayanthi et al., 1994), many conventional doctors have simply concluded that significant vitamin C supplementation will lead to kidney stones. For this reason alone, it would seem that many patients are still warned by their physicians that vitamin C supplementation "might" cause problems and increase their chance of developing a kidney stone.

However, there exists a large amount of literature from respected research centers that indicates otherwise. In patients with known kidney disease, some reasonable cautions are in order. However, a healthy person who avoids dehydration and ingests even very large amounts of vitamin C does not need to have any concern about kidney stone formation. In fact, there is a strong suggestion in some studies that regular supplementation of vitamin C actually decreases the chances of kidney stone development. Two recent and extensive studies at Harvard have clearly demonstrated that vitamin C is not a factor in the development of kidney stones in healthy adults. Curhan et al. (1999) looked at a group of 85,557 women with no history of kidney stones. Over a follow-up period of 14 years, 1,078 cases of kidney stones developed in this group. Vitamin C intake had no statistical association with any increased risk of stone development.

a study followed 85,557 women for 14 years and found no statistical association with vitamin C and increased risk of kidney stone development — a similar study with 45,251 men reached the same conclusion

A bit earlier, Curhan et al. (1996) looked at a group of 45,251 men with no history of kidney stones. They also found that vitamin C was not a risk factor for stone formation over their six years of follow-up, and it did not matter whether the men were consuming 250 mg or 1,500 mg of vitamin C daily.

Gerster (1997) noted that a statistical study revealed that individuals with the highest vitamin C intake actually had a *lower* risk of kidney stones compared to individuals taking the least vitamin C. Analyzing the relationship more precisely, Simon and Hudes (1999) found that every 1.0 mg/dL increase in blood vitamin C levels was "independently associated" with approximately a 28% decrease in the prevalence of kidney stones in men. Gaker and Butcher (1986) reported that an 81-year-old woman successfully dissolved her very large kidney stone over an eight-week period with only diuretics, antibiotics, and vitamin C.

In veterinary work, Belfield and Zucker (1993) reported two cases in which vitamin C administration dissolved documented bladder stones. A 10-year-old female terrier was found to have bladder stones. Since the owner did not want an operation for only that reason, the dog was placed on 500 mg of vitamin C daily. After six months the animal had unrelated uterine surgery, and an operative examination of the bladder revealed that the stones were gone. In another case, a veterinarian gave a small-breed dog 8,000 mg of vitamin C as ascorbic acid daily for four months. This successfully dissolved a large bladder stone.

Many factors are involved in the precipitation of calcium oxalate out of the urine, leading to stone formation, and increased vitamin C supplementation is but one of these factors. It is important to realize that a given risk factor can only produce a given medical condition when other surrounding circumstances favor the development of that condition as well. These risk factors, with appropriate references, include the following:

1. Increased urinary oxalate (Hagler and Herman, 1973b; Ogawa et al., 2000)

2. Increased vitamin C supplementation (Pru et al., 1985; Urivetzky et al., 1992; Auer et al., 1998)

3. Calcium ascorbate as the type of supplemental vitamin C (Kalokerinos et al., 1981; Tsugawa et al., 1999)

4. Presence and concentration of other dissolved substances (solutes) in the urine (Oke, 1969; Lawton et al., 1985)

5. Presence of heavy metal chelation agents, such as DMPS, DMSA, and EDTA, which have their own independent kidney toxicities, due to increased urinary solute load and toxin damage to the kidneys (Oke, 1969)

6. Increased urinary calcium (Noe, 2000; Kinder et al., 2002; Bushinsky et al., 2002; Borghi et al., 2002)

7. Decreased urinary magnesium (Schwartz et al., 2001)

8. Decreased urinary citrate (Alvarez et al., 1992; Tekin et al., 2000; Yagisawa et al., 2001)

9. Decreased urinary potassium (Kinder et al., 2002)

10. Increased urinary cystine (Martins et al., 2002)

11. Increased urinary phosphorus (Prie et al., 2001)

12. Increased urinary uric acid (Koide, 1996; Yagisawa et al., 1999)

13. Increased urinary lipids and cholesterol (Khan et al., 1988; Khan and Glenton, 1996)

14. Increased age, with age-associated decrease in glomerular filtration rate (Mousson et al., 1993)

15. Intake of hard water (Bellizzi et al., 1999)

16. Overall state of hydration (Sakhaee et al., 1987; Borghi et al., 1996)

17. Decreased daily volume of urine flow and formation (Riobo et al., 1998; Borghi et al., 1999a)

18. Urinary pH (Wall and Tiselius, 1990; Hokama et al., 2000; Murayama et al., 2001; Kinder et al, 2002; Hsu et al., 2002)

19. Low dietary calcium (Curhan et al., 1997a)

20. Supplemental calcium (Curhan et al., 1997a); supplemental calcium causing calcium gallstones (Powell, 1985)

21. Vitamin D supplementation (Black, 1945; Hodgkinson and Zarembski, 1968; Broadus et al., 1980; Ichioka et al., 2002)

22. Low intake of magnesium and vitamins (Williams and Smith, 1968)

23. Preexisting calcium deposits throughout the body, especially in the vascular system

24. Presence of preexisting kidney insufficiency or failure; being on hemodialysis (Oren et al., 1984; Chen et al., 1990; Daudon et al., 1992)

25. Any injury to the cells lining those parts of the urinary system susceptible to stone formation (Khan and Thamilselvan, 2000)

26. Intake of oxalate stone-generating or oxalate-containing foods (Hagler and Herman, 1973a; Bakane et al., 1999; Massey et al., 2001)

27. Intake of oxalate stone-generating or oxalate-containing beverages (McKay et al., 1995; Curhan et al., 1996a; Terris et al., 2001)

28. Intake of oxalate stone-generating or oxalate-containing supplements and medicines (Shields and Simmons, 1976; Fleisch, 1978; Ettinger et al., 1980; Wolf et al., 1985; Ahlstrand and Tiselius, 1987; Daudon et al., 1987; Michelacci et al., 1992; Kohan et al., 1999; Sundaram and Saltzman, 1999; Gonzalez et al., 2000; Wu and Stoller, 2000)

29. Intake of oxalate stone-generating toxins (Hagler and Herman, 1973c; Conyers et al., 1990; Muthukumar and Selvam, 1998)

30. Receiving total parenteral nutrition (Friedman et al., 1983; Swartz et al., 1984)

31. Deficiency of pyridoxine [vitamin B6] (Gershoff et al., 1959; Faber et al., 1963; Gershoff, 1964; Mitwalli et al., 1988; Alkhunaizi and Chan, 1996; Curhan et al., 1999)

32. Deficiency of thiamine [vitamin B1] (Buckle, 1963; Alkhunaizi and Chan, 1996)

33. Having had intestinal bypass or resection surgery, or small bowel malabsorption from any cause (Gregory et al., 1977; Drenick et al., 1978; Nightingale, 1999; Nightingale, 2001)

34. Urinary tract infection, or presence of bacteria (Trinchieri et al., 1996; Dewan et al., 1997; Daskalova et al., 1998; Hokama et al., 2000; Sohshang et al., 2000; Kim et al., 2001)

35. Presence of increased oxidative stress in the urinary tract (Scheid et al., 1996; Muthukumar and Selvam, 1998)

36. Primary hyperoxaluria, a hereditary disorder (Daudon et al., 1998)

37. Hyperparathyroidism (Ralph-Edwards et al., 1992; Yamaguchi et al., 2001)

38. Urinary stasis, or incomplete voiding (Nikakhtar et al., 1981; Sarkissian et al., 2001)

39. Obstructive urinary disease (Kim et al., 2001)

40. Polycystic kidney disease (Torres et al., 1988; Torres et al., 1993)

41. Cirrhosis (Hagler and Herman, 1973c)

42. Diabetes (Hagler and Herman, 1973c)

43. Congestive heart failure (Hagler and Herman, 1973c)

44. Crohn's disease (Shiraishi et al., 1998; Buno et al., 2001; McConnell et al., 2002)

45. Cystic fibrosis (Turner et al., 2000; Perez-Brayfield et al., 2002)

46. Renal tubular acidosis (Hagler and Herman, 1973c)

47. Sarcoidosis (Sharma, 1996; Rodman and Mahler, 2000)

48. Klinefelter's syndrome (Hagler and Herman, 1973c)

49. Parasitic diseases, including amebiasis, schistosomiasis, giardiasis, and ascariasis (Hagler and Herman, 1973c)

50. Antibiotic therapy (Bohles et al., 2002)

51. Increased fluoride intake (Singh et al., 2001)

52. Prolonged bedrest (Hwang et al., 1988)

53. Kidney transplantation (Torrecilla et al., 2001)

54. Hypertension (Borghi et al., 1999; Hall et al., 2001)

55. Increased alcohol intake (Hughes and Norman, 1992)

56. Increased glucose intake (Burns et al., 1951; Nguyen et al., 1989)

57. Pregnancy (Hildebrandt and Shanklin, 1962; Maikranz et al., 1989)

58. Methoxyflurane anesthesia (Mazze et al., 1971; Mazze et al., 1971a; Silverberg et al., 1971)

59. Ketogenic diet (Furth et al., 2000)

60. Space travel (Whitson et al., 1997; Whitson et al., 1999)

One of the primary reasons why the vitamin C/kidney stone connection continues to generate concern is because vitamin C does increase the urinary concentration of oxalate. Therefore, it just seems logical to assume that more and prolonged vitamin C administration will continue to increase this concentration until calcium oxalate stones begin to form.

However, research proves that this is not the case, although vitamin C is one of many risk factors (see above) for increased oxalate formation and the subsequent formation of calcium oxalate stones. Schmidt et al. (1981) determined that there was actually a leveling off of oxalate production even though the vitamin C dosing was continued. The researchers noted that a significant amount of the vitamin C does not even get metabolized to oxalate and is excreted unchanged in the urine.

When very high doses of vitamin C are administered for any significant medical condition, the active, non-oxidized form of vitamin C is much more readily regenerated from the oxidized vitamin C than the metabilic breakdown products. This process further inhibits the irreversible metabolism of vitamin C to the oxalate end product. Takenouchi et al. (1966) noted that about 80% of vitamin C administered to human subjects was eliminated as dehydroascorbic acid, the oxidized form of vitamin C. They concluded that the metabolic breakdown of vitamin C in humans does not necessarily have to follow the entire sequence down to oxalate. They also noted that as the vitamin C dose is increased, urinary excretion of diketogulonic acid increased. This is a clear indication that further oxidative breakdown of the diketogulonic acid to oxalate does not have to occur for a metabolic breakdown product of vitamin C to be excreted.

In healthy men, Lamden and Chrystowski (1954) showed that vitamin C doses of 4,000 mg or less "produced no significant increase in oxalate excretion" over non-supplementers. Fituri et al. (1983) found that the ingestion of 8,000 mg of vitamin C daily for seven days by eight normal subjects did not "significantly alter urinary or plasma oxalate during or after ingestion." Other investigators have found that vitamin C administration will raise urinary oxalate levels (Tiselius and Almgard, 1977; Hatch et al., 1980; Hughes et al, 1981). As noted in the list above, vitamin C is only one of many risk factors that can affect whether calcium oxalate stones are ultimately formed.

Unfortunately, many of the research studies examining this issue have not even looked for most of the other risk factors itemized above, resulting in conflicting findings on the ability of vitamin C to increase urinary oxalate. Fituri et al. even noted that some studies have used a tablet form of vitamin C, and they suggested that the tartaric acid and sucrose present in some tablets could convert to oxalate in the body. The amounts of such additional agents in pills can be significant, as Wilk (1976) noted that 100 mg vitamin C pills weighed 400 mg, with the additional 300 mg due to fillers. Auer et al. (1998a) also showed that urine specimens not preserved with EDTA registered erroneously high oxalate levels in their testing, possibly indicating a reason for some of the higher oxalate levels noted in other urine studies of vitamin C supplementers.

Logically, there have to be multiple other ways to metabolize and excrete vitamin C rather than by urinary oxalate. Casciari et al., (2001) showed that 50,000 mg daily doses of intravenous vitamin C have already been given to cancer patients for eight-week periods without problem. If urinary oxalate was the only excreted metabolic product of vitamin C, such doses would cause such a supersaturation of oxalate in the urine that crystal deposition and eventual stone formation would have to occur. Yet, this does not occur.

Since oxalate is a primary component of so many kidney stones, it is also very important to know about the many other potential sources of increased oxalate concentration in the urine. In addition to vitamin C, glyoxylate and glycolate are the primary substances that can be metabolized to oxalate (Ogawa et al., 2000). Also, there are numerous other lesser precursors to oxalate, including gelatin, certain amino acids (such as tryptophan, phenylalanine, aspartic acid, tyrosine, threonine, and asparagine), creatinine, purines, glucose, other carbohydrates, and probably several unidentified substances (Hagler and Herman, 1973).

A lesser precursor can assume a great deal of importance in the generation of oxalate when one has a peculiar diet rich in the precursor, such as occurs in the regular excessive ingestion of aspartame-containing diet drinks and other diet foods. Aspartame is primarily a combination of phenylalanine and aspartic acid, two of the amino acids that can lead to oxalate. Also, if a patient is receiving hyperalimentation with a high concentration of amino acids, increased oxalate formation can result. Glycine, the simplest of the amino acids, is likely the major source of glyoxylate, which is a major immediate precursor to oxalate (Hagler and Herman, 1973).

Important dietary sources of oxalate include spinach, rhubarb, parsley, citrus fruits, and tea. Tea is probably the most important source of oxalate in the average English diet (Zarembski and Hodgkinson, 1962). Other significant dietary sources of oxalate include Swiss chard, cocoa, chocolate, beet tops, peppers, wheat germ, pecans, peanuts, okra, chocolate, refried beans, lentils, and lime peel. Various soy-based foods can also contain large amounts of oxalate (Massey et al., 2001).

High-purine foods, such as sardines and herring roes, also substantially increase oxalate excretion (Zarembski and Hodgkinson, 1969). Oxalate poisoning has been reported in the literature secondary to an excessive intake of rhubarb (Tallquist and Vaananen, 1960; Kalliala and Kauste, 1964). Clearly, a detailed dietary history is critical in the proper management of any patient with kidney stone risk or disease, and merely lessening or discontinuing vitamin C intake as the only significant intervention is not in the patient's best interests. Eliminating one or several of the patient's favorite oxalate-containing foods should always take precedence over lessening or eliminating any regular supplementation of vitamin C.

Calcium also plays several roles in the propensity for calcium oxalate stone formation. Reducing the dietary (*not* supplemental) intake of calcium increases the intestinal absorption of oxalate (Hodgkinson, 1958). Conversely, in a study on 45,619 men Curhan et al. (1993) found that a high dietary intake of calcium decreased the risk of symptomatic kidney stones. In looking at 91,731 women, Curhan et al. (1997) again found that the high dietary intake of calcium decreased the risk of symptomatic kidney stones, "whereas intake of supplemental calcium may increase risk." It was also found that vitamin D supplementation increased the excretion of oxalate in humans (Hodgkinson and Zarembski, 1968).

Some researchers have actually demonstrated that vitamin C probably lessens the likelihood of kidney stone formation in those individuals who already have a history of stone formation, indicating a possible *therapeutic* role for vitamin C in the treatment of kidney stone disease. Schwille et al. (2000) found that vitamin C actually inhibited the development of calcium oxalate crystals in these individuals. Not surprisingly, they also concluded that vitamin C does not play a role in helping the formation of kidney stones "under normal conditions."

researchers have actually demonstrated that vitamin C probably lessens the likelihood of kidney stone formation in individuals with a history of stone formation

Grases et al. (1998) were able to demonstrate that free radical-damaged cells in an experimental model using living epithelial cells tended to produce a "favorable environment" for the development of calcium oxalate crystals. They found the vitamin C "exerted the most remarkable effects" in preventing the formation of calcium oxalate crystals.

Selvam (2002) found that "antioxidant therapy prevented calcium oxalate precipitation in the rat kidney and reduced oxalate excretion in stone patients." Gotz et al. (1986) showed that another antioxidant, lipoic acid, helped prevent the precipitation of calcium oxalate crystals in dogs. Jayanthi et al. (1994) also showed that lipoic acid was effective in lowering oxalate levels in the kidneys and urine of rats. As a powerful antioxidant, vitamin C may well have the same effects as lipoic acid. Certainly, vitamin C also quenches free radicals, prevents oxidant-induced damage, and facilitates tissue healing after such damage has been inflicted. Perhaps eliminating focal areas of such tissue damage makes it that much more difficult to initiate an abnormal deposit of calcium oxalate. This may be one significant way in which vitamin C can reduce kidney stone formation. McCormick (1946) long ago asserted that his research on vitamin C indicated that a vitamin C deficiency was "the basic etiological factor" for stone formation anywhere in the body.

A Typical Research Report Relating Vitamin C and Kidney Stone Formation

There have been isolated reports associating vitamin C administration with the formation of kidney stones and/or the worsening of kidney function. Lawton et al. (1985) reported on the case of a 58-year-old woman who developed acute kidney failure from calcium oxalate crystals depositing in the kidneys after the administration of 45,000 mg of vitamin C as ascorbic acid intravenously. However, this woman had pre-existing kidney disease (nephrotic syndrome), and a disease called amyloidosis, which was spilling large amounts of proteins (immunoglobulins) in the urine.

Amyloidosis often causes nephrotic syndrome, and that was probably the situation with this lady. Prior to the vitamin C administration, the patient was on a regimen that included doses of prednisone (steroid), melphalan and busulfan (cancer chemotherapy drugs), furosemide (diuretic), vitamin B complex, vitamin E, sodium selenite, trazodone hydrochloride (antidepressant), doxycycline (antibiotic), levothyroxine (thyroid hormone), and docusate sodium (stool softener).

This patient's urine was already concentrated with abnormal proteins, and the diuretic therapy likely depleted the body's fluids and concentrated the urine even more. The more urine is concentrated with any solutes, such as the abnormal proteins, the more likely any other dissolved substances (such as calcium oxalate) will precipitate out of solution. Congestive heart failure, an additional diagnosis suggested to be present by the authors, can also decrease the amount and rate of fluid flow in the kidney, contributing to the development of crystal formation and subsequent kidney failure. Furthermore, vitamin B12 can sometimes have toxic effects on certain individuals who take it in supplemental form rather than ingest it in dietary form. The thyroid supplement implies the lady was hypothyroid, which predisposes to even more unforeseen problems. Also, there is no evidence as to what other medicines, vitamins, and/or nutrients were added to the IV bottle along with the vitamin C.

Many adult women, especially the elderly, take regular doses of calcium supplements that are often in a rock-like form like dolomite. Excess calcium looking for a way to fall out of solution in the urine finds a ready partner with the oxalate already concentrated there. If this patient had occasion to take a significant amount of aspirin, this is yet another factor that has been shown to substantially increase urinary oxalate (El-Dakhakhny and El-Sayed, 1970). The only thing that can be stated with certainty is that vitamin C was one of many possible contributing factors to this unfortunate patient's kidney failure.

Singh et al. (1993) were able to demonstrate in guinea pigs that vitamin C alone did not cause the formation of kidney and bladder stones. However, they did show that vitamin C given in combination with calcium carbonate and an additional source of oxalate (sodium oxalate), did contribute to stone formation. This also strongly suggests that many patients who develop kidney stones after supplementing vitamin C are taking calcium ascorbate (rather than sodium ascorbate or ascorbic acid), calcium supplements, or both.

Cathcart (1993), in his experience with thousands of patients, routinely gave vitamin C infusions as sodium ascorbate in lactated Ringer's solution and nothing else (except for tiny amounts of EDTA to prevent oxidation of the vitamin C). As a result, he never reported any catastrophic events, or even any significant minor side effects. Whenever a multitude of other vitamins, minerals, and nutrients are added to a vitamin C infusion, negative outcomes cannot be reliably blamed on only the vitamin C. Furthermore, Lawton et al. even acknowledged that the wrong pH in a vitamin C infusion was capable of causing a significant conversion of the vitamin C into oxalate before it was ever given to the patient.

While the vitamin C infusion was likely a contributing factor to the unfortunate clinical outcome in the patient of Lawton et al. noted above, it would appear that multiple other factors played strong contributory roles in the precipitation of calcium oxalate crystals in the kidneys. Preexisting kidney disease should always invoke extra care in the administration of supplemental vitamin C, and additional factors such as possible dehydration secondary to chronic diuretic therapy and slow-flowing, thick urine already concentrated with abnormal amounts of protein merit close attention.

Caution and close monitoring should always be part of any additional therapies that impose more of a solute (dissolved substance) load to sick and compromised kidneys already being taxed with an abnormally high solute load. Also, as long as water retention with a disease such as congestive heart failure is not present, vigorous hydration should always accompany vitamin supplementation.

A number of other papers and case reports have attempted to connect vitamin C and increased calcium oxalate deposition with various degrees of kidney failure. However, no report could be found in which an extensive analysis of the other potential sources of oxalate and calcium was made (see itemized list above). Only rarely were *any* of the stone-promoting items previously listed even mentioned as being specifically present or absent. Every report appeared content to place all or most of the blame upon intravenous or oral vitamin C for the oxalate-related consequences. Some of these reports include the following, in which the presence of only a few of many other stone risk factors is noted:

1. Swartz et al. (1984) reported on a 22-year-old woman who developed compromised kidney function after receiving home parenteral nutrition with intravenous vitamin C following resection of nearly the entire small intestine. Both the parenteral nutrition and the small intestine resection can produce increased oxalate along with the vitamin C. Such patients also tend to be dehydrated.

2. Mashour et al. (2000) reported on a 31-year-old man who developed acute renal failure after a six-day history of headache and a three-day history of nausea and vomiting. No mention is made of what kind of vitamin C was taken,

except that it was in the form of a large number of tablets, which would have had other ingredients that could lead to oxalate production. Also, the nausea and vomiting made it highly likely he was very dehydrated, a strong predisposing condition for the formation of calcium oxalate crystals.

3. Other cases have been reported with preexisting kidney disease, a factor that will always substantially increase the risk of stone disease, regardless of what sources of oxalate production are present. Wong et al. (1994): acute renal failure after vitamin C; patient already had renal insufficiency secondary to malignant obstructive uropathy and was also ingesting large amounts of oxalate-rich herbs, including turkey rhubarb. McAllister et al. (1984): acute renal failure after intravenous vitamin C; patient already had advanced renal insufficiency; no evaluation of other possible risk factors was presented.

All sources of oxalate, including vitamin C therapy, must be carefully monitored when administered to a patient with chronic renal failure and undergoing chronic hemodialysis (Balcke et al., 1984). Indeed, a majority of patients on hemodialysis already have calcium oxalate deposits in their kidneys and hearts (Salyer and Keren, 1973), and other hemodialysis patients have established calcium oxalate deposits in their bones (Ott et al., 1986). However, the answer is also not to completely avoid vitamin C supplementation since increased oxidative stress is generated during hemodialysis and needs to be chronically addressed as well (Hultqvist et al., 1997). Recommendations vary, but multiple authors have shown the need for some vitamin C supplementation in hemodialysis patients (Ponka and Kuhlback, 1983; Ha et al., 1996).

In rat studies, Thamilselvan and Selvam (1997) have shown that oxalate itself increases oxidative stress that initiates microprecipitates in the kidney. This mandates that good antioxidant therapy should be maintained to help prevent further crystal precipitation from taking place. These authors also showed that this oxalate challenge reliably decreased the kidney levels of vitamin C, vitamin E, and glutathione. This again supports the concept that a proper balance of antioxidant therapy, which includes vitamin C, must be found in order to maintain optimal health for chronic renal failure patients.

One point needs to be clearly emphasized at this point. In reviewing the scientific literature, no report was found in which vitamin C was identified as the sole factor responsible for causing renal failure secondary to excess calcium oxalate crystal formation in a normal person. Dehydration and preexisting kidney disease are probably the two most consistent conditions and risk factors that would facilitate a dramatic decline in kidney function after vitamin C therapy. Furthermore, it is clear in reviewing the literature that very few of the many risk factors for increased oxalate formation are addressed with any precision, especially once it is known that a patient with stone disease took any vitamin C.

Would it be possible to cause calcium oxalate stone disease in an otherwise normal person with enough vitamin C? Possibly, but it would almost have to involve a situation in which substantial dehydration and/or several other of the risk factors noted above were already present. Vitamin C, as with many other nutrients and medications, should always be accompanied by generous hydration. High solute intake with low urine volume will always increase concentrations of everything present, inviting crystal precipitation. I feel that vitamin C should be given in minimal doses only if someone simply will not drink water. Even normal physiology can be pushed only so far. Specific vitamin C dosing recommendations, along with suggestions for dosing the patient at a slighter higher risk for stone formation, will be addressed in Chapter 6.

Vitamin C: Antioxidant and Prooxidant

In discussing this topic, it is first very important to know the differences between an *in vivo* research study and an *in vitro* research study. *In vivo* means the research looked at the reaction and interaction of the entire body with the substance(s) being studied, while *in vitro* means the research looked at how one thing interacted with something else outside of the body, as in the test tube. Furthermore, *in vitro* research systems can be very remote from the circumstances of the body, as in observing how two of the body's chemicals interact in a solute unrelated to the body. However, an *in vitro* study can be much closer to an *in vivo* study when, for example, living cells and tissues are researched outside of the body. Whenever trying to appreciate how much validity a given study may have to a clinical situation, one must always look at what type of study was done, how close that study reproduces the environment of the body if done outside of the body, and how many other researchers have successfully repeated similar research studies.

Under varying conditions, vitamin C has been demonstrated to have either prooxidant or antioxidant properties (Giulivi and Cadenas, 1993; Otero et al., 1997; Paolini et al., 1999). A prooxidant promotes oxidation and the increased presence of oxidative stress and free radicals, while an antioxidant does the opposite. That vitamin C can sometimes display prooxidant properties should not come as too great a surprise since it is such an effective antiviral and general antimicrobial agent. Logically, there have to exist some circumstances that allow vitamin C to attack and destroy invading microorganisms or cancer cells, often through destructive prooxidative processes, while still having a protective antioxidant effect for the normal cells of the body.

Carr and Frei (1999) reviewed 44 *in vivo* studies while addressing the question of whether vitamin C can act as a prooxidant under physiological conditions (Dillard et al., 1982; Kunert and Tappel, 1983; Blondin et al., 1986; Harats et al., 1990; Tsao et al., 1990; Fraga et al., 1991; Kimura et al., 1992; Rifici and Khachadurian, 1993; Barja et al., 1994; Green et al., 1994; Cadenas et al., 1996; Cadenas et al., 1996a; Reilly et al., 1996; Fuller et al., 1996; Mannick et al., 1996; Mulholland et al., 1996; Alessio et al., 1997; Wen et al., 1997; Samman et al., 1997; Nyyssonen et al., 1997; Helen and Vijayammal, 1997; Collis et al., 1997; Anderson et al., 1997; Tanaka et al., 1997; Cadenas et al., 1997; Prieme et al., 1997; Panayiotidis and Collis, 1997; Yamaguchi et al., 1997; Cadenas et al., 1998; Harats et al., 1998; Reddy et al., 1998; Sanchez-Quesada et al., 1998; Podmore et al., 1998; Cooke et al., 1998; Rehman et al., 1998; Lee et al., 1998; Kang et al., 1998). They found that 38 of these studies "showed a reduction in markers of oxidative DNA, lipid, and protein damage," a total of 14 demonstrated no change, and six showed laboratory evidence of increased oxidative stress after vitamin C supplementation. Carr and Frei concluded that any studies looking for a prooxidant effect from vitamin C should "be evaluated carefully as to their choice of biomarkers, methodology, study system, and experimental design to rule out any oxidation artifacts." They further concluded that vitamin C does not act as a prooxidant under typical physiological conditions.

Buettner and Jurkiewicz (1996) demonstrated that vitamin C can serve as either a prooxidant or an antioxidant depending upon its concentration in an experimental system. However, it is important to realize that vitamin C can only *directly* have an antioxidant function, meaning it can only lose electrons to another chemical in the process of becoming its oxidized form, dehydroascorbic acid. In the presence of metals like copper and iron that readily exchange electrons, the antioxidant loss of the electrons from vitamin C to these metals results in an increased ability of the metals to subsequently have a prooxidant activity in their immediate microenvironment.

In their reduced form, these catalytic metals greatly facilitate the formation of free radicals and increased oxidative stress in the form of superoxide radicals, hydroxyl radicals, and hydrogen peroxide (Miller et al., 1990). Therefore, the net effect is that vitamin C in the presence of the right concentration of iron and/or copper ions can result in prooxidant activity even though the direct and immediate effect exerted by the vitamin C was an antioxidant one. Typically, in such a catalytic metal environment, lower vitamin C concentrations favor prooxidant effects, while higher concentrations favor antioxidant effects. The researchers also observed that virtually all experimental systems where vitamin C facilitated prooxidant activity also had metal catalysts, usually as iron (Fe_3+) or copper (Cu_2+) ions. They termed the transition from prooxidant activity to antioxidant activity the "crossover" effect. They also noted that this crossover point was variable in the research published by many others (Will, 1966; Wills, 1969; Wills, 1969a; Girotti et al., 1985; Girotti et al., 1985a; Rees and Slater, 1987; Burkitt and Gilbert, 1990; Lin and Girotti, 1993; Wagner et al., 1993; Buettner et al., 1993; Wagner et al., 1994). However, the consistent finding was that where catalytic metal concentrations were relatively lower, antioxidant properties predominated. Conversely, relatively higher catalytic metal concentrations could promote prooxidant effects. This proposition also fits well with the observed clinical fact that many people have taken extremely large doses of vitamin C without ever showing any prooxidant effect.

Generally, it is only in daily dose ranges from the small recommended dietary allowance of 60 mg for the adult up to about 2,000 mg that vitamin C can ever exert a prooxidant effect. Furthermore, this would still require an unusual clinical situation in which the supplementing individual has high circulating levels or tissue levels of one or more catalytic metals.

generally, it is only in daily dose ranges from the small recommended dietary allowance of 60 mg for the adult up to about 2,000 mg that vitamin C can ever exert a prooxidant effect

Practically speaking, if a low dose of vitamin C has someone feeling at all poorly, a larger dose will almost always be the solution for feeling better when there are no exceptionally large catalytic metal excesses present. The simple reason for this suggestion is that a large amount of "excess" vitamin C is the single best immediate therapy to either quench freshly produced free radicals or undo their immediate damage to the surrounding tissues. Even if localized concentrations of catalytic metals continue to produce free radicals, extra vitamin C will always immediately neutralize them or their acute harm before chronic damage is done.

Furthermore, this is consistent with the results seen repeatedly with individuals taking mega-gram dosages of vitamin C. Podmore et al. (1998) concluded that 500 mg daily of vitamin C for six weeks increased the levels of a marker substance that indicated DNA damage resulting from increased free radicals. No analysis of the iron status in these volunteers was reported. Nevertheless, the result does raise some concern about chronically supplementing with a dose of vitamin C as low as 500 mg, which is probably roughly the amount that very many supplementers take. The many positive observed effects of much higher doses of vitamin C must be considered here, in spite of the theoretical concern that if a little is bad, more has to be worse. In fact, at least in the case of vitamin C and perhaps antioxidants in general, the exact opposite appears to be true: a little might be bad, but more is always good.

Halliwell (1996) also pointed out that vitamin C is not the only antioxidant that can be demonstrated to induce prooxidant activity. Rather, prooxidant activity is a characteristic of any compound that can receive or donate electrons in the typical oxidation-reduction chemical reaction. Many such agents, including glutathione, NADH, NADPH, and flavonoids, can be shown to promote prooxidant activities in addition to displaying their more commonly recognized antioxidant activities. Again, the presence of enough catalytic metals is typically required for the prooxidant properties to emerge (Rowley and Halliwell, 1982; Rowley and Halliwell, 1985; Hodnick et al., 1986; Laughton et al., 1989; Canada et al., 1990; Fazal et al., 1990; Sahu and Washington, 1991; Milne et al., 1993; Sahu and Gray, 1993; Ahmed et al., 1994).

Since it appears that the presence of catalytic metals is the primary requirement for causing vitamin C and other antioxidants to sometimes demonstrate prooxidant activity, it is important to know what causes these metallic ions to be available inside the body and why they are unavailable most of the time. In a healthy state, ionic copper and iron remain in forms that keep them from promoting oxidative reactions. In normal human plasma, these metallic ions remain bound and sequestered in the circulating blood proteins. No freely circulating or protein-unbound iron and copper ions are normally present (Halliwell and Gutteridge, 1986; Halliwell and Gutteridge, 1990).

Hemochromatosis is a disease characterized by a generalized overload of iron that eventually results in damage to tissues where iron is deposited. Hemochromatosis can be inherited, or it can occur secondary to a number of other predisposing factors or diseases. These secondary forms are much more common than the inherited form. Secondary hemochromatosis is commonly associated with certain types of anemia, and it is frequently seen in persons receiving too many blood transfusions or ingesting too much iron, often as supplementation. One of the initial laboratory abnormalities to appear in evolving hemochromatosis is an increased transferrin level.

Transferrin is the serum protein (ß-globulin) that binds and transports iron throughout the body. Iron bound to transferrin is not generally available for exerting a prooxidant effect with vitamin C and other antioxidants. In hemochromatosis and other iron overload disorders, a significant portion of the total plasma iron is not bound to transferrin but "circulates in the form of low molecular weight complexes" (Brissot et al., 1985). These researchers also suggested that this non-transferrin-bound iron was a likely important source of the iron that eventually deposits in the liver in iron overload disorders.

Furthermore, as iron stores increase and the transferrin in the blood approaches 100% iron saturation, the deposition of iron throughout the body in the storage form known as hemosiderin increases. Then, as hemosiderin deposits continue to grow, localized oxidative tissue damage from excess iron becomes more manifest as well. Probably because of this, hemochromatosis patients have low serum and white blood cell levels of vitamin C (Wapnick et al., 1968; O'Brien, 1974; Charlton and Bothwell, 1976; Brissot et al., 1978).

Several case reports have asserted that the administration of vitamin C to iron-overloaded patients was likely associated with negative clinical consequences (Nienhuis, 1981; McLaran et al., 1982; Rowbotham and Roeser, 1984). McLaran et al. reported that a 29-year-old man who ultimately died from congestive cardiomyopathy (poorly contracting enlarged heart) associated with hemochromatosis had been taking 1,000 mg of supplemental vitamin C daily for his last year. However, significant clinical deterioration had taken place over the last two months of his life. Generally, the median survival time after the diagnosis of hemochromatosis is only two years, and heart failure is often the immediate cause of death.

One could also hypothesize that the vitamin C supplementation had actually benefited this man for nine or 10 months, but that the disease finally prevailed. The case reported by Rowbotham and Roeser was somewhat similar. A 47-year-old man had a declining clinical picture with increasing heart failure for the prior three months leading up to his clinical presentation. He had taken 500 mg of vitamin C daily for three years, and this dose was increased to 1,000 mg daily for another year. This patient did not die, but responded well to iron chelation therapy. Again, it is very unclear whether the vitamin C supplementation was the culprit causing the clinical decline.

If vitamin C was responsible for worsening the clinical condition of either patient involved in these case reports, the relationship between vitamin C and iron becomes even more difficult to fully understand, especially in light of studies looking at the effects of vitamin C on iron-overloaded patients *in vivo*.

Berger et al. (1997) looked at the plasma vitamin C levels of 29 preterm infants and five adult controls. In these patients the authors also looked at levels of a certain form of iron felt to be biologically active and capable of causing oxidative damage *in vivo*. After looking at the laboratory markers of oxidative stress and levels of oxidized vitamin C, they concluded that vitamin C acted as an antioxidant in iron-overloaded plasma *in vivo*. Furthermore, they asserted their data indicated that vitamin C, in the presence of excess iron *in vivo*, did not cause any oxidative damage to lipids or proteins.

In healthy volunteers, Rehman et al. (1998) showed that the increased oxidative stress seen after six weeks of supplementation with both vitamin C (either 60 mg or 260 mg daily) and iron disappeared after 12 weeks of supplementation. This may indicate that longer supplementation with even small amounts of vitamin C may result in early prooxidant effects eventually giving way to antioxidant effects as body stores of vitamin C gradually increase.

This may also help to explain why a study by Shilotri and Bhat (1977), which lasted only 15 days, showed that a daily vitamin C supplement resulted in impaired white blood cell immune function rather than the anticipated improvement. Based on the work of Rehman et al., vitamin C supplementation studies should probably be extended to at least 12 weeks to better observe the long-term effects of chronic supplementation on what is being studied.

Chen et al. (2000) looked at vitamin C and iron overload in guinea pigs. They were able to demonstrate that vitamin C acted as an antioxidant to lipids *in vivo,* even in the presence of an iron overload. They also noted that iron loading by itself did not cause oxidative lipid damage, but was associated with a growth retardation and tissue damage that were not affected by the doses of vitamin C given. It was further noted that iron loading in animals with a low vitamin C status lowered vitamin E levels and increased plasma triglycerides.

This indicates that the iron in this situation probably had a nonspecific toxic effect. Such an effect would increase the triglycerides and deplete vitamin E, which was the available antioxidant. Also studying guinea pigs, Collis et al. (1997) performed *in vivo* studies looking at the effects of vitamin C and iron supplementation. Vitamin C displayed no prooxidant activity in the face of simultaneous iron supplementation. In fact, it actually *lessened* the evidence of oxidative stress induced by the iron supplementation alone. In other words, vitamin C remained a powerful protective antioxidant in this *in vivo* experimental setting, even in the presence of extra iron.

Vitamin C also plays a role in the absorption of iron from the digestive tract. In persons with low iron stores, vitamin C can significantly enhance the absorption of iron from plant sources (Gerster, 1999). Gerster also noted that a "prolonged intake of high-dose vitamin C has been shown not to change iron balance in iron replete persons." However, Gerster further commented that a proper study has not yet been done to determine whether vitamin C further enhances iron absorption in people with hemochromatosis, an effect that would be highly undesirable.

Cathcart (1993) reported treating over 20,000 patients with daily vitamin C doses ranging from 4,000 to 200,000 mg. Although he reported no significant vitamin C side effects in these patients, he also failed to mention whether any undesirable gradual accumulations of iron were taking place in any of these patients. Such a side effect would require specific blood testing since it would not show up in the routine blood testing done on most people having general checkups. Even though this side effect would be unlikely, it cannot be completely ruled out as a possibility at this time in patients with or without hemochromatosis.

Until one or more definitive studies can be conducted, blood testing of very high-dose vitamin C users should probably include at least an annual check on the levels of ferritin and iron to make sure no subclinical accumulations of iron are developing.

Vitamin C and G6PD Deficiency

Glucose-6-phosphate dehydrogenase (G6PD) is an enzyme in the red blood cell (RBC) that is critical to the physical stability of the cell. The prime function of G6PD appears to be in protecting the red blood cell from oxidative damage (Beutler, 1971). G6PD deficiency is a genetic disease inherited as an X-linked trait, predisposing the patient to episodes of mild to serious RBC rupture, known as hemolytic crises (WHO report, 1967; Marks, 1967). Multiple oxidant compounds such as primaquine, acetylphenylhydrazine, and sulfonamides have been known to provoke hemolytic crises in G6PD-deficient individuals (Jacob and Jandl, 1966).

For unclear reasons, G6PD deficiency is probably a condition that warrants some concern when giving higher doses of vitamin C, especially intravenously. Rees et al. (1993) reported on a 32-year-old man of Nigerian descent who initially did quite well in his ingestion of vitamin C and other nutrients as treatment for an HIV-positive status with generalized lymphadenopathy. Even though the patient received 40,000 mg of intravenous vitamin C three times weekly for about a month, along with 20,000 to 40,000 mg of oral vitamin C daily, he immediately sustained a hemolytic crisis with blackened urine the day after having an 80,000 mg intravenous administration of vitamin C.

This response did not appear to be readily predictable since no problem with the vitamin C dosing had been encountered for the entire month leading up to the increased dose. Subsequent testing confirmed a G6PD deficiency along with sickle cell trait. Vigorous hydration facilitated his uneventful recovery. Campbell et al. (1975) reported on a 68-year-old black man who eventually died from acute renal failure after a massive hemolytic crisis following the administration of 80,000 mg of vitamin C intravenously on two consecutive days. Testing later showed he had G6PD-deficient red blood cells.

In vitro research by Winterburn (1979) showed that a low concentration of vitamin C protected against the rupture of G6PD-deficient red blood cells. However, a higher dose of vitamin C was found to actually promote rupture. Udomratn et al. (1977) also demonstrated a reduced survival rate of G6PD-deficient red blood cells in the presence of vitamin C in rats.

Although the results of the above research and clinical reports warrant some concern when giving vitamin C to anyone with a documented G6PD deficiency, the mechanisms involved in stimulating a hemolytic crisis are not clear. Furthermore, the vast quantities of vitamin C taken throughout the world today would suggest that reports of such hemolytic crises would be far more frequent if vitamin C reliably caused red blood cell rupture whenever a G6PD deficiency is present.

The work of Marva et al. (1992) suggested that the relationship between increased vitamin C and increased rupture of G6PD deficient red blood cells is related to an increased immediate availability of iron in these cells. The ability of iron to evoke a prooxidant effect by vitamin C was addressed in the previous section.

Marva et al. looked at malaria parasite-infected red blood cells. They found that vitamin C was highly toxic to advanced forms of the malaria parasite in infected red blood cells. As the malaria parasite grows in a red blood cell, hemoglobin is progressively digested (Sherman, 1979; Vander Jagt et al., 1986; Grellier et al., 1989). This digestive process releases the iron-containing heme core from hemoglobin within the red blood cell. This may make iron more available to any vitamin C or other antioxidant present, thereby facilitating the destruction of the parasite and red blood cell through the prooxidant effect discussed in the previous section.

Consistent with this reasoning, the G6PD-deficient red blood cell has been shown to allow the release of the iron-containing heme from the hemoglobin even more readily than the normal red blood cell (Janney et al., 1986). Since locally released iron can readily be provoked to induce prooxidant activity, this provides at least one good reason why these cells are more susceptible to oxidative stress and rupture (Clark et al., 1989; Golenser and Chevion, 1989). The study of Marva et al. gives an excellent example of how vitamin C can have a very focal prooxidant effect in the destruction of an invading microbe while retaining its primary protective antioxidant effects over the remaining cells and tissues.

Calabrese et al. (1983) demonstrated that G6PD-deficient red blood cells incubated with copper and vitamin C developed "pre-hemolytic" changes. However, the authors acknowledged that the copper levels used were 15 to 30 times greater than normally found in plasma. Nevertheless, such a study does suggest that when a large enough amount of a catalytic metal such as copper is accompanied by a low enough amount of vitamin C, the "crossover" effect discussed earlier can result in a positive net amount of prooxidant activity.

Cathcart (1985) hypothesized that a high enough dose of vitamin C would tend to keep the glutathione in the G6PD-deficient red blood cells at risk in the reduced state, able to better buffer the red blood cell against any potentially hemolytic oxidant stress. A low reduced glutathione level in a G6PD-deficient red blood cell is a finding that indicates an increased risk of oxidant-induced rupture because adequate levels of reduced glutathione are needed by the red blood cell to repair any oxidant-induced damage (Kondo, 1990).

A reasonable conclusion regarding G6PD deficiency is that definite evidence exists to show that at least rarely vitamin C can promote a hemolytic crisis in individuals with this condition. It is unclear, however, exactly what circumstances will reliably predict when a hemolytic crisis will occur. Some evidence indicates that higher doses of vitamin C should have a protective effect against a hemolytic crisis in susceptible red blood cells. However, one case report clearly showed that a lower dose of vitamin C was tolerated well while a higher dose seemed to be the hemolysis-inducing factor. Certainly, many large doses of intravenous vitamin C have already been given throughout the world, and there are still very few reports of problems with G6PD-deficient patients in the literature. This is especially significant since G6PD deficiency causes some degree of anemia in over 100 million people, and it is considered the most common inborn error of metabolism.

Nevertheless, at the very least, screening for G6PD-deficient persons should be done in the patient populations considered to be at risk for this condition. The clinician would then have an early warning of any possible problems that could develop with vitamin C administration. Groups at primary risk include American blacks, black Africans, and the Mediterranean, Indian, and Southeast Asian populations.

Vitamin C and Cancer

Lee and Blair (2001) published a paper in *Science* that received widespread media coverage. It was a test tube study that concluded vitamin C facilitated the production of DNA-damaging agents known to produce mutations, which were associated with a variety of cancers.

Blair, in a press interview, wanted to emphasize the point that the study results did not mean that vitamin C causes cancer. However, the implication remained. Also, the amount of vitamin C used in the experiment of Lee and Blair was considered to be roughly the equivalent of a human supplementing 200 mg daily. Such a low dose of vitamin C is much more likely to result in a prooxidant effect compared to much larger doses. Furthermore, similar findings had already been demonstrated by numerous researchers before the work of Lee and Blair.

In addition to reaching a scientifically unsound conclusion, Lee and Blair asserted that vitamin C was "ineffective" for the prevention of cancer. A number of very current studies argue very strongly otherwise (Kromhout et al., 2000; Loria et al., 2000; Khaw et al., 2001; Simon et al., 2001). In light of the vast amounts of existing research, advising patients against a significant daily supplementation of vitamin C borders on medical malpractice, and the omission of daily vitamin C certainly opens the door to multiple degenerative diseases processes that need not otherwise develop.

While test tube research has an invaluable place in scientific research, it simply cannot be relied upon in reaching definitive clinical conclusions. What takes place in a test tube is often quite different from what takes place in humans. The primary value of an *in vitro* study is to determine how two or more chemicals react in a well-defined, reproducible, and tightly controlled environment. As already discussed in this chapter, vitamin C can easily and consistently be observed to induce prooxidant activity in the right microenvironment.

Vitamin C has already been proven as a very safe form of supplementation and therapy for chronic cancer patients. As was already noted at the start of this chapter, Casciari et al. (2001) reported that multiple cancer patients were given up to 50,000 mg of intravenous vitamin C daily for as long as eight weeks without any noteworthy negative effects. Riordan et al. (1996) gave 100,000 mg intravenous doses of vitamin C over five-hour periods daily for about a week to a terminal cancer patient with no negative effect noted. The only effects noted were a significant improvement in strength and general well-being.

100,000 mg intravenous doses of vitamin C over five-hour periods daily for about a week to a terminal cancer patient with no negative effect noted ... the only effects noted were a significant improvement in strength and general well-being

Riordan et al. (1990) reported on another cancer patient who responded well to receiving multiple 30,000 mg intravenous doses of vitamin C over an extended period of time. These authors commented that "during and after the treatments, the patient showed no toxic or unusual side effects" from the vitamin C infusions. Riordan et al. (1995) also reported on six cancer patients receiving multiple intravenous infusions of vitamin C over eight-hour periods. The amounts infused ranged from 57,500 mg to 115,000 mg, with no reported negative effects.

Although intravenous vitamin C therapy is very well-tolerated by most patients, including severely ill cancer patients, a few negative acute reactions to this form of therapy have been reported. Campbell and Jack (1979) reported negative side effects in three cancer patients, two with Hodgkin's disease and one with bronchial cancer. All three patients had evidence of a significant cancer mass in their bodies. One patient developed an acute fever and pain in the cancer mass in his chest after receiving 30,000 mg of oral and intravenous vitamin C over a period of 36 hours. Another patient had symptoms of acute mediastinal compression following a total dose of 100,000 mg of vitamin C. It would appear that some patients who have received no prior regular vi-

tamin C supplementation can be very susceptible to the effects of vitamin C on their tumor mass. Especially when the tumor mass is greater,
the vitamin C effect can cause acute cell death in the tumor, which can
release toxic by-products into the blood and/or cause an acute swelling
of the tumor mass.

Although these possibilities are rare, initial vitamin C supplementation should be no more than 3,000 to 5,000 mg daily by mouth for
at least the first week or two. Initial intravenous vitamin C infusions
should contain only 5,000 to 10,000 mg before proceeding to higher
doses. Hydration should always be vigorous, and a high volume of urinary output should be consistently maintained.

Another possible concern to some cancer patients has been reported by Basu (1977) and Calabrese (1979). In cancer patients who choose
to take laetrile as one of their chemotherapy agents, a possible side effect from the simultaneous dosing of vitamin C has been suggested.
Laetrile contains cyanide, which is normally detoxified by cysteine, a
sulfur-containing amino acid. Vitamin C, in doses of 3,000 mg daily,
has been observed to reduce both cysteine and thiocyanate levels in
the urine. This has been interpreted to mean that vitamin C lessens the
cysteine available for cyanide detoxification, and the lower thiocyanate
level means that less cyanide has been effectively metabolized.

Basu (1983) later showed that urinary thiocyanate levels in guinea pigs were significantly elevated after laetrile administration, even
though these elevations were less marked when vitamin C was also
given. No mention of any clinical evidence of cyanide toxicity was
made, however, in the guinea pigs given both vitamin C and laetrile.

Even if the above data actually indicates a degree of acutely increased cyanide toxicity in the tissues of a vitamin C supplementer
taking laetrile, lessening or eliminating vitamin C intake is not necessarily the solution. Generally, larger amounts of vitamin C will successfully address many different toxicities, even when the benefits of lower
doses of vitamin C are not clear. Cyanides are potent poisons that readily induce increased oxidative stress and the formation of free radicals
in the tissues. Kanthasamy et al. (1997) demonstrated this effect in rat
cell cultures exposed to cyanide. These authors also showed that vita-

min C lessened the cyanide-induced oxidative stress and blocked the cyanide-induced cell death in these cultures. It is a good possibility that any potential side effect of increased cyanide levels produced by laetrile and lower levels of vitamin C would be completely negated by giving more vitamin C.

Vitamin C and Intentional Immune System Suppression

There are certain medical conditions that are treated with immunosuppressive drugs. Some of these medical conditions, such as systemic lupus erythematosis or multiple sclerosis, are considered to be at least partially due to an overactive immune system. Because of this reasoning, such diseases are traditionally felt to be best treated by a combination of prescription medicines that will suppress aspects of the immune system.

In fact, many of these diseases may be largely due to unneutralized toxins. Clinically, both lupus and multiple sclerosis respond well to high-dose vitamin C therapy. If a strengthened immune system truly made these diseases worse, vitamin C therapy would not be a reasonable treatment. However, if the presence of toxins is the cause of such diseases, then vitamin C with its antitoxic properties is arguably one of the best treatment choices for such diseases.

There are other medical conditions in which immunosuppressive medical therapy is absolutely essential. Such conditions are best characterized by organ transplantations. When a patient receives a donor heart or kidney, the process of rejection mediated by the immune system must be continuously suppressed for the life of the patient, or the organ will eventually be rejected. If no new organ is available for repeat transplantation dire or even fatal consequences will likely result. Although it is not clear whether it is best to supplement such patients with multigram doses of vitamin C for an indefinite period of time, there is no doubt that some vitamin C and chronic antioxidant therapy is of great benefit to these patients.

However, it is unclear if a certain dosage level of vitamin C might increase the chances of organ rejection by strengthening the suppressed immune system too effectively. Although no definite evidence was found indicating that vitamin C in any dosage would be a problem for the transplant patient, it remains a theoretical possibility.

At least one study that supports giving vitamin C in very large doses to transplant patients came from Slakey et al. (1993). These researchers found that vitamin C increased the survival times of transplanted rat hearts. The recipient rats also received cyclosporine for immunosuppression, but vitamin C was not found to enhance the immunosuppressive effect of cyclosporine as measured by mixed lymphocyte response testing. Nevertheless, the dose of vitamin C that was successful in prolonging transplanted heart survival was approximately equivalent to 100,000 mg daily for a 200-pound person. This study certainly suggests that any of the theoretical negative effects of vitamin C on the rejection process of transplanted organs are more than outweighed by its many other positive effects since the heart transplants in rats with high-dose vitamin C clearly outlasted the heart transplants without the vitamin C.

Some clinicians may consider it better to omit vitamin C supplementation in transplant patients in order to avoid any chances of stimulating the suppressed immune systems and accelerating the rejection process. However, Williams et al. (1999) suggested that increased oxidative stress may play a major role in the rejection process for lung transplant patients. Furthermore, these authors found that this increased oxidative stress was accompanied by a compromised antioxidant status in patients. Although a study such as this confirms the need for some antioxidant supplementation, it still does not suggest the most appropriate dose.

Further evidence that some vitamin C should be given to transplant patients comes from the work of Fang et al. (2002). In a double-blind, prospective study these researchers looked at the progression of arteriosclerosis in the blood vessels of transplanted hearts. The treated group received 500 mg of vitamin C and 400 IU of vitamin E, each twice daily for one year. The researchers concluded that this regimen of vitamins C and E "retards the early progression of transplant-associated coronary arteriosclerosis."

Thorner et al. (1983) studied the white blood cells in patients who received kidney transplants. They found that the chronic steroid therapy given to these patients caused a defect in the delivery response of these immune cells to sites of bacterial invasion, which "leads to increased susceptibility to infection." These researchers found that 4,000 mg of vitamin C daily for several weeks significantly improved this delivery function in the white blood cells, "with no change noted in graft function."

The proper doses of vitamin C and other antioxidants in transplant patients will be variable, just as they are with patients who have not undergone a transplant procedure. Different people, depending upon their underlying diseases and daily toxin exposures, will require different doses of vitamin C to maintain a given blood level. Whether there is a daily dose of vitamin C in a transplant patient that should never be exceeded has not been determined.

Vitamin C and the Rebound Effect

Some authors have expressed concern that taking large doses of vitamin C can put the supplementing person at risk for developing a suddenly diminished level of vitamin C when abruptly discontinuing supplementation. To a limited degree, this assertion is valid. Tsao and Salimi (1984) looked at the urinary excretion pattern of vitamin C in two volunteers who took 10,000 mg daily. One volunteer took this dose for two weeks before discontinuation, and the other took it for six weeks. Discontinuing the vitamin C after two weeks of supplementation resulted in a drop of urinary vitamin C excretion below basal levels on the eighth day after discontinuation, and the levels remained low for two days before coming back up. The subject who supplemented for six weeks dropped less dramatically, but remained on the lower side of normal for a longer period of 12 days.

Tsao and Salimi hypothesize that vitamin C supplementation induces the increased activity of enzymes that metabolically break it down. When supplementation is abruptly discontinued, the increased enzyme activity is felt to persist temporarily while continuing to break down vitamin C at an accelerated rate. In turn, the levels of vitamin C temporarily drop below levels considered normal. Pauling (1981) had earlier hypothesized this enzyme activity induction by vitamin C.

Practically speaking, the sudden discontinuation of vitamin C will rarely have clinically significant consequences. However, if one discontinues a long-term supplementation while members of the family are sick with colds or flu, the opportunity for contracting such an infection would probably be somewhat increased. Perhaps the scenario of greatest concern involves the sudden discontinuation of long-term supplementation after being acutely hospitalized for trauma or medical illness. At such times the need for vitamin C will be greatly increased while body levels are dropping. Unless vitamin C supplementation can be continued in the hospital at perhaps even larger doses, an increased rate of complications during the hospitalization, with increased morbidity and mortality, is quite possible.

Summary

Many researchers in numerous different studies have clearly established that vitamin C is one of the safest supplements or nutrient substances that can be taken. Multigram doses of vitamin C taken daily over a period of years are virtually devoid of any side effects. Furthermore, even very high oral (200,000 mg) and intravenous (300,000 mg) doses of vitamin C over a 24-hour period have also been shown to be safe.

One of the biggest misunderstandings and ongoing misrepresentations about vitamin C is that it might place a normal person at a greater risk of developing kidney stone disease. Multiple large studies have clearly shown this concern to be completely without any basis. To the contrary, vitamin C probably lessens the incidence of kidney stones in the populations of people who supplement it regularly. Although vitamin C is known to be a contributor to the production of oxalate, which is a principal ingredient in most kidney stones, more than 50 other risk factors in addition to vitamin C have been identified for developing this type of stone disease. In patients with chronic kidney insufficiency and failure, however, vitamin C supplementation must be conservative and closely monitored. It should be added that this same concern applies to monitoring the other risk factors for stone disease, which will also become more problematic as kidney function declines. An analysis of a typical research report relating vitamin C and kidney stone formation showed that many risk factors other than vitamin C are usually present, even though the many other potential risk factors do not appear to have been considered by the authors.

Vitamin C has been documented to occasionally promote prooxidant activity in addition to its regular role as a powerful antioxidant. The prooxidant properties are found most commonly in test tube, or *in vitro*, studies. However, the presence of catalytic metals with a low enough concentration of vitamin C can result in prooxidant activity, even inside the body. Generally, however, larger doses of vitamin C protect against any possible damage that could result from focal sites of prooxidant activity, rendering this entire issue as primarily only a theoretical concern.

Because of the potential prooxidant activity of vitamin C in the face of catalytic metals, diseases that feature iron excess require careful evaluation and supplementation. Once again, using larger rather than smaller doses of vitamin C is usually a practical solution for many such patients.

G6PD deficiency, in at least a handful of reports, appears to precipitate a hemolytic crisis in the blood when vitamin C is given at a certain dosage level. From a practical standpoint, however, the very limited number of reports in light of the widespread incidence of this disorder and the widespread administration of vitamin C suggests such hemolysis is quite rare. Minimizing or eliminating vitamin C supplementation if the patient is G6PD-deficient is not necessarily in the best interests of long-term health. Testing for this disease is still appropriate so that any potential problems after initial vitamin C supplementation can be anticipated and properly monitored.

Vitamin C is an especially effective supplement for most cancer patients. The vitamin C is generally well-tolerated, and most cancer patients positively respond to this treatment. A limited number of case reports suggests that the daily vitamin C dosage for cancer patients should be built up gradually before proceeding directly to high-dose supplementation. Cancer patients who take laetrile may be at a theoretical risk of increased cyanide exposure. However, this has not been clearly demonstrated to be of clinical concern, especially when larger doses of vitamin C are regularly supplemented.

Regular high-dose vitamin C therapy over an extended time seems to induce more enzyme activity, which helps to metabolize the greater vitamin C presence. A sudden stopping of significant long-term supplementation can drop vitamin C levels significantly lower than normal for a few days. Practically, this is of little concern unless someone is acutely hospitalized and in need of greater doses of vitamin C at a time when vitamin C levels are dropping lower than normal.

Transplant patients definitely need vitamin C supplementation for optimal health and optimal organ graft function. However, whether extra-high doses of vitamin C for prolonged periods of time could stimulate immune function to more readily reject transplanted organs remains only a theoretical possibility. It is yet to be proved but worthy of clinical consideration on an individual basis.

References

Ahlstrand, C. and H. Tiselius. (1987) Urine composition and stone formation during treatment with acetazolamide. *Scandinavian Journal of Urology and Nephrology* 21(3):225-228.

Ahmed, M., K. Ainley, J. Parish, and S. Hadi. (1994) Free radical-induced fragmentation of proteins by quercetin. *Carcinogenesis* 15(8):1627-1630.

Alessio, H., A. Goldfarb, and G. Cao. (1997) Exercise-induced oxidative stress before and after vitamin C supplementation. *International Journal of Sport Nutrition* 7(1):1-9.

Alkhunaizi, A. and L. Chan. (1996) Secondary oxalosis: a cause of delayed recovery of renal function in the setting of acute renal failure. *Journal of the American Society of Nephrology* 7(11): 2320-2326.

Alvarez, M., M. Traba, and A. Rapado. (1992) Hypocitraturia as a pathogenic risk factor in the mixed (calcium oxalate/uric acid) renal stones. *Urologia Internationalis* 48(3):342-346.

Anderson, D., B. Phillips, T. Yu, A. Edwards, R. Ayesh, and K. Butterworth. (1997) The effects of vitamin C supplementation on biomarkers of oxygen radical generated damage in human volunteers with "low" or "high" cholesterol levels. *Environmental and Molecular Mutagenesis* 30(2):161-174.

Auer, B., D. Auer, and A. Rodgers. (1998) Relative hyperoxaluria, crystalluria and haematuria after megadose ingestion of vitamin C. *European Journal of Clinical Investigation* 28(9):695-700.

Auer, B., D. Auer, and A. Rodgers. (1998a) The effect of ascorbic acid ingestion on the biochemical and physicochemical risk factors associated with calcium oxalate kidney stone formation. *Clinical Chemistry and Laboratory Medicine* 36(3):143-147.

Bakane, B., S. Nagtilak, and B. Patil. (1999) Urolithiasis: a tribal scenario. *Indian Journal of Pediatrics* 66(6):863-865.

Balcke, P., P. Schmidt, J. Zazgornik, H. Kopsa, and A. Haubenstock. (1984) Ascorbic acid aggravates secondary hyperoxalemia in patients on chronic hemodialysis. *Annals of Internal Medicine* 101(3):344-345.

Barja, G., M. Lopez-Torres, R. Perez-Campo, C. Rojas, S. Cadenas, J. Prat, and R. Pamplona. (1994) Dietary vitamin C decreases endogenous protein oxidative damage, malondialdehyde, and lipid peroxidation and maintains fatty acid unsaturation in the guinea pig liver. *Free Radical Biology & Medicine* 17(2):105-115.

Bass, W., N. Malati, M. Castle, and L. White. (1998) Evidence for the safety of ascorbic acid administration to the premature infant. *American Journal of Perinatology* 15(2):133-140.

Basu, S., S. Som, S. Deb, D. Mukherjee, and I. Chatterjee. (1979) Dehydroascorbic acid reduction in human erythrocytes. *Biochemical and Biophysical Research Communications* 90(4): 1335-1340.

Basu, T. (1977) Possible toxicological aspects of megadoses of ascorbic acid. *Chemico-Biological Interactions* 16(2):247-250.

Basu, T. (1983) High-dose ascorbic acid decreases detoxification of cyanide derived from amygdalin (laetrile): studies in guinea pigs. *Canadian Journal of Physiology and Pharmacology* 61(11):1426-1430.

Belfield, W. and M. Zucker. (1993) *The Benefits of Vitamin and Minerals for Your Dog's Life Cycles. How to Have a Healthier Dog.* San Jose, CA: Orthomolecular Specialties.

Bellizzi, V., L. De Nicola, R. Minutolo, D. Russo, B. Cianciaruso, M. Andreucci, G. Conte, and V. Andreucci. (1999) Effects of water hardness on urinary risk factors for kidney stones in patients with idiopathic nephrolithiasis. *Nephron* 81(Suppl 1):66-70.

Bendich, A. and L. Langseth. (1995) The health effects of vitamin C supplementation: a review. *Journal of the American College of Nutrition* 14(2):124-136.

Berger, T., M. Polidori, A. Dabbagh, P. Evans, B. Halliwell, J. Morrow, L. Roberts, and B. Frei. (1997) Antioxidant activity of vitamin C in iron-overloaded human plasma. *The Journal of Biological Chemistry* 272(25):15656-15660.

Beutler, E. (1971) Abnormalities of the hexose monophosphate shunt. *Seminars in Hematology* 8(4):311-347.

Black, J. (1945) Oxaluria in British troops in India. *British Medical Journal* 1:590.

Blondin, J., V. Baragi, E. Schwartz, J. Sadowski, and A. Taylor. (1986) Delay of UV-induced eye lens protein damage in guinea pigs by dietary ascorbate. *Journal of Free Radicals in Biology & Medicine* 2(4):275-281.

Bode, A., C. Yavarow, D. Fry, and T. Vergas. (1993) Enzymatic basis for altered ascorbic acid and dehydroascorbic acid levels in diabetics. *Biochemical and Biophysical Research Communications* 191(3):1347-1353.

Bohles, H., B. Gebhardt, T. Beeg, A. Sewell, E. Solem, and G. Posselt. (2002) Antibiotic treatment-induced tubular dysfunction as a risk factor for renal stone formation in cystic fibrosis. *Journal of Pediatrics* 140(1):103-109.

Borghi, L., T. Meschi, F. Amato, A. Briganti, A. Novarini, and A. Giannini. (1996) Urinary volume, water and recurrences in idiopathic calcium nephrolithiasis: a 5-year randomized prospective study. *The Journal of Urology* 155(3):839-843.

Borghi, L., T. Meschi, A. Guerra, A. Briganti, T. Schianchi, F. Allegri, and A. Novarini. (1999) Essential arterial hypertension and stone disease. *Kidney International* 55(6):2397-2406.

Borghi, L., T. Meschi, T. Schianchi, A. Briganti, A. Guerra, F. Allegri, and A. Novarini. (1999a) Urine volume: stone risk factor and preventive measure. *Nephron* 81(Suppl 1):31-37.

Borghi, L., T. Schianchi, T. Meschi, A. Guerra, F. Allegri, U. Maggiore, and A. Novarini. (2002) Comparison of two diets for the prevention of recurrent stones in idiopathic hypercalciuria. *The New England Journal of Medicine* 346(2):77-84.

Brissot, P., Y. Deugnier, A. Le Treut, F. Regnouard, M. Simon, and M. Bourel. (1978) Ascorbic acid status in idiopathic hemochromatosis. *Digestion* 17(6):479-487.

Brissot, P., T. Wright, W. Ma, and R. Weisiger. (1985) Efficient clearance of non-transferrin-bound iron by rat liver. Implications for hepatic iron loading in iron overload states. *The Journal of Clinical Investigation* 76(4):1463-1470.

Broadus, A., R. Horst, R. Lang, E. Littledike, and H. Rasmussen. (1980) The importance of circulating 1,25-dihydroxyvitamin D in the pathogenesis of hypercalciuria and renal-stone formation in primary hyperparathyroidism. *The New England Journal of Medicine* 302(8):421-426.

Brox, A., K. Howson-Jan, and A. Fauser. (1988) Treatment of idiopathic thrombocytopenic purpura with ascorbate. *British Journal of Haematology* 70(3):341-344.

Buckle, R. (1963) The glyoxylic acid content of human blood and its relationship to thiamine deficiency. *Clinical Science* 25:207.

Buettner, G., E. Kelley, and C. Burns. (1993) Membrane lipid free radicals produced from L1210 murine leukemia cells by photofrin photosensitization: an electron paramagnetic resonance spin trapping study. *Cancer Research* 53(16):3670-3673.

Buettner, G. and B. Jurkiewicz. (1996) Catalytic metals, ascorbate and free radicals: combinations to avoid. *Radiation Research* 145(5):532-541.

Buno, A., R. Torres, A. Olveira, I. Fernandez-Blanco, A. Montero, and F. Mateos. (2001) Lithogenic risk factors for renal stones in patients with Crohn's disease. *Archivos Espanoles de Urologia* 54(3):282-292.

Burkitt, M. and B. Gilbert. (1990) Model studies of the iron-catalysed Haber-Weiss cycle and the ascorbate-driven Fenton reaction. *Free Radical Research Communications* 10(4-5):265-280.

Burns, J., H. Burch, and C. King. (1951) The metabolism of 1-C14-L-ascorbic acid in guinea pigs. *The Journal of Biological Chemistry* 191:501.

Bushinsky, D., J. Asplin, M. Grynpas, A. Evan, W. Parker, K. Alexander, and F. Coe. (2002) Calcium oxalate stone formation in genetic hypercalciuric stone-forming rats. *Kidney International* 61(3): 975-987.

Bussey, H., J. DeCosse, E. Deschner, A. Eyers, M. Lesser, B. Morson, S. Ritchie, J. Thomson, and J. Wadsworth. (1982) A randomized trial of ascorbic acid in polyposis coli. *Cancer* 50(7):1434-1439.

Cadenas, S., S. Lertsiri, M. Otsuka, B. Barja, and T. Miyazawa. (1996) Phospholipid hydroperoxides and lipid peroxidation in liver and plasma of ODS rats supplemented with alpha-tocopherol and ascorbic acid. *Free Radical Research* 24(6):485-493.

Cadenas, S., C. Rojas, J. Mendez, A. Herrero, and G. Barja. (1996a) Vitamin E decreases urine lipid peroxidation products in young healthy human volunteers under normal conditions. *Pharmacology & Toxicology* 79(5):247-253.

Cadenas, S., G. Barja, H. Poulsen, and S. Loft. (1997) Oxidative DNA damage estimated by oxo8dG in the liver of guinea-pigs supplemented with graded dietary doses of ascorbic acid and alpha-tocopherol. *Carcinogenesis* 18(12):2373-2377.

Cadenas, S., C. Rojas, and G. Barja. (1998) Endotoxin increases oxidative injury to proteins in guinea pig liver: protection by dietary vitamin C. *Pharmacology & Toxicology* 82(1):11-18.

Calabrese, E. (1979) Conjoint use of laetrile and megadoses of ascorbic acid in cancer treatment: possible side effects. *Medical Hypotheses* 5(9):995-997.

Calabrese, E., G. Moore, and M. McCarthy. (1983) Effect of ascorbic acid on copper-induced oxidative changes in erythrocytes of individuals with a glucose-6-phosphate dehydrogenase deficiency. *Bulletin of Environmental Contamination and Toxicology* 30(3): 323-330.

Campbell, A. and T. Jack. (1979) Acute reactions to mega ascorbic acid therapy in malignant disease. *Scottish Medical Journal* 24(2): 151-153.

Campbell, G., M. Steinberg, and J. Bower. (1975) Ascorbic acid-induced hemolysis in G-6-PD deficiency. *Annals of Internal Medicine* 82(6):810.

Canada, A., E. Giannella, T. Nguyen, and R. Mason. (1990) The production of reactive oxygen species by dietary flavonols. *Free Radical Biology & Medicine* 9(5):441-449.

Carr, A. and B. Frei. (1999) Does vitamin C act as a pro-oxidant under physiological conditions? *The FASEB Journal* 13(9):1007-1024.

Casciari, J., N. Riordan, T. Schmidt, X. Meng, J. Jackson, and H. Riordan. (2001) Cytotoxicity of ascorbate, lipoic acid, and other antioxidants in hollow fibre *in vitro* tumours. *British Journal of Cancer* 84(11):1544-1550.

Cathcart, R. (1981) Vitamin C, titrating to bowel tolerance, anascorbemia, and acute induced scurvy. *Medical Hypotheses* 7(11):1359-1376.

Cathcart, R. (1984) Vitamin C in the treatment of acquired immune deficiency syndrome (AIDS). *Medical Hypotheses* 14(4):423-433.

Cathcart, R. (1985) Vitamin C: the nontoxic, nonrate-limited, antioxidant free radical scavenger. *Medical Hypotheses* 18(1):61-77.

Cathcart, R. (1993) The third face of vitamin C. *Journal of Orthomolecular Medicine* 7(4):197-200.

Charlton, R. and T. Bothwell. (1976) Iron, ascorbic acid, and thalassemia. *Birth Defects Original Article Series* 12(8):63-71.

Chen, K., J. Suh, A. Carr, J. Morrow, J. Zeind, and B. Frei. (2000) Vitamin C suppresses oxidative lipid damage *in vivo*, even in the presence of iron overload. *American Journal of Physiology. Endocrinology and Metabolism.* 279(6):E1406-E1412.

Chen, S., T. Chen, Y. Lee, W. Chu, and T. Young. (1990) Renal excretion of oxalate in patients with chronic renal failure or nephrolithiasis. *Journal of the Formosan Medical Association* 89(8):651-656.

Clark, I., G. Chaudhri, and W. Cowden. (1989) Some roles of free radicals in malaria. *Free Radical Biology & Medicine* 6(3):315-321.

Collis, C., M. Yang, A. Diplock, T. Hallinan, and C. Rice-Evans. (1997) Effects of co-supplementation of iron with ascorbic acid on anti-oxidant—pro-oxidant balance in the guinea pig. *Free Radical Research* 27(1):113-121.

Conyers, R., R. Bais, and A. Rofe. (1990) The relation of clinical catastrophes, endogenous oxalate production, and urolithiasis. *Clinical Chemistry* 36(10):1717-1730.

Cooke, M., M. Evans, I. Podmore, K. Herbert, N. Mistry, P. Mistry, P. Hickenbotham, A. Hussieni, H. Griffiths, and J. Lunec. (1998) Novel repair action of vitamin C upon *in vivo* oxidative DNA damage. *FEBS Letters* 439(3):363-367.

Creagan, E., C. Moertel, J. O'Fallon, A. Schutt, M. O'Connell, J. Rubin, and S. Frytak. (1979) Failure of high-dose vitamin C (ascorbic acid) therapy to benefit patients with advanced cancer. A controlled trial. *The New England Journal of Medicine* 301(13):687-690.

Curhan, G., W. Willett, E. Rimm, and M. Stampfer. (1993) A prospective study of dietary calcium and other nutrients and the risk of symptomatic kidney stones. *The New England Journal of Medicine* 328(12):833-838.

Curhan, G., W. Willett, E. Rimm, and M. Stampfer. (1996) A prospective study of the intake of vitamins C and B6, and the risk of kidney stones in men. *Journal of Urology* 155(6):1847-1851.

Curhan, G., W. Willett, E. Rimm, D. Spiegelman, and M. Stampfer. (1996a) Prospective study of beverage use and the risk of kidney stones. *American Journal of Epidemiology* 143(3):240-247.

Curhan, G., W. Willett, F. Speizer, D. Spiegelman, and M. Stampfer. (1997) Comparison of dietary calcium with supplemental calcium and other nutrients as factors affecting the risk for kidney stones in women. *Annals of Internal Medicine* 126(7):497-504.

Curhan, G., W. Willett, F. Speizer, D. Spiegelman, and M. Stampfer. (1997a) Comparison of dietary calcium with supplemental calcium and other nutrients as factors affecting the risk for kidney stones in women. *Annals of Internal Medicine* 126(7):497-504.

Curhan, G., W. Willett, F. Speizer, and M. Stampfer (1999) Intake of vitamins B6 and C and the risk of kidney stones in women. *Journal of the American Society of Nephrology* 10(4):840-845.

Daskalova, S., S. Kostadinova, D. Gauster, R. Prohaska, and A. Ivanov. (1998) Are bacterial proteins part of the matrix of kidney stones? *Microbial Pathogenesis* 25(4):197-201.

Daudon, M., R. Reveillaud, M. Normand, C. Petit, and P. Jungers. (1987) Piridoxilate-induced calcium oxalate calculi: a new drug-induced metabolic nephrolithiasis. *The Journal of Urology* 138(2):258-261.

Daudon, M., R. Lacour, P. Jungers, T. Drueke, R. Reveillaud, A. Chevalier, and C. Bader. (1992) Urolithiasis in patients with end stage renal failure. *The Journal of Urology* 147(4):977-980.

Daudon, M., L. Estepa, B. Lacour, and P. Jungers. (1998) Unusual morphology of calcium oxalate calculi in primary hyperoxaluria. *Journal of Nephrology* 11(Suppl 1):51-55.

Davies, M., J. Austin, D. Partridge. (1991) *Vitamin C: Its Chemistry and Biochemistry.* Cambridge: The Royal Society of Chemistry.

Dewan, B., M. Sharma, N. Nayak, and S. Sharma. (1997) Upper urinary tract stones & *Ureaplasma urealyticum. The Indian Journal of Medical Research* 105:15-21.

Dillard, C., K. Kunert, and A. Tappel. (1982) Effects of vitamin E, ascorbic acid and mannitol on alloxan-induced lipid peroxidation in rats. *Archives of Biochemistry and Biophysics* 216(1):204-212.

Drenick, E., T. Stanley, W. Border, E. Zawada, L. Dornfield, T. Upham, and F. Llach. (1978) Renal damage with intestinal bypass. *Annals of Internal Medicine* 89(5):594-599.

El-Dakhakhny, M. and M. El-Sayed. (1970) The effect of some drugs on oxalic acid excretion in urine. *Arzneimittelforschung* 20(2): 264-267.

Ettinger, B., N. Oldroyd, and F. Sorgel. (1980) Triamterene nephrolithiasis. *The Journal of the American Medical Association* 244(21): 2443-2445.

Faber, S., W. Feitler, R. Bleiler, M. Ohlson, and R. Hodges. (1963) The effects of an induced pyridoxine and pantothenic acid deficiency on excretions of oxalic and xanthurenic acids in the urine. *The American Journal of Clinical Nutrition* 12:406.

Fang, J., S. Kinlay, J. Beltrame, H. Hikiti, M. Wainstein, D. Behrendt, J. Suh, B. Frei, G. Mudge, A. Selwyn, and P. Ganz. (2002) Effect of vitamins C and E on progression of transplant-associated arteriosclerosis: a randomized trial. *Lancet* 359(9312):1108-1113.

Fazal, F., A. Rahman, J. Greensill, K. Ainley, S. Hadi, and J. Parish. (1990) Strand scission in DNA by quercetin and Cu(II): identification of free radical intermediates and biological consequences of scission. *Carcinogenesis* 11(11):2005-2008.

Fituri, N., N. Allawi, M. Bentley, and J. Costello. (1983) Urinary and plasma oxalate during ingestion of pure ascorbic acid: a re-evaluation. *European Urology* 9(5):312-315.

Fleisch, H. (1978) Inhibitors and promoters of stone formation. *Kidney International* 13(5):361-371.

Fraga, C., P. Motchnik, M. Shigenaga, H. Helbock, R. Jacob, and B. Ames. (1991) Ascorbic acid protects against endogenous oxidative DNA damage in human sperm. *Proceedings of the National Academy of Sciences of the United States of America* 88(24): 11003-11006.

Friedman, A., R. Chesney, E. Gilbert, K. Gilchrist, R. Latorraca, and W. Segar. (1983) Secondary oxalosis as a complication of parenteral alimentation in acute renal failure. *American Journal of Nephrology* 3(5):248-252.

Fuller, C., S. Grundy, E. Norkus, and I. Jialal. (1996) Effect of ascorbate supplementation on low density lipoprotein oxidation in smokers. *Atherosclerosis* 119(2):139-150.

Furth, S., J. Casey, P. Pyzik, A. Neu, S. Docimo, E. Vining, J. Freeman, and B. Fivush. (2000) Risk factors for urolithiasis in children on the ketogenic diet. *Pediatric Nephrology* 15(1-2):125-128.

Gaker, L. and N. Butcher. (1986) Dissolution of staghorn calculus associated with amiloride-hydrochlorothiazide, sulfamethoxazole and trimethoprim, and ascorbic acid. *The Journal of Urology* 135(5):933-934.

Gershoff, S., F. Faragalla, D. Nelson, and S. Andrus. (1959) Vitamin B6 deficiency and oxalate nephrocalcinosis in the cat. *The American Journal of Medicine* 27:72.

Gershoff, S. (1964) Vitamin B6 and oxalate metabolism. *Vitamins and Hormones* 22:581.

Gerster, H. (1997) No contribution of ascorbic acid to renal calcium oxalate stones. *Annals of Nutrition & Metabolism* 41(5):269-282.

Gerster, H. (1999) High-dose vitamin C: a risk for persons with high iron stores? *International Journal for Vitamin and Nutrition Research* 69(2):67-82.

Girotti, A., J. Thomas, and J. Jordan. (1985) Lipid photooxidation in erythrocyte ghosts: sensitization of the membranes toward ascorbate- and superoxide-induced peroxidation and lysis. *Archives of Biochemistry and Biophysics* 236(1):238-251.

Girotti, A., J. Thomas, and J. Jordan. (1985a) Prooxidant and antioxidant effects of ascorbate on photosensitized peroxidation of lipids in erythrocyte membranes. *Photochemistry and Photobiology* 41(3):267-276.

Giulivi, C. and E. Cadenas. (1993) The reaction of ascorbic acid with different heme iron redox states of myoglobin. Antioxidant and prooxidant aspects. *FEBS Letters* 332(3):287-290.

Godeau, B. and P. Bierling. (1990) Treatment of chronic autoimmune thrombocytopenic purpura with ascorbate. *British Journal of Haemotology* 75(2):289-290.

Golenser, J. and M. Chevion. (1989) Oxidant stress and malaria: host-parasite interrelationships in normal and abnormal erythrocytes. *Seminars in Hematology* 26(4):313-325.

Gonzalez, C., I. Jimenez, J. Perez, R. Montero, M. Cancho, and R. Vela. (2000) [Renal colic and lithiasis in HIV(+)-patients treated with protease inhibitors]. Article in Spanish. *Actas Urologicas Espanolas* 24(3):212-218.

Gotz, F., L. Gimes, J. Hubler, G. Temes, and D. Frang. (1986) Induced precipitation of calcium-oxalate crystals and its prevention in laboratory animals. *International Urology and Nephrology* 18(4): 363-368.

Grases, F., L. Garcia-Ferragut, and A. Costa-Bauza. (1998) Development of calcium oxalate crystals on urothelium: effect of free radicals. *Nephron* 78(3):296-301.

Green, M., J. Lowe, A. Waugh, K. Aldridge, J. Cole, and C. Arlett. (1994) Effect of diet and vitamin C on DNA strand breakage in freshly-isolated human white blood cells. *Mutation Research* 316(2):91-102.

Gregory, J., K. Park, and H. Schoenberg. (1977) Oxalate stone disease after intestinal resection. *The Journal of Urology* 117(5): 631-634.

Grellier, P., I. Picard, F. Bernard, R. Mayer, H. Heidrich, M. Monsigny, and J. Schrevel. (1989) Purification and identification of a neutral endopeptidase in *Plasmodium falciparum* schizonts and merozoites. *Parasitology Research* 75(6):455-460.

Ha, T., N. Sattar, D. Talwar, J. Cooney, K. Simpson, D. O'Reilly, and M. Lean. (1996) Abnormal antioxidant vitamin and carotenoid status in chronic renal failure. *QJM: Monthly Journal of the Association of Physicians* 89(10):765-769.

Hagler, L. and R. Herman. (1973) Oxalate metabolism. I. *The American Journal of Clinical Nutrition* 26(7):758-765.

Hagler, L. and R. Herman. (1973a) Oxalate metabolism. II. *The American Journal of Clinical Nutrition* 26(8):882-889.

Hagler, L. and R. Herman. (1973b) Oxalate metabolism. III. *The American Journal of Clinical Nutrition* 26(9):1006-1010.

Hagler, L. and R. Herman. (1973c) Oxalate metabolism. IV. *The American Journal of Clinical Nutrition* 26(10):1073-1079.

Hall, W., M. Pettinger, A. Oberman, N. Watts, K. Johnson, E. Paskett, M. Limacher, and J. Hays. (2001) Risk factors for kidney stones in older women in the southern United States. *The American Journal of the Medical Sciences* 322(1):12-18.

Halliwell, B. and J. Gutteridge. (1986) Oxygen free radicals and iron in relation to biology and medicine: some problems and concepts. *Archives of Biochemistry and Biophysics* 246(2):501-514.

Halliwell, B. and J. Gutteridge. (1990) The antioxidants of human extracellular fluids. *Archives of Biochemistry and Biophysics* 280(1):1-8.

Halliwell, B. (1996) Vitamin C: antioxidant or pro-oxidant *in vivo*? *Free Radical Research* 25(5):439-454.

Hanck, A. (1982) Tolerance and effects of high doses of ascorbic acid. *Dosis facit venenum*. *International Journal for Vitamin and Nutrition Research. Supplement* 23:221-238

Harats, D., M. Ben-Naim, Y. Dabach, G. Hollander, E. Havivi, O. Stein, and Y. Stein. (1990) Effect of vitamin C and E supplementation on susceptibility of plasma lipoproteins to peroxidation induced by acute smoking. *Atherosclerosis* 85(1):47-54.

Harats, D., S. Chevion, M. Nahir, Y. Norman, O. Sagee, and E. Berry. (1998) Citrus fruit supplementation reduces lipoprotein oxidation in young men ingesting a diet high in saturated fat: presumptive evidence for an interaction between vitamins C and E *in vivo*. *The American Journal of Clinical Nutrition* 67(2):240-245.

Hatch, M., S. Mulgrew, E. Bourke, B. Keogh, and J. Costello. (1980) Effect of megadoses of ascorbic acid on serum and urinary oxalate. *European Urology* 6(3):166-169.

Helen, A. and P. Vijayammal. (1997) Vitamin C supplementation on hepatic oxidative stress induced by cigarette smoke. *Journal of Applied Toxicology* 17(5):289-295.

Hildebrandt, R. and D. Shanklin. (1962) Oxalosis and pregnancy. *American Journal of Obstetrics and Gynecology* 84:65.

Hodgkinson, A. (1958) The urinary excretion of oxalic acid in nephrolithiasis. *Proceedings of the Royal Society of Medicine* 51:970-
971.

Hodgkinson, A. and P. Zarembski. (1968) Oxalic acid metabolism in
man: a review. *Calcified Tissue Research* 2(2):115-132.

Hodnick, W., F. Kung, W. Roettger, C. Bohmont, and R. Pardini. (1986)
Inhibition of mitochondrial respiration and production of toxic oxy-
gen radicals by flavonoids. A structure-activity study. *Biochemical
Pharmacology* 35(14):2345-2357.

Hokama, S., C. Toma, M. Jahana, M. Iwanaga, M. Morozumi, T.
Hatano, and Y. Ogawa. (2000) Ascorbate conversion to oxalate
in alkaline milieu and *Proteus mirabilis* culture. *Molecular Urology*
4(4):321-328.

Hsu, T., J. Chen, H. Huang, and C. Wang. (2002) Association of
changes in the pattern of urinary calculi in Taiwanese with diet
habit change between 1956 and 1999. *Journal of the Formosan
Medical Association* 101(1):5-10.

Hughes, C., S. Dutton, and A. Truswell. (1981) High intakes of ascorbic acid and urinary oxalate. *Journal of Human Nutrition* 35(4):
274-280.

Hughes, J. and R. Norman. (1992) Diet and calcium stones. *Canadian
Medical Association Journal* 146(2):137-143.

Hultqvist, M., J. Hegbrant, C. Nilsson-Thorell, T. Lindholm, P. Nilsson,
T. Linden, and U. Hultqvist-Bengtsson. (1997) Plasma concentrations of vitamin C, vitamin E and/or malondialdehyde as markers
of oxygen free radical production during hemodialysis. *Clinical
Nephrology* 47(1):37-46.

Hwang, T., K. Hill, V. Schneider, and C. Pak. (1988) Effect of prolonged bedrest on the propensity for renal stone formation. *The
Journal of Clinical Endocrinology and Metabolism* 66(1):109-112.

Ichioka, K., S. Moroi, S. Yamamoto, T. Kamoto, H. Okuno, A. Terai, T.
Terachi, and O. Ogawa. (2002) [A case of urolithiasis due to vitamin D intoxication in a patient with idiopathic hypoparathyroid-
ism]. Article in Japanese. *Hinyokika Kiyo. Acta Urologica Japonica*
48(4):231-234.

Jacob, H. and J. Jandl. (1966) A simple visual screening test for glu-
cose-6-phosphate dehydrogenase deficiency employing ascorbate
and cyanide. *The New England Journal of Medicine* 274(21):1162-
1167.

Janney, S., J. Joist, and C. Fitch. (1986) Excess release of ferriheme in G6PD-deficient erythrocytes: possible cause of hemolysis and resistance to malaria. *Blood* 67(2):331-333.

Jayanthi, S., N. Saravanan, and P. Varalakshmi. (1994) Effect of DL alpha-lipoic acid in glyoxylate-induced acute lithiasis. *Pharmacological Research* 30(3):281-288.

Kalliala, H. and O. Kauste. (1964) Ingestion of rhubarb leaves as cause of oxalic acid poisoning. *Annales Paediatriae Fenniae* 10: 228-231.

Kalokerinos, A., I. Dettman, and G. Dettman. (1981) Vitamin C. The dangers of calcium and safety of sodium ascorbate. *The Australasian Nurses Journal* 10(3):22.

Kalokerinos, A., I. Dettman, and G. Dettman. (1982) Ascorbate—the proof of the pudding! A selection of case histories responding to ascorbate. *The Australasian Nurses Journal* 11(2):18-21.

Kang, S., Y. Jang, and H. Park. (1998) *In vivo* dual effects of vitamin C on paraquat-induced lung damage: dependence on released metals from the damaged tissue. *Free Radical Research* 28(1):93-107.

Kanthasamy, A., B. Ardelt, A. Malave, E. Mills, T. Powley, J. Borowitz, and G. Isom. (1997) Reactive oxygen species generated by cyanide mediate toxicity in rat pheochromocytoma cells. *Toxicology Letters* 93(1):47-54.

Khan, S., P. Shevock, and R. Hackett. (1988) Presence of lipids in urinary stones: results of preliminary studies. *Calcified Tissue International* 42(2):91-96.

Khan, S. and P. Glenton. (1996) Increased urinary excretion of lipids by patients with kidney stones. *British Journal of Urology* 77(4): 506-511.

Khan, S. and S. Thamilselvan. (2000) Nephrolithiasis: a consequence of renal epithelial cell exposure to oxalate and calcium oxalate crystals. *Molecular Urology* 4(4):305-312.

Khaw, K., S. Bingham, A. Welch, R. Luben, N. Wareham, S. Oakes, and N. Day. (2001) Relation between ascorbic acid and mortality in men and women in EPIC-Norfolk prospective study: a prospective population study. European Prospective Investigation into Cancer and Nutrition. *Lancet* 357(9257):657-663.

Kim, H., J. Cheigh, and H. Ham. (2001) Urinary stones following renal transplantation. *The Korean Journal of Internal Medicine* 16(2): 118-122.

Kimura, H., Y. Yamada, Y. Morita, H. Ikeda, and T. Matsuo. (1992) Dietary ascorbic acid depresses plasma and low density lipoprotein lipid peroxidation in genetically scorbutic rats. *The Journal of Nutrition* 122(9):1904-1909.

Kinder, J., C. Clark, B. Coe, J. Asplin, J. Parks, and F. Coe. (2002) Urinary stone risk factors in the siblings of patients with calcium renal stones. *The Journal of Urology* 167(5):1965-1967.

Kohan, A., N. Armenakas, and J. Fracchia. (1999) Indinavir urolithiasis: an emerging cause of renal colic in patients with human immunodeficiency virus. *The Journal of Urology* 161(6):1765-1768.

Koide, T. (1996) [Hyperuricosuria and urolithiasis]. Article in Japanese. *Nippon Rinsho* 54(12):3273-3276.

Kondo, T. (1990) [Impaired glutathione metabolism in hemolytic anemia]. Article in Japanese. *Rinsho Byori. The Japanese Journal of Clinical Pathology* 38(4):355-359.

Kromhout, D., B. Bloemberg, E. Feskens, A. Menotti, and A. Nissinen. (2000) Saturated fat, vitamin C and smoking predict long-term population all-cause mortality rates in the Seven Countries Study. *International Journal of Epidemiology* 29(2):260-265.

Kunert, K. and A. Tappel. (1983) The effect of vitamin C on *in vivo* lipid peroxidation in guinea pigs as measured by pentane and ethane production. *Lipids* 18(4):271-274.

Lamden, M. and G. Chrystowski. (1954) Urinary oxalate excretion by man following ascorbic acid ingestion. *Proceedings of the Society for Experimental Biology and Medicine* 85:190-192.

Laughton, M., B. Halliwell, P. Evans, and J. Hoult. (1989) Antioxidant and pro-oxidant actions of the plant phenolics quercetin, gossypol and myricetin. Effects on lipid peroxidation, hydroxyl radical generation and bleomycin-dependent damage to DNA. *Biochemical Pharmacology* 38(17):2859-2865.

Lawton, J., L. Conway, J. Crosson, C. Smith, and P. Abraham. (1985) Acute oxalate nephropathy after massive ascorbic acid administration. *Archives of Internal Medicine* 145(5):950-951.

Lee, B., S. Lee, and H. Kim. (1998) Inhibition of oxidative DNA damage, 8-OhdG, and carbonyl contents in smokers treated with antioxidants (vitamin E, vitamin C, beta-carotene and red ginseng). *Cancer Letters* 132(1-2):219-227.

Lee, S. and I. Blair. (2001) Vitamin C-induced decomposition of lipid hydroperoxides to endogenous genotoxins. *Science* 292(5524): 2083-2086.

Lin, F. and A. Girotti. (1993) Photodynamic action of merocyanine 540 on leukemia cells: iron-stimulated lipid peroxidation and cell killing. *Archives of Biochemistry and Biophysics* 300(2):714-723.

Long, W. and P. Carson. (1961) Increased erythrocyte glutathione reductase activity in diabetes mellitus. *Biochemical and Biophysical Research Communications* 5:394-399.

Loria, C., M. Klag, L. Caulfield, and P. Whelton. (2000) Vitamin C status and mortality in US adults. *The American Journal of Clinical Nutrition* 72(1):139-145.

Ludvigsson, J., L. Hansson, and O. Stendahl. (1979) The effect of large doses of vitamin C on leukocyte function and some laboratory parameters. *International Journal of Vitamin and Nutrition Research* 49(2):160-165.

Lux, B. and P. May. (1983) Long-term observation of young cystinuric patients under ascorbic acid therapy. *Urologia Internationalis* 38(2):91-94.

McAllister, C., E. Scowden, F. Dewberry, and A. Richman. (1984) Renal failure secondary to massive infusion of vitamin C. *The Journal of the American Medical Association* 252(13):1684.

McConnell, N., S. Campbell, I. Gillanders, H. Rolton, and B. Danesh. (2002) Risk factors for developing renal stones in inflammatory bowel disease. *BJU International* 89(9):835-841.

McCormick, W. (1946) Lithogenesis and hypovitaminosis. *Medical Record* 159:410-413.

McKay, D., J. Seviour, A. Comerford, S. Vasdev, and L. Massey. (1995) Herbal tea: an alternative to regular tea for those who form calcium oxalate stones. *Journal of the American Dietetic Association* 95(3):360-361.

McKeown-Eyssen, G., C. Holloway, V. Jazmaji, E. Bright-See, P. Dion, and W. Bruce. (1988) A randomized trial of vitamins C and E in the prevention of recurrence of colorectal polyps. *Cancer Research* 48(16):4701-4705.

McLaran, C., J. Bett, J. Nye, and J. Halliday. (1982) Congestive cardiomyopathy and haemochromatosis—rapid progression possibly accelerated by excessive ingestion of ascorbic acid. *Australian and New Zealand Journal of Medicine* 12(2):187-188.

Maikranz, P., J. Holley, J. Parks, M. Lindheimer, Y. Nakagawa, and F. Coe. (1989) Gestational hypercalciuria causes pathological urine calcium oxalate supersaturations. *Kidney International* 36(1): 108-113.

Mannick, E., L. Bravo, G. Zarama, J. Realpe, X. Zhang, B. Ruiz, E. Fontham, R. Mera, M. Miller, and P. Correa. (1996) Inducible nitric oxide synthase, nitrotyrosine, and apoptosis in *Helicobacter pylori* gastritis: effect of antibiotics and antioxidants. *Cancer Research* 56(14):3238-3243.

Marks, P. (1967) Glucose-6-phosphate dehydrogenase in mature erythrocytes. *The American Journal of Clinical Pathology* 47(3): 287-295.

Martins, M., A. Meyers, N. Whalley, and A. Rodgers. (2002) Cystine: a promoter of the growth and aggregation of calcium oxalate crystals in normal undiluted human urine. *The Journal of Urology* 167(1):317-321.

Marva, E., J. Golenser, A. Cohen, N. Kitrossky, R. Har-El, and M. Chevion. (1992) The effects of ascorbate-induced free radicals on *Plasmodium falciparum*. *Tropical Medicine and Parasitology* 43(1): 17-23.

Mashour, S., J. Turner, and R. Merrell. (2000) Acute renal failure, oxalosis, and vitamin C supplementation. *Chest* 118(2):561-563.

Massey, L., R. Palmer, and H. Horner. (2001) Oxalate content of soybean seeds (Glycine max: Leguminosae), soyfoods, and other edible legumes. *Journal of Agricultural and Food Chemistry* 49(9): 4262-4266.

Mazze, R., G. Shue, and S. Jackson. (1971) Renal dysfunction associated with methoxyflurane anesthesia. A randomized, prospective clinical evaluation. *The Journal of the American Medical Association* 216(2):278-288.

Mazze, R., J. Trudell, and M. Cousins. (1971a) Methoxyflurane metabolism and renal dysfunction: clinical correlation in man. *Anesthesiology* 35(3):247-252.

Melethil, S., D. Mason, and C. Chang. (1986) Dose-dependent absorption and excretion of vitamin C in humans. *International Journal of Pharmacology* 31:83-89.

Michelacci, Y., M. Boim, C. Bergamaschi, R. Rovigatti, and N. Schor. (1992) Possible role for chondroitin sulfate in urolithiasis: *in vivo* studies in an experimental model. *Clinica Chimica Acta* 208(1-2): 1-8.

Miller, D., G. Buettner, and S. Aust. (1990) Transition metals as catalysts of "autoxidation" reactions. *Free Radical Biology & Medicine* 8(1):95-108.

Milne, L., P. Nicotera, S. Orrenius, and M. Burkitt. (1993) Effects of glutathione and chelating agents on copper-mediated DNA oxidation: pro-oxidant and antioxidant properties of glutathione. *Archives of Biochemistry and Biophysics* 304(1):102-109.

Mitwalli, A., A. Ayiomamitis, L. Grass, and D. Oreopoulos. (1988) Control of hyperoxaluria with large doses of pyridoxine in patients with kidney stones. *International Urology and Nephrology* 20(4): 353-359.

Moertel, C., T. Fleming, E. Creagan, J. Rubin, M. O'Connell, and M. Ames. (1985) High-dose vitamin C versus placebo in the treatment of patients with advanced cancer who have had no prior chemotherapy. A randomized double-blind comparison. *The New England Journal of Medicine* 312(3):137-141.

Mousson, C., E. Justrabo, G. Rifle, C. Sgro, J. Chalopin, and C. Gerard. (1993) Piridoxilate-induced oxalate nephropathy can lead to end-stage renal failure. *Nephron* 63(1):104-106.

Mulholland, C., J. Strain, and T. Trinick. (1996) Serum antioxidant potential, and lipoprotein oxidation in female smokers following vitamin C supplementation. *International Journal of Food Sciences and Nutrition* 47(3):227-231.

Murayama, T., N. Sakai, T. Yamada, and T. Takano. (2001) Role of the diurnal variation of urinary pH and urinary calcium in urolithiasis: a study in outpatients. *International Journal of Urology* 8(10): 525-531.

Muthukumar, A. and R. Selvam. (1998) Role of glutathione on renal mitochondrial status in hyperoxaluria. *Molecular and Cellular Biochemistry* 185(1-2):77-84.

Nguyen, N., G. Dumoulin, J. Wolf, and S. Berthelay. (1989) Urinary calcium and oxalate excretion during oral fructose or glucose load in man. *Hormone and Metabolic Research* 21(2):96-99.

Nienhuis, A. (1981) Vitamin C and iron. *The New England Journal of Medicine* 304(3):170-171.

Nightingale, J. (1999) Management of patients with a short bowel. *Nutrition* 15(7-8):633-637.

Nightingale, J. (2001) Management of patients with a short bowel. *World Journal of Gastroenterology* 7(6):741-751.

Nikakhtar, B., N. Vaziri, F. Khonsari, S. Gordon, and M. Mirahmadi. (1981) Urolithiasis in patients with spinal cord injury. *Paraplegia* 19(6):363-366.

[No authors listed] (1967) Standardization of procedures for the study of glucose-6-phosphate dehydrogenase. Report of a WHO scientific group. *World Health Organization Technical Report Series* 366:1-53.

Noe, H. (2000) Hypercalciuria and pediatric stone recurrences with and without structural abnormalities. *The Journal of Urology* 164(3 Pt 2):1094-1096.

Nyyssonen, K., H. Poulsen, M. Hayn, P. Agerbo, E. Porkkala-Sarataho, J. Kaikkonen, R. Salonen, and J. Salonen. (1997) Effect of supplementation of smoking men with plain or slow release ascorbic acid on lipoprotein oxidation. *European Journal of Clinical Nutrition* 51(3):154-163.

O'Brien, R. (1974) Ascorbic acid enhancement of desferrioxamine-induced urinary iron excretion in thalassemia major. *Annals of the New York Academy of Sciences* 232:221-225.

Ogawa, Y., T. Miyazato, and T. Hatano. (2000) Oxalate and urinary stones. *World Journal of Surgery* 24(10):1154-1159.

Oke, O. (1969) Oxalic acid in plants and in nutrition. *World Review of Nutrition and Dietetics* 10:262-303.

Oren, A., H. Husdan, P. Cheng, R. Khanna, A. Pierratos, G. Digenis, and D. Oreopoulos. (1984) Calcium oxalate kidney stones in patients on continuous ambulatory peritoneal dialysis. *Kidney International* 25(3):534-538.

Osilesi, O., L. Trout, J. Ogunwole, and E. Glover. (1991) Blood pressure and plasma lipids during ascorbic acid supplementation in borderline hypertensive and normotensive adults. *Nutrition Research* 11:405-412.

Otero, P, M. Viana, E. Herrera, and B. Bonet. (1997) Antioxidant and prooxidant effects of ascorbic acid, dehydroascorbic acid and flavonoids on LDL submitted to different degrees of oxidation. *Free Radical Research* 27(6):619-626.

Ott, S., D. Andress, and D. Sherrard. (1986) Bone oxalate in a long-term hemodialysis patient who ingested high doses of vitamin C. *American Journal of Kidney Diseases* 8(6):450-454.

Panayiotidis, M. and A. Collins. (1997) *Ex vivo* assessment of lymphocyte antioxidant status using the comet assay. *Free Radical Research* 27(5):533-537.

Paolini, M., L. Pozzetti, G. Pedulli, E. Marchesi, and G. Cantelli-Forti. (1999) The nature of prooxidant activity of vitamin C. *Life Sciences* 64(23):PL-273-PL-278.

Pauling, L. (1981) *Vitamin C, the Common Cold & the Flu.* New York, NY: Berkley Books.

Perez-Brayfield, M., D. Caplan, J. Gatti, E. Smith, and A. Kirsch. (2002) Metabolic risk factors for stone formation in patients with cystic fibrosis. *The Journal of Urology* 167(2 Pt 1):480-484.

Podmore, I., H. Griffiths, K. Herbert, N. Mistry, P. Mistry, and J. Lunec. (1998) Vitamin C exhibits pro-oxidant properties. *Nature* 392(6676):559.

Ponka, A. and B. Kuhlback. (1983) Serum ascorbic acid in patients undergoing chronic hemodialysis. *Acta Medica Scandinavica* 213(4):305-307.

Powell, R. (1985) Pure calcium carbonate gallstones in a two year old in association with prenatal calcium supplementation. *Journal of Pediatric Surgery* 20(2):143-144.

Prie, D., V. Ravery, L. Boccon-Gibod, and G. Friedlander. (2001) Frequency of renal phosphate leak among patients with calcium nephrolithiasis. *Kidney International* 60(1):272-276.

Prieme, H., S. Loft, K. Nyyssonen, J. Salonen, and H. Poulsen. (1997) No effect of supplementation with vitamin E, ascorbic acid, or coenzyme Q10 on oxidative DNA damage estimated by 8-oxo-7,8-dihydro-2'-deoxyguanosine excretion in smokers. *The American Journal of Clinical Nutrition* 65(2):503-507.

Pru, C., J. Eaton, and C. Kjellstrand. (1985) Vitamin C intoxication and hyperoxalemia in chronic hemodialysis patients. *Nephron* 39(2):112-116.

Ralph-Edwards, A., M. Deitel, D. Maziak, E. Stone, D. Thompson, and T. Bayley. (1992) A jejuno-ileal bypass patient presenting with recurrent renal stones due to primary hyperparathyroidism. *Obesity Surgery* 2(3):265-268.

Reaven, P., A. Khouw, W. Beltz, S. Parthasarathy, and J. Witztum. (1993) Effect of dietary antioxidant combinations in humans. Protection of LDL by vitamin E but not by beta-carotene. *Arteriosclerosis and Thrombosis* 13(4):590-600.

Reddy, V., F. Giblin, L. Lin, and B. Chakrapani. (1998) The effect of aqueous humor ascorbate on ultraviolet-B-induced DNA damage in lens epithelium. *Investigative Ophthalmology & Visual Science* 39(2):344-350.

Rees, D., H. Kelsey, and J. Richards. (1993) Acute haemolysis induced by high dose ascorbic acid in glucose-6-phosphate dehydrogenase deficiency. *BMJ* 306(6881):841-842.

Rees, S. and T. Slater. (1987) Ascorbic acid and lipid peroxidation: the cross-over effect. *Acta Biochimica et Biophysica Hungarica* 22:241-249.

Rehman, A., C. Collis, M. Yang, M. Kelly, A. Diplock, B. Halliwell, and C. Rice-Evans. (1998) The effects of iron and vitamin C co-supplementation on oxidative damage to DNA in healthy volunteers. *Biochemical and Biophysical Research Communications* 246(1): 293-298.

Reilly, M., N. Delanty, J. Lawson, and G. FitzGerald. (1996) Modulation of oxidant stress *in vivo* in chronic cigarette smokers. *Circulation* 94(1):19-25.

Rifici, V. and A. Khachadurian. (1993) Dietary supplementation with vitamins C and E inhibits *in vitro* oxidation of lipoproteins. *Journal of the American College of Nutrition* 12(6):631-637.

Riobo, P., O. Sanchez, S. Azriel, J. Lara, and J. Herrera. (1998) [Update on the role of diet in recurrent nephrolithiasis]. Article in Spanish. *Nutricion Hospitalaria* 13(4):167-171.

Riordan, H., J. Jackson, and M. Schultz. (1990) Case study: high-dose intravenous vitamin C in the treatment of a patient with adenocarcinoma of the kidney. *Journal of Orthomolecular Medicine* 5(1): 5-7.

Riordan, H., H. Riordan, X. Meng, Y. Li, and J. Jackson. (1995) Intravenous ascorbate as a tumor cytotoxic chemotherapeutic agent. *Medical Hypotheses* 44(3):207-213.

Riordan, N., J. Jackson, and H. Riordan. (1996) Intravenous vitamin C in a terminal cancer patient. *Journal of Orthomolecular Medicine* 11(2):80-82.

Rodman, J. and R. Mahler. (2000) Kidney stones as a manifestation of hypercalcemic disorders. Hyperparathyroidism and sarcoidosis. *The Urologic Clinics of North America* 27(2):275-285, viii.

Rose, R. and A. Bode. (1992) Tissue-mediated regeneration of ascorbic acid: is the process enzymatic? *Enzyme* 46(4-5):196-203.

Rowbotham, B. and H. Roeser. (1984) Iron overload associated with congenital pyruvate kinase deficiency and high dose ascorbic acid ingestion. *Australian and New Zealand Journal of Medicine* 14(5): 667-669.

Rowley, D. and B. Halliwell. (1982) Superoxide-dependent formation of hydroxyl radicals from NADH and NADPH in the presence of iron salts. *FEBS Letters* 142(1):39-41.

Rowley, D. and B. Halliwell. (1985) Formation of hydroxyl radicals from NADH and NADPH in the presence of copper salts. *Journal of Inorganic Biochemistry* 23(2):103-108.

Sahu, S. and M. Washington. (1991) Quercetin-induced lipid peroxidation and DNA damage in isolated rat-liver nuclei. *Cancer Letters* 58(1-2):75-79.

Sahu, S. and G. Gray. (1993) Interactions of flavonoids, trace metals, and oxygen: nuclear DNA damage and lipid peroxidation induced by myricetin. *Cancer Letters* 70(1-2):73-79.

Sakhaee, K., S. Nigam, P. Snell, M. Hsu, and C. Pak. (1987) Assessment of the pathogenetic role of physical exercise in renal stone formation. *The Journal of Clinical Endocrinology and Metabolism* 65(5):974-979.

Salyer, W. and D. Keren. (1973) Oxalosis as a complication of chronic renal failure. *Kidney International* 4(1):61-66.

Samman, S., A. Brown, C. Beltran, and S. Singh. (1997) The effect of ascorbic acid on plasma lipids and oxidisability of LDL in male smokers. *European Journal of Clinical Nutrition* 51(7):472-477.

Sanchez-Quesada, J., O. Jorba, A. Payes, C. Otal, R. Serra-Grima, F. Gonzalez-Sastre, and J. Ordonez-Llanos. (1998) Ascorbic acid inhibits the increase in low-density lipoprotein (LDL) susceptibility to oxidation and the proportion of electronegative LDL induced by intense aerobic exercise. *Coronary Artery Disease* 9(5):249-255.

Sarkissian, A., A. Babloyan, N. Arikyants, A. Hesse, N. Blau, and E. Leumann. (2001) Pediatric urolithiasis in Armenia: a study of 198 patients observed from 1991 to 1999. *Pediatric Nephrology* 16(9): 728-732.

Scheid, C., H. Koul, W. Hill, J. Luber-Narod, L. Kennington, T. Honeyman, J. Jonassen, and M. Menon. (1996) Oxalate toxicity in LLC-PK1 cells: role of free radicals. *Kidney International* 49(2): 413-419.

Schmidt, K., V. Hagmaier, D. Hornig, J. Vuilleumier, and G. Rutishauser. (1981) Urinary oxalate excretion after large intakes of ascorbic acid in man. *American Journal of Clinical Nutrition* 34(3):305-311.

Schwartz, B., J. Bruce, S. Leslie, and M. Stoller. (2001) Rethinking the role of urinary magnesium in calcium urolithiasis. *Journal of Endourology* 15(3):233-235.

Schwille, P., A. Schmiedl, U. Herrmann, M. Manoharan, J. Fan, V. Sharma, and D. Gottlieb. (2000) Ascorbic acid in idiopathic recurrent calcium urolithiasis in humans—does it have an abettor role in oxalate, and calcium oxalate crystallization? *Urology Research* 28(3):167-177.

Selvam, R. (2002) Calcium oxalate stone disease: role of lipid peroxidation and antioxidants. *Urological Research* 30(1):35-47.

Sharma, D. and R. Mathur. (1995) Correction of anemia and iron deficiency in vegetarians by administration of ascorbic acid. *Indian Journal of Physiology and Pharmacology* 39(4):403-406.

Sharma, O. (1996) Vitamin D, calcium, and sarcoidosis. *Chest* 109(2):535-539.

Sherman, I. (1979) Biochemistry of *Plasmodium* (malarial parasites). *Microbiological Reviews* 43(4):453-495.

Shields, M. and R. Simmons. (1976) Urinary calculus during methazolamide therapy. *American Journal of Ophthalmology* 81(5): 622-624.

Shilotri, P. and K. Bhat. (1977) Effect of mega doses of vitamin C on bactericidal activity of leukocytes. *The American Journal of Clinical Nutrition* 30(7):1077-1081.

Shiraishi, K., M. Yamamoto, K. Takai, Y. Tei, A. Suga, A. Aoki, K. Ishizu, and K. Naito. (1998) [Urolithiasis associated with Crohn's disease: a case report]. Article in Japanese. *Hinyokika Kiyo. Acta Urologica Japonica.* 44(10):719-723.

Silverberg, D., J. McIntyre, R. Ulan, and E. Gain. (1971) Oxalic acid excretion after methoxyflurane and halothane anaesthesia. *Canadian Anaesthetists' Society Journal* 18(5):496-504.

Simon, J. and E. Hudes. (1999) Relation of serum ascorbic acid to serum vitamin B12, serum ferritin, and kidney stones in US adults. *Archives of Internal Medicine* 159(6):619-624.

Simon, J., E. Hudes, and J. Tice. (2001) Relation of serum ascorbic acid to mortality among US adults. *Journal of the American College of Nutrition* 20(3):255-263.

Singh, P., R. Kiran, A. Pendse, R. Gosh, and S. Surana. (1993) Ascorbic acid is an abettor in calcium urolithiasis: an experimental study. *Scanning Microscopy* 7(3):1041-1047; discussion 1047-1048.

Singh, P., M. Barjatiya, S. Dhing, R. Bhatnagar, S. Kothari, and V. Dhar. (2001) Evidence suggesting that high intake of fluoride provokes nephrolithiasis in tribal populations. *Urological Research* 29(4):238-244.

Slakey, D., A. Roza, G. Pieper, C. Johnson, and M. Adams. (1993) Delayed cardiac allograft rejection due to combined cyclosporine and antioxidant therapy. *Transplantation* 56(6):1305-1309.

Sohshang, H., M. Singh, N. Singh, and S. Singh. (2000) Biochemical and bacteriological study of urinary calculi. *The Journal of Communicable Diseases* 32(3):216-221.

Sundaram, C. and B. Saltzman. (1999) Urolithiasis associated with protease inhibitors. *Journal of Endourology* 13(4):309-312.

Swartz, R., J. Wesley, M. Somermeyer, and K. Lau. (1984) Hyperoxaluria and renal insufficiency due to ascorbic acid administration during total parenteral nutrition. *Annals of Internal Medicine* 100(4):530-531.

Takenouchi, K., K. Aso, K. Kawase, H. Ichikawa, and T. Shiomi. (1966) On the metabolites of ascorbic acid, especially oxalic acid, eliminated in urine, following the administration of large amounts of ascorbic acid. *The Journal of Vitaminology* 12(1):49-58.

Tallquist, H. and I. Vaananen. (1960) Death of a child from oxalic acid poisoning due to eating rhubarb leaves. *Annales Paediatriae Fenniae* 6:144-147.

Tanaka, K., T. Hashimoto, S. Tokumaru, H. Iguchi, and S. Kojo. (1997) Interactions between vitamin C and vitamin E are observed in tissues of inherently scorbutic rats. *The Journal of Nutrition* 127(10): 2060-2064.

Taylor, A., P. Jacques, D. Nadler, F. Morrow, S. Sulsky, and D. Shepard. (1991) Relationship in humans between ascorbic acid consumption and levels of total and reduced ascorbic acid in lens, aqueous humor, and plasma. *Current Eye Research* 10(8):751-759.

Tekin, A., S. Tekgul, N. Atsu, A. Sabin, H. Ozen, and M. Bakkaloglu. (2000) A study of the etiology of idiopathic calcium urolithiasis in children: hypocitruria is the most important risk factor. *The Journal of Urology* 164(1):162-165.

Terris, M., M. Issa, and J. Tacker. (2001) Dietary supplementation with cranberry concentrate tablets may increase the risk of nephrolithiasis. *Urology* 57(1):26-29.

Thamilselvan, S. and R. Selvam. (1997) Effect of vitamin E and mannitol on renal calcium oxalate retention in experimental nephrolithiasis. *Indian Journal of Biochemistry & Biophysics* 34(3): 319-323.

Thorner, R., C. Barker, and R. MacGregor. (1983) Improvement of granulocyte adherence and *in vivo* granulocyte delivery by ascorbic acid in renal transplant patients. *Transplantation* 35(5): 432-436.

Tiselius, H. and L. Almgard. (1977) The diurnal urinary excretion of oxalate and the effect of pyridoxine and ascorbate on oxalate excretion. *European Urology* 3(1):41-46.

Torrecilla, C., C. Gonzalez-Satue, L. Riera, S. Colom, E. Franco, F. Aguilo, and N. Serrallach. (2001) [Incidence and treatment of urinary lithiasis in renal transplantation]. Article in Spanish. *Actas Urologicas Espanolas* 25(5):357-363.

Torres, V., S. Erickson, L. Smith, D. Wilson, R. Hattery, and J. Segura. (1988) The association of nephrolithiasis and autosomal dominant polycystic kidney disease. *American Journal of Kidney Diseases* 11(4):318-325.

Torres, V., D. Wilson, R. Hattery, and J. Segura. (1993) Renal stone disease in autosomal dominant polycystic kidney disease. *American Journal of Kidney Diseases* 22(4):513-519.

Trinchieri, A., F. Rovera, R. Nespoli, and A. Curro. (1996) Clinical observations on 2086 patients with upper urinary tract stone. *Archivio Italiano di Urologia, Andrologia* 68(4):251-262.

Tsao, C. and S. Salimi. (1984) Evidence of rebound effect with ascorbic acid. *Medical Hypotheses* 13(3):303-310.

Tsao, C., L. Xu, and M. Young. (1990) Effect of dietary ascorbic acid on heat-induced eye lens protein damage in guinea pigs. *Ophthalmic Research* 22(2):106-110.

Tsugawa, N., T. Yamabe, A. Takeuchi, M. Kamao, K. Nakagawa, K. Nishijima, and T. Okano. (1999) Intestinal absorption of calcium from calcium ascorbate in rats. *Journal of Bone and Mineral Metabolism* 17(1):30-36.

Turner, M., D. Goldwater, and T. David. (2000) Oxalate and calcium excretion in cystic fibrosis. *Archives of Disease in Childhood* 83(3):244-247.

Udomratn, T., M. Steinberg, G. Campbell, and F. Oelshlegel. (1977) Effects of ascorbic acid on glucose-6-phosphate dehydrogenase-deficient erythrocytes: studies in an animal model. *Blood* 49(3): 471-475.

Urivetzky, M., D. Kessaris, and A. Smith. (1992) Ascorbic acid overdosing: a risk factor for calcium oxalate nephrolithiasis. *The Journal of Urology* 147(5):1215-1218.

Vander Jagt, D., L. Hunsaker, and N. Campos. (1986) Characterization of a hemoglobin-degrading, low molecular weight protease from *Plasmodium falciparum*. *Molecular and Biochemical Parasitology* 18(3):389-400.

Wagner, B., G. Buettmer, and C. Burns. (1993) Increased generation of lipid-derived and ascorbate free radicals by L1210 cells exposed to the ether lipid edelfosine. *Cancer Research* 53(4):711-713.

Wagner, B., G. Buettner, and C. Burns. (1994) Free radical-mediated lipid peroxidation in cells: oxidizability is a function of cell lipid bis-allylic hydrogen content. *Biochemistry* 33(15):4449-4453.

Wall, I. and H. Tiselius. (1990) Long-term acidification of urine in patients treated for infected renal stones. *Urologia Internationalis* 45(6):336-341.

Wapnick, A., S. Lynch, P. Krawitz, H. Seftel, R. Charlton, and T. Bothwell. (1968) Effects of iron overload on ascorbic acid metabolism. *British Medical Journal* 3(620):704-707.

Wen, Y., T. Cooke, and J. Feely. (1997) The effect of pharmacological supplementation with vitamin C on low-density lipoprotein oxidation. *British Journal of Clinical Pharmacology* 44(1):94-97.

Whitson, P., R. Pietrzyk, and C. Pak. (1997) Renal stone risk assessment during Space Shuttle flights. *The Journal of Urology* 158(6): 2305-2310.

Whitson, P., R. Pietrzyk, and C. Pak. (1999) Space flight and the risk of renal stones. *Journal of Gravitational Physiology* 6(1):P87-P88.

Wilk, I. (1976) Problem-causing constituents of vitamin C tablets. *Journal of Chemical Education* 53(1):41-43.

Williams, A., G. Riise, B. Anderson, C. Kjellstrom, H. Schersten, and F. Kelly. (1999) Compromised antioxidant status and persistent oxidative stress in lung transplant recipients. *Free Radical Research* 30(5):383-393.

Williams, H. and L. Smith. (1968) Disorders of oxalate metabolism. *The American Journal of Medicine* 45(5):715-735.

Wills, E. (1966) Mechanisms of lipid peroxide formation in animal tissues. *The Biochemical Journal* 99(3):667-676.

Wills, E. (1969) Lipid peroxide formation in microsomes. General considerations. *The Biochemical Journal* 113(2):315-324.

Wills, E. (1969a) Lipid peroxide formation in microsomes. The role of non-haem iron. *The Biochemical Journal* 113(2):325-332.

Wolf, C., G. Maistre-Charransol, C. Barthelemy, E. Thomas, J. Thomas, G. Arvis, and A. Steg. (1985) [Calcium oxalate stones and hyperoxaluria secondary to treatment with pyridoxilate]. Article in French. *Annales d'urologie* 19(5):313-317.

Wong, K., C. Thomson, R. Bailey, S. McDiarmid, and J. Gardner. (1994) Acute oxalate nephropathy after a massive intravenous dose of vitamin C. *Australian and New Zealand Journal of Medicine* 24(4):410-411.

Wu, D. and M. Stoller. (2000) Indinavir urolithiasis. *Current Opinion in Urology* 10(6):557-561.

Yagisawa, T., T. Hayashi, A. Yoshida, H. Okuda, H. Kobayashi, N. Ishikawa, N. Goya, and H. Toma. (1999) Metabolic characteristics of the elderly with recurrent calcium oxalate stones. *BJU International* 83(9):924-928.

Yagisawa, T., C. Kobayashi, T. Hayashi, A. Yoshida, and H. Toma. (2001) Contributory metabolic factors in the development of nephrolithiasis in patients with medullary sponge kidney. *American Journal of Kidney Diseases* 37(6):1140-1143.

Yamaguchi, S., S. Yachiku, M. Okuyama, M. Tokumitsu, S. Kaneko, and H. Tsurukawa. (2001) Early stage of urolithiasis formation in experimental hyperparathyroidism. *The Journal of Urology* 165(4):1268-1273.

Yamaguchi, T., T. Hashizume, M. Tanaka, M. Nakayama, A. Sugimoto, S. Ikeda, H. Nakajima, and F. Horio. (1997) Bilirubin oxidation provoked by endotoxin treatment is suppressed by feeding ascorbic acid in a rat mutant unable to synthesize ascorbic acid. *European Journal of Biochemistry* 245(2):233-240.

Zarembski, P. and A. Hodgkinson. (1962) The oxalic acid content of English diets. *The British Journal of Nutrition* 16:627-634.

Zarembski, P. and A. Hodgkinson. (1969) Some factors influencing the urinary excretion of oxalic acid in man. *Clinica Chimica Acta* 25(1):1-10.

Chapter Five

Liposome Technology and Intracellular Bioavailability

*Real knowledge is to know the extent
of one's ignorance.*

CONFUCIUS (551-479 B.C.)

Overview

Since Frederick Klenner, MD established the enormous therapeutic utility of vitamin C in a wide variety of diseases and medical conditions, the added clinical benefit of intravenous administration over all other routes of administration became readily apparent and increasingly indisputable over time. Patients with diseases resistant to oral vitamin C administration repeatedly demonstrated dramatic responses to vitamin C given intravenously. Indeed, the intravenous administration of vitamin C rapidly established itself as the "gold standard" of vitamin C treatment modalities. Similarly, the technique of intravenous administration, in general, has long been considered the optimal way to deliver virtually any drug or nutrient into the body. It has always been intuitively reasoned that the delivery of a drug or nutrient directly into the bloodstream had to be the most beneficial and effective form of administration.

435

Although still little known to many active health care practitioners, the science of liposome technology initially emerged in the 1960s (Bangham et al., 1965) and has continued to be refined in its scientific development and practical clinical applications over the last 40 years or so (Gregoriadis, 2007). The huge potential of this exciting technology is only really beginning to be appreciated now. In a nutshell, the oral administration of liposome encapsulated nutrients and drugs has many defined and unequivocal advantages over their intravenous administration. Why this technology may someday soon make many intravenous therapies effectively obsolete or at least secondary forms of administration will be addressed in the rest of this chapter.

The Liposome

Liposomes are microscopic spheres of phospholipids that are stable in water and able to contain water-soluble substances (Walde et al., 1990; Walde and Ichikawa, 2001). Simplistically, a conventional liposome is structurally similar to many of the cells in the body. Phospholipids, particularly phosphatidylcholine, are prominent components of both natural cell walls as well as liposome walls. When phospholipids are placed in a water environment, they naturally form these liposomal spheres spontaneously, similar to when oil is put in water. This occurs because a phospholipid is a long molecule with a water-soluble (hydrophilic or water-seeking) end and a fat-soluble (hydrophobic or fat-seeking) end. The fat-seeking ends are driven to avoid the water and to clump together, resulting in the natural formation of a membrane that is comprised of the fat-seeking ends of the phospholipid molecules on the inside and the water-seeking tails of the molecules facing to the outside. This membrane then naturally collapses into many tiny spheres containing the water in which it was formed. Depending on what is already dissolved in the water when the phospholipids are added, any of a wide variety of substances can be encapsulated in liposomes.

Liposome Characteristics (Conventional)

The basic, unmodified ("nontargeted") liposome has certain characteristics making it an extraordinarily useful tool for the efficient and typically nontoxic administration of a wide variety of drugs and nutrients. These characteristics include the following:

1. Excellent absorption after oral administration. Regardless of the substance encapsulated in the liposomes, an excellent absorption into the blood, or lymph, can be expected (Ling et al., 2006)

2. Protection of the encapsulated substance from digestion or degradation. Until the substance is released from the liposome, it will remain largely inert to its environment inside the body. The substance will not be broken down or metabolized by enzymes in the gut or in the blood, and the substance will exert none of its chemical/biological effects while inside the liposome. For substances with a deliberately toxic profile, like cancer-killing agents, much less clinical toxicity can be expected because of these liposome properties.

3. Supplemental value of the lipid content of the liposome by itself. The typical unmodified and unloaded liposome contains a large amount of phosphatidylcholine (PC). PC and its closely related components appear to have a multitude of different positive effects even when given alone. These effects include the following:

   a. Antioxidant (Das et al., 2007)

   b. Anti-atherosclerotic (Altman et al., 1980; Levy, 2006)

   c. Cholesterol-lowering (Mastellone et al., 2000)

   d. Tissue protection from ischemia (Aabdallah and Eid, 2004; Demirbilek et al., 2006)

   e. Treatment and prevention of liver disease (Lieber, 2004; Buang et al., 2005; Lamireau et al., 2007)

   f. Treatment and prevention of cell membrane damage (Lubin et al., 1972; Demirbilek et al., 2004)

    g. Protection against pancreatic damage (Lee et al., 2003)

    h. Protection against gallstone formation (Kasbo et al., 2003)

    i. Vital role in the metabolism of the nucleus and its membrane (Albi et al., 2008)

4. Deep intracellular access. The similarity of the liposome membrane to the cell membranes in the body allow absorption/passage of the liposome to the intracellular space (cytoplasm), as well as into structures within the cells, such as mitochondria (Yamada and Harashima, 2008), endoplasmic reticula, and even the nuclei (Rawat et al., 2007).

5. Absorption without energy consumption. An unmodified liposome can result in the absorption of a substance from the gut into the blood, and from the blood into the cytoplasm and organelles within the cells, in an *energy-sparing* way. Many large molecules require energy-consuming, active membrane transport mechanisms for intracellular access (Baumrucker, 1985). For even a relatively small molecule like vitamin C, much of its delivery from the blood into the cells — in both its active form and its oxidized (dehydroascorbate) form — requires the expenditure of cellular energy (Goldenberg and Schweinzer, 1994; Puskas et al., 2000; Liang et al., 2001; Wilson, 2005). In addition cellular energy (as glutathione) must ultimately be spent, or oxidized, to restore the dehydroascorbate form of vitamin C to its active, reduced state inside the cell (Meister, 1994). This is especially inefficient since the function of vitamin C as an antioxidant is to deliver electrons, not deplete them. However, when vitamin C is given in its most common forms (not in liposomes), the ultimate goal of increased intracellular levels of active vitamin C requires the depletion of other antioxidants to be achieved.

6. Greater uptake by macrophages (scavenger cells) relative to other cells. When the encapsulated substance is a potent antioxidant such as vitamin C, the function of these important immune cells can be enhanced.

7. Distribution throughout the body. This is a feature of the unmodified liposome. Such a property is highly desirable when the encapsulated substance is a nutrient that is useful to all the cells of the body. Liposome modifications can be introduced that can target certain cells, such as cancer cells, with encapsulated drugs that are highly toxic and not desirable for distribution throughout the body. Many modifications to liposomes can be introduced, including the following:
   a. Encapsulated contents
   b. Size
   c. Surrounding membrane thickness (multilamellar)
   d. Type of phospholipids in the membranes
   e. Membrane-entrapped drugs or substances (fat-soluble)
   f. Membrane-attached immunoglobulins, protein antigens, antibodies, or polyethylene glycol (PEG) [surface-modified] (Cattel et al., 2004; Schnyder and Huwyler, 2005)
   g. Sensitivity to pH
   h. Positive charge (cationic liposomes)

A Unique Marriage: Liposomes and Antioxidants

A wide variety of antioxidant and nutrient substances have already been effectively administered therapeutically and in research models with the use of liposome technology. These include, but are not limited to, the following:

1. Vitamin C (Hickey et al., 2008)

2. Vitamin E (Yao et al., 1994; Wu and Zern, 1999)

3. Vitamin A (Lee et al., 2002; Sato et al., 2008)

4. Beta carotene, carotenoids (Chen and Djuric, 2001; Socaciu et al., 2002; Pintea et al., 2005; Gouranton et al., 2008)

5. Glutathione (Wendel, 1983; Rosenblat et al., 2007; Mirahmadi et al., 2008)

6. L-cysteine (El Kateb et al., 2008)

7. N-acetylcysteine (Hoesel et al., 2008)

8. Superoxide dismutase (Chan et al., 1987; Imaizumi et al., 1990; Nakae et al., 1990)

9. Silibinin, silymarin (Maheshwari et al., 2003; El-Samaligy et al., 2006)

10. Adenosine triphosphate [ATP] (Chapat et al., 1991; Puisieux et al., 1994; Konno et al., 1996; Verma et al., 2005; Korb et al., 2008)

11. Quercetin [flavonoid antioxidant] (Sarkar and Das, 2006; Mandal et al., 2007; Rivera et al., 2008)

12. Rutin [flavonoid antioxidant] (Goniotaki et al., 2004; Xi and Guo, 2007)

13. Catalase (Yoshimoto et al., 2006; Jubeh et al., 2006)

14. Coenzyme Q10 [ubiquinone] (Verma et al., 2007)

15. Resveratol (Caddeo et al., 2008)

16. Melatonin (Dubey et al., 2007; Dubey et al., 2008)

17. Combination antioxidants [carotenoids and glutathione] (Junghans et al., 2000); [vitamin C and vitamin E] (Waters et al., 1997)

The above list, which is but a minimal sampling of the wide array of such substances that can be administered to the body in a liposomal form, is reflective of the enormous potential utility of this type of drug/nutrient delivery system.

Intravenous Impact with Oral Administration

Vitamin C is an ideal substance for delivery by the basic, nontargeted liposome technology. Already documented to deliver roughly twice the maximum amount of vitamin C to the blood previously believed to be possible with other more "traditional" forms of oral vitamin C (Hickey et al., 2008), the clinical impact of liposome encapsulated vitamin C appears to exceed even the clinical impact of intravenous vitamin C. It would appear that the ability of liposomes to deliver their contents inside the cells, often without the consumption of energy (electrons) in the process, makes this intracellular bioavailability of the encapsulated substance to be superior to even intravenous infusion.

While the 100% delivery of something directly into the blood offers a tremendous advantage over all known forms of oral administration, intravenous infusion of any substance does not assure a direct, non-energy-depleting, access to the inside of cells, which is where the "sickness" is in most ill individuals. However, this is not to suggest that intravenous vitamin C is not highly beneficial and should never be used. Much of the incredible information and research in this book clearly attests otherwise. Because of this, a sick, possibly toxic, individual is best advised to receive vitamin C by both the oral liposome encapsulated route and the intravenous route whenever possible. These two routes of administration work synergistically in optimizing the antioxidant capacity for treating a given condition. However, given the choice of only one or the other, adequately dosed oral liposome encapsulated vitamin C will prove to be clinically superior to intravenous vitamin C in most instances.

When the condition is very acute and largely contained in the blood, as with an acute intoxication such as a venomous snakebite, an intravenous infusion may well prove to be superior to any oral preparation, liposome-based or otherwise. However, the emphasis is on the immediacy of the clinical situation, as snakebite toxins will likely prove to be more responsive to the liposome encapsulated vitamin C after they have entered the cells and poisoned them from within. Given together, however, intravenous vitamin C and oral liposome encapsulated vitamin C are proving to be a combination that would have even made Dr. Klenner envious.

The dosing of oral liposome encapsulated vitamin C is approached in the same empirical manner that Dr. Klenner used on all of his patients. As the liposome encapsulated vitamin C is absorbed very rapidly when taken on an empty stomach, additional dosing can follow the initial dosing by as little as 30 to 60 minutes in the pursuit of a satisfactory clinical response. This is similar to the initial time frame of clinical response seen with intravenous dosing. When it is clear that the patient is responding positively and the clinical condition is clearly resolving, dosing may be maintained at the same frequency without further increase in dose amount. As with all vitamin C and antioxidant therapy, never discontinue therapy for at least 24 to 48 hours after the condition of the patient is felt to be completely cured or resolved. This is especially the case with rapidly evolving viral diseases. As with all other forms of vitamin C therapy, a poor or inadequate clinical response to liposome encapsulated vitamin C is best approached with a more vigorous and protracted dosing schedule.

Summary

Drug delivery systems utilizing liposome technology are revolutionizing the medical therapies for a variety of different medical diseases and conditions, although they still remain enormously overlooked or neglected. The biochemical characteristics of liposomes allow ready intracellular access for their encapsulated substances. The clinical responses of infected and toxic patients with adequate amounts of oral liposome encapsulated therapy, particularly vitamin C, are even often surpassing the clinical responses seen with intravenous therapies. In the case of vitamin C, the difference can be dramatic. A much smaller oral dose of liposome encapsulated vitamin C (5 to 10 grams) often results in a clearly superior clinical response than a much larger dose of vitamin C given intravenously (25 to 100 grams). Of course, when a critically ill individual has access to both intravenous and liposome encapsulated forms of therapy, it is best to take both. However, intravenous therapy is time-consuming, expensive, and of limited availability to many people. It is also associated with occasional but significant side effects (for example, inflamed veins or infection at the site), and it is often uncomfortable or even painful during administration. Liposome encapsulated vitamin C can now extend the amazing benefits of properly-dosed vitamin C to very many more people than ever before.

References

Aabdallah, D. and N. Eid. (2004) Possible neuroprotective effects of lecithin and alpha-tocopherol alone or in combination against ischemia/reperfusion insult in rat brain. *Journal of Biochemical and Molecular Toxicology* 18(5):273-278.

Albi, E., R. Lazzarini, and M. Viola Magni (2008) Phosphatidylcholine/ sphingomyelin metabolism crosstalk inside the nucleus. *The Biochemical Journal* 410(2):381-389.

Altman, R., G. Schaeffer, C. Salles, A. Ramos de Souza, and P. Cotias. (1980) Phospholipids associated with vitamin C in experimental atherosclerosis. *Arzneimittelforschung* 30(4):627-630.

Bangham, A., M. Standish, and J Watkins. (1965) Diffusion of univalent ions across the lamellae of swollen phospholipids. *Journal of Molecular Biology* 13(1):238-252.

Baumrucker, C. (1985) Amino acid transport systems in bovine mammary tissue. *Journal of Dairy Science* 68(9):2436-2451.

Buang, Y., Y. Wang, J. Cha, K. Nagao, and T. Yanagita (2005) Dietary phosphatidylcholine alleviates fatty liver induced by orotic acid. *Nutrition* 21(7-8):867-873.

Caddeo, C., K. Teskac, C. Sinico, and J. Kristl. (2008) Effect of resveratol incorporated in liposomes on proliferation and UV-B protection of cells. *International Journal of Pharmaceutics* 363(1-2): 183-191.

Cattel, L., M. Ceruti, and F. Dosio. (2004) From conventional to stealth liposomes: a new frontier in cancer chemotherapy. *Journal of Chemotherapy* 16 Suppl 4:94-97.

Chan, P., S. Longar, and R. Fishman. (1987) Protective effects of liposome-entrapped superoxide dismutase on posttraumatic brain edema. *Annals of Neurology* 21(6):540-547.

Chapat, S., V. Frey, N. Claperon, C. Bouchaud, F. Puisieux, P. Couvreur, P. Rossignol, and J. Delattre. (1991) Efficiency of liposomal ATP in cerebral ischemia: bioavailability features. *Brain Research Bulletin* 26(3):339-342.

Chen, G. and Z. Djuric. (2001) Carotenoids are degraded by free radicals but do not affect lipid peroxidation in unilamellar liposomes under different oxygen tensions. *FEBS Letters* 505(1):151-154.

Das, S., G. Gupta, D. Rao, and D. Vasudevan. (2007) Effect of lecithin with vitamin-B complex and tocopheryl acetate on long-term effect of ethanol induced immunomodulatory activities. *Indian Journal of Experimental Biology* 45(8):683-688.

Demirbilek, S., M. Ersoy, S. Demirbilek, A. Karaman, M. Akin, M. Bayraktar, and N. Bayraktar. (2004) Effects of polyenylphosphatidylcholine on cytokines, nitrite/nitrate levels, antioxidant activity and lipid peroxidation in rats with sepsis. *Intensive Care Medicine* 30(10):1974-1978.

Demirbilek, S., A. Karaman, A. Baykarabulut, M. Akin, K. Gurunluoglu, E. Turkman, E. Tas, R. Aksoy, and M. Edali (2006) Polyenylphosph atidylcholine pretreatment ameliorates ischemic acute renal injury in rats. *International Journal of Urology: Official Journal of the Japanese Urological Association* 13(6):747-753.

Dubey, V., D. Mishra, and N. Jain. (2007) Melatonin loaded ethanolic liposomes: physicochemical characterization and enhanced transdermal delivery. *European Journal of Pharmaceutics and Biopharmaceutics* 67(2):398-405.

Dubey, V., D. Mishra, M. Nahar, and N. Jain. (2008) Elastic liposomes mediated transdermal delivery of an anti-jet lag agent: preparation, characterization and *in vitro* human skin transport study. *Current Drug Delivery* 5(3):199-206.

El Kateb, N., L. Cynober, J. Chaumeil, and G. Dumortier. (2008) L-cysteine encapsulation in liposomes: effect of phospholipids nature on entrapment efficiency and stability. *Journal of Microencapsulation* 25(6):399-413.

El-Samaligy, M., N. Afifi, and E. Mahmoud. (2006) Evaluation of hybrid liposomes-encapsulated silymarin regarding physical stability and *in vivo* performance. *International Journal of Pharmaceutics* 319(1-2):121-129.

Goldenberg, H. and E. Schweinzer. (1994) Transport of vitamin C in animal and human cells. *Journal of Bioenergetics and Biomembranes* 26(4):359-367.

Goniotaki, M., S. Hatziantoniou, K. Dimas, M. Wagner, and C. Demetzos. (2004) Encapsulation of naturally occurring flavonoids into liposomes: physicochemical properties and biological activity against human cancer cell lines. *The Journal of Pharmacy and Pharmacology* 56(10):1217-1224.

Gouranton, E., C. Yazidi, N. Cardinault, M. Amiot, P. Borel, and J. Landrier. (2008) Purified low-density lipoprotein and bovine serum albumin efficiency to internalize lycopene into adipocytes. *Food and Chemical Toxicology* Oct. 11. [Epub ahead of print]

Gregoriadis, G. [ed.] (2007) *Liposome Technology. Third edition. Volume I: Liposome Preparation and Related Techniques.* New York, NY: Informa Healthcare USA, Inc.

Gregoriadis, G. [ed.] (2007) *Liposome Technology. Third edition. Volume II: Entrapment of Drugs and Other Materials into Liposomes.* New York, NY: Informa Healthcare USA, Inc.

Gregoriadis, G. [ed.] (2007) *Liposome Technology. Third edition. Volume III: Interactions of Liposomes with the Biological Milieu.* New York, NY: Informa Healthcare USA, Inc.

Hickey, S., H. Roberts, and N. Miller. (2008) Pharmacokinetics of oral vitamin C. *Journal of Nutritional & Environmental Medicine* July 31.

Hoesel, L., M. Flierl, A. Niederbichler, D. Rittirsch, S. McClintock, J. Reuben, M. Pianko, W. Stone, H. Yang, M. Smith, J. Sarma, and P. Ward. (2008) Ability of antioxidant liposomes to prevent acute and progressive pulmonary injury. *Antioxidants & Redox Signaling* 10(5):973-981.

Imaizumi, S., V. Woolworth, R. Fishman, and P. Chan. (1990) Liposome-entrapped superoxide dismutase reduces cerebral infarction in cerebral ischemia in rats. *Stroke* 21(9):1312-1317.

Jubeh, T., M. Nadler-Milbauer, Y. Barenholz, and A. Rubinstein. (2006) Local treatment of experimental colitis in the rat by negatively charged liposomes of catalase, TMN and SOD. *Journal of Drug Targeting* 14(3):155-163.

Junghans, A., H. Sies, and W. Stahl. (2000) Carotenoid-containing unilamellar liposomes loaded with glutathione: a model to study hydrophobic-hydrophilic antioxidant interaction. *Free Radical Research* 33(6):801-808.

Kasbo, J., B. Tuchweber, S. Perwaiz, G. Bouchard, H. Lafont, N. Domingo, F. Chanussot, and I. Yousef. (2003) Phosphatidylcholine-enriched diet prevents gallstone formation in mice susceptible to cholelithiasis. *Journal of Lipid Research* 44(12):2297-2303.

Konno, H., A. Matin, Y. Maruo, S. Nakamura, and S. Baba. (1996) Liposomal ATP protects the liver from injury during shock. *European Surgical Research* 28(2):140-145.

Korb, V., K. Tep, V. Escriou, C. Richard, D. Scherman, L. Cynober, J. Chaumeil, and G. Dumortier. (2008) Current data on ATP-containing liposomes and potential prospects to enhance cellular energy status for hepatic applications. *Critical Reviews in Therapeutic Drug Carrier Systems* 25(4):305-345.

Lamireau, T., G. Bouchard, I. Yousef, H. Clouzeau-Girard, J. Rosenbaum, A. Desmouliere, and B. Tuchweber. (2007) Dietary lecithin protects against cholestatic liver disease in cholic acid-fed Abcb4- deficient mice. *Pediatric Research* 61(2):185-190.

Lee, S., H. Yuk, D. Lee, K. Lee, Y. Hwang, and R. Ludescher. (2002) Stabilization of retinol through incorporation into liposomes. *Journal of Biochemistry and Molecular Biology* 35(4):358-363.

Lee, S., Y. Han, B. Min, and I. Park. (2003) Cytoprotective effects of polyenoylphosphatidylcholine (PPC) on beta-cells during diabetic induction by streptozotocin. *The Journal of Histochemistry and Cytochemistry* 51(8):1005-1015.

Levy, T. (2006) *Stop America's #1 Killer. Reversible Vitamin Deficiency Found to be Origin of ALL Coronary Heart Disease.* Henderson, NV: LivOn Books.

Liang, W., D. Johnson, and S. Jarvis. (2001) Vitamin C transport systems of mammalian cells. *Molecular Membrane Biology* 18(1): 87-95.

Lieber, C. (2004) Alcoholic fatty liver: its pathogenesis and mechanism of progression to inflammation and fibrosis. *Alcohol* 34(1): 9-19.

Ling, S., E. Magosso, N. Khan, K. Yuen, and S. Barker. (2006) Enhanced oral bioavailability and intestinal lymphatic transport of a hydrophilic drug using liposomes. *Drug Development and Industrial Pharmacy* 32(3):335-345.

Lubin, B., S. Shohet, and D. Nathan. (1972) Changes in fatty acid metabolism after erythrocyte peroxidation: stimulation of a membrane repair process. *The Journal of Clinical Investigation* 51(2): 338-344.

Maheshwari, H., R. Agarwal, C. Patil, and O. Katare. (2003) Preparation and pharmacological evaluation of silibinin liposomes. *Arzneimittelforschung* 53(6):420-427.

Mandal, A., S. Das, M. Basu, R. Chakrabarti, and N. Das. (2007) Hepatoprotective activity of liposomal flavonoid against arsenite-induced liver fibrosis. *The Journal of Pharmacology and Experimental Therapeutics* 320(3):994-1001.

Mastellone, I., E. Polichetti, S. Gres, C. de la Maisonneuve, N. Domingo, V. Marin, A. Lorec, C. Farnarier, H. Portugal, G. Kaplanski, F. Chanussot. (2000) Dietary soybean phosphatidylcholines lower lipidemia: mechanisms at the levels of intestine, endothelial cell, and hepato-biliary axis. *The Journal of Nutritional Biochemistry* 11(9):461-466.

Meister, A. (1994) Glutathione-ascorbic acid antioxidant system in animals. *The Journal of Biological Chemistry* 269(13):9397-9400.

Mirahmadi., N., M. Babaei, A. Vali, F. Daha, F. Kobarfard, and S. Dadashzadeh. (2008) 99mTc-HMPAO-labeled liposomes: an investigation into the effects of some formulation factors on labeling efficiency and *in vitro* stability. *Nuclear Medicine and Biology* 35(3):387-392.

Nakae, D., K. Yamamoto, H. Yoshiji, T. Kinugasa, H. Maruyama, J. Farber, and Y. Konishi. (1990) Liposome-encapsulated superoxide dismutase prevents liver necrosis induced by acetaminophen. *American Journal of Pathology* 136(4):787-795.

Pintea, A., H. Diehl, C. Momeu, L. Aberle, and C. Socaciu. (2005) Incorporation of carotenoid esters into liposomes. *Biophysical Chemistry* 118(1):7-14.

Puisieux, F., E. Fattal, M. Lahiani, J. Auger, P. Jouannet, P. Couvreur, and J. Delattre. (1994) Liposomes, an interesting tool to deliver a bioenergetic substrate (ATP). *In vitro* and *in vivo* studies. *Journal of Drug Targeting* 2(5):443-448.

Puskas, F., P. Gergely, Jr., K. Banki, and A. Perl. (2000) Stimulation of the pentose phosphate pathway and glutathione levels by dehydroascorbate, the oxidized form of vitamin C. *The FASEB Journal* 14(10):1352-1361.

Rawat, A., B. Vaidya, K. Khatri, A. Goyal, P. Gupta, S. Mahor, R. Paliwal, S. Rai, and S. Vyas. (2007) Targeted intracellular delivery of therapeutics: an overview. *Die Pharmazie* 62(9):643-658.

Rivera, F., G. Costa, A. Abin, J. Urbanavicius, C. Arruti, G. Casanova, and F. Dajas. (2008) Reduction of ischemic brain damage and increase of glutathione by a liposomal preparation of quercetin in permanent focal ischemia in rats. *Neurotoxicity Research* 13(2): 105-114.

Rosenblat, M., N. Volkova, R. Coleman, and M. Aviram. (2007) Antioxidant and anti-atherogenic properties of liposomal glutathione: studies *in vitro*, and in the atherosclerotic apolipoprotein E-deficient mice. *Atherosclerosis* 195(2):e61-e68.

Sarkar, S. and N. Das. (2006) Mannosylated liposomal flavonoid in combating age-related ischemia-reperfusion induced oxidative damage in rat brain. *Mechanisms of Ageing and Development* 127(4):391-397.

Sato, Y., K. Murase, J. Kato, M. Kobune, T. Sato, Y. Kawano, R. Takimoto, K. Takada, K. Miyanishi, T. Matsunaga, T.Takayama, and Y. Niitsu. (2008) Resolution of liver cirrhosis using vitamin A-coupled liposomes to deliver siRNA against a collagen-specific chaperone. *Nature Biotechnology* 26(4):431-442.

Schnyder, A. and J. Huwyler. (2005) Drug transport to brain with targeted liposomes. *NeuroRx: The Journal of the American Society for Experimental NeuroTherapeutics* 2(1):99-107.

Socaciu, C., P. Bojarski, L. Aberle, and H. Diehl. (2002) Different ways to insert carotenoids into liposomes affect structure and dynamics of the bilayer differently. *Biophysical Chemistry* 99(1):1-15.

Verma, D., T. Levchenko, E. Bernstein, and V. Torchilin. (2005) ATP-loaded liposomes effectively protect mechanical functions of the myocardium from global ischemia in an isolated rat heart model. *Journal of Controlled Release* 108(2-3):460-471.

Verma, D., W. Hartner, V. Thakkar, T. Levchenko, and V. Torchilin. (2007) Protective effect of coenzyme Q10-loaded liposomes on the myocardium in rabbits with an acute experimental myocardial infarction. *Pharmaceutical Research* 24(11):2131-2137.

Walde, P., A. Giuliani, C. Boicelli, and P. Luisi. (1990) Phospholipid-based reverse micelles. *Chemistry and Physics of Lipids* 53(4): 265-288.

Walde, P. and S. Ichikawa. (2001) Enzymes inside lipid vesicles: preparation, reactivity and applications. *Biomolecular Engineering* 18(4):143-177.

Waters, R., L. White, and J. May. (1997) Liposomes containing alpha-tocopherol and ascorbate are protected from an external oxidant stress. *Free Radical Research* 26(4):373-379.

Wendel, A. (1983) Hepatic lipid peroxidation: caused by acute drug intoxication, prevented by liposomal glutathione. *International Journal of Clinical Pharmacology Research* 3(6):443-447.

Wilson, J. (2005) Regulation of vitamin C transport. *Annual Review of Nutrition* 25:105-125.

Wu, J. and M. Zern. (1999) NF-kappa B, liposomes and pathogenesis of hepatic injury and fibrosis. *Frontiers in Bioscience* 4:D520-D527.

Xi, J. and R. Guo. (2007) Interactions between flavonoids and hemoglobin in lecithin liposomes. *International Journal of Biological Macromolecules* 40(4):305-311.

Yamada, Y. and H. Harashima. (2008) Mitochondrial drug delivery systems for macromolecule and their therapeutic application to mitochondrial diseases. *Advanced Drug Delivery Reviews* 60(13-14):1439-1462.

Yao, T., S. Esposti, L. Huang, R. Arnon, A. Spangenberger, and M. Zern. (1994) Inhibition of carbon tetrachloride-induced liver injury by liposomes containing vitamin E. *The American Journal of Physiology* 267(3 Pt 1):G476-G484.

Yoshimoto, M., Y. Miyazaki, Y. Kudo, K. Fukunaga, and K. Nakao. (2006) Glucose oxidation catalyzed by liposomal glucose oxidase in the presence of catalase-containing liposomes. *Biotechnology Progress* 22(3):704-709.

Chapter Six

Practical Suggestions

*I've been guilty myself, in many instances, of
thinking, when some new exciting idea comes
along, "This can't be right."*

PAUL GREENGARD
AWARDED THE 2000 NOBEL PRIZE
IN PHYSIOLOGY OR MEDICINE

Balancing Antioxidant Supplementation

While the evidence clearly demonstrates that vitamin C is the premier antioxidant and arguably the premier nutrient in the body, a supplementation regimen that features exclusively vitamin C is certainly not being recommended. However, the importance of vitamin C is such that taking it alone may well be of greater benefit than taking any other combination of supplements that completely exclude vitamin C. The recommendations in this chapter should be regarded as my opinions and general guidelines only, and the reader is advised to obtain the guidance of a qualified health care professional before adopting any long-term supplementation regimens.

A good supplementation program, in addition to vitamin C as ascorbic acid or sodium ascorbate, should include vitamin A (as beta

451

carotene), vitamin E, and the B vitamins. However, B12 supplementation should be limited to documented states of deficiency, and hydroxy-cobalamin should be taken rather than cyanocobalamin to gradually restore B12 levels. Important antioxidants that can be added include alpha lipoic acid, coenzyme Q10, silibinin or silymarin, glutathione, and N-acetyl cysteine. Taking a variety of the important antioxidants has certain direct benefits in addition to keeping vitamin C levels up by continuously converting oxidized vitamin C back to the metabolically active reduced form. Flavonoids, such as quercetin and rutin, are also important supporters of vitamin C's metabolic functions.

There is no magic dosage for any of the supplements. Like vitamin C, much higher doses of a given supplement might be indicated for a given medical condition versus a much lower maintenance dose to support and maintain good health. Cost is a consideration, as well as the decision on how many pills one is willing to take each day.

Optidosing with Regular Oral Vitamin C

For the average healthy adult, taking a daily dose of vitamin C ranging between 6,000 and 12,000 mg will generally meet the body's metabolic needs. Most adults will need a dosage closer to 12,000 mg than to 6,000 mg. Taking less than 6,000 mg of vitamin C a day would be an optidose for only a few individuals. It should be taken into consideration, however, that the only real chance of encountering a prooxidant effect with vitamin C occurs in the context of lower dose ranges (see Chapter 4). A prooxidant effect is rare at any dose, but doses of 500 mg or less will increase the chance of its occurrence. The practical determination of a vitamin C optidose for an individual is best calculated after determining one's bowel tolerance as described by Cathcart (1981). Depending upon one's underlying medical diseases or daily toxin exposure, this bowel tolerance can vary widely from person to person. Chronic cancer patients and chronic infection patients like those with AIDS can have bowel tolerances of 100,000 mg of vitamin C or higher. However, most healthy individuals with an average body size will demonstrate a bowel tolerance effect between 10,000 and 15,000 mg of vitamin C.

Once the bowel tolerance has been determined, taking approximately the same dose of vitamin C in three or four divided doses throughout the day will meet the body's daily need for vitamin C without causing the bowel tolerance "flushing" effect. If diarrhea or loosened bowels are experienced even with the divided dosing regimen, then the dose should be adjusted downward until the effect is no longer present. Remember, however, that vitamin C-induced diarrhea is a good thing to periodically undergo since it cleans out the bowels and detoxifies pockets of toxicity that are harbored in the gut. Therefore, if the bowel tolerance symptoms are not an inconvenience it is likely even better for long-term health to keep vitamin C doses at levels inducing these symptoms. Generally, if one's baseline health remains stable, and new infections or new medical conditions do not develop, the vitamin C bowel tolerance dosage should remain stable. Sometimes you may be able to infer that your body has encountered a new infective challenge when your vitamin C bowel tolerance rather suddenly increases. This generally indicates that the body's requirement for vitamin C has acutely increased. If you notice this, increase your vitamin C dosing accordingly. As you maintain your vitamin C doses near your bowel tolerance, you should also gradually develop a greater health "intuition." Unless there is exposure to a very high titer of infectious microorganisms all at once, you should remain common cold- and flu-free. However, you will sometimes notice days where you are not clearly sick, but you are also not completely well. Your energy level might be off a bit, but it probably will not prevent you from doing whatever you need to do. The end result is that when you maintain a regular optidose of vitamin C, just being a bit "off" will usually be as sick as you get when faced with even the biggest of infectious and toxic challenges.

Discussed at greater length in Chapter 5, there is now available an oral liposome encapsulated form of vitamin C. As it is proving to be more effective clinically than even intravenous vitamin C, it should always be the vitamin C form of choice if available. However, if either liposome encapsulated vitamin C orally or regular vitamin C intravenously is not available, these optidosing principles in the context of bowel tolerance should be followed carefully to maximize the attainable benefits of vitamin C therapy. Even in this most traditional form of administration, vitamin C can offer much more clinical benefit than many of the different traditional medical therapies offered today.

Treating Infections and Toxin Exposure

Klenner lead the way in establishing the optimal doses of vitamin C for treating individuals with an acute infection or significant toxin exposure. Klenner (1971) asserted that in order to "bring about quick reversal" of both infectious and toxic insults to the body, the initial vitamin C must be given intravenously, in doses ranging from 350 mg to 1,200 mg/kg body weight. He added that when the dose of vitamin C was under 400 mg/kg of body weight, the injection could be made directly by syringe as long as the solution was adequately buffered to neutral pH with sodium bicarbonate, and every 1,000 mg of vitamin C was diluted to at least a five cc volume. The injecting solution could be dextrose in water, saline in water, or Ringer's lactate. This IV push application should be limited to very critically ill patients who could die before an IV bottle for continuous infusion can be prepared.

Intravenous dosing is straightforward. Sterile water, saline, and Ringer's lactate solution are probably the best choices of IV fluid. Vitamin C as sodium ascorbate or ascorbic acid buffered to pH neutrality with sodium bicarbonate can be added directly to these fluids. A final fluid volume of 500 cc in the IV bottle or bag with a total of 50,000 mg of vitamin C works very well. As a general rule, when combating infection or toxicity, do not add anything else to the IV. Mixing a wide variety of supplements in with the vitamin C can have mixed results, and any other nutrients or supplements can be given orally. Future research may produce superior IV combinations, but pure vitamin C solutions without additions have been shown to work exceptionally well.

As Klenner demonstrated on numerous occasions, intravenous vitamin C can be given very quickly or slowly, depending upon the circumstances. For acute toxic exposures, such as occurs with a poisonous snake bite, let the IV run in rapidly since the toxin increases its damage the longer it remains unneutralized, and a certain dosage level of vitamin C must ultimately be reached to completely neutralize the venom dose. A 500 cc IV bottle with 50,000 mg vitamin C can be infused in as few as 50 to 60 minutes under such circumstances.

When treating less critical toxin exposures and most clinically stable infections, infusing the 500 cc bottle of vitamin C should take from two to four hours. With comatose or mentally confused encephalitis patients, however, go as fast as you can since death can occur very quickly. Starting with 5,000 to 15,000 mg of vitamin C IV push is a good way to initiate therapy in such patients.

There is no absolute cookbook approach for the best vitamin C doses to finish out a treatment plan after the patient initially shows a positive response. Fever, pulse rate, and the lessening of the patient's primary presenting symptoms dictate how aggressive the continuing dosing of vitamin C must be. What is probably most important to remember is that you should err on the side of excess vitamin C and duration of therapy to assure no unexpected clinical relapse occurs some time after the last high doses.

Patients must be vigorously hydrated, and high volumes of urine output must be maintained. Of course, this is generally good medical advice, but it is especially important when giving high doses of vitamin C or any other medicines to critically ill patients with fever, increased rates of fluid loss, and generally decreased fluid intakes.

Patients with Kidney Disease

Hydration to insure high urine volume is especially important when administering vitamin C to patients with kidney disease. This can generally be accomplished if the patient is still producing normal amounts of urine and has not proceeded to a state of acute or chronic renal failure requiring dialysis. Most patients should drink at least two quarts of water daily. If urine flow does not immediately pick up with increased water intake, oral or intravenous doses of rapidly acting diuretics can be given when highest blood levels of vitamin C are felt to be present. Such diuretic therapy ensures brisk urine flow when the blood presents a high solute load to the kidneys.

It is absolutely essential that any patient with compromised renal function review completely all of the risk factors leading to increased urinary oxalate listed in Chapter 4. The patient needs to take some personal responsibility in reviewing these risk factors since the literature seems to indicate that many doctors are not nearly thorough enough in this risk factor review on their kidney stone-prone patients.

The form of vitamin C supplementation should never be calcium ascorbate. Sodium ascorbate and ascorbic acid are the supplement forms of choice. Calcium ascorbate provides an additional source of calcium to associate with oxalate and possibly precipitate out in the urinary tract as stones. Furthermore, there is no evidence that calcium ascorbate has any therapeutic advantages over sodium ascorbate and ascorbic acid. Supplemental forms of vitamin C also include what are known as mineral ascorbates. An example of a mineral ascorbate is magnesium ascorbate. There is nothing wrong with taking such a supplement. However, mineral ascorbates should not be your sole source of vitamin C. The dosage level of vitamin C that you need to take on a daily basis would require an overdose of associated mineral forms if mineral ascorbates were your only forms of supplemented vitamin C.

Calcium supplements should also be avoided while taking large daily doses of vitamin C. This is not to infer that taking both calcium and vitamin C assures the formation of kidney stones. However, many patients who do end up with stone formation are older and have been taking calcium supplements and multiple prescription medications in addition to their vitamin C doses. Furthermore, there is significant evidence to support the assertion that most calcium supplements are not in a bioavailable form and are probably quite toxic to those who take them. Non-bioavailable forms of calcium can lead to an increased risk of heart disease, cancer, and other chronic degenerative diseases (Levy, 2001). Taking calcium supplements for years is sometimes associated with extensive deposits of calcium throughout the body. Vitamin C dissolves calcium very readily, and when a patient starts taking vitamin C for the first time, greater amounts of calcium will be dissolved from these deposits than when vitamin C has already been taken for an extended time. In older patients, greater hydration and smaller doses of vitamin C should be given initially, and vitamin C doses should only be increased at a later time. For those seeking objective measurements to follow, vitamin C dosage should only be increased at a time when periodic urinary calcium measurements clearly indicate that the amounts of calcium being mobilized from the body are lessening.

The patient needs to drink properly purified water. Tap water can contain significant amounts of calcium and other minerals that are not in a biologically available form. This presents an increased solute load to the kidney, which poses an increased risk of stone formation. The water should be distilled, or it can be purified by reverse osmosis or any filtration method documented to significantly reduce the solute load in the water. Any satisfactory filtration method must also be able to remove fluoride.

Probably the most important factor in supplementing well to maintain good health is to find a qualified health care practitioner who is willing to help you and periodically monitor routine blood tests. Your practitioner should be open and receptive to any and all questions that you may have. Unless you have specific medical problems that need to be treated and monitored, you should at least have a complete blood count, full biochemistry panel, iron and ferritin levels, and thyroid function tests performed annually. A test for G6PD deficiency should be taken once.

Summary

There is no perfect or precise approach to properly supplementing vitamin C and other nutrients. However, you should find a qualified health practitioner who will agree to be your partner in working toward maintaining your best health. Some vitamin C supplementation is absolutely essential to staying healthy, and very often it may be the only way to restore good health. Determine and take your optidose of vitamin C daily, include the other important vitamins and antioxidants discussed, and, above all, don't be afraid to listen to your body. If everything is done correctly, you will rarely have to feel worse before you feel better.

The current availability of liposome encapsulated vitamin C (see Chapter 5) makes the goal of optidosing much less difficult and problematic while affording superior antioxidant protection. However, if only the traditional forms of vitamin C are available to you, then the suggestions above need to be kept in mind.

References

Cathcart, R. (1981) Vitamin C, titrating to bowel tolerance, anascorbemia, and acute induced scurvy. *Medical Hypotheses* 7(11):1359-1376.

Klenner, F. (1971) Observations on the dose and administration of ascorbic acid when employed beyond the range of a vitamin in human pathology. *Journal of Applied Nutrition* 23(3&4):61-88.

Levy, T. (2001) *Optimal Nutrition for Optimal Health. The Real Truth About Eating Right for Weight Loss, Detoxification, Low Cholesterol, Better Digestion, and Overall Well-Being.* New York, NY: Keats Publishing.

RESOURCES

Suggested Readings

Adams, R. and F. Murray. (1972) *Vitamin C, the Powerhouse Vitamin, Conquers More Than Just Colds.* New York, NY: Larchmont Press.

Burns, J., J. Rivers, and L. Machlin. [eds.] (1987) *Third Conference on Vitamin C.* New York, NY: The New York Academy of Sciences.

Cheraskin, E., W. Ringsdorf, and E. Sisley. (1983) *The Vitamin C Connection. Getting Well and Staying Well with Vitamin C.* New York, NY: Harper & Row, Publishers, Inc.

Cheraskin, E. (1988) *The Vitamin C Controversy. Questions & Answers.* Wichita, KS: Bio-Communications Press.

Cheraskin, E. (1993) *Vitamin C . . . Who Needs It?* Birmingham, AL: Arlington Press & Company.

Clemetson, C. (1989) *Vitamin C. Volume I.* Boca Raton, FL: CRC Press, Inc.

Clemetson, C. (1989) *Vitamin C. Volume II.* Boca Raton, FL: CRC Press, Inc.

Clemetson, C. (1989) *Vitamin C. Volume III.* Boca Raton, FL: CRC Press, Inc.

Davies, M., J. Austin, and D. Partridge. (1991) *Vitamin C: Its Chemistry and Biochemistry.* Cambridge, UK: The Royal Society of Chemistry.

Goodman, S. (1991) *Vitamin C: The Master Nutrient.* New Canaan, CT: Keats Publishing, Inc.

Gutteridge, J. and B. Halliwell. (1994) *Antioxidants in Nutrition, Health, and Disease.* New York, NY: Oxford University Press.

Harris, J. [ed.] (1996) *Subcellular Biochemistry. Volume 25. Ascorbic Acid: Biochemistry and Biomedical Cell Biology.* New York, NY: Plenum Press.

Huggins, H. and T. Levy. (1999) *Uninformed Consent. The Hidden Dangers in Dental Care.* Charlottesville, VA: Hampton Roads Publishing Company, Inc.

King, C. and J. Burns. [eds.] (1975) *Second Conference on Vitamin C.* New York, NY: The New York Academy of Sciences.

Kulacz, R. and T. Levy. (2002) *The Roots of Disease. Connecting Dentistry and Medicine.* Philadelphia, PA: Xlibris Corporation.

Levy, T. (2001) *Optimal Nutrition for Optimal Health. The Real Truth About Eating Right for Weight Loss, Detoxification, Low Cholesterol, Better Digestion, and Overall Well-Being.* New York, NY: Keats Publishing.

Levy, T. (2006) *Stop America's #1 Killer! Reversible Vitamin C Deficiency Found to be Origin of ALL Coronary Heart Disease.* Henderson, NV: LivOn Books.

Packer, L. and J. Fuchs. [eds.] (1997) *Vitamin C in Health and Disease.* New York, NY: Marcel Dekker, Inc.

Pauling, L. (1981) *Vitamin C, the Common Cold & the Flu.* New York, NY: Berkley Books.

Pauling, L. (1987) *How to Live Longer and Feel Better.* New York, NY: Avon Books, Inc.

Seib, P. and B. Tolbert. [eds.] (1982) *Ascorbic Acid: Chemistry, Metabolism, and Uses.* Washington, D.C.: American Chemical Society.

Smith, L. (1988) *The Clinical Experiences of Frederick R. Klenner, M.D.: Clinical Guide to the Use of Vitamin C.* Portland, OR: Life Sciences Press.

Stone, I. (1972) *The Healing Factor. "Vitamin C" Against Disease.* New York, NY: Grosset & Dunlap.

Webster, J. (1972) *Vitamin C—The Protective Vitamin.* New York, NY: Award Books.

For Further Education and Assistance

1. To order additional copies of *Curing the Incurable,* or Dr. Levy's books *Stop America's #1 Killer* and *GSH: The Master Defender:*

   LivOn Books
   800-334-9294
   www.LivOnBooks.com
   Orders@LivOnBooks.com
   2654 W. Horizon Ridge Pkwy - Suite B-5, Dept 108
   Henderson, NV 89052

2. For information on dental toxicity and for assistance in receiving a Total Dental Revision (TDR):
   Scientific Health Solutions, Inc.
   Website: www.shslab.com
   Email: peakenenergymail@yahoo.com
   Phone: 719-548-1600; 800-331-2303
   Fax: 719-572-8081

3. Information regarding Dr. Levy and his other books:
   Website: www.tomlevymd.com
   Email: televymd@yahoo.com

4. Online information on liposomal encapsulation technology and products:
   www.livonlabs.com/liposomal-encapsulation.html
   www.pubmedcentral.nih.gov/articlerender.fcgi?artid=162866
   http://www.phospholipid.jp/cancerres.aacrjournals.org/cgi/content/full/60/13/3389
   www.nsec.ohio-state.edu/briefs/Liposomal.pdf

About the Author

Thomas E. Levy, M.D., J.D.

Dr. Levy received his bachelor of arts degree in biology from the Johns Hopkins University in 1972. He later graduated from the Tulane University School of Medicine in 1976. Continuing his training at Tulane, he specialized first in internal medicine and then in cardiology, receiving board certification in both of these disciplines. After completing his postgraduate training, Dr. Levy served as an assistant professor of medicine at Tulane Medical School for another three years.

After a private practice of adult cardiology, Dr. Levy started his research on the medical impact of dental toxicity with Dr. Hal Huggins in 1994. In 1998, he received his law degree from the University of Denver and was subsequently admitted to practice law in Colorado and the District of Columbia.

Vitamin C, Infectious Diseases, and Toxins is Dr. Levy's fourth book. His previous books are *Uninformed Consent: The Hidden Dangers in Dental Care,* co-authored with Dr. Huggins; *The Roots of Disease: Connecting Dentistry and Medicine,* co-authored with Robert Kulacz, D.D.S.; and *Optimal Nutrition for Optimal Health.* For further information on Dr. Levy, you can review his curriculum vitae on the web at www.TomLevyMD.com.